Leg over Leg

Volume One

Letter from the General Editor

The Library of Arabic Literature is a new series offering Arabic editions and English translations of key works of classical and pre-modern Arabic literature, as well as anthologies and thematic readers. Our books are edited and translated by distinguished scholars of Arabic and Islamic studies, and are published in parallel-text format with Arabic and English on facing pages. The Library of Arabic Literature will include texts from the pre-Islamic era to the cusp of the modern period, and will encompass a wide range of genres, including poetry, poetics, fiction, religion, philosophy, law, science, history and historiography.

Supported by a grant from the New York University Abu Dhabi Institute, and established in partnership with NYU Press, the Library of Arabic Literature will produce authoritative Arabic editions and modern, lucid English translations, with the goal of introducing the Arabic literary heritage to scholars and students, as well as to a general audience of readers.

Philip F. Kennedy
General Editor, Library of Arabic Literature

كتاب

الساق على الساق

في ما هو الفارياق

فارس الشدياق

المجلد الأول

LIBRARY OF
المكتبة
ARABIC
العربية
LITERATURE

Leg over Leg

or

The Turtle in the Tree

concerning

The Fāriyāq

What Manner of Creature Might He Be

by

Fāris al-Shidyāq

Volume One

Edited and translated by
HUMPHREY DAVIES

NEW YORK UNIVERSITY PRESS
New York and London

NEW YORK UNIVERSITY PRESS
New York and London

Library of Congress Cataloging-in-Publication Data

Shidyaq, Ahmad Faris, 1804?-1887.
Leg over leg or, : The turtle in the tree / Faris al-Shidyaq ; edited and translated by Humphrey Davies.
volumes cm
Bilingual edition In English and Arabic on facing pages.
Includes bibliographical references and index.
ISBN 978-0-8147-2937-3 (cl : alk. paper) -- ISBN 978-0-8147-4524-3 (e-book) -- ISBN 978-0-8147-4541-0 (e-book) 1. Shidyaq, Ahmad Faris, 1804?-1887. 2. Shidyaq, Ahmad Faris, 1804?-1887--Travel--Middle East. 3. Arabic language--Lexicography. 4. Middle East--Description and travel. I. Davies, Humphrey T. (Humphrey Taman) translator, editor. II. Shidyaq, Ahmad Faris, 1804?-1887. Saq ʻala al-saq. III. Shidyaq, Ahmad Faris, 1804?-1887. Saq ʻala al-saq. English. IV. Title. V. Title: Turtle in the tree.
PJ7862.H48S213 2013
892.7'8503--dc23
2013007540
CIP

New York University Press books are printed on acid-free paper, and their binding materials are chosen for strength and durability.

Series design by Titus Nemeth.

Typeset in Tasmeem, using DecoType Naskh and Emiri.

Typesetting and digitization by Stuart Brown.

Manufactured in the United States of America
c10 9 8 7 6 5 4 3 2 1

Table of Contents

Foreword

Rebecca C. Johnson

> While I do not claim to be the first writer in the world to follow this path or thrust a pinch of it up the noses of those who pretend they are dozing, I do notice that all the authors in my bookcase are shackled to a single stylistic chain . . . . Once you've become familiar with one link of the chain, you feel as though you know all the others, so that each one of them may truly be called a chain-man, given that each has followed in the footsteps of the rest and imitated them closely. This being established, know that I have exited the chain, for I am no chain-man and will not form the rump of the line; nor do I have any desire to be at its front, for the latter is an even more calamitous place to be than the former.
>
> —*Leg over Leg* (1.17.10)

For most Anglophone readers, this will be their first introduction to the writing of Fāris al-Shidyāq (later Aḥmad Fāris al-Shidyāq, born in 1805 or 1806 and died in 1887), a foundational figure in Arabic literary modernity.[1] For, although he is the author of at least four published works of literary prose, ten linguistic studies of Arabic, Turkish, English, and French, over 20,000 lines of poetry, and at least four unpublished manuscripts (not to mention his many translations, journalistic and critical essays, or those works that have been lost), his work has never appeared in English until now. For specialists in Arabic literature and many native readers of Arabic, however, he needs little introduction. As belletrist, poet, travel writer, translator, lexicographer, grammarian, literary historian, essayist, publisher, and newspaper editor, he is known as a pioneer of modern Arabic literature, a reviver of classical forms, the father of Arabic journalism, and no less than a modernizer of the Arabic language itself. His masterwork, *Al-Sāq ʿalā l-sāq fī mā huwa al-Fāriyāq* (*Leg over Leg or the Turtle in the Tree concerning the Fāriyāq, What Manner of Creature Might He Be*, 1855), is acknowledged as one of the most distinguished works of the nineteenth century and an inaugural text of Arab modernity. It is also among the most controversial: generically impossible to characterize, it is a critical, self-referential, learned, and irreverent book of observations on the lives and manners of "The Arabs and their Non-Arab Peers" that includes scathing attacks on authority, both ecclesiastical and worldly, as well as liberal and libertine discussions of relations between the sexes.

Yet, while virtually all studies of Arabic literature acknowledge his central place in literary history, the works of al-Shidyāq, as Nadia Al-Bagdadi writes, have largely been "merely read, but not seriously known" in Arabophone and Anglo-European academies alike.[2] Although a growing number of essays on his work has been published in English, no monograph on his work has yet been written, and, although several biographies and studies exist in Arabic, his oeuvre was still so little known in 1995 that an edited volume of his selected works could be published in a series entitled *Unknown Works*.[3] *Leg over Leg* itself has been seldom reprinted and often abridged (as often for moral as for aesthetic reasons), making a thorough study of its contents difficult. Moreover, it has suffered from more general scholarly neglect, as the nineteenth century has, until recently, remained one of the lesser-studied periods of Arabic literature. Known as the *Nahḍah*, a term derived from the verb meaning "to rise" or "to stand up," it is commonly translated as the "awakening" or "revival" of Arabic literary culture—a flowering often attributed to the salutary influence of European culture, for which reason it has also been called the "Arab rediscovery of Europe," beginning with Napoleon's invasion of Egypt in 1798.[4] Following a clearly Eurocentric paradigm, scholarship has tended for many years to emphasize the innovative aspects of the period—most notably the introduction of European genres and styles—and to sideline works following classical models, as well as works that fall between the two. Works such as *Leg over Leg* have been overlooked by those scholars who have seen it as a transitional curiosity between the "intellectually frivolous" and decadent post-classical literary age and the twentieth-century flowering of the modern novel.[5]

Looking at al-Shidyāq's complete work, however, helps scholars to re-evaluate this assessment, to engage critically with the *Nahḍah* and its output, to understand the importance of both translation and philology to modern Arabic literature, and to reconceptualize global frameworks of literature and Arabic's place in them. As al-Shidyāq writes, he is no "chain-man" and does not seek to replicate the style of those authors who have come before him. Yet he has as much distaste for appearing at the front of the chain as he does for appearing at its rear. For this reason, *Leg over Leg* can be seen as a portrait in miniature of Arabic literary modernity, if we understand that modernity as it has been described more recently in scholarship: a contested category marked by self-interrogation and a "constant reworking of the meaning of community" through language, created not by being imported from the West, but through interaction with Europe.[6] Historically contingent rather than inevitable and ambivalent in its relationship to both universalist claims and Eurocentric enunciations, Arabic modernity in *Leg over Leg* appears not as a stage on a single linear trajectory of history but as the name given to all of the competing "discrepant histories" which are themselves intertwined.[7]

Engaged with both the literary heritage of the past and the social and political conditions of the present, written in conversation with European languages and literature, and following the path of a burgeoning print industry, *Leg over Leg* is a portrait of a world where material and literary culture are in simultaneous flux. As al-Shidyāq writes:

> I tell you, the world in your late grandfather's and father's day was not as it is now. In their day, there were no steamboats or railway *tracks* to bring close far-off *tracts* and create new *pacts*, to connect the *disconnected*, and make accessible what was *once protected*. Then, one didn't have to learn many languages. It could be said of anyone who knew a few words of Turkish—Welcome, my lord! How nice to see you, my lord!—that he'd make a fine interpreter at the Imperial court. (1855 4.1.9)

The "new age" [*al-ʿaṣr al-jadīd*], the subject of many *Nahḍah*-era writings, was one in which the disconnected were being rapidly and frequently connected—through technologies of travel, of course, as well as through imperialist military expansion, missionary activities, and trade. Yet as al-Shidyāq hints here, these connections were formed as much by the production of knowledge and literature as they were by material innovations. Languages, translation, and even print culture—as printing presses gradually replaced the scriptoria of the imperial court—are what draw distant places closer in *Leg over Leg*, as it follows its protagonist from his native Lebanon to Malta, Egypt, Tunisia, France, and England, while he searches for gainful employment in the literary sphere, as a scribe, then poet, translator, editor, and author.

* * *

Leg over Leg is not only emblematic of his age; it is also largely autobiographical and, in this sense, irreducibly idiosyncratic. Al-Shidyāq followed the same peregrinations as his protagonist, whose name, al-Fāriyāq (or "the Fāriyāq," as he retains the definite article from his family name), is a condensation of his given and last names.[8] In the absence of consistent historical records, biographers have even gone so far as to use *Leg over Leg* as a historical document, although this practice—considering the text's satirical and highly stylized mode of narration—seems to obscure more than it illuminates.[9] It cannot, for example, help settle the question of al-Shidyāq's birth date (which is variously given as 1801, 1804, or 1805), as the Fāriyāq is only specified as being "born with the misfortune of having misfortune in the ascendant everywhere, the Scorpion raising its tail to strike at the Kid, or Billy Goat, and the Crab set on a collision course with the horn of the Ox" (1.1.13). What is known is that Fāris al-Shidyāq was probably born in the village of Ashqūt, in what is now Lebanon, to a prominent family in the Maronite community. Like many in his family, which had for generations provided clerks, teachers, and secretaries for local emirs and their sons, al-Shidyāq entered the local village school in Ḥadath, where the family later moved. An intelligent child of a literary family, he learned in large part at home and afterward took up the family profession as copyist and instructor in the service of the emir Ḥaydar al-Shihābī and helped him to compile his family chronicle and history of Lebanon, *Al-Ghurar al-ḥisān fī tārīkh ḥawādith al-zamān*.

Al-Shidyāq might have kept to this well-trodden path had he not come into contact with some of those forces that "connect the disconnected." In 1825 his older brother Asʿad began working as an Arabic instructor and translator for two American evangelical missionaries in Beirut and eventually converted to Protestantism and declared his desire to interpret the Gospel independently and preach it to others. Distraught and probably fearful of the social and financial repercussions of his leaving the church, his family begged him to renounce his new faith and his vocal skepticism of what he called their "custom and upbringing"; when he did not, he was taken into Patriarchal custody.[10] In the Qannūbīn monastery in Mount Lebanon, whether from torture or poor living conditions—he was kept for some time in a small cell that was blocked entirely by earth and stone except for a small window through which rations were passed to him—Asʿad died in 1830.[11] In the meantime Fāris al-Shidyāq—who "anticipated trouble," according to a missionary account of Asʿad's case, but possibly also out of disgust for the general approbation among the elites in his community for his brother's punishment—fled with several of the Americans to Alexandria and then British-protected Malta, where he entered their employ.[12]

This would mark al-Shidyāq's exile from Lebanon and the beginning of his lifetime of wandering, as he would return only once, in 1840, to visit his family in secret. He stayed in Malta from early 1827 to 1828 and again from 1834 to 1848, working primarily for the London-based Church Missionary Society (CMS). At first, he was employed as a tutor in Arabic for several of the missionaries, but they soon recognized the full extent of his abilities and enlisted him in their most precious and frustrating project—their Arabic printing press, which they hoped would produce translations of religious materials but was stalled by the lack of printing materials and qualified personnel. Al-Shidyāq soon began translating texts, as well as editing and correcting others' translations; as Jurjī Zaydān remarks in the biographical entry for al-Shidyāq in his *A History of Arabic-Language Literature*, "he was responsible, as the author, translator, or editor, for every single Arabic book printed at the Malta press" during his tenure there.[13] Zaydān's description, as later scholars have pointed out, is probably an exaggeration—there were other translators employed by the press, and the missionaries themselves took an active role in the production of literary materials. But it is nonetheless clear that al-Shidyāq became essential to the operations of the press, as the missionaries found him indispensable, despite the fact that he remained unconvinced of the truth of Protestant Christianity and the validity of the missionary project as a whole.

Upon his arrival, as his supervisor notes, al-Shidyāq was "very much in need of a sound knowledge of the truth of the Gospel, and . . . gives good hope of receiving it."[14] But if they hoped that they would find him to be like his brother, open to evangelical teachings and eager to join the missionary ranks himself, then they were deeply disappointed. Al-Shidyāq maintained a steadfast skepticism in matters ecclesiastical, which is evident in his sometimes ambivalent adoption of Protestantism.[15] As one of the American missionaries writes, "Fares has always expressed a wish to be free, and <u>loudly</u> sometimes."[16] Yet he was also the most qualified and learned of any of those they could find to work with them; he "probes things to the very bottom," as his supervisor wrote of him, an often vexing quality—as it meant long sessions of debate (as the same missionary also wrote, "were it not for his disputing I scarcely knew labours more pleasant to me than those I perform with him")—but one that was ultimately beneficial.[17] Al-Shidyāq translated religious tracts, secular educational materials, and grammars for the CMS and was often the only translator in their employ.

Al-Shidyāq was unhappy in Malta. In *Leg over Leg* he calls it as "the Island of Scoundrels" (*Jazīrat al-mulūṭ*, a word-play with the root letters of Malta) and "the Island of the Foul of Breath" (an allusion to the Maltese language, which he sometimes referred to as a corrupt version of Arabic). In his *Travel Narrative of the Known Conditions of Malta* he found fault with almost every aspect of Maltese culture and geography, describing the climate as so inhospitable that vegetables, even when grown abroad, lose their taste when eaten there.[18] He likewise bristled under missionary life: he could not tolerate the missionaries' food or austere lifestyle—he visited taverns, to the missionaries' chagrin, and was rumored to have had "conversation with bad women"[19]—and wished to be more fairly compensated for his work.

Yet his years in Malta also gave him his first opportunity to work in print, allowing him to develop skills and interests in many aspects of the printing process, all of which would allow him to hold editorial and managing positions in Arabic presses throughout the region. In Egypt, where he traveled when he left CMS employ between 1828 and 1834, he worked on the editorial staff of the first Arabic periodical, *Al-Waqāʾiʿ al-Miṣriyyah* (*Egyptian Events*), and he would later found his own journal and printing press in Istanbul. Little is known about his life in Egypt, except that he seemed dissatisfied with his government position—he approached the missionaries in 1829 to return to Malta, and in 1832 was employed as an Arabic instructor in a missionary school. When his replacement translator left to participate in an expedition to the Euphrates, he returned to Malta and resumed his former post, remaining there from the end of 1834 until the press closed in 1842.

When al-Shidyāq finally left CMS employ, it was to complete a translation of the Bible under the auspices of the Society for Promoting Christian Knowledge (SPCK), another Anglican mission organization operating in Malta. In 1845, this brought al-Shidyāq to the small village of Barley, in Hertfordshire, and then (after a brief return to Malta) to Cambridge, in order to work with Professor Reverend Samuel Lee (d. 1852), an Orientalist and missionary. After Lee's death, al-Shidyāq continued to work on the Bible, while living alternately in London and Paris until its publication in 1857. This was the first of his periods of great literary productivity, enabled by the steady salary he received from the SPCK (and supplemented by a job as the commercial correspondent for the trading company of Butrus Ḥawwā, to whom he dedicates *Leg over Leg*[20]). In England, he lived near the Cambridge University Library and the British Museum and their substantial Arabic manuscript holdings—he was impressed by the access readers were granted to rare and important manuscripts—and came into contact with scholars of Arabic literature there and in Paris (including Thomas Jarrett at Cambridge, John Nicholson at Oxford, and Caussin de Perceval in Paris). In Paris he also met Arab litterateurs and reformers on their travels (including Fransīs Fatḥallah Marrāsh and Khayr al-Dīn al-Tūnusī). It was in this atmosphere of intellectual stimulation (as opposed to the "Panegyricon," or "praise factory," of the Egyptian press office) that al-Shidyāq wrote and published *Leg over Leg* (at the Paris press of Benjamin Duprat, in 1855) and began his travel narratives of Malta and Europe and several other minor projects, including a French grammar for Arabic students and an Arabic grammar for English students.

Although he worked with Protestant missionaries for nearly half of his career, he rigorously maintained an independent-minded scholarly agenda. While translating texts in Malta, he held a post as lecturer in Arabic at the university in Valletta. In Egypt, while working for Muḥammad ʿAlī's state-run newspaper and then a CMS-run school, he began to attend Muslim scholarly and literary circles, studying jurisprudence, grammar, and literature with al-Azhar shaykhs, as well as acquiring or copying "as many classical texts as he could find."[21] Later, when he moved to England in order to collaborate on a translation of the Bible, he not only copied manuscripts of some of the most important works produced during the golden age of Islam but also began to compose a refutation of the Gospels.[22] That is, during the same years that al-Shidyāq worked to establish a faithful and correct translation of the Bible, in accordance with the Hebrew and Syriac source texts, he was also working on a treatise arguing for the unreliability of the Gospels on the very basis of source criticism. In this treatise, al-Shidyāq presents the contradictions of source criticism and faith as irresolvable—a gesture that perhaps most concretely points to his own resolute skepticism that remained the basis of his literary and scholarly endeavors, whether he worked under Christian or under Ottoman Muslim patronage, which he did after leaving Europe in 1857.

The year 1857 marks al-Shidyāq's final departure from missionary employment (though it may be argued that the true break came in 1855, with the publication of his scathing depiction of the missionaries in *Leg over Leg*). In 1842, while in Malta, he had written a poem in praise of the ruler of Tunis, Aḥmad Bāy, and had received a diamond in recognition of it. Later, in Paris, on one of the Bāy's journeys there, al-Shidyāq wrote another laudatory poem; this one elicited an invitation from the Bāy to Tunis to establish a state printing press and newspaper. While this project was eventually realized by one of his contemporaries, al-Shidyāq remained in Tunis for nearly two years, where he continued to work on his European travelogue, *Uncovering the Hidden Arts of Europe* (published in Tunis in 1863). Scholars believe that it was here that he converted to Islam, taking the name Aḥmad—though evidence in *Al-Sāq* seems to point to his having converted even earlier, while still in Europe.[23]

Soon afterward, he was invited by the Sublime Porte to the capital, and it was there, as *Aḥmad* Fāris al-Shidyāq, that he would attain the greatest recognition. He arrived in Istanbul/Constantinople in 1859, where he was first employed as chief corrector at the imperial press, and, in 1861, he became the founder and editor in chief of *Al-Jawāʾib* (*Tidings from Afar*), the first Arabic periodical to be published there and perhaps the most influential Arabic publication to be produced in the *Nahḍah*. *Al-Jawāʾib* ran weekly from 1861 to 1883, and for the first nine years it was subsidized by the imperial ministry of finance and printed at the government press.[24] Thus beholden, as were most other periodicals of the time, to "our master, the great sultan," as al-Shidyāq puts it, *Al-Jawāʾib* reproduced government bulletins and produced news reports that corresponded with official accounts of events and yet maintained a partial independence, for which it was occasionally punished.[25] More than merely a mouthpiece for the Ottoman sultan and his provincial governors, *Al-Jawāʾib* was also a source for domestic and international news and might have been best known as a venue for cultural and literary debates. A lover and defender of the Arabic language, al-Shidyāq used *Al-Jawāʾib* as a vehicle for his philological scholarship and as a place where he could hold fierce linguistic debates with his contemporaries and publish poems satirizing his critics. He engaged in international debates about Arabic usage with the editors of the Paris journal *Birjīs Bārīs* (*The Paris Jupiter*, 1858–63) and an intergenerational argument about orthography with Ibrāhīm al-Yāzijī and the editors of *Al-Jinān* in Beirut. These were so heated as to inspire a critic to launch a periodical devoted entirely to satirizing al-Shidyāq, *Rujūm wa-ghassāq ilā Fāris al-Shidyāq* (*Fire and Brimstone upon Fāris al-Shidyāq*, 1868); it only lasted a few issues.

During this period, al-Shidyāq launched the Jawāʾib Press; in 1870 he began printing his periodical himself (with the assistance of his son, Salīm), as well as his book-length works, the works of his supporters and friends, and classical works on Arabic language and literature. Many of these were devoted to philological inquiry, including works on the morphology, lexicography, and phonology of

Arabic, most notably *Al-Jāsūs ʿalā l-Qāmūs* (*Spying on the Dictionary*, 1884) and *Sirr al-Layāl fī l-qalb wa-l-ibdāl* (*The Secrets of Morphology and Metathesis*, 1884) as well as a comparative study of Arabic, French, and Turkish (*Kanz al-lughāt*; *The Treasury of Languages*, 1876). As Geoffrey Roper notes, al-Shidyāq "did not just passively accept and make use of the printing press" but was "an active protagonist and propagandist of the print revolution."[26] Al-Shidyāq helped to establish many of the norms of modern printing—from language to typesetting—including the addition of tables of contents and title pages with dates. As he argued, "all the crafts that have been invented in this world are inferior to the craft of printing."[27]

Al-Shidyāq operated the Jawāʾib Press from 1870 until three years before his death, when he was perhaps able to devote his full attention to his final project—a critical edition and introduction to the seventh/thirteenth-century dictionary, *Lisān al-ʿArab* (*The Arab Tongue*, 1883–89) of Ibn Manẓūr. Published in twenty volumes at the Bulāq Press in Cairo, it remains one of the largest dictionaries in Arabic and a near-exhaustive source for rare words—one of al-Shidyāq's particular passions, as evidenced in *Leg over Leg*'s extensive lists of synonyms and near-synonyms. His final journey, in a life of traveling, was to Cairo in 1886, in order to confer with the press about its publication. A fellow author and literary biographer described his visit:

> Old age had overtaken him, dimmed his eyes, and bent his back; but he had lost nothing of his keenness or intelligence. He was, until the last of his days, a pleasant conversationalist with graceful expressions, amiable—with a tendency towards profanity.[28]

Eloquent and profane until the last, al-Shidyāq died, shortly after his return from Egypt, in the village of Kadiköy, on September 20, 1887. Some biographers claim that he converted back to Maronite Catholicism on his deathbed, but his own final wishes seem to contradict this. Never one to settle such questions simply, he requested to be buried in a Christian cemetery near his family home in Hazmiyyah, Lebanon, in a grave marked not by a cross but by a crescent.[29]

Al-Shidyāq, then, was paradoxical even in death, as is fitting, considering the broadest strokes of his biography. In the (perhaps understated) words of the missionary society's annual report, "Fāris is a man of excellent mind, but strong and wayward passions"—an apt way to describe many of his political and religious affiliations. He wrote poems in praise of Aḥmad Bāy of Tunis but also of Queen Victoria and the rebel leader ʿAbd al-Qādir of Algeria, and he became a British citizen before leaving England to work as a subject of the Ottoman Empire. To quote Kamran Rastegar, he was a "Muslim Christian. A sedentary traveler. An ascetic sensualist. A modernist classicist. A literary gutter-mouth. A pious unbeliever."[30] He was, intellectually and personally, a series of irresolvable paradoxes.

* * *

Al-Shidyāq's body of work—seen as a whole—is equally difficult to categorize neatly. Most frequently, al-Shidyāq is seen as a modernizer, a renovator of Arabic letters who "had little regard for literary tradition" and who instead looked to Europe for literary modes that would replace those discredited indigenous ones.[31] In a certain sense this is true: he was a pioneer of narrative forms new to the Arab public sphere, including the modern travelogue and experimental narrative prose such as we find in *Leg over Leg*. Known as the father of Arabic journalism for his work on *Al-Waqāʾiʿ al-Miṣriyyah* and *Al-Jawāʾib*, he was invested in the modernization of the Arabic language, so as to preserve its usefulness and expressiveness in modern daily life. Thus, he introduced many surviving neologisms that described his contemporary reality, including *jarīdah* "newspaper," *intikhāb* "election," and *jawāz* "passport," and he translated and edited English translations of religious, geographical, pedagogical, natural historical, and narrative works. His literary career, that is, showed a sustained engagement with European languages, scholarship, and literary forms.

And yet much of his published work consists of works one might classify as neo-classical, or even "revivalist," including influential studies in classical lexicography and critical editions of classical Arabic texts, as well as original compositions in neo-classical style, such as his poetry and his examples of *maqāmāt* (a rhyming prose form that originated in the fourth/tenth century but that was produced by many during the *Nahḍah*).[32] These works, comprising much of his prolific production, signal that al-Shidyāq was not interested simply in abandoning inherited Arabic literary modes and rhetorical styles: he was equally interested in reviving classical rhetoric and forms and publishing them for the new reading public.[33] His modernity, that is, was pioneered precisely *through* an interest in Arabic literary pre-modernity.

In this sense, al-Shidyāq's oeuvre exemplifies the diverse trajectories of the *Nahḍah*. Yet, despite the diversity of its output, the *Nahḍah* had for many years been seen as an enlightenment movement with its primary origins in "Western influences, the introduction of unknown or barely known genres such as the theatre or the European-style novel" or which "loosened the attachment of Arab societies to traditions reckoned inappropriate to modern civilization." [34] In recent years, however, scholars have looked at the production of the *Nahḍah* as more ambivalent in its attitude toward Western literary and cultural models and less categorical in its rejection of indigenous ones. Studies of translation and literary contact in the *Nahḍah* now tend to see experimentations in Western forms not as admiring imitations of a dominant culture but as creative acts of cultural resistance or indifference that "cared nothing for origins and genealogies."[35] And intra-regional studies have questioned the extent to which these works should be viewed solely in conversation with the West. These studies point to more continuities than discontinuities with the literary heritage of the East, and show us that looking at the literature of the *Nahḍah* solely in the context of its relationship with the West writes out a significant part of the period's output: not only "revivalist" literature (classical and neo-classical publications) but also those works that lie between revivalist and "modernist," such as *Leg over Leg*.[36]

The *Nahḍah,* in light of these recent studies, might more precisely be understood as a period of dynamic social and literary change, which oriented its modernity simultaneously inward, toward a classical heritage, and outward, in the direction of Europe. Indeed, Samah Selim has gone as far as to suggest abandoning the singular term *Nahḍah,* in order to "speak of two intertwined literary *Nahḍahs*": "one that, partly looking backwards to an antediluvian 'golden age,' was invested in an act of genetic and linguistic recuperation (re-naissance) and another that was strictly materialist in the play of its textual and social articulations."[37] That is, one *Nahḍah* that recovers a *literary* past and another that *represents,* in varying degrees of realism, a material present, which included goods and people from both inside and outside the Arabic-speaking world, or the "Arabs and their non-Arab peers" of *Leg over Leg*'s subtitle, or those disconnected and newly connected by steamships and railways, to paraphrase the Fāriyāq.

Al-Shidyāq's—and the Fāriyāq's—steamship fare to England was, of course, paid by missionaries. The missionary presence in the Middle East, mostly American and British, began in Egypt and the eastern Mediterranean in the early nineteenth century and was aimed mainly toward the conversion of Eastern Christian sects such as the Maronites in Lebanon and the Copts in Egypt (and, to a lesser extent, Jewish Ottoman subjects). While they failed to convert many—in 1830, the entire "Protestant community" of the Ottoman empire reportedly consisted of six people[38]—they did establish important institutions of learning and foster intellectual relationships with several influential literary figures. Yet missionary societies are just one example of international contact in the Middle East; far more influential and commonplace than the "Biblemen," as they were sometimes called—or "bag-men," as al-Shidyāq satirizes them, because they, like itinerant merchants, would hawk their wares in the spiritual marketplace—were European merchants and manufacturers, who appeared more often in the region during the nineteenth century.

During this period, economic ties between European countries and the larger Ottoman Empire (of which modern-day Syria and Lebanon were a part) deepened: beginning in the 1840s with a series of laws called the *tanẓīmāt*, Istanbul rapidly opened its empire to foreign investment and trade. In Egypt this meant that European banks began to establish themselves in Alexandria as early as the 1850s, lending money to the soon-to-be bankrupt Egyptian government.[39] In Lebanon the consequence of these changes was the rapid growth in the export of agricultural products in the 1850s and 1860s; the silk-thread trade alone accounted for over eighty percent of the region's exports to Europe.[40] At the same time, the quantity of European manufactured goods consumed in the region increased: the Middle East became incorporated into the new world economic system as a dependent region, with prices and exports determined by demand in Europe, and with locally-based European merchants reaping much of the profit.[41]

Foreign travel and immigration to the Middle East rose apace; the silk trade brought French capitalists and merchants (especially from Lyon) to Mount Lebanon to set up silk factories, and a booming cotton industry and transport construction lured workers and investors to Egypt. (The number of Europeans who came into Egypt alone rose from between 8,000 and 10,000 in 1838 to 30,000 in 1861 and 80,000 by 1865.[42]) At the same time that foreign travel and immigration to the Middle East became more frequent, so did Arab migration and travel to Europe. While it was once a scholarly commonplace to consider Muslims and Arabs as generally uncurious about Europe—a view popularized, at least in academic contexts, by Bernard Lewis in *Islam and the West* and *The Muslim Discovery of Europe*—recent work has made lesser-known travelogues of the seventeenth through nineteenth centuries known and available to English readers.[43] Putting this period's travel literature into the long history of Arab contact with Europe makes it clear that there was no sudden nineteenth-century "discovery" of Europe.

Nonetheless, a new dimension to this contact emerged in the nineteenth century—national consolidation, with the goal of strengthening Arab scientific and military capabilities in the wake of European encroachment. After Napoleon's short-lived occupation of Egypt, from 1798 to 1801, Egypt's ruler, Muḥammad ʿAlī, launched his own scientific campaign to Europe by dispatching educational missions in various disciplines.[44] First sending a group of students to Italy to train as printers and type-founders, he later sent missions to France and England to study shipbuilding, engineering, medicine, law, diplomacy, and languages. During what Muḥammad ʿAlī envisioned as a cultural and technical revival, these missions stood at the core of a national education project—as they not only brought home valuable skills and information, but also disseminated them through university teaching and the translation of technical textbooks.[45] Printing presses, then, including the press that Napoleon brought to print his military bulletins and the still-operating Bulāq Press (founded in 1821), were instrumental to Muḥammad ʿAlī's modernizing agenda, as they published official news and the scientific and academic works that Egyptian delegates translated upon their return.

Not all publishing, however, was produced in the service of the state. Any author could have a book printed at Muḥammad ʿAlī's press, provided that the costs were paid, and private presses began to compete with state publishing houses for the emerging print market.[46] By mid-century, there were more than a dozen presses operating in the Levant alone, with six privately owned commercial presses opening in the 1850s.[47] In addition to missionary presses like the CMS Press in Malta, authors themselves also became printer-publishers, founding their own presses and publishing their own writing or journals. In Cairo, Alexandria, Beirut, Baghdad, Mosul, Aleppo, Damascus, Jerusalem, and Valletta, authors and translators published a range of texts for the emerging commercial market.[48] The nineteenth-century Arabic print sphere emerged as one that was profoundly heterogeneous, producing editions of classical Arabic texts as well as translations from English and French literature. Alongside these, original Arabic prose works appeared, some in neoclassical style, and others written in a form called *riwāyah*, the word now used to mean "novel" but which then signified a category more fluid, such as "narrative" (literally, it is the verbal noun for "telling"), as well as works in between.

In doing so, the *Nahḍah*'s print market forged new alliances, not simply within the imagined community of the nation, but intra-regionally—creating, in effect, something that could for the first time be called a public Arabic print sphere, where "the sounds from Beirut, Cairo, and Alexandria reached other Arab provinces, and educated groups in the towns of Syria, Palestine, Iraq, and even the Hejaz became involved in the new exchange in print across provincial boundaries."[49] Periodicals published in Beirut would advertise or review novels written by Egyptian colleagues, and journals of various affiliations would engage each other in debate about the correct use of Arabic, the relative merits of different literary translators, or editorial policy. The picture that emerges is of an Arabic print sphere that was intricately interlinked, making alliances across provincial borders, confessional boundaries, and even across continents. Early journals and newspapers were sometimes the product of either foreign investment (as was the case with the Franco-Egyptian ventures of *L'Echo des Pyramides*, 1827, and *Al-Tanbīh*, founded in 1800) or direct intellectual exchange,[50] and featured an international news section often translated from European newspapers and wire services, thanks to the widespread use of the telegraph and the establishment of Reuters's first office outside Europe, in Alexandria in 1865.[51] Their audience, too, was international—composed not just of readers in Beirut or Cairo but also immigrant readers and Orientalists in Europe and, later, in North America.[52] An English traveler to the Arabian Peninsula in the 1870s, Charles Montagu Doughty, remarked that al-Shidyāq's *Al-Jawāʾib* was "current in all countries of the Arabic speech" and that he had seen it even "in the Nejd merchants' houses at Bombay."[53]

The links established by trade and travel, then, were formed simultaneously in the print sphere, and it was there that they were debated. What was shared in print, perhaps even more than a sense of a bounded national or imperial space, was the *Nahḍah* reader's relationship to the world around him, the sense both of being a local actor and participating in global phenomena. Indeed, by the end of the nineteenth century it was possible to see journalists referring an international or even global *Nahḍah*, consisting of Arab authors or litterateurs who traveled and published abroad.[54] The *Nahḍah*, then, might be understood as an attempt to negotiate Arab modernity, identity, and enlightenment in the context of what authors identified as a new age of technological, social, literary, commercial, and even moral change, which they were joining by virtue of a new sense of global interconnectedness.[55] One intellectual project that concerned the writers and thinkers of the *Nahḍah*, then, was how—and on what terms—to understand their participation in this global process. Debates about modernity, oriented toward the issue of *tamaddun* (loosely translated as "progress toward civilization"), emerged. Journalistic essays asked, "Who are we?" as a way to seek answers to the larger question of what it means to be Arab (and not necessarily an Egyptian or a Lebanese) and modern, or Arab and enlightened, in the cross-currents of global capitalism, empire, and the trans-regional and potentially global community of the faithful, the *umma.*[56] To do so was to demarcate local specificity within the global, rather than against it. Thus *Nahḍah* intellectuals did not necessarily seek either to preserve or to abandon authentic traditions in the face of foreign encroachment. The common understanding of the choice intellectuals made, between the position of "reformer" and "reactionary," might be a false dichotomy. As Shaden Tageldin writes, "For most of the elite Egyptian intellectuals of the *Nahḍah,* becoming modern was never a question of abandoning Arabic and writing in the languages of their European colonizers—in French or English. The *Nahḍah* unfolded in translation: it transported French or English into Arabic. Thus it appeared to 'preserve' Arabic—all the while *translating* it."[57] In other words, these intellectuals theorized modernity as a comparative project, as something taking shape alongside Europe.[58]

* * *

One can see this comparative tendency in the title page of *Leg over Leg.* As its subtitle announces ("Days, Months, and Years spent in Critical Examination of the Arabs and their Non-Arab Peers"), the narrative takes the outward form of a travelogue that follows the Fāriyāq between Europe and the Arab Middle East. In his "critical examination," he looks outward at a cultural other, but he also reflects inwardly upon his own social background, leaving no society safe from his satirizing gaze. It takes place on the road between cultures; though influenced by Laurence Sterne and François Rabelais, it takes equal interest in the wandering scholars of the classical Arabic tradition, such as Badīʿ al-Zamān al-Hamadhānī (d. 398/1008), who—like the Fāriyāq—traveled in search of literary patronage. Though nominally Christian at the time of its publication (he added "Aḥmad" several years later), he invokes Islamic motifs and values that seem to identify him ambivalently as already Muslim.[59] And though avowedly a work devoted to linguistic preservation—and indeed taking antiquarian delight in stringing together lists of rare words and in lampooning authors and orators for using incorrect language—he also claims to eschew the dominant rhetorical tendencies of the preceding centuries that produced texts "marinated in the spices of paronomasia and morphological parallelism, of metaphor and metonymy" (1.1.11).

This final contradiction helps to describe the work's complex prose style. *Leg over Leg* contains many elaborate displays of linguistic erudition—in the form of its lists of synonyms but also his repeated demonstrations of rhetorical and generic mastery. Al-Shidyāq intersperses his narrative with original verse compositions and sections in rhymed prose (*saj*ʿ), as well as the four *maqāmāt* he includes, along with other more occasional usages. These passages, combined with his quotations and intertextual references to poets and linguistic scholars, give the reader a full sense of his scholarly abilities and qualifications—he makes clear that he could hold his own with the literary masters of his time. In this sense, we can see *Leg over Leg* as "a last glance at a fading language," in which the author is conscious of "the precarious state written classical Arabic reached under the growing impact of European languages and local attempts at reforming the Arab language in the Ottoman world."[60] One cannot help but wonder, however, if this final glance did not contain a glint of irony. In the opening pages, as the reader will see, he preserves classical erudition by recalling over 250 synonyms and euphemisms for "penis," "vagina," and "sexual intercourse." He may have aimed to unseat literary authority even as he claimed it for himself.

In other sections, he renders events in clear and direct language that can approach the style of present-day Arabic novels. He even, on rare occasions, writes in colloquial Arabic—an act that remains controversial even today. For many scholars, the shifting of registers between formal and informal Arabic and between ornate and simple styles, marks *Leg over Leg* as a text produced during the transition to modernity and is one of the sources of the notorious difficulty in categorizing the work. While its title seems to present it as a travelogue, and its story follows the author's real-life travels, its characters and events are abstracted and stylized, with rhetorical acrobatics often seeming to take precedence over attempts at ethnographic verisimilitude. Long philosophical and literary digressions frequently interrupt the plot, so that the narrative often takes on the form of a miscellany. As the narrator admits, "I committed myself to writing a book that would be a repository for every idea that appealed to me, relevant or irrelevant, for it seemed to me that what was irrelevant to me might be relevant to someone else, and vice versa" (1.10.6).

Despite this hint at formlessness, the author's preface gives two possible generic possibilities: to "give prominence to the oddities of the language, including its rare words" (0.2.1) and to "discuss the praiseworthy and blameworthy qualities of women" (0.2.12). Yet no study exists that treats the work as either a linguistic treatise or a sociology of gender. Instead, scholars have categorized it as belonging to a variety of literary genres. Luwīs ʿAwaḍ and Shawqī Ḍayf, for example, classify it as a *maqāmah* or neo-*maqāmah*, Radwa ʿAshour as a novel ("the first and most important Arabic novel"), Matityahu Peled as Menippean, and Paul Starkey as fictional autobiography or a "voyage of self-definition."[61] For Nadia Al-Bagdadi, the work transcends categorization: she argues that it should be understood both as a novel and as "a unique literary expression of its time," or "a genre of its own."[62] Al-Shidyāq might have agreed with this characterization. As he warns in his prefatory poem, his art is "an orphan" and "unique"; "so be well disposed toward it," he begs his reader (0.4.5). In this verse description (and anticipatory list of complaints) of *Leg over Leg*, he identifies what might be the central difficulty in characterizing it: it appears as if he "pieced it together and cobbled it up by hand" (0.4.2). It might not be categorizable because it is pieced together from many genres and literary modes, as it contains passages in verse (*madīḥ, hijāʾ, ghazal, rithāʾ*), prose (with passages that imitate or make reference to historical writing, sermons, aphorisms, ethnographic writing, linguistic studies, and philosophical critiques), and prosody (it includes four original *maqāmāt*, as well as other passages written in rhyming prose, or *sajʿ*). Alongside these Arabic exemplars, he includes sections translated from European authors, such as the travel narratives of Chateaubriand and Lamartine, and original passages written in "the Frankish way" (1.7.5). And he intersperses in these lists (many quoted, as Humphrey Davies notes in his Afterword, from *Al-Qāmūs*), anecdotes, and typographical jokes which punctuate the text.

In cobbling together this multigeneric work, he renders no mode privileged over any other. Instead, he incorporates all into his narrative archive, to praise and discredit equally. As a result, there is no stable position of narrative authority in *Leg over Leg*, a fact perhaps announced by the work's title itself. In a text abounding in sexual puns and innuendos, "leg over leg" could refer to an intimate union of limbs or the detached posture of an armchair academic. Moreover, this single phrase signals the linguistic and structural play built into all aspects of the work: "*al-sāq ʿalā l-sāq*" also appears within the text in a list of the conventional topoi of courtship narratives, which interrupts the very courtship story that the narrator is trying to tell:

> It is the custom of my fellow writers sometimes to go back and leap over a period of time and connect an event that happened before it to an event that

> happened after it. This is called analepsis (*tawriyah*), that is, "taking backward (*warā'*)." They also may start by mentioning everything about the protagonist, from his first whisperings into his beloved's ear until his reappearance as a married man. In the course of this, the author will relate such long and tedious matters as how his face paled and his pulse raced when he met her, how he was reduced to a tizzy and felt ill while he waited for her answer, how he sent her an old woman or a missive, how he met with her at such and such a time and place, and how she changed color when he spoke to her of the bed, of drawing her close, of embracing, of *leg over leg*, of kissing, of kissing tongue to tongue, of intercourse, and the like. (3.4.1)

The "and the like" that mockingly ends this list opens it up to parodic criticism, gesturing simultaneously toward infinite substitutability on the one hand and the impossibility of precise equivalence on the other—signaling both the mechanisms and limits of representation that will be explored throughout the text (which reaches the absurd in the secondary reading of the title, "The Turtle in the Tree"). Thus al-Shidyāq, in his display of mastery over these genres, also leads the reader through a series of generic parodies, anatomizing literary forms—interrupting his *maqāmah* to talk about the limitations of *saj'* (likening it to walking with a wooden leg), interrupting his protagonist's poetry with literary-critical commentary, or (as above) disrupting the narrative episodes to discuss the conventions of the narrative discourse.

Furthermore, these interruptions, digressions, and lists create an endless leg after leg of narrative, where text seems to generate only more text. This itself points to the work's operative hermeneutic mode: it is contiguity, not equivalence, that serves as the driving force behind meaning. It is by the juxtaposition of events, characters, and even adjectives that the plot, as nonlinear as it is, moves forward (or sideways, which is often the case). Al-Shidyāq even goes so far as to reject explicitly the very notion of equivalence, in the form of synonymity, in its opening pages. He writes:

> In addition, I have imposed on the reader the condition that he not skip any of the "synonymous" words in this book of mine, many though they be (for it may happen that, on a single road, a herd of fifty words, all with the same meaning, or with two meanings that are close, may pass him by). If he cannot commit to this, I cannot permit him to peruse it and will not offer him my congratulations if he does so. I have to admit that I cannot support the idea that all "synonyms" have the same meaning, or they would have called them "equi-nyms." (1.1.7)

As al-Shidyāq points out here, the Arabic root for "synonym," *r-d-f*, does not necessarily connote equivalence. The verbs derived from it can mean to pile up in layers, to become stratified, to flock, to throng, to form a single line, or to follow one after another. Or, to put one foot after another, follow leg upon leg, as another reading of *al-sāq ʿalā l-sāq* allows.[63] Thus does *Leg over Leg*, in its very title, "lay bare the device," as Victor Shklovsky wrote of *Tristram Shandy*.[64]

Leg over Leg, then, might be more precisely characterized as meta-generic—as al-Shidyāq seems to comment *on* genre more often than he writes *in* a generic mode. Yet his interruptions of literary convention are not only a commentary on style; they are also the foundation of his larger social and political critiques. The linguistic authority that al-Shidyāq undermines is always tied to political authority: he lampoons emirs for their misguided overconfidence in grammatical studies, satirizes Maronite priests for their hypocritical lack of scholarly goals—when staying at a monastery and in need of a dictionary to compose poetry, he inquires after a copy of the *Qāmūs*, Muḥammad ibn Yaʿqūb Fīrūzābādī's lexicon, and is given answers about *jāmūs* and *kābūs*, or buffaloes and nightmares—ridicules Protestant missionaries for their inability to communicate with their congregations in their native language, and criticizes Orientalist scholars for their errors in translation (he devotes an entire appendix to correcting the errors found in the works of the French scholars he came into contact with in Paris). Yet his attacks on ecclesiastical authority should not be seen solely in light of his well-known disagreements and injuries. His position against ecclesiastical authority is more than a reaction to his brother's treatment in Lebanon, just as his critiques of Orientalist scholarship are more than simply a reaction to his reported failure to find an academic post in Europe.[65] Both are part of a sustained critique of institutionalized interpretations of sacred texts, canonical works of literature, and even social conventions—and especially of any person who blindly accepts them. Instead, al-Shidyāq subtly suggests skepticism—based on individual perception and self-improving study—as the guiding principle for spiritual enlightenment, political leadership, judicial decisions, and moral principles, as well as for scholarly research. Or, as his narrator tells us early on: "Observe, then, how people differ with regard to a single word and a single meaning!" (1.2.7) The linguistic indeterminacy that reigns in *Leg over Leg*—with simple definitions of words seeming to collapse under the weight of his lists of subtly differentiated synonyms—does not establish him as the ultimate linguistic authority as much as it shows that language itself is the key to dissidence. It is not a coincidence, in this sense, that his protagonist's name also means "he who distinguishes."

It might not be possible to tease a coherent political doctrine from his work, but al-Shidyāq expressed in his writings values that today would be associated with liberalism. He repeatedly advocated a separation of religious and political life and a respect for "personal freedoms" (so long as they are in the interest of society). Both in his travels and in his observations on life within the Ottoman Empire, he called attention to the need to improve working conditions for farmers and workers, approaching (but never wholly identifying with) some of the socialist ideas being debated in Europe during his sojourn there, chief among them the responsibility of the ruling classes toward the poor and the importance of equality under the law.[66] His promotion of the value of equality, in fact, might be considered among his most radical, as he advocated for it not only among religious sects and social classes but also between genders. In *Leg over Leg* and elsewhere he promotes absolute equality between men and women, advocating—nearly fifty years before Qāsim Amīn's *The Liberation of Women* (1899)—for the right of women to be educated. (As he explains in *Al-Jawāʾib*, "knowledge and education are the light of the mind . . . and if you cannot entrust this light to woman, then you cannot trust her with any light whatsoever, for fear that she might use it to burn down the house."[67]) Unlike many of his contemporary reformers, however, he did not write of an idealized woman whose education was in the service of a better performance of her domestic duties or the education of a new generation of children. As he writes in *Leg over Leg*, if one reads him in order to hear about women "possessing peculiar skills in terms of the excellent management of such household tasks as sewing, embroidery, and the like, these are mentioned in many a book and you'll have to look them up yourselves" (2.16.72). In his book, women appear not as angels of the house but as full and equal participants in society who have a right to work as well as stay at home. "There can be no *Nahḍah* in the East," al-Shidyāq is reported to have said, "without a *Nahḍah* of women."[68]

In *Leg over Leg*, written, as he claims, with so much interest in women and sympathy for them that one might believe his protagonist had been transformed into one, his interest in women's equality is centered less on female education than on female emotional and sexual fulfillment. Through conversations with the protagonist's wife, the Fāriyāqiyyah, al-Shidyāq decries sexual double standards, advocating for the right of women to choose their own husbands, to divorce, and to demand sexual pleasure (see Volume Three). These conversations reveal her as a witty social satirist in her own right, or, as al-Shidyāq writes in the preface, one who "argues with theorist and practitioner alike and provides excellent critiques of the political issues and conditions, mundane and spiritual, of the countries she has seen" (0.2.12). Rastegar argues for reading "the Fāriyāqiyyah" not as a name—if it were a feminization of Fāriyāq, it would be Fāriyāqah, as he points out—but as "Fāriyāq-ness," rendered in the feminine form.[69] She might thus be thought of not as a stand-in for a historical personage (al-Shidyāq's wife, Wardah al-Ṣūlī) but as a second apparition of the self. Writing not simply *about* women but *as if a woman*, al-Shidyāq uses gender as another permutation of his thought-experiment in radical difference and belonging. And he reveals that above all, it is an experiment in subjectivity—which does not result in a definition of the self or of something one might call the modern Arab subject, but examines "the ways the self cannot be accommodated by social frameworks the world around."[70] The self, in *Leg over Leg*, seems always to exceed its narrative frame and multiply. As if to see himself from the inside and out, he appears as the author on the title page ("Fāris al-Shidyāq") and as his textual doubles: the unnamed narrator (who narrates in the first person), the Fāriyāq, the Fāriyāqiyyah, and the interpolated narrator of the four *maqāmāt* that appear in the work.

But even the lisping narrator of these *maqāmāt*, "al-Hāwif ibn Hifām," has his own textual doubles, in the form of the narrators of the most famous series of *maqāmāt*, ʿĪsā ibn *Hishām* and *al-Ḥārith* ibn Hammām. Indeed, as Humphrey Davies points out, the name in its "lisped" form is no name at all but may be translated as "Masher, son of Pulverizer." At every turn, al-Shidyāq does violence to the very presumption of verisimilitude; word and thing never correspond neatly, even in the attempt simply to name a character. Instead, he holds up art and artifice as the substance that underlies the world and even constitutes it. To navigate it, one must travel not only through space but through texts; when one reads *Leg over Leg* one also reads those innumerable authors he quotes or invokes, like the authors of the *maqāmāt*, al-Hamadhānī and al-Ḥarīrī ("men who have rendered their reputations white by covering pages in black," 1.1.1), or the English and French authors whom he quotes. It is no wonder that the text begins with eleven synonyms for the command, "be quiet!" (1.1.1), as al-Shidyāq attempts to speak alongside, and often over, the voices that crowd the text.

This multi-register and multi-lingual cacophony sets the stage for many of the travel narrative's comic scenes, where intercultural encounters are not always entirely fungible. As in *Tristram Shandy*, its closest English analogue, communication more often leads to misunderstanding and misinterpretation than to understanding. The result can hardly be used as a guide for East–West relations but instead parodies intercultural communication and its institutional forms—chief among them Orientalist scholarship. If this period's literature was partly looking to the West, what it saw was the West looking at it. Perhaps, then, there was no other way to write about that encounter than as a self-reflexive one. It looks to the West as a way to reflect on itself, not to imitate it but to critique and reformulate it. If we see *Leg over Leg* as an archive of Arabic literary modernity, we must take this double refraction into account.

What al-Shidyāq ultimately gives us in *Leg over Leg* is a theory of world literature—from a particular, *Nahḍawī* perspective. It imagines and constructs the world anew, through an omnivorous textuality, absorbing texts and literary forms through juxtaposition, quotation, imitation, and parody. Far from holding up Sterne or Lamartine as culturally distinct and inviolable paradigms, he incorporates them into Arabic literary categories, aligning *Tristram Shandy* with the *maqāmāt*. Rather than a choice between the two, or a straight line of filiation connecting them, literary history in al-Shidyāq appears as a winding one—modernity is staged on the road and does not always appear in the guise of "progress" (to use the language of modernity's evil twin, modernization). It sometimes appears to move sideways, to digress.

As an alternative translation of the work's subtitle allows, al-Faryāq's travels track the *ʿujm*, or mistakes, of the Arabs and "non-Arabs" (*al-ʾaʿjām* can also be translated as "barbarians," or those whose speech is unintelligible to Arabic-speakers). Traveling along linguistic boundaries, al-Shidyāq pieces together an unruly patchwork of a text whose unity is in danger of disintegration, threatening to dissolve into mere *ʿujmah*, or "babble." *Leg over Leg* thus creates a literary sphere that reminds us that the "world" in world literature is not a given; it must be manufactured. It is not merely "there" to be observed but is itself a dynamic constitutive process. It creates trouble—generic and otherwise—and it is always in danger of collapse. That is, world literature during the *Nahḍah* age is constructed out of the migrations and cross-fertilizations that define the era. Or, as the Fāriyāq reminds us, it was produced in the time of steamboats and railways, of "connecting the disconnected."

Rebecca C. Johnson
Northwestern University

A Note on the Text

The Arabic text presented here is that of the first edition of *Al-Sāq ʿalā l-sāq*, printed in Paris in 1855 under the author's supervision. The sole omission is of the Corrigenda (1855 pp. 25–26, "Arabic").[71] The only other deliberate changes are the adoption, without comment in the apparatus, of the contents of the Corrigenda and the corrections, noted in the apparatus, of a small number of apparent additional misprints, including amendment of the vowelling of lexical items taken directly from al-Fīrūzābādī's *Al-Qāmūs* where required to make the text conform to the 1344/1925–6 edition of the latter. This edition of *Al-Sāq ʿalā l-sāq* also follows the order in which the opening and closing sections of the book were printed in 1855. Inconsistencies in the original, such as differences between the titles of chapters as they appear in the list of contents versus the body of the text, have been maintained.

I stress the completeness and faithfulness to the original order of this edition, because al-Shidyāq's text has elsewhere been subjected to significant editorial intervention. Darwīsh Juwaydī's[72] edition omits the celebrated pointing-hand graphic element both from the list of contents and from its place in the text (2.15 in the present edition); it also omits the verses from the 1855 title page, the author's notice (0.2) and the publisher's introduction (0.3) and places the dedication (0.1) at the end of the book between the Conclusion and the Appendix (see Volume Four); at the end of the book, in addition to changing the order of elements, he omits the original conclusion, gives the originally untitled letter in Egyptian Arabic the heading "Conclusion," and omits the list of synonym lists and the author's remarks on the printing of the edition. Nasīb Wahībah al-Khāzin's edition[73] is complete with the exception of the omission of the hand, but it reverses the order of the author's notice and the publisher's introduction, while interleaving the opening pages with a considerable amount of editorial comment; at the end of the book, he changes the order of the sections entirely. By changing the order of elements at the end of the book, both Juwaydī and al-Khāzin obliterate al-Shidyāq's playful division of the work into two parts, whereby the Conclusion marks the end of Part I (*tamma l-juzʾ al-awwal*), consisting of 703 "Hindi"-numbered pages in the 1855 edition, while Part II (by implication; this heading is not used) consists of only eleven pages (the list of synonym lists), followed by the Appendix, consisting of twenty-six "Arabic"-numbered pages. ʿImād al-Ṣulḥ's edition, published under the title *Iʿtirāfāt al-Shidyāq fī Kitāb al-Sāq ʿalā l-sāq*,[74] which I have not seen, is apparently both radically shortened (through the omission of the lexical lists and much of the poetry)[75] and bowdlerized.[76]

That the 1855 edition faithfully represents the author's intentions is made clear in the last lines of the work, where he asks, "Do you not observe that M. Perrault, rue de Castellane, 15, Paris . . . has followed with the utmost care our instructions in terms of corrections and changes and gone to great lengths to compose the letters correctly and produce an excellent piece of printing—so much so that he has ended up, praise God, with the best thing ever printed in our language in Europe?" (1855 p. 24, "Arabic"). In another work of his, he states that he corrected all the proofs of *Al-Sāq* himself.[77]

The orthography—which is often, though not always, at variance with current norms and conventions—has also, therefore, been left unchanged. This both honors the intentions of the author and will, it is hoped, provide material for the study of the development of orthography and printing in Arabic and of its relation to wider issues of language change during the Arabic literary *nahḍah*, or "renaissance," to which Fāris al-Shidyāq was so important a contributor. In addition, retention of such forms may on occasion be imposed by the internal demands of the text, especially in terms of rhymed prose as when, to take but one of several examples, *al-yās* (for *al-ya's*) rhymes with *al-nās* (2.13.11).

Examples of orthographies at variance with modern convention are:

- omission of dots below final *yā'* (e.g., الثانى for الثاني); this practice is notably inconsistent in the case of فى/في, where two different type-pieces are used apparently randomly, one (the more common) with an undotted ى , and the other with backward-facing ي which is always dotted, the dot being omitted from the associated *fā'*, giving ڡي .
- the opposite of the preceding, i.e., dots below final *alif maqṣūrah* (المعني for المعنى).
- omission of *hamzat al-qaṭʿ* in initial (اثارة for إثارة), medial (قرآتى for قرآءتي; شيا for شيئا), and final (شى for شيء; تقرا for تقرأ) position; this also occurs where a short vowel is written (اَصح for أصح; الاَشكال for الأشكال) above initial *alif*.

- use of *maddah* above *alif* where the latter would, under modern conventions, be followed by *hamzat al-qaṭʿ* (جآ for جاء).
- *scriptio defectiva* (ثلثة ايام for ثلاثة ايام; ثلثون يوما for ثلاثون يوما).
- writing of the vocative particle يا as part of the following word (ياسيدي; يالحكمة الله)
- use of ح as an abbreviation for حينئذ

In the same spirit, unusual graphic features of the 1855 edition, such as the pointing hand in Book Two, Chapter 15 (omitted in all other editions) and the caudate line compositions at the end of many chapters, have been preserved. On the other hand, there is no compelling argument for retaining the original Arabic typeface, which the author himself described as being of "alien form."[78]

Notes to the Frontmatter

Foreword

1 Al-Shidyāq's biographers differ as to the date of his birth, with dates ranging from 1801 to 1805. We have used Geoffrey Roper's calculations, based on al-Shidyāq's British naturalization record submitted September 26, 1851, which lists his age as 45. Public Record Office, Home Office Papers—Naturalisation, 1278A, 26.9.1851.

2 Nadia Al-Bagdadi, "The Cultural Function of Fiction: From the Bible to Libertine Literature. Historical Criticism and Social Critique in Aḥmad Fāris al-Šidyāq," *Arabica,* 46, no. 3 (1999): 377.

3 ʿAzīz al-ʿAẓmah and Fawwāz Ṭarābulsī, *Aḥmad Fāris al-Shidyāq: Silsilat al-aʿmāl al-majhūlah* (London: Riad El-Rayyes Books, 1995).

4 See Ibrahim Abu-Lughod, *The Arab Rediscovery of Europe: A Study in Cultural Encounters* (Princeton: Princeton University Press, 1963).

5 Examples of this opinion abound; see, for example, M. M. Badawi, *A Critical Introduction to Modern Arabic Poetry* (Cambridge: Cambridge University Press, 1975), 25.

6 Samah Selim, *The Novel and the Rural Imaginary in Egypt, 1880–1985* (New York: Routledge, 2004), 90.

7 Timothy Mitchell, "The Stage of Modernity," in *Questions of Modernity,* edited by Timothy Mitchell (Minneapolis: University of Minnesota Press, 2000), 24; see also Stephen Sheehi, *Foundations of Modern Arab Identity* (Gainesville: University of Florida Press, 2004).

8 The following biographical information is taken largely from M. B. Alwan, "Aḥmad Fāris ash-Shidyāq and the West" (PhD diss., University of Indiana, 1970) and Geoffrey Roper, "Arabic Printing in Malta 1825–1845: Its History and Its Place in the Development of Print Culture in the Arab Middle East," supplemented by archival research in the CMS Archives in Birmingham, UK.

9 See, e.g., Muḥammad al-Hādī al-Maṭwī, *Aḥmad Fāris al-Shidyāq, 1801–1887: Ḥayātuhu wa-āthāruhu wa-ārāʾuhu fī l-nahḍah al-ʿarabiyyah al-ḥadīthah,* 2 vols. (Beirut: Dār al-Gharb al-Islāmī, 1989) and ʿImād al-Ṣulḥ, *Aḥmad Fāris al-Shidyāq: Āthāruhu wa-ʿaṣruhu* (Beirut: Sharikat al-Maṭbūʿāt li-l-Tawzīʿ wa-l-Nashr, 1987).

10 Ussama Makdisi, *Artillery of Heaven: American Missionaries and the Failed Conversion of the Middle East* (Ithaca: Cornell University Press, 2008), 114. For a complete account of the As'ad al-Shidyāq affair, see Makdisi, 103–37, Buṭrus al-Bustānī, *Qiṣṣat As'ad al-Shidyāq* (1860; Beirut: Dār al-Ḥamrā', 1992) and Isaac Bird, *The Martyr of Lebanon* (Boston: American Tract Society, 1864).

11 Makdisi, *Artillery of Heaven*, 127.

12 Bird, *Martyr of Lebanon*, 145.

13 Jurjī Zaydān, *Tārīkh ādāb al-lugha al-'arabiyyah*, vol. 16 of *Mu'allaffāt Jurjī Zaydān al-Kāmilah* (Beirut: Dār al-Jīl, 1982), 222. Originally published in 1911–3 by Maṭba'at al-Hilāl.

14 Christopher Schlienz, letter to Society Secretary, 18 May 1827, Church Missionary Society Archives CMS/CMO 65/1, University of Birmingham Special Collections.

15 The matter of al-Shidyāq's two conversions is difficult to settle using archival sources. Though Theodor Müller writes that he has received a "confession of belief with which [he] was satisfied" from al-Shidyāq in 1832, his colleague, William Krusé, writes three years later that, in his opinion, "Fares … is not yet converted." Theodor Müller to Christopher Schlienz, April 2, 1832, Church Missionary Society Archives CMS/CMO/65/20; William Krusé to Lay Secretary, January 25, 1835, Church Missionary Society Archives CMS/CMM 5/39. For references to the Fāriyāq's beliefs, see 1.19.4 and 1.19.5: "[H]e concluded that, in view of his said perseverance and mild manners, the Bag-man must be following the right path and that the metropolitan, with his vehemence and eagerness to do evil, must be among the misguided. (1.19.4) So he said to the Bag-man, 'Sir, I have heeded everything with which you've filled my ears and believe the truth to lie with you alone. I am your partisan, your follower, and the co-carrier of your bag.'" (1.19.5)

16 Daniel Temple to William Jowett, July 25, 1828, Church Missionary Society Archives CMS/CMO/ 39/121; emphasis Temple's.

17 Christopher Schlienz to Society Secretary, February 3, 1836, Church Missionary Archives CMO/65/44A; Christopher Schlienz to William Jowett, May 20, 1828, Church Missionary Society Archives CMO/65/4A.

18 Aḥmad Fāris al-Shidyāq, *Al-Wāsiṭah fī ma'rifat aḥwāl Mālṭa* (Beirut: al-Mu'assasah al-'Arabiyyah li-l-Dirāsāt wa-l-Nashr, 2004), chap. 2.

19 Theodor Müller to Christopher Schlienz, June 15, 1830, Church Missionary Society Archives CMS/CMO 73/47.

20 Buṭrus Yūsuf Ḥawwā: one of a group of Lebanese merchants living in London, on whom al-Shidyāq depended for financial and moral support during his third sojourn there,

between June 1853 and the summer of 1857, during which period he was also visiting Paris to oversee the printing of *Al-Sāq*; Ḥawwā provided al-Shidyāq with employment as a clerk in his offices.

21 See Geoffrey Roper, "Aḥmad Fāris al-Shidyāq and the Libraries of Europe and the Ottoman Empire," *Libraries & Culture* 33, no. 3 (Summer 1998), 235. For the names of the scholars with whom al-Shidyāq made contact, see Alwan, 42–45.

22 Aḥmad Fāris al-Shidyāq, *Mumāḥakāt al-ta'wīl fī munāqiḍāt al-injīl* [*Altercations of Interpretation: On Contradictions in the Gospels*] (Amman: Dār Wā'il li-l-Nashr wa-Tawzīʿ, 2003). For a discussion of its contents and technique, see Nadia al-Bagdadi, "The Cultural Function of Fiction: From the Bible to Libertine Literature: Historical Criticism and Social Critique in Aḥmad Fāris al-Šidyāq," *Arabica*, 46, no. 3 (1999): 375–401.

23 There is no empirical evidence for the exact date or place of his conversion, which might also have occurred while he was in Tunis, Paris, or London. Al-Shidyāq, in fact, began an intellectual relationship with Islamic scholars while in Egypt and continued to pursue, in the libraries of Cambridge and London, his interest in linguistic and literary texts produced during Islam's golden age. And, as Humphrey Davies notes in the translator's Afterword, his invocation of Islamic motifs in *Leg over Leg* might indicate that he converted before its 1855 publication—as he deploys specifically Islamic formulae on more than one occasion, even going so far as to say, regarding a Christian woman, that "she had converted to Islam, praise be to God, Lord of the Worlds" (2.4.16). For more on al-Shidyāq's textual studies in England see Roper, "Aḥmad Fāris al-Shidyāq and the Libraries of Europe and the Ottoman Empire," 236–41.

24 Ami Ayalon, *The Press in the Arab Middle East: A History* (Oxford: Oxford University Press, 1995), 30.

25 Ayalon, 30.

26 Geoffrey Roper, "Fāris al-Shidyāq and the Transition from Scribal to Print Culture," in *The Book in the Islamic World: The Written Word and Communication in the Middle East*, edited by George N. Atiyeh (Albany: State University of New York Press, 1995), 214.

27 Al-Shidyāq, *Al-Wāsiṭah*, 382. Cited in Roper, "Scribal to Print Culture," 214.

28 Jurjī Zaydān, *Tarājim mashāhīr al-Sharq fī l-qarn al-tāsiʿ ashar* (Cairo: Maṭbaʿat al-Hilāl, 1922), 2:87.

29 Walid Hamarneh, "Ahmad Fāris al-Shidyāq," *Essays in Arabic Literary Biography: 1850–1950*, edited by Roger Allen (Wiesbaden: Otto Harrassowitz, 2010), 327.

30 Kamran Rastegar, *Literary Modernity between the Middle East and Europe: Textual Transactions in Nineteenth-century Arabic, English, and Persian Literatures* (New York: Routledge, 2007), 109.

31 Sabry Hafez, *Genesis of Arabic Narrative Discourse: A Study in the Sociology of Modern Arabic Literature* (London: Saqi Books, 1993), 47.

32 The *maqāmah* (plural *maqāmāt*), or "session," is a genre popularized by Aḥmad Badīʿ al-Zamān al-Hamadhānī in the fourth/tenth century. Considered the first avowedly fictional literary genre in Arabic, al-Hamadhānī's *maqāmāt* narrated, in rhyming prose, the adventures of Abū l-Fatḥ al-Iskandarī, a vagabond trickster figure who earns his living by outwitting his companions with his verbal dexterity. For an introduction to the *maqāmāt*, see Abdelfattah Kilito, *Les séances* (Paris: Sindbad, 1983).

33 These include a commentary on al-Fīrūzābādī's *Al-Qāmūs*, entitled *Al-Jāsūs ʿalā l-Qāmūs* (Istanbul: al-Jawāʾib, 1882), an edition (with introduction) to Ibn al-Manẓūr's fourteenth-century lexicon, *Lisān al-ʿArab*, 20 vols. (Cairo: Bulāq, 1883–9), and a lost commentary on classical Arabic poetry, *Malḥūẓāt ʿalā l-shiʿr al-ʿarabī*. For a complete bibliography of the works of al-Shidyāq, see al-ʿAẓmah and Ṭarābulsī, 408–40.

34 Robert Brunschvig, *Classicisme et déclin culturel dans l'histoire de l'Islam: Actes du symposium international d'histoire de la civilisation musulmane, Bordeaux 25–29 juin 1956*, organized by R. Brunschvig and G. E. Von Grunebaum (Paris: Chantemerle, 1957), 284; cited in Nada Tomiche, "Nahḍah," in *Encyclopaedia of Islam*, edited by P. Bearman et al., 2nd ed. (Leiden: E. J. Brill, 2008), 7:900.

35 Samah Selim, "The People's Entertainments: Translation, Popular Fiction, and the Nahdah in Egypt," in *Other Renaissances: A New Approach to World Literature*, edited by Brenda Deen Schildgen et al. (New York: Palgrave Macmillan, 2006), 38.

36 See Rastegar, *Literary Modernity*, and the essays in "The Novelization of Islamic Literatures: The Intersections of Western, Arabic, Persian, Urdu, and Turkish Traditions," a special issue of *Comparative Critical Studies*, 4, no. 3 (2007), guest editor Mohamed Salah Omri.

37 Samah Selim, "The Nahda, Popular Fiction, and the Politics of Translation," *MIT Electronic Journal of Middle East Studies* 4 (Fall 2004): 71.

38 Henry Harris Jessup, *Fifty-three Years in Syria* (New York: Fleming H. Revell, 1910), 2:713.

39 Roger Owen, *The Middle East in the World Economy, 1800–1914* (London: Methuen, 1981), 116.

40 Akram Fouad Khater, *Inventing Home: Emigration, Gender, and the Middle Class in Lebanon, 1870–1920* (Berkeley: University of California Press, 2001), 22–29.

41 Owen, *Middle East in the World Economy*, 160.

42 Roger Owen, "Egypt and Europe: From French Expedition to British Occupation," in *The Modern Middle East*, edited by Albert Hourani et al., 2nd ed. (London: I. B. Tauris, 2005), 117, and Fritz Steppat, "National Education Projects in Egypt before the British Occupation," in *Beginnings of Modernization in the Middle East: The Nineteenth Century*, edited by William R. Polk and Richard L. Chambers (Chicago: University of Chicago Press, 1968), 283–4.

43 See Nabil Matar, *Europe through Arab Eyes, 1578–1727* (New York: Columbia University Press, 2009), Nabil Matar (ed.), *In the Lands of the Christians: Arabic Travel Writing in the Seventeenth Century, First English Translations* (New York: Routledge, 2003), and Roxanne L. Euben, *Journeys to the Other Shore: Muslim and Western Travelers in Search of Knowledge* (Princeton: Princeton University Press, 2006).

44 On these early educational missions, see Ibrahim Abu-Lughod, *The Arab Rediscovery of Europe* (Princeton: Princeton University Press, 1963), Alain Silvera, "The First Egyptian Student Mission to France under Muhammad Ali," *Middle Eastern Studies*, 16, no. 2 (May 1980): 1–22, and Lisa Pollard, "The Habits and Customs of Modernity: Egyptians in Europe and the Geography of Nineteenth-Century Nationalism," *The Arab Studies Journal*, 7–8, no. 2/1 (1999/2000): 52–74.

45 Headed by Rifāʿa Rāfiʿ al-Ṭahṭāwī, the scholar selected to accompany the first *Mission égyptienne* to Paris in 1824, Muḥammad ʿAlī opened the School of Languages [Kulliyat al-Alsān] in Cairo in 1837 in order to centralize these translation efforts that were earlier performed out of individual schools and institutes. (Al-Ṭahṭāwī himself had worked as a translator out of the School of Medicine and the Artillery School.) While the purview of the school was by no means strictly literary—they published more than 2,000 scholarly and scientific books—al-Ṭahṭāwī himself is commonly considered the initiator of what became known as the "Translation Movement" of Arabic literature (*ḥarakat al-tarjamah*) with his 1867 translation of François Fénelon's *Aventures de Télémaque*.

46 John Heyworth-Dunne, "Printing and Translations under Muhammad Ali of Egypt: The Foundation of Modern Arabic," *Journal of the Royal Asiatic Society*, no. 3 (1940): 332.

47 Heyworth-Dunne, 332; see also Ayalon, 565.

48 These presses were international also in their day-to-day operations, with translators sometimes working with the European authors (who were employed in government schools, for example) to produce Arabic versions of textbooks; Heyworth-Dunne, 346.

49 Ayalon, 561.

50 Elisabeth Kendall, "Between Politics and Literature: Journals in Alexandria and Istanbul at the End of the Nineteenth Century," in *Modernity and Culture: From the*

Mediterranean to the Indian Ocean, edited by Leila Tarazi Fawaz, Christopher Alan Bayly, and Robert Ilbert (New York: Columbia University Press, 2002), 332.

51 Kendall, 350.

52 See for example Stephen Sheehi, "Arabic Literary-scientific Journals: Precedence for Globalization and the Creation of Modernity," *Comparative Studies of South Asia, Africa, and the Middle East,* 25, no. 2 (2005).

53 Charles Montagu Doughty, *Travels in Arabia Deserta* (Cambridge: Cambridge University Press, 1888), 2:371.

54 In an article entitled "Al-Jarā'id al-ʿarabiyyah fī Amrīkā" ("Arabic Periodicals in America"), appearing in Ibrāhīm al-Yāzijī's journal *al-Ḍiyā'*, for example, the author refers to Arab writers in the United States as part of a worldwide *Nahḍah*: "Al-Jarā'id al-ʿarabiyyah fī Amrīkā," *Al-Ḍiyā': Majallah ʿilmiyyah adabiyyah ṣiḥḥiyyah ṣināʿiyyah* 16 (Cairo, April 30, 1899): 502.

55 As Lital Levy puts it, *Nahḍah* authors "viewed themselves as local agents of this global process" of historical change; Lital Levy, "Jewish Writers in the Arab East: Literature, History, and the Politics of Enlightenment, 1863–1914" (PhD diss., University of California Berkeley, 2007), 23.

56 Both of these are titles of articles in Buṭrus and Salīm al-Bustānī's biweekly *Al-Jinān* (Beirut, 1870), 1:160–4.

57 Shaden Tageldin, *Disarming Words: Empire and the Seductions of Translation in Egypt* (Berkeley: University of California Press, 2011), 5.

58 This description is not exclusive to Arab modernity. As the essays in Timothy Mitchell's *Questions of Modernity* make clear, modernity in Western and non-Western contexts alike "had its origins in reticulations of exchange and production encircling the world," making it "a creation not of the West but of an interaction between West and non-West;" Mitchell, "The Stage of Modernity," 2.

59 For an example, see the translator's Afterword in Volume Four, and Rastegar, 113–25.

60 Al-Bagdadi, 392.

61 Luwīs ʿAwaḍ, *Al-Mu'aththirāt al-ajnabiyya fī l-adab al-ʿarabī al-ḥadīth* (Cairo 1962), 28, and Shawqī Ḍayf, *Al-Matāmāt* (Cairo: 1964), both cited in Mattityahu Peled, "Al-Sāq ʿalā al-Sāq: A Generic Definition," *Arabica* 32, no. 1 (March 1985): 35; Raḍwah ʿĀshūr, *Al-Ḥadātha al-mumkina: Al-Shidyāq wa-l-Sāq ʿalā l-sāq, al-riwāyah al-ūlā fī l-adab al-ʿarabī al-ḥadīth* (Cairo: Dār al-Shurūq, 2009), 10; Paul Starkey, "Voyages of Self-definition: The Case of [Ahmad] Faris al-Shidyāq," in *Sensibilities of the Islamic Mediterranean: Self-Expression in a Muslim Culture from Post-Classical Times to the Present Day*, edited by Robin Ostle (London; I. B. Tauris, 2008), 118–32.

62 Al-Bagdadi, 394–5.

63 Lexically, the adverbial phrase *sāqan ʿalā l-sāq* is also a figurative way of saying "one after another"—which is fitting for the text's self-conscious attention to narrative sequence. Lane gives the example, "So-and-So had three children one after the other [*sāqan ʿalā l-sāq*]." Edward Lane, *Arabic-English Lexicon* (Beirut: Librairie du Liban, 1968), 4:1472.

64 Viktor Shklovsky, *Theory of Prose*, translated by Benjamin Sher (Normal IL: Dalkey Archive Press, 1991), 147.

65 For a reading of *Leg over Leg* in the context of al-Shidyāq's intellectual challenge to ecclesiastical authority, see Al-Bagdadi, 391–401.

66 See al-Ṣulḥ, 109.

67 Aḥmad Fāris al-Shidyāq, in *Kanz al-raghāʾib fī muntakhabāt al-Jawāʾib*, edited by Salīm Fāris (Istanbul: Maṭbaʿat al-Jawāʾib, 1288–98/1871–81), cited in al-Ṣulḥ, 215.

68 ʿAẓmah and Ṭarābulsī, 34.

69 Rastegar, 104–5.

70 Rastegar, 104–5.

Note on the Text

71 The Corrigenda occupies pp. 25–26 of the Appendix (*Dhanab*), which is numbered using "Arabic" forms and follows p. 712 of the "Hindi"-numbered text.

72 Sidon and Beirut: al-Dār al-Namūdhajiyyah, 2006.

73 Beirut: Dār Maktabat al-Ḥayāh, n.d.

74 Beirut: Dār al-Rāʾid al-ʿArabī, 5th ed., 1982.

75 Matityahu Peled, "The enumerative style in *al-Sâq ʿalâ al-sâq*," *Journal of Arabic Literature* 22 (1991), 127; Katia Zakharia, "Aḥmad Fāris al-Šidyāq, auteur de maqāmāt," *Arabica* 52, no. 4 (2005), 509–10.

76 Peled, "Enumerative," 137.

77 Geoffrey Roper, "Fāris al-Shidyāq and the Transition from Scribal to Print Culture," in *The Book in the Islamic World: The Written Word and Communication in the Middle East*, edited by George N. Atiyeh (Albany: State University of New York Press, 1995), 213.

78 Roper, "Fāris al-Shidyāq," 219.

الساق على الساق

المجلّد الأوّل

Leg Over Leg

Volume One

كتاب

الساق على الساق فى ما هو الفارياق

او

ايام وشهور واعوام فى عجم العرب والاعجام

تاليف العبد الفقير الى ربه الرزاق

فارس بن يوسف الشدياق

تاليف زيد وهند فى زمانك ذا   اشهى الى الناس من تاليف سفرين
ودرس ثورين قد شُدّا الى قَرَن   اقنى وانفع من تدريس حبرين[١]

---

١ بعدها في ١٨٥٥: طبعه بنفقته العبد الفقير الى رحمة ربه الموقى رافائيل كحلا الدمشقي وذلك فى مدينة باريس المحمية سنة ١٨٥٥ مسيحية ١٢٧٠ هجرية ثم باللغة الفرنساوية

LA VIE ET LES AVENTURES
DE FARIAC
RELATION DE SES VOYAGES
AVEC SES OBSERVATIONS CRITIQUES
SUR LES ARABES ET SUR AUTRES PEUPLES
Par FARIS EL-CHIDIAC.

PARIS
BENJAMIN DUPRAT, LIBRAIRIE DE L'INSTITUT,
DE LA BIBLIOTHÈQUE IMPERIALE, DES SOCIÉTÉS ASIATIQUES DE PARIS, DE LONDRES, DE MADRAS,
DE CALCUTTA, etc.
Rue du Cloître-Saint-Benoît, no. 7.
1855

Leg over Leg

or

The Turtle in the Tree

concerning

The Fāriyāq

What Manner of Creature Might He Be

otherwise entitled

Days, Months, and Years

spent in

Critical Examination

of

The Arabs

and

Their Non-Arab Peers

by

The Humble Dependent on His Lord the Provider

Fāris ibn Yūsuf al-Shidyāq

The writings of Zayd and Hind these days speak more to the common taste
  Than any pair of weighty tomes.
More profitable and useful than the teachings of two scholars
  Are what a yoke of oxen from the threshings combs.

فهرست الكتاب

Contents of the Book

في اهدآ هذا الكتاب البديع

الحمد لله

لما جرت عادة المولفين من الافرنج ان يهدوا مولفاتهم الى من تميّز فى عصرهم ١،٠
بالفضائل والمحامد و رُويت عنه مآثر جليلة فى اكرام العلم واهله رايت هنا ان احذو
حذوهم في اهدآ هذا الكتاب البديع الى الجناب المكرم الخواجا بطرس يوسف
حوّا المقيم بلندرة اذ كان قد اتصف فى عصرنا هذا بالمزايا الحميدة التى يتحلّى بها
مدح كل مطرئ وقول كل مولّف وهو الان كبير هذا البيت المشهور من قديم
الزمان بالحسب والفخر ورفعة القدر وكثيرا ما اعان على تحصيل الفضايل وامدّ
بنى جنسه وغيرهم بما افازهم بمنتهى الامال وادرك بهم منتأى الاوطار فانثنوا
عنه حامدين وعلى آلائه شاكرين هذا وان يكن مقامه الكريم يجلّ عن بعض
جُمَل فى الكتاب لكنه فى الجملة جدير بان يختص به فالمرجو منه قبوله واجارته
وترويجه واجازته فان الحقير بالانتمآ اليه يعود جليلا والناقص يكتسب تكميلا *

من الداعى لجنابه
فارس الشدياق

The Dedication of This Elegantly Eloquent Book

Praise Be to God

It being the custom of Frankish authors to dedicate their works to those distinguished in their day by virtues and praiseworthy qualities and of whom great achievements are reported regarding the patronage of scholarship and its servants, I have decided here to follow their example by dedicating this elegantly eloquent book to the esteemed and honorable Khawājā Buṭrus Yūsuf Ḥawwā,[1] of London, for he is well known in this age of ours for all the commendable merits with which the eulogist adorns his songs and the author his words, while he is now also head of that house[2] so long celebrated for its pedigree, pride, and elevated status. Many a time has he assisted in the attainment of virtuous qualities and provided those of his race, and others, with the means to obtain their highest hopes and realize their most distant goals, so that they leave him uttering *praise,* grateful to him for his generous *ways.* Moreover, albeit his standing exceeds what little may be contained in *summary* form in this book, it is nevertheless fitting that the latter be dedicated to him in *sum.* We ask that he accept it, take it under his wing, promote it, and grant it his approval, for whatever is unworthy regains, through appurtenance to him, its worth, and all that is incomplete is made whole. 0.1

From Fāris al-Shidyāq
Who Prays for His Honorable Person

تنبيه من المولف

الحمد لله الموفّق الى السداد والملهم الى الرشاد وبعد فان جميع ما اودعته فى هذا ١،٢،٠
الكتاب فانما هو مبنىّ على امرين احدهما ابراز غرائب اللغة ونوادرها فيندرج تحت ٢،٢،٠
جنس الغريب نوع المترادف والمتجانس وقد ضمّنت منهما هنا اشهر ما تلزم معرفته
واهمّ ما تمسّ الحاجة اليه على نمط بديع ولو ذكر على اسلوب كتب اللغة مقتضبا على
العلائق لجآء مملاّ وقد راعيت سرده مرة على ترتيب حروف المعجم ومرّة نسقته بفقر
مسجعة وعبارات مرصعة * ومن ذلك القلب والابدال كما فى التورور والثورور ٣،٢،٠
والتوثور والترتور وتمطّى وتمتى وتمطط وتمدد * ومنه ايراد الفاظ كثيرة متقاربة
اللفظ والمعنى من حرف واحد من حروف المعجم نحو الغطش والغمش والبهز والبحز
والبغز والحفز تنبيها على ان كل حرف يختص بمعنى من المعانى دون غيره وهو
من اسرار اللغة العربية التى قلّ من تنبّه لها * وقد وضعت لهذا كتابا مخصوصا
سميته منتهى العجب فى خصائص لغة العرب فمن خصائص حرف الحآء السعة ٤،٢،٠
والانبساط نحو الابتحاح والبداح والبراح والابطح والابلنداح والجحّ والرحرح والمرتدح
والرَوح والتركح والتسطيح والمسفوح والمسح فى قولهم ان فيه لمَسْحًا اى متسعا

Author's Notice

Praise be to God, who each happy thought *inspires*, and to guide man to righteous acts *conspires*. To proceed: everything that I have set down in this book is determined by one of two concerns. The first of these is to give prominence to the oddities of the language, including its rare words.[3] 0.2.1

Under the category of oddities fall words that are similar in meaning and words that are similar in lexical association. Here I have included the most celebrated, important, and necessary items that need to be known, and in elegantly eloquent form, for, had they been set out in the style typical of our books on language, divorced from any context, the effect would have been wearisome. I have also taken care on some occasions to present them in alphabetical order and on others to arrange them in paragraphs of rhymed prose and morphologically parallel expressions.[4] 0.2.2

Another consists of substitution and swapping,[5] as in *tuʾrūr, thuʾrūr, tuʾthūr*, and *turtūr* ("police officer or his assistant"[6]), or *tamaṭṭā, tamattā, tamaṭṭaṭ*, and *tamaddad* ("to stretch"). Another is the production of numerous words of similar sound and meaning from a single letter of the alphabet, such as *ghaṭash* ("going blind from hunger") and *ghamash* (ditto), and *bahz* ("shoving"), *baḥz* (ditto), *baghz* ("striking with the foot or a stick"), and *ḥafz* ("pushing from behind"), for it is to be noted that each letter is associated with a specific meaning distinct from that of every other letter—a peculiarity of the Arabic language of which few have taken note. I have written a book devoted to this topic entitled *Muntahā l-ʿajab fī khaṣāʾiṣ lughat al-ʿArab* (*Wonder's Apogee Concerning Every Arab Linguistic Particularity*).[7] 0.2.3

Thus, among the characteristic associations of the letter *ḥ*, for example, are amplitude and expansiveness, as in the words *ibtiḥah* ("affluence and abundance"), *badāḥ* ("broad tract of land"), *barāḥ* ("broad uncultivated tract of land"), *abṭaḥ* ("wide watercourse"), *iblindāḥ* ("widening out (of a place)"), *jaḥḥ* ("leveling out (of a thing)"), *raḥraḥ* ("wide and spread out"), *murtadaḥ* ("scope, freedom"), *rawḥ* ("breeze"), *tarakkuḥ* ("spaciousness"), *tasṭīḥ* ("roof-laying"), *masfūḥ* ("spreading (of water)"), *masmaḥ* ("ample room") as in the saying "Keep thou to the truth, for in it is ample room, i.e., 0.2.4

والساحة والانسياح والشُدحة والشرح والصفيحة والصلدح والاصلنطاح والمصلنفح والطح والمفرطح والفشح والفطح والفلطحة الى آخر الباب * ويلحق به الفاظ كثيرة خفية الاتصال لا تدرك الا بامعان النظر نحو الاسجاح والتسريح والسماحة والسنح * ومن خصائص حرف الدال اللين والنعومة والغضاضة نحو البرخداة ٥،٢،٠
والتيد والثأد والثعد والمثمعد والمثمغد والثوهد والثهمد والخبنداة والخود والرادة والرَخْودة والرهادة والعبرد والفرهد والاملود والفلهود والقرهد والقشدة والمأد والمرد والمغد والملَدَ الى اخر الباب * ويلحق به من الامور المعنوية الرغد والسرهدة والمجد وغير ذلك * وربما عادلوا فى بعض الحروف اى راعوا فيها الاكثار من ٦،٢،٠
النقيض فان حرف الدال يشتمل ايضا على الفاظ كثيرة تدل على الصلابة والقوة والشدة * وذلك نحو التادّد والتاكيد والتاييد والجلعد والجلمد والجد والحديد والسحدد والسخدود والسمهد والتشدد والصفد والصلد والصلخد والصمغد والعجرد والتجلد والعرد والعِربَد والعرقدة والعصلد والعطوّد والعطرّد والعلد الى آخره *

space,"[8] *sāḥah* ("courtyard"), *insiyāḥ* ("bigness of belly"), *shudḥah* ("roominess"), *sharḥ* ("laying open"), *ṣafīḥah* ("slab of stone"), *ṣaldaḥ* ("wide stone"), *iṣlinṭāḥ* ("widening out (of a valley)"), *muṣalfaḥ* ("large-headed"), *ṭaḥḥ* ("spreading"), *mufalṭaḥ* ("large-headed"), *fashḥ* ("standing astraddle"), *fatḥ* ("broadening"), *falṭaḥah* ("flattening"), and so on to the end of that rubric. To these may be added numerous words whose connection to the idea of amplitude and expansiveness is not obvious and can be detected only with careful scrutiny, such as *sujāḥ* ("air"), *tasrīḥ* ("divorce"), *samāḥah* ("generosity"), and *sunḥ* ("good fortune and blessing").

Among characteristic associations of the letter *d* are softness, smoothness, and tenderness, as in the words *burakhdāh* ("a smooth, limp woman"), *tayd* ("kindness"), *tha'ad* ("soft, tender plants"), *tha'd* ("soft dates"), *mutham'idd* ("clear-faced (of a boy)"), *muthamghidd* ("fatty (of a kid)"), *thawhad* ("fat and well-formed (of an adolescent boy)"), *thahmad* ("large and fat"), *khabandāh* ("fat and full (of a woman)"), *khawd* ("young and well-formed (of a girl)"), *ra'dah* ("early matured due to good nourishment (of a girl)"), *rakhwaddah* ("soft (of a woman)"), *rahādah* ("softness and pliancy"), *'ubrud* ("white and soft (of a girl)"), *furhud* ("plump and handsome (of an adolescent boy)"), *umlūd* ("soft and pliable"), *fulhūd* ("fat and comely (of a youth)"), *qurhud* ("smooth, fleshy, and soft"), *qishdah* ("clotted cream"), *ma'd* ("large and fat"), *murd* ("boys with downy upper lips but no beards"), *maghd* ("smooth and fleshy"), *malad* ("youthfulness, softness, and wobbliness"), and so on to the end of the rubric. To these may be added, under the heading of figurative usages, such words as *raghd* ("generous and kindly"), *sarhadah* ("ease of living"), *majd* ("glory, generosity"), and so on. 0.2.5

It may be that the ancient Arabs sought to bring a balance to certain letters or, in other words, took care to give the opposite meaning full play too, for the letter *d* also encompasses many words indicating hardness, strength, and force, as in *ta'addud* ("harshness"), *ta'kīd* ("asserting"), *ta'yīd* ("confirming"), *jal'ad* ("hard and strong"), *jalmad* ("a rock"), *jamad* ("ice"), *ḥadīd* ("iron"), *suḥdud* ("strong and rebellious"), *sukhdūd* ("a man of iron"), *samhad* ("a thing hard and dry"), *tashaddud* ("harshness, severity"), *ṣafad* ("shackle"), *ṣald* ("hard and smooth"), *ṣalkhad* ("a tall, strong, aged camel"), *ṣimaghd* ("hard"), *'ajrad* ("thick and strong"), *ta'ajlud* ("to grow large and strong"), *'ard* ("erect, strong, and hard"), *'irbadd* ("strong"), *'arqadah* ("to twist tightly"), *'aṣlad* ("strong and hard"), *'aṭawwad* ("harsh and difficult"), *'aṭarrad* ("harsh and difficult"), *'ald* ("hard and strong"), and so on. 0.2.6

ومن خصائص حرف الميم القطع والاستئصال والكسر نحو اَرَم وازم وثَرِم وثلم ٧،٢،٠
وجذم وجرم وجزم وجلم وحذم وحذلم وحسم وحطم وحلقم وخذم وخرم وخزم
وخضم الى اخر الباب * ويلحق به من الامور المعنوية حُمَّ الامر اى قُضى وحرم
وحتم وحزم فان معنى القطع ملحوظ فيها * ويكثر فى هذا الحرف ايضا معنى
الظلام والسواد * ومن خصائص حرف الهآ الحمق والغفلة والرثء اى قلة ٨،٢،٠
الفطنة نحو اَلِه واُمِه وبله والبُوهة وتفه والتَوَه والدله والسَبَه وشُده لغة فى دُهش
او مقلوب منه وعُتِه وعَلِه وعمه ونمه ووَرِه وقس على ذلك سائر الحروف *
ومن هذا الغريب ايضا كون بعض الصيغ يختص بمعنى من المعانى نحو اجرهدّ ٩،٢،٠
واسمهرّ وكل ذلك مشار اليه فى هذا الكتاب فينبغى التفطّن له * وقد طالعت ١٠،٢،٠
كتاب المزهر فى اللغة للامام السيوطى رحّمه مما ذكر فيه خصائص اللغة نقلا عن
الامام اللغوىّ ابن فارس فلم اجده تعرّض لهذا النوع بل ربما اورد من الخصائص
احيانا ما لا ينبغى ايراده كجعله مثلا اطلاق لفظة الحمار على البليد منها *

Among the characteristic associations of the letter *m* are cutting, uprooting, and breaking, as in the words *arama* ("to seize and bite"), *azima* ("to bite hard using the whole of the mouth"), *tharima* ("to be gap-toothed"), *thalama* ("to nick or notch (a blade or the like)"), *jadhama* ("to chop off"), *jarama* ("to bone (meat)"), *jazama* ("to cut short"), *jalama* ("to clip"), *ḥadhama* ("to cut quickly"), *ḥadhlama* ("to sharpen to a point"), *ḥasama* ("to sever"), *ḥaṭama* ("to smash"), *ḥalqama* ("to cut the throat of (s.o.)"), *khadhama* ("to cut"), *kharama* ("to pierce"), *khazama* ("to thread (pearls)"), *khaḍama* ("to bite into (s.th.)"), and so on to the end of the rubric. To these may be added, under the heading of figurative usages, *ḥumma* meaning "it (a certain matter) was decreed," *ḥaruma* ("to be forbidden"), *ḥatama* ("to declare necessary") and *ḥazuma* ("to be resolute"), in all of which the sense of "cutting" is clearly observable. Also common in this letter are the meanings "darkness" and "blackness." 0.2.7

Among the characteristic associations of the letter *h* are stupidity, heedlessness, and *rath'*, or lack of native wit, examples being *aliha* ("to be perplexed"), *umiha* ("to become demented"), *baliha* ("to be stupid"), *būhah* ("a stupid, inconstant, and disordered man"), *tafiha* ("to become stupid"), *tawh* ("disturbance of the mind"), *dalh* ("being maddened by love"), *sabah* ("senile dementia"), *shudiha* ("to become amazed and confused") (a dialectal variant of *duhisha*, or formed from it by metathesis), *'utiha* ("to lose one's mind"), *'aliha* ("to become confused and amazed"), *'amiha* ("to hesitate as though lost and confused (in an argument or on a road)"), *namiha* ("to become somewhat confused"), and *wariha* ("to become stupid"). It is the same with the rest of the letters. 0.2.8

Another oddity of the language is that certain patterns are associated with a specific meaning, examples being *ijrahadda* ("to hasten one's pace when walking") and *ismaharra* ("to become hard and strong").[9] 0.2.9

All these things are alluded to in this book and must be quickly grasped. I have perused what Imam al-Suyūṭī[10] (God show him mercy) has to say on the distinguishing characteristics of the language in his *Al-Muzhir fī l-lughah* (*The Luminous Work on Language*),[11] copying from the master linguist Ibn Fāris,[12] and found that it fails to deal at any length with this type of association of form and sense; even worse, it sometimes seems to provide examples of "associations" that shouldn't be considered as such—for example, the application of the term *ḥimār* ("donkey") to a dim-wit.[13] 0.2.10

١١،٢،٠ ومن ذلك الغريب النوادر من الالفاظ وذلك نحو قولى اكهى فى صفة الرجل
المتقرقف من البرد قال فى القاموس اكهى سخّن اطراف اصابعه بنَفَس * ونحو
العنقاش للذى يطوف فى القرى يبيع الاشيآ * والضوطار وهو من يدخل السوق
بلا راس مال فيحتال للكسب * والذُبابة[١] اى بقية الدَين * وثرمل يقال ثرمل
الطعام لم يحسن اكله فانتثر على لحيته وفمه * وتكظكظ وهو ان ينتصب الانسان
عند الاكل قاعدا كلّما امتلا بطنه * ونحو الجلهزة والتلحزّ والوَذم والارغال وغير
١٢،٢،٠ ذلك مما فُسّر بعضه وترك الباقى فرارا من تكبير جرم الكتاب * والامر الثانى ذكر
محامد النسآء ومذامهنّ فمن هذه المحامد ترقى المرأة فى الدراية والمعارف بحسب
اختلاف الاحوال عليها كما يظهر مما اثرت عن الفارياقية * فانها بعد ان كانت لا
تفرق بين الامرد والمحلوق اللحية وبين البحر الملح وبحر النيل تدرّجت فى المعارف بحيث
صارت تجادل اهل النظر والخبرة وتنتقد الامور السياسية والاحوال المعاشية
والمعادية فى البلاد التى راتها احسن انتقاد * فان قيل انه قد نقل عنها الفاظ
غريبة غير مشهورة لا فى التخاطب ولا فى الكتب فلا يمكن ان تكون قد نطقت
بها * قلت ان النقل لا يلزم هنا ان يكون بحروفه وانما المدار على المعنى * ومن
تلك المحامد ايضا حركات النسآ الشائقة وضروب محاسنهن المتنوعة التى لم يتصوّر
منها شى الّا وذكرته فى هذا الكتاب لا بل قد اودعته ايضا معظم خواطرهن
وافكارهن وكل ما اختصّ بهن *

---

١ ١٨٥٥: الذبابة.

Among other such oddities are the rare words, as when I use *akhā* to describe a man shivering with cold; in the *Qāmūs*, it states that "*akhā* means 'he warmed the ends of his fingers by blowing on them'." Further examples are *ʿinqāsh* for "the man who goes around the villages selling things," *ḍawṭār* for "one who enters the market without capital and swindles people for gain," *dhubābah* meaning "the amount outstanding on a debt," *tharmala* as in *tharmala l-ṭaʿām* meaning "he ate messily, so that it was scattered over his beard and mouth," *yatakaẓkaẓ* meaning that a person "straightens up in his seat every time he feels his belly is full." Further examples are *jalhazah* ("pretending ignorance of something of which one is aware"), *talaḥḥuz* ("drooling from the mouth on eating a pomegranate or the like"), *wadham* ("a penis with its testicles"), *arghāl* ("orache plants"), and so on. Some such words are explained while others have been left without explanation to avoid inflating the size of the book. 0.2.11

My other concern has been to discuss the praiseworthy and blameworthy qualities of women. One such praiseworthy quality is the distance a woman may advance in knowledge and education depending on the varying circumstances to which she is subjected, as will appear in my reports on the Fāriyāqiyyah,[14] for the latter, who once didn't know the difference between a beardless boy and a clean-shaven one, or between the ocean and the Nile, has made such progress in education that she now argues with theorist and practitioner alike and provides excellent critiques of the political issues and conditions, mundane and spiritual, of the countries she has seen. If it be said that the book attributes to her rare words that are little-known either in speech or in books and which she could not have uttered, I reply that such attributions do not, in this case, have to be literal; the thought is what matters. Other praiseworthy qualities of women are their alluring ways of moving and all their various charms, no imaginable form of which have I left unmentioned in this book. Nay, I have put into it 0.2.12

most of their thoughts and ideas as well,
and everything else that has
to do with them.

مقدمة لناشر هذا الكتاب

الحمد لله تعالى على ما اسبغ من نعمه علينا ووالى وبعد فيقول العبد الفقير الى رحمة ربه ١،٣،٠
الحافظ الموقِّي رافائيل كحلا الدمشقى انى لما طالعت هذا الكتاب المسمى بالساق على
الساق رايته قد اشتمل على فوائد جزيلة من سرد الفاظ كثيرة من المترادف والمتجانس
باسلوب رائق معجب وتمهيد شائق مطرب وخصوصا لاشتماله على اخص ما يلزم
معرفته من الالات والادوات واستيفائه لجميع اصناف الماكول والمشروب والمشموم
والملبوس والمفروش والمركوب والحلى والجواهر مما لم يوجد في كتاب غيره على هذا
النمط وما أُغفل من تلك الاشياء فى بابه وهو قليل فقد ذكره المولف فى الجدول
المبيِّن للالفاظ المترادفة وقد رأيت من محاسن هذا الكتاب ايضا انه اشتمل على
نثر ونظم وخطب ومقامات وملاحظات حكمية وانتقادات فلسفية ومطارحات
وكنايات وتوريبات وتوريات ومحاورات وعبارات مضحكة يكلا يملّ القارى من
مطالعته المرة بعد المرة * فمن ملح تلك المحاورات ما ذكر فى الفصل التاسع من الكتاب ٢،٣،٠
الاول وفى الفصل الثامن عشر والعشرين من الكتاب الثالث وفى الفصل الثانى
من الكتاب الرابع وفى الفصل السادس منه وفى الفصل العاشر وفى غيره ومن
الكنايات ما ذكر فى الفصل الثامن عشر من الكتاب الاول وفى الفصل العشرين وفى
خطبة الكتاب الثانى وفى الفصل الخامس منه وفى وضع أخرى كثيرة فاما التوريات
فانها لا تكاد تحصى كثرةً فالمرجو من مطالعه ان يتصفّحه بروية واعمال نظر ليتبيّن
خفيّ ما اودع فى فصوله المفصلة من النكات والمحاسن * ومن محاسنه ايضا انه
اذا ذكر شيا استوفى كل ما امكن ان يقال فيه وراعى النظير له من جميع طرقه

An Introduction by the Publisher of This Book

To Almighty God be *praise*, for the blessings with which He has showered us throughout our *days*. To proceed: Rāfā'īl Kaḥlā, of Damascus,[15] humble seeker of the mercy of his Lord the Preserver and Protector, declares: When I perused this book entitled *Leg over Leg*, I found it provided a wealth of useful information through its enumeration of many synonymous and lexically associated words in a style clear and *admirable*, presented in a manner both fascinating and *delectable*. This is especially so, given that it encompasses all the names of instruments and tools that need to be known and provides a complete reckoning of all types of foods, drinks, perfumes, clothes, furniture, shoes, jewelry, and gems, the like of which is to be found in no other book in this form, while any items that may have been omitted in the relevant chapter—and they are few—have been mentioned by the author in the table enumerating synonyms.[16] I also found that a further excellent feature of the book is its inclusion of prose and poetry, sermons and *maqāmahs*, aphorisms and philosophical critiques, conversations and idioms, double entendres and puns, and amusing dialogues and expressions, so that the reader will never grow bored perusing it, even if he reads it over and over again. 0.3.1

Among the most entertaining of the aforesaid conversations are those to be found in Chapter 9 of Book One, chapters 18 and 20 of Book Three, chapters 2, 6, and 10 of Book Four, and elsewhere, and of the idioms, those to be found in chapters 18 and 20 of Book One, in the sermon in Book Two,[17] and in Chapter 5 of Book Two, as well as in many other places. The puns are almost too many to count; anyone reading the book is asked to turn the pages slowly and focus closely in order to uncover the hidden meanings conveyed through jokes and the other excellent features that have been placed within its separate chapters. Another of the book's excellent qualities is that, when it mentions something, it says everything there is to say about it, while also taking into consideration every aspect of any similar words. 0.3.2

٣،٣،٠ وبالجملة فانى اتجاسر على ان اقول ان المولف قد فتح باب هذا الاسلوب الغريب فى
التاليف ثم ما لبث ان قفله فلا يمكن تحدّيه من بعده لان الكتاب انطوى على
اشهر ما يروم القارى معرفته من غرائب اللغة * هذا ولما رايت ما فيه من جمّ
الفوائد الادبية والنوادر اللغوية وثبت لديّ انه يكون مقبولا لدى اهل العلم والذوق
٤،٣،٠ الصحيح استخرت الله فى طبعه واشتهاره ليعمّ نفعه ويسهل تحصيله فاما ما يظهر
منه فى بادى الامر من الاساّة فى حق اشخاص صرّح المولف بأسمآئهم فقد كنت
اود لو ان هذه الاسمآ لم تكن شيا مذكورا الا انه اشترط عليّ قبل الشروع فى
الطبع ان لا انقص منه شيا كما انه اشترط ذلك ايضاً على جميع القارئين واليه
اشار فى الفاتحة بقوله او ترتأى استعماله محذوفا * فرايت ان قليل اللوْم الذى
ينشأ عن اثبات تلك الاسمآء بالنسبة الى كثرة الفوائد التى تحصل منه غير مانع من
٥،٣،٠ اشتهاره وقبوله فدونكه ايها المطالع تحفة مبتكرة لم يسبق اليها وهدية نفيسة يجب
الحرص عليها فامعن عند تلاوتها النظر وادم عليها الفكر لتبرز لك مجبّات[1] معانيها
وتنجلى عليك مُجْيات مبانيها ولا تعاملها معاملة ما سواها مما قد اشتهر فانها بِدْع
٦،٣،٠ عزّ عن ان ينظّر * ثم انّا نعتذر اليك عن بعض غلطات وقعت فى الطبع غالبها
مقصور على شكل الفاظ غير مشهورة على انها قليلة جدّا ولا توجد فى جميع النسخ
المطبوعة فانّا تدراكنا بعضها بالاصلاح وقلّ ان يوجد كتاب فى غريب اللغة خاليا
من ذلك فالمامول من كرمك ان تقابلها على جدول التصحيح وتصلحها بالقلم والمولف
معترف بالقصور والاعتراف يمحو الاقتراف وليس الكامل الّا الله وحده ومنه
نستمد المغفرة والمعونة *

١ ١٨٥٥: محجباب.

In sum, I would make so bold as to say that the author, having once opened the door to this strange style of writing, has as quickly shut it again and that hereafter the book will never be challenged, for it has covered all the most celebrated oddities of the language that the reader might want to know. This being the case, when I saw the abundant useful literary items and linguistic rarities that it contained and became convinced that it would appeal to scholars and people of sound taste, I asked God for proper guidance as to its printing and promotion, so that its benefits might be generally enjoyed and it might be easy to obtain. 0.3.3

As to what it contains at the beginning by way of disrespectful comments directed against persons named by the author, I would have preferred that those names "had not been mentioned,"[18] but the author imposed the condition on me—before printing went ahead—that I should leave nothing out of the book, and he has imposed the same on all his readers, a fact to which he alludes in the *Proem* when he says, "[Beware lest you] . . . think of using it in abbreviated form." I decided therefore that the small amount of condemnation that might result from making those names explicit was no reason—when measured against the many benefits that would accrue from the book as a whole—to stop its promotion and acceptance. 0.3.4

Here then, Reader, is a novel and unprecedented treasure for you, a precious gift to be treated with care. Scrutinize it closely when reading it and give it your undivided attention, so that its veiled meanings may *appear*, its enigmatic constructions become *clear*, and do not treat it as you would any other well-known work, for it is an innovation singular beyond *compare*. 0.3.5

Finally, we apologize to you for certain mistakes that occurred during printing, most of which are limited to the vowelling of little known words and are, anyway, very few. Nor do they occur in all the copies printed, as we managed to catch and correct some. Few books on the oddities of language are completely without such errors and we hope you will be gracious enough to match them against the table of corrigenda and correct them with your pens; the author confesses his shortcomings, confession erases commission, and none is perfect but God alone, from whom we ask forgiveness and aid. 0.3.6

الحمدلله تعالى

فاتحة الكتاب

هذا كتابى للظريف ظريفا   طَلِقَ اللسان وللسخيف سخيفا ١،٤،٠

اودعتُه كَلِماً والفاظا حلت   وحشوتُه نقطا زهت وحروفا

وبداهةً وفكاهة ونزاهة   وخلاعة وقناعة وعُزوفا

كالجسم فيه غيرُ عُضوٍ تعشق المستور منه وتحمد المكشوفا

فصّلته لكن على عقلى فما   مِقياس عقلك كان لى معروفا

قعّرته بمحافر الافكار كى   يسع الكلام وسُمته تجويفا ٢،٤،٠

لفّقته وخصفته بيدى فقل   نِعمَ الكتابُ ملفَّقا مخصوفا

افرغت فيه كل حبرٍ راقه   وله بريت من اليراع الوفا

وكانما بيدىّ قد نمّقته   حتى اتى مستحكما مرصوفا

الّفته والليل اسود حالك   فلذاك جآء مسخَّما مسجوفا

Praise Be to God Almighty

Proem

This book of mine to the sophisticate will be sophisticated 0.4.1
And smooth-tongued, while to the foolish it will be foolish.
I have set down in it words and lexical items to bejewel it
And filled it with dots that shine[19] and letters,
With natural style, humor, and purity of intent
As well as with license, temperance, and abstinence.
Like a body, it has more than one member. Those that are concealed
May earn your passion, those that are in plain sight your praise.
I have tailored it, but to fit my own way of thinking, for
The measure of yours is to me unknown.
I beat a path for it with the hooves of my thoughts 0.4.2
To make it wide enough for the words and forced it to be hollowed out.
I pieced it together and cobbled it up by hand. Say then,
"What a well-pieced-together and cobbled-up book it is!"
I emptied into it every sort of ink that might make it appealing
And for it I sharpened thousands of pens.
One might almost say that with my very hands I shaped it, down to the last detail,
So that it came out tightly constructed and compactly built.
I composed it on a night black as pitch
Which is why it emerged so filled with animus and darkling allusion.

تبلّته لك دون طاهى القوم بالرَّ   بلات فهى تزيل منك خُلوفا ٣،٤،٠
وتُصِحُّ ما بك من طُلاطِلَة ومن   ضَرَسٍ فتَلْقَم بعد ذاك الفوفا
يُغنيك عن مَين الطبيب وسَحْله   ما من جراه تخازم الحتروفا
قد انبتت غَضرآء ارض سطوره   روضاً وجنّاتٍ تروق وريفا
فتشمّ منها عَرْف كل رِبَحْلة   دَهْسآء يفتن حسنها الغطريفا
وترى الملعَّظة الشِناط بجنبها   والفارض القِرطاس والسُرعوفا ٤،٤،٠
ووراءها وامامها مُرمُورة   وغُرانقٌ ما ان تزال انوفا
واذا بدت لك من خلال حروفه   رُدُح وثائر فاخطبنّ رَشوفا
فاذا عجزتَ عن المؤنة واستقلْ   تَ وجدت فى اعقابهن الهيفا
فاختر هداك الله ما تهوى ولا   تتراخ عن ان تُدْرك الخرنوفا[1]
غيرى من الوصّاف فى ذا صنّفوا   لكنهم لم يحسنوا التصنيفا ٥،٤،٠
اذ كان ما قالوه مبتذلا ولم   يتقصَّ منهم واصف موصوفا
لكن كتابى او انا بخلاف ذا   نكفى الحفىَّ الحدّ والتعريفا
لا عيب فينا غير انك لا ترى   صنوا لنا فى فنّنا وحريفا
فهو اليتيم المستحيل اِخاؤه   وهو الفريد فكن عليه عطوفا

---

١ ١٨٥٥: الحرنوفا.

Outdoing the best of cooks, I seasoned it for you with pulicaria 0.4.3
Plants, for these will dispel the bad breath of fasting from your mouths[20]
And set right whatever misfortunes may afflict you and whatever
Sets your teeth on edge; after which you'll be ready to gobble up the pellicle of a date stone.
It will allow you to dispense with doctors' lies and their fees—
Nor on its account will you have to face a struggle to feed your children.
From the clayey ground of its lines has sprouted
A meadow, and gardens excelling in luxuriance.
From them will come to you the scent of statuesque girls,[21]
Ruddy-colored, whose beauty charms the comely youth.
At her side you will see tall plump girls 0.4.4
And well-endowed ones, white and tall, and tall smooth women
While behind them and to their fore are smooth girls whose flesh wobbles
And fair women, ever proud.
And should there emerge before you from among its letters
Heavy-haunched women, fat and ready to be bedded, then propose marriage to a girl whose saliva is sweet and vagina dry.
Should you lack what it takes to do so and excuse
Yourself from this obligation, you will find, hot on their tails, slim-bellied lasses;
So choose, God guide you, what you desire
And be not lazy in pursuing and realizing cunsummation.[22]
Other describers of such things have made their categorizations, 0.4.5
But did not do so well,
For what they said was trite and not one
Among them studied minutely what was to be described.
My book, however, or I myself, have done the opposite:
We save the enquirer the task of delimiting and defining.
We have no blemish, though you will not find
Any like us in our art nor any co-worker.
For this art is an orphan to find whose brother is impossible,
And it is unique, so be well disposed toward it.

الفضل لى ولصاحب القاموس اذ   من لُجّـه قولى غـدا مغروفـا ٦،٤،٠
حبلتْ بـه راسى خلافا للنسا   عـامـا وكل العـام كان خريفـا
لكـن تولّد فى ٣ِ اشـهـر   وحبا عـلى عَجَل وشبّ لطيفـا
لم ادرِ هل رَجَلَته او مخطته او   بصقـتـه او القتـه ثـمّ كنيفـا
عانيت فيه من الزحير اجارك الـــمولى عنـآء لا يُكال جـزيفـا
وقطعت سُرَّتـه على اهـل الحجى   وعلى اسمهـم لا يبرحَنْ موقوفـا
ماكان من ظئر له عندى سوى   فكرى ومـع ذا خـلتُه مسروفـا ٧،٤،٠
قِـدْماً عـليه توحمت نفسى ولم   يكُ شوقها عن نحوه مـصروفـا
ورشحتُ لذّاتٍ قُـبَيل نتـاجـه   حتى اذا باشرت عدت نَشوفـا
اولدت لى ولدين لا لك ثـم ذا   لك ثالثاً لا لى فَعُـلُهُ القُوَفـا
عـهدى الى ولدىّ ان يتحـدّيا   اسـلوبـه وبدفّـتـيه يُطيفـا
ليؤمّناه من الحريق اذا احتمى   احـد عـليه لكونـه حِرّيفـا
انى بـرىٓء منهما ان يعـدلا   عنـه ويتّخذا عـليه حليفـا
مَن كان يرغب فيه فهو موفّق   اَوْ لا فقد ضَلّ السبيل وإِيفـا ٨،٤،٠
فى الليل يسمع منه غطغطة يطيـــب نعـاسه بدوامها وجحيفـا
ولرُبّ نور سـاطع يغـدو اذا   قـابلتـه يومـا بـه مكسوفـا
وكبيرِ بطن ضاق عـنه وفاتك   ذى شِرّةٍ عنه يخيم ضعيفـا
كالزئبق الفـرّار ينـظـره ولا   يسطيع يُمسك من قفاه صوفـا

To me and to the author of the *Qāmūs* must go the credit 0.4.6
Since it is from his fathomless sea that my words have been scooped.
Unlike a woman, my head was pregnant with it
For a year, and the whole year was a season of storms.
But it took only three months to be born
And quickly it learned to crawl and grew into a delightful youth.
I could not tell if my head gave birth to it feet first or blew it out of its nose or
Spat it out or dumped it there at the latrine.
I suffered over it in groans, may the Lord protect
You, suffering such as cannot be measured haphazardly
And cut its umbilical cord to suit only the people of discernment
To whose name alone it is dedicated.
It had no wet nurse other than 0.4.7
My thoughts, and even so I thought it too well suckled.
From days of old, my soul had craved it, like a pregnant woman, and
Its longing could not be distracted
And I sweated with pleasure just before it was born,
So much so that when I ejaculated the book, I was left drained.
I fathered two sons for myself, not for you, O Reader, then this one
Which is for you—a third, not for me, so lend it your ears.
My behest to my two true sons is that they should emulate
Its style and make a ritual circuit around its covers
So that they make keep it safe from burning, should any
Grow hot with anger against it, because of its spiciness.
I wash my hands of the doings of both, should they turn aside
From it and take an ally against it.
Any who longs to find it will be granted success, 0.4.8
Or if not and he loses his way and is stricken,
At night he will hear a burbling sound coming from it
That will sweeten his slumber with its unceasing gurgling—
And how many a shining light will appear if
You find yourself faced with it on a gloomy day!
How many a one large of belly has given up on it in dudgeon!
How many a murderous killer recoils from it, now weak!
To him like elusive mercury it seems and he cannot
Grasp any of the wool on its nape.

يهوِى هوىَّ الريح فى الوادى اذا   مـا هِـيج ثـمّ يُسنِم الشُنعوفا ٩،٤،٠
هو خير داجٍ للذى لم يرضَ من   لُعَب الزمـان ولهوه خذروفا
ان تتلُه يطربْك حسن بُغامه   او تُلغه يُسْمِعْك منه عزيفا
فيه ترى فى البرد مشتى ثم اِن   ثارت خَجَوجاة السَّهام مَصِيفا
واذا ثقلتَ من الطعام وغيره   تلقى بـه من ثَقَلة تخفيـفا ١٠،٤،٠
واذا اتخذت حديقةً فاغرس بها   منه كُلَيمات تـزدك قُطوفا
تغنيك عن نصب الخيال بها فلو   اضحى شِظاظا لصّها لأُخيفا
انى ضمنتُ لك الفُدور فما تُرَى   من بعـده عـَزها ولا منجوفا
كلّا ولا مستثـقِلا نومـا ولا   اَرِقًا ولا تشكو صَدًى وعُجوفا
لا تُقدمنَّ على ركوب الصعب ان   لم تتخـذه صـاحبا ورديفـا ١١،٤،٠
حتى اذا تُعتعت اصبح عاصما   لك اَن تـزل فتخطى الخر__فا
انى لاَعـلم والسـداد يـدلُّنى   اَن الجناب يرَى الاَبيل مخيفا
فاَخِفْه انت بكل حـرف باتـر   قد خُطّ فيه يكّف عنك كفيفا
هو حصرم فى طَرْف مَن يغتابه   مـا زال ان ذُكِرَ اسمـه مطروفا
وهو الحديد القاطع الماضى الذى   يبرى العظام ويحسم الشرسوفا

It falls like the wind in the valley when 0.4.9
Stirred up, and wears the mountain peak down to a bump.
It is the best of levelers for any who has found no humming top
Among Fate's toys and games to please him.
If you recite it, the beauty of its sound, like a gazelle calling to its young, will delight you
And if you seek to drown it out with your talk, it will give out a musical sound to which you will have no choice but to hearken.
In it you will find a winter refuge in the cold; then,
When the burning wind of summer gusts, a summer resort.
If you grow tired of food and other things, 0.4.10
You will find in it relief for your boredom
And if you acquire a garden, plant there
Little words from it that will give you yet more posies
That will relieve you of having to erect a scarecrow in it;
Should even Shiẓāẓ[23] come to steal them, he'll be affrighted.
I guarantee[24] you will find it so absorbing that you will lose all interest in sex,
But no one thereafter will think you're strait-laced or no longer able—
No indeed!—nor that you're one who doesn't want to sleep or is kept awake
By insomnia, or because he suffers thirst or hunger.
Make not bold to mount life's challenges 0.4.11
Unless you are ready to take them as your companion and pillion rider,
So that, should you be shaken in your seat, it may protect
You from slipping and so missing . . . summation.[25]
Well I know, and common sense instructs me,
That Your Honored Self finds monks frightening.
Scare them yourself, then, using every cutting character[26]
That's in it inscribed, and any monk will pull back from you blinded.[27]
It is sour grape juice in the eye of its calumniator,
Whose eye, if its title is ever mentioned, will weep and weep.
It is the sharp cutting steel that
Slices bones and cleaves cartilage.

ان شئت تلبسه على علاّته فاهنأ به اَوْ لا فدعه نظيفا ١٢،٤،٠
ولقد اجزتك سفَّه او لَعْقَهُ او ان تَخَفْ قَيْئاً فخذه مدوفا
لكن حذارِ من الزيادة فيه او ان ترتأى استعماله محذوفا
اذ ليس فيه من محلّ قابل للحذف او لزيادة تشقيفا
لو كان يُعشَق جامدٌ لجماله لغدا الورى طُراًّ به مشغوفا ١٣،٤،٠
ولَئن نزحتُ عن الانام فانه يمشى اليه حيث كان زحوفا
واذا تخاصم كاذبان فلحية الاشقى يغادر شعرها منتوفا
حتى كأنّ الشَعر من لَحييهما قطن الحشايا ناعما مندوفا
وحياة راسك ان راسى عارف انى به لن استفيد رغيفا
كلاّ ولا اقطا ولا حَشَفا ولا خزاً على وتدى ولا كرسوفا
لكن بقرنى حِكَّة هاجت على انى اعالج مرة تاليفا ١٤،٤،٠
من كان يُؤجَر كى يولّفَ خطبة فهو الخليق بان يُعدّ عسيفا
ما راجَ من قولى فخذه وما تجدْ من زائف فاتركه لى ملفوفا
لابدّ اَن تجد الصيارف مّرة بين الدراهم درهما مزيوفا
ولربَّ دينار يجرُّ اليك مَن تهوى بلحيته وليس مشوفا

If you wish to dress yourself in it, despite its shortcomings, **0.4.12**
Then enjoy it; if not, then leave it be, still clean.
I have licensed you to swallow it whole or to lick it
Or, if afraid of vomiting, to take it diluted.
Beware, though, lest you add to it or
Think of using it in abbreviated form,
For no place in it is susceptible
To abbreviation, or to addition, to make it better.
If an inanimate object may be fallen in love with for its beauty, **0.4.13**
Then all humanity will be enamored of it.
After I have bidden mankind farewell,
They will find their way to it, wherever it be, in droves.
And if two liars quarrel, the hair of the beard
Of the more unjust will end up plucked out
And finally the hair on both their jawbones will be like
Mattress cotton, smooth and carded.
By the life of your head, my head knows that
I'll never benefit from it by even a loaf—
No indeed!—nor cottage cheese, nor poor-quality dates,
Nor silk mixed with wool to hang on my peg, nor a cotton wad for my inkwell.
But on my pate I had an itch that spurred me **0.4.14**
To practice writing, if only once,
Though he who is hired to compose a sermon for money,
Such a one is well suited to be considered a laborer of no worth.
Take of my words such as will find a market, and what you find
Counterfeit, leave for me in their wrappings.
The money changers are bound on occasion to find
Among the silver coins one that is of bad metal.
Many a gold coin will drag to you by his beard one whom you
May love, even if its face cannot be clearly read.

لا يعلقن بزجاج عقلك ما ترى   فيه من الصدأ القديم كثيفا ١٥،٤،٠
من كان فى بلد لطيفا طبعه   يجد الغليظ من المحبّ لطيفا
لا ترفسن ما سَرَّ منه لاجل ما   قد ساء بل لا تُولِهِ تافيفا
ان المصنف لا يكون مصنّفا   الا اذا جعل الكلام صنوفا
او ليس ان الضرب مثل الصنف فى المعنى وقرع عصا اليه أُضيفا
حاشاك ان تقضى علىّ تهافتا   من قبل ان تتحقق التوقيفا ١٦،٤،٠
فتقول قد كفر المولف فاحشدوا   ياقوم صاحبكم اتى تجديفا
فتهيجَ ارباب الكنائس هَيجة   شُؤمَى فيخترطوا عليه سيوفا
بينى وبينك من صِلات مودَّة   ما يقطع التفسيق والتسقيفا
لا تزبئرّ الى القتال ولا الى الشكوى ولا تك بيننا قِذِّيفى[1]
ان كنتُ إحسانًا اتيت فدونكالتحبيذ لى او لا فلا تقذيفا ١٧،٤،٠
لا يُشتَمَنَّ ابى ولا امى ولا   عرضى ولا تك لى بذاك اليفا
اثمى على انفى يناط مدلدلا   ما ان يُصيبُ من العباد انوفا
ولربَّ فِسّيق اللسان مُباذئٍ   يغدو وقد فسق العفيف عفيفا
ونزيه نفس ان يزر ذا زوجة   ويكون ان ضحكت له عِتريفا

---

١ ١٨٥٥: قِذِّيفى ا [كذا].

The old patina that you see thick 0.4.15
Upon it will not adhere to the glass of your mind.
He whose nature is refined, be he where he may,
Will believe what is gross in his beloved to be as refined as he.
Do not spurn what has gladdened you in him just because of what
Has hurt you. Nay, turn not your back on him in disgust.
The classifier is no classifier
If he doesn't put things into classes.
Isn't "of a certain stamp" the same in meaning as
"Of a certain type," with the addition of the thwack of a stick?[28]
God forbid that you should judge me incoherently 0.4.16
Before you have properly studied it
And say, "The author has committed blasphemy, so gather,
You people—your friend has uttered unbelief,"
Causing the masters of the churches to rise up in dread
Outrage and unsheathe their swords against it.
The bonds of affection between you and me are such
As to cut short any accusations of my being either a sinner or a saint.
Raise not your hackles in preparation for a quarrel, or a complaint,
And let there be between us no dogfight.
If I have come with good intentions, you should acclaim 0.4.17
Me. If not, at least do not calumniate me.
Do not let my father, my mother, or my
Honor be insulted, and do not get used to doing so.
My sin is suspended, dangling, from my nose.
It does not strike the noses of other mortals.[29]
Many a foul-tongued loud-mouth
Has become, when the chaste have become sinners, himself chaste,
And many a man of pure soul, if he visits a man who has a wife,
Becomes, if she smiles at him, a rascal.

كِلَبُ الكواعب ليس يُعدى غيره   ودواؤه كُعُبٌ يليه مَنُوفا ١٨،٤،٠
ماذا على مُهدٍ الى اخوانه   شيا الذَّ من المدام طريفا
سهر الليالى مُحكما تفصيله   وهمُ رقود يُحكمون جحيفا
ارايت ذاكرم يردّ هدية   ويسوم مهديها له تعنيفا
او ليس ان الدهر اصبح مازحا   يَهذى ويأتى المضحكات جنوفا ١٩،٤،٠
فاشتقَّ من خَرَف الجنَى خِرَفا ومن   حَصَفٍ تَهِى الاظفار منه حصيفا
دع عنك تعبيس الاسود وكن اخاً   لابى الحُصَيْن مراوغا يَهفوفا
من اضحك السلطان صوت رُدامه   فهو الذى فى الناس عُدّ عريفا
تمت بهذا البيت فاتحتى وقد   صيّرته لبنائها تسقيفا
لا تقرأنّ من بعده شيا ولو   كُلِّفتَ حرفا واحدا تكليفا
فتكون قد أُزلقتَ ثم تجاوزتْ   بك رجلك اليسرى له تاريفا
انى ارى كالريح فى اذنيك عر   ف نصيحتى راحت سدى وطليفا

One rabid for young girls with firm breasts infects none but himself 0.4.18
And his medicine's a breast abreast of him that's well-risen.
What blame can attach to one who gives to his brethren
Something more delicious than wine, something exquisite?
He spent the nights carefully crafting its details
While they were sleeping, snoring loudly as they did so.
Did you ever see a noble man return a gift,
Humiliating the one who gave it to him with harsh words?
Could it not be that Fate has taken to playing the fool, 0.4.19
To raving and making jokes unfairly?
It derives *kharif* ("dotard") from *kharf al-janā* ("the gathering in of the harvest") and
From the *ḥaṣaf* ("mange") that weakens the fingernails it derives *ḥaṣīf* ("man of clear judgment").
Avoid making the lion frown, and be a brother
To the fox, a crafty fellow, of iron will.
He the sound of whose bow-string when plucked makes the sultan laugh
Is the one whom the people consider an expert.
My proem finishes with this line,
Which I have made as a roof to complete its construction.
Read nothing after this, even should you be
Charged with reading a single letter of any other book,
For then you'll be on a slippery path, where you'll go wrong foot first
And so slide across the line.
(Though I think that the scented air of my advice,
Like wind is in your ears—passing, leaving no trace, as though it were nought.)

الكتاب الاول

Book One

الفصل الاول

في اثارة رياح

مه صه اسكت اصمت انصت اَيبس اِعقَم اسمع اِئْذن اِصخ اصغَ اعلم انى شرعت ١،١،١
فى تاليف كتّيبى هذا المشتمل على اربعة كتب فى ليالى راهصة ضاغطة احوجتنى
الى الجؤار قائما وقاعدا حتى لم اجد لصُنبور افكارى ما يسّده عن ان يتبعّق على
ميزاب القلم فى وجوه هذه الصحائف * فلما رايت القلم مِطواعا لانامِلى والدواة
مطواعا للقلم قلت فى نفسى لا باس ان اقفو القوم الذين بيّضوا وجوههم بتسويد
الطروس فان كانوا قد احسنوا فانا اُعدّ ايضا من المحسنين * وان كانوا قد اساوا
فلعل عدد كتبهم يحتاج الى تكملة فيكون كتابى على كل حال متّصفا بالكمال * لان
ما كمّل غيره كان جديرا بان يكمل نفسه * فمن ثم لم اتوقف فيما قصدته ولم اتحاش
ان اودعه من الالفاظ الشائقة الرائقة والمعانى الفائقة الآفقة كل ما خَفَّ على
السمع * ولذَّ للطبع * مع عملى انه لا يكاد مُولِّفٌ يعجب الناس جميعا * وكانى ٢،١،١
بمتعنّت يقول فى نفسه او لغيره لوكان المولف اجهد قريحته فى تاليف كتاب مفيد
لاستحق ان يثنى عليه * لكنى اراه قد اضاع وقته عبثا بذكر ما لا ينبغى ذكره
حينا * وحينا بذكر ما لا يجدى نفعا * والجواب عن الاول * ومحترِسٍ من مثله
وهو حارس[١] * وعاد الحَيْسُ يُحاس * وخذ من جِذْع ما اعطاك * وشحمتى فى

[١] ١٨٥٥: حارسُ.

Chapter 1

Raising a Storm[30]

Gently! Hush! Silence! Quiet! Cock an ear! Listen up! Hold your tongue! Quit talking! Hear! Hark! Hearken!—and know that I embarked upon the composition of this four-book opuscule of mine during wearing, grinding nights that had me praying to God standing and seated, until finally I found no further impediment to stop the faucet of my thoughts from emptying like rain clouds into the drainpipe of my pen and onto the surfaces of these pages; and that when I found the pen obedient to my fingertips and the inkpot to the pen, I said to myself, "There can be no harm to my following in the footsteps of that company of men who have rendered their reputations white by covering pages in black, for if they did well, then I too may be considered to have done well, and if they did badly, it may be that one more book is needed to add to their efforts, in which case my book, at least, may be described as perfect, for whatever has perfected something else must be capable itself of being perfect." Taking this as my starting point, I never paused in the pursuit of my goal and felt no compunction in consigning to it all such words attractive and *fascinating* and figures admirable and *scintillating* as bring pleasure to the *ear* and to the constitution *cheer*; this, despite knowing that scarce an author can please everyone. 1.1.1

I picture myself, then, as one confronted by some picky fault-finder who says to himself, or to another, "If the author had put his talent to work to compose a book that was of some use, he'd deserve to be praised for it; but it seems to me he has wasted his time for nothing by mentioning on some occasions things that should not be mentioned and on others things that yield no benefit." My reply to the first point is "How many a pot has called the kettle black!,"[31] and "You've made a bad business worse!,"[32] and "Make the most 1.1.2

قَلْعى * واهتبِلْ هَبَلك * وعين الرضى عن كل عيب كليلةٌ * وعن الثانى * اربع على ظَلْعك * وارقَ على ظلعك * وارقأ على ظلعك * وقِ على ظلعك * وكانى
٣،١،١ بآخر يقول حديث خرافة ياام عمرو * وجوابه وكم من عائب قولاً سليما * ثم كاني بجوقة عظيمةٍ من الجلاذىّ والنهاميّين والاَنهمة والوَقَفة والوَفَهة والوهفة والابيلين والزرازرة والقمامسة وامامهم الجاثليق الاكبر وامام هذا العَسطوس الاعظم وهم يضجون ويعجون ويجأرون ويعرون ويلجبون ويصخبون ويزأطون ويلغطون ويتقتّرون ويتوغّرون ويتوعدون ويتهددون ويتذمرون ويتنكرون ويتنمرون ويتشذرون ويتشزرون ويتغذمرون ويحمون وينهمون ويلغمون * فاقول لهم مهلا مهلا مهلا انكم قضيتم عمركم كله فى حرفة التاويل فما يضركم لو اوّلتم ما تنكرونه فى كتابى من اول وهلة * وتمحّلتم كما هو دابكم لان تجعلوا منه حسنا ما يظهر قبيحا ومستظرفا ما يلوح من خِلال عبارته فاحشاً * فان ابا نواس قد اوجب عليكم ذلك مذ مئين من السنين بقوله *

لا تحظر العفو ان كنت امرءا ورعا　　فـانّ حـظركه بالدّين ازرآء

وبقوله

كن كيفما شئت ان الله ذو كرم　　وما عـليك اذا اذنبت من باسِ
الا اثنتين فـلا تقـربهما ابـدًا　　الشرك بالله والاضرار بالنـاس

٤،١،١ فاما ان قلتم ان عبارته صريحة بحيث لا تقبل التاويل * فاقول لكم انكم بالامس كنتم تخطأون وتحضرمون وتهرأون وتلحنون وتلكنون وتغلطون وتوهمون وتعفكون وتُلبكون وتَلتكّون وتلفتون وتعصدون وتخلطون وتخطلون وتهذون وتهذرون وتحصرون وتلخّون وتلخلخون وتعجمون وتجعمون وتفدمون وتلفُّون وتتبلتعون وتتلهيعون

of what you're given!,"[33] and "So what are you going to do about it?!,"[34] and "Mind your own business!," and "The accepting eye to every fault is blind!," while to the second it is to point out that one who limps (a) should go easy on himself, (b) shouldn't try to climb mountains, (c) should tend to his own limp before anyone else's, and (d) shouldn't call attention to his limping;[35] or as though confronted by someone else who says, "Another of Khurāfah's tales, Umm ʿAmr!,"[36]—to which I reply, "Many a true word has been spoken by the less than perfect!"

Next, I am confronted by a mighty crowd of priests, abbots, and monks, bequeathers of pious bequests, churchwardens, and sacristans, board-beaters,[37] patriarchs, and hegumens, before whom goes the Great Catholicos[38] with, before him, the Supreme Pontiff,[39] all of them clamoring and havering, mooing and snorting, raging and roaring, shouting and shrieking, fuming and furious, threatening and fulminating, complaining and calumniating, venting, ventilating, and hyperventilating, yelling and gasping, praying and spittle-spraying, thus causing me to say, "*Hold your horses! Hold your horses!* You have spent your whole lives in the craft of exegesis, so what harm would it do if you were to explain away what it is you don't like about my book from the get-go, making arguments, as is your wont, that whatever is malformed is in fact comely and whatever seems hideously phrased is in fact elegant? This is something Abū Nuwās made incumbent on you hundreds of years ago, when he said, 1.1.3

Be not stingy in forgiveness if you be a pious man
For your illiberality is but contempt of religion

"and

Be as you wish, for God is kind—
No harm shall befall you if you sin.
Two things alone you must eschew in full—
Ascribing partners[40] to God and injuring men."

If, on the other hand, you say, "Its words are too plain to explain away," I say to you that only yesterday you were making mistakes, mispronouncing, and maledicting, uttering solecisms and stuttering, erring and aberring, speaking randomly and raggedly, misspeaking and randomly mouthing off, rambling and roaming, raving, ranting, and talking irrationally, faltering and 1.1.4

وتلغلغون وتلقلقون وتقلقلون وترترون وتثرثرون وتحصرون وتفرفرون وتجمجمون
وتمجمجون وتمغمغون وتمغمغون وتعتعون وتتعتغون وتشعثعون وتشغشغون وتبعبعون وتبغبغون
وتوتغون وتضغضغون وتَعْيَون وتفههون فمتى جاكم العلم حتى فهمتموها * وان قلتم ١،١،٥
ان بعضها وهو السيئ مفهوم وبعضها غير مفهوم * قلت لعلّ ما لم تفهموه هو
من الحسنات التى تذهب السيئات فلا ينبغى لكم على ايّة حالة[١] كانت ان
تحرقوه * ولعمرى لو لم يكن من شافع لقبوله واجرآئه عند الادبآء وعندكم انتم ايضا
مجرى كتب الادب سوى سَرْد الفاظ كثيرة من المترادف لكفى * بل فيه من ذكر
الجمال واهله ادام الله عزهنّ ما يوجب اعظامه وتقريظ مولّفه حيّا ثم تأبينه بعد
مفارقته اياهن برغم انفه * على انى اعرف كثيرا من الوفهة الكرام المشهود لهم ١،١،٦
بالفضل بين الانام لا يتحرّجون من قولهم شى مجمجٌ وشى متدملك وشى مفرَّم وشى
ازيَبّ وشى مُهدِف وشى قازح وبَكْبَك * ومن ذكر الكَعْثَب والكثعب والكثم
والجَلْهوب[٢] والعَرَكْرَك والاكثم والاخثم والخثيم[٣] والحَزَنْبَل والدِعَكْنة والجُدجُد والنّيْزج
والبَوْص والنامة والبُلْغص والقَلْذم والاكبس والضّراطمىّ والعُمارطىّ والحَضْر
والهَيَدَب والمَحلوس والبُوْص والعِضْرِط والعُضارطىّ والجميش والجمشآ والبدّآء

١ ١٨٥٥: حالت. ٢ ١٨٥٥: والجُلْهوم. ٣ كذا في القاموس وفي ١٨٥٥: الخشيم.

floundering, babbling like foreigners, bumbling as though you had plums in your mouths and mumbling as though your mouths were covered, dragging out your words and wagging your tongues mischievously (and at great length too), stammering, yammering, and pronouncing letters like Qur'ān readers,[41] tripping over your *t*s, prattling, faltering,[42] and battologizing, hemming and hawing and hawing and hemming, talking as though you had a bone in your throats, swallowing your words, lifping your *f*s, mumbling as though you'd lost your teeth, speaking as though you were belching and vomiting, prattling incoherently, burbling like emptying water jars and squawking like parrots, talking nonsense, snarling like wolves tearing at their prey, howling, and ending up running out of breath like winded horses—so at what point did you acquire the knowledge that would allow you to understand it?

And if you say that one part (the bad part) is comprehensible and the other part incomprehensible, I reply, "Perhaps the part you don't understand consists of precisely those good features that compensate for the work's bad, and, anyway, under no circumstances do you have the right to burn the book." I swear by my life, even if the only thing it had to intercede for it and give it currency with the literati, and with you too, as a literary work, were its enumeration of so many synonyms, that would be enough! Yet, in fact, there is more: the book contains sufficient discussion of beauty and beautiful women—God prolong their glory!—to require that it be extolled and its author be lauded while alive and eulogized when the time comes for him, unwillingly, to part their company. 1.1.5

In addition to which, I know many a noble churchwarden whose virtues are acknowledged among men and yet has no compunction about referring to "things quivering," "things rounded," "things tightened,"[43] "things huge," "things 'the size of mountains,'" or "things hard and vigorously thrusting," nor about making mention of the pudendum big, the pudendum large, the pudendum swollen, the pudendum huge, enormous, the pudendum vast, the thick, raised pudendum and the raised, thick pudendum,[44] the pudendum thick of lip, the vulva huge, the vulva mighty, the vulva long of clitoris, the buttocks, the vulva's inner chamber and space, the wide wet one and the bulgy one, the big brutish one and the just plain large one,[45] the genitals of either sex, the woman's droopy one, the skinny one, the buttocks but with a slightly different spelling,[46] the anus, the flabby vulva, the pudendum shaven, the woman whose vulva is huge, the woman with a huge vulva with widely 1.1.6

والفَشُوش واللَّطعآ والمَهلوسة والمرصوفة والمستودفة والجالقة والحارقة والخَبُوق والخقوق والغَقوق والرَبُوخ والمُخَرْبقة والسَلَقْلق والشَّقآ والمُتلاحمة والنِجام والنَجُوم والاَتُوم والشريم والهَوْجَل والمَتَكآ والحَلِقيّة والمرفوغة والمَصُوص والمِنْفاص والمِيْراص والعَضُوض والِمنخار والشفيرة والزَّخّاخة والبَخّاخة والخُنُنّة والشَفَلَّح والعُنْبُلة والجَليع ومن العِلَّوْز والقُنب والنَوْف والخُنُتُب والاُيَّل والبَيْظ والثُعْرُورِن والحِتار والاَشْعَر والطَبَق والاسكتين والحسكلتين والعُنْتُل والقُحْقُح والمأْنة والجُعْب والطِرْث والعكبز والمجرم والعُجارِم والوَبيل والفَنْجليس والفِلْطيس والحَطاط والكوتعة والجُوفان والمَتَك والحوقلة والكوشلة

separated edges, the woman whose vulva squeaks when it's entered, the woman with the dry little scrawny one, the woman with the emaciated one, the woman with the tiny vagina a man can't get at, the woman who holds the man's semen inside her womb, the woman who flashes her "thing" and her belly folds, the woman the clefts at the head of whose womb are narrow and who holds herself rigid on her side for the man,[47] the woman whose vagina makes a sound when entered, the woman broad-buttocked as a donkey whose vulva also makes a sound, the one whose vagina makes another kind of sound, the woman who swoons during intercourse and the woman who faints during intercourse, the woman who menstruates from her anus, the woman with a wide vagina, the woman the meaty parts of whose vagina are tight, the woman whose vagina is wide open and the woman whose vagina is open wide,[48] the woman whose vagina may be either small or capacious, the woman whose vagina and rectum have been torn so that they have become one, the broad-vagina-ed and debauched woman, the uncircumcised woman with torn vagina and rectum who is also incontinent, the women so much fucked that, like an overused she-ass, she's developed a medical condition in her womb, the woman with the tiny vagina a man can't get at (again, but a different word),[49] the woman who covets the man during intercourse,[50] the woman who wets her bed, the woman who excretes when laid, the tight woman, the woman who whinnies through her nostrils during intercourse like a lunatic, the woman who derives her pleasure from the edges of her vagina, the woman who gushes water during intercourse, the woman whose belly's so big they say, "Bravo!", the woman who's no good at intercourse, the woman whose vagina is droopy with large edges, the woman with the long clitoris, or the woman who doesn't keep herself covered when alone with her husband; nor about the thick clitoris, the clitoris *tout court*, the prepuce of the clitoris or that of the girl before she's been cut, the semen in the womb, the woman's womb itself,[51] the folds that protect the clitoris, the part between the backside and the front, the side of the vagina, the back of the vagina, the edges or sides of the womb, the testicles, the clitoris said with a funny accent,[52] the pelvic bone, the navel, the flabby belly between the navel and the pelvis, the tip of the clitoris, the glans, the "knotty rod," the man with a strong penis, the "thick stick," the large glans, the tip of the glans if it's broad, the edges of the glans, the donkey's glans, the donkey's penis, the fly's penis, the large limp penis, the large glans, the foreskin of a boy if it widens

والقُصْعة والدُلْعة ومن الاِقْماد والتوتيد والاستعناد والتفنشخ والشَمْذ والفَهْر والاِفهار والوجس والنشنشة والاستخلاط والتشيّط والهُكاع والخّةّ والسَغْم والاِكسال والدَعْم والزَجْل والهُقُق والنَيْطل والعُتُر والطَرُوح والعجيز والفِنْخر والاختضار والترفّغ والاصفآ والعَصْد والحَمْق والتعفيل والتبارخ والعُرْوة والاِسواع والسِباع والاِلْهاط والعَصْد والرُفْغ والعَفَل والقُرْنة والكَيْن والطَّوْطُوْة ومن ذكر الاِرْزَبّ والبَزْباز والفاعوسة والخُرنوف والمشرح والغُضارطي والمَصُوص والخاق باق والزَرْدان والطَّنْبَرِيز والفَلْهَم والقبْقاب واللُهْمُوم والجُحُوم والمَزَخّة والنُغنغ والخَشَنْفل والمُعْرَنْفِط والمقرنفط والفُوق والقوق والرَكْوة والقحفليز والعَفَلّق وغير ذلك من ادوات النصب ومن البنُّودة والجِعِبّى والحَذّافة

so far that the glans emerges, and a vein in the penis; nor about extra hard erections, ordinary erections, pricks that commit fornication, women's stuffing of their vaginas with rags so that their wombs won't come out, women's spreading their legs wide during coitus, a man's practicing coitus with one woman and then another before ejaculating and a man's practicing coition with one women and then another before ejaculating,[53] one slave-girl's hearing the sounds made by her master when he's with another slave-girl, and a little-used word for plain copulation,[54] the spontaneous leaping of she-camels by he-camels, emaciation resulting from incessant intercourse, lusting for intercourse, sleep taken after intercourse, having intercourse with one's slave girl by merely inserting and withdrawing because not wishing to ejaculate, withdrawing before ejaculation because not wanting children, thrusting it into her the whole way, ejaculating into the womb, people who fuck frequently, men with long genitalia, vaginas that excite, men intercourse with whom is sure to result in pregnancy, men who find it difficult to have intercourse with a woman, the hard man who keeps on fucking, the deflowering of pre-pubescent girls, sitting between a woman's thighs in order to have intercourse with her, women's emptying a man of all his seed, a noun meaning copulation from which no verb is formed,[55] something white that comes out of the vulva, the curing of the thing resembling a scrotal hernia that emerges from a woman's vulva and makes intercourse impossible, having protuberant buttocks (of a woman), the nympha at the base of the clitoris, to push forth its penis (of a donkey), women voracious as lionesses, dashing water on one's vagina,[56] the external parts of the vulva, the thing resembling a scrotal hernia that emerges from a woman's vulva and makes intercourse impossible, the protuberant part of the womb, and the flesh of the inner part of the vulva[57]; nor about the vulva (especially when large), the vulva said four other ways,[58] the flabby vagina,[59] the vagina that dries the liquid from the surface of the penis,[60] the gaping vagina, the tight vagina, and another name for the vagina,[61] the large ugly vagina with long womb flaps, the large wet squeaky vagina, the women's sexual parts in general, the "bulge," the "sprayer," the fleshy vagina, the bizarrely spelled,[62] the "shrunken," the "gripper," the "nock,"[63] the woman sent mad by the cravings of her crevice, the woman's "wide well," and the vagina again in another exotic spelling,[64] the large floppy one, and other "instruments of erection"[65]; nor about mentioning the backside, the posterior, "the thrower,"[66] "the

والمِخذفة والمَخْذَقة والخوّارة والخفّاقة والعزّاقة والمِحسّة والمحشّة والخَنْفَثة والرّمّاعة والصُمارى والرُّبم والطِبّيخة والحمّآ والعوّآ والعَزْلا والجعْمآ والسّحآ والفُنقُصة والفُرقُعة والصَّفّارة والنبُّور والنبّاعة والنبّاغة والوبّاعة والجوّانة والخوّانة والصوانة والبُرْعُث والبُعْثُط وغير ذلك من ادوات الجزم ومن الأُداف والبَيْزار والجُمَيْح والجُعْثُوم والأَذْلعيّ والحوْقل والمِطْوَل والزُنْقُطة والخَدَرْنَق والسُحادِل والضَبيْز والعُلْعُل والدَوْقَل والقُسْطَبِيْنة والفِنْطِيس والشاقول والقَهْبَلِيس والعَرْدَل والقَصْطَبير والجُزاجِز والقِرْزِميلة والمُتَمَئِّز والدَوْسَر والسَمَهْدر وغير ذلك من ادوات الجرّ ومن ذحَّ وذحا ودحَّ ودَحْبَى ورصع ورطأ وشفتن وشكز وضهز وطعز وطنخ وعزط وعزلب وقرفط وقنطر وقسبر وقحطر وقمطر ولطز ولج ولمذ ومشق ومتر ومهج ومعج ونيرج وزخزخ ودعظ * وكنت احملق في وجوههم عند ذكرهم ذلك فلم اكن ارى عليها حمرة الخجل ولا صفرة الوجل * بل كانت ناضرة مستبشرة مبتهجة مسفرة * فان ابَى المنكر اِلّا عناداً وتقاضاني جدول اسمآئهم قلت له هاك اوله يبتدي بالالف
وآخره بالياء * فاحسبوني اذاً وافهاً من هولآء * ثم ان شرطي على القاري الا ٧،١،١
يُسطر شيا من الالفاظ المترادفة في كتابي هذا على كثرتها * فقد يتفق ان يمر به في طريق واحدة سرب خمسين لفظة بمعني واحد او بمعان متقاربة * والّا فلا اجيز له مطالعته ولا اهنّؤه به * علي اني لا اذهب الى ان الالفاظ المترادفة هى بمعني واحد والّا لسموها المتساوية وانما هي مترادفة بمعني ان بعضها قد يقوم مقام

catapult," "the podex," "the bellower," "the dunger," "the winnower," "the currycomb," "the sickle," the *khabanfatha*,[67] "the fontanel,"[68] "the dry and sweaty-smelling,"[69] "the slimy," "the watermelon," "the heater," "the howler," "the draining vent,"[70] "the toothless one," "the black one,"[71] "the exploder," "the whistler," "the greatly swollen," "the gusher," "the prominent," "the swallower," "the blackener," "the betrayer," "the flintstone," the bunghole, the butthole,[72] and other "instruments of cutting off,"[73] nor about mentioning the penis, "the falcon's stand," "the little bolter," the huge penis, the huge long penis, the flaccid penis incapable of erection, "the lengthener," "the little man," "the big spider," another rare word for the penis,[74] "the strong, crafty wolf,"[75] the erect but not very hard penis, "the mast," "the thimble,"[76] "the snub nose," "the plumb line," the prick,[77] the penis distended and erect, the *qaṣṭabīr*,[78] "the tassels,"[79] "the short ugly thing," "the straight, thick lance," the huge, strong penis, the hard, dry thing, and other "instruments of attraction"[80], nor about using words meaning to lie with, to have sex with, to compress, to lie with one's slave girl, to have intercourse, to perform coitus, to have sex with in or out of wedlock, "to prod," to copulate with, to "push," to "jab," to shtup,[81] another word of similar form but dubious status,[82] to double up like a she-goat during mating, to "bridge,"[83] to fuck hard,[84] to "string her bow," to "fill her up,"[85] to "kick"[86] her, to "nibble" her and a variant,[87] to "chafe" her, to "cut" her, to "suckle" her, to "stick the kohl-stick in her kohl-pot," to "furrow" her, to "push" her, or to "ram it in all the way to the hilt." I would stare into their faces while they were using such words and see there no trace of either embarrassment's *red* or the yellow of *dread*. On the contrary, their faces would be verdant and *cheerful*, radiant and *joyful*—and should anyone, out of sheer pigheadedness, deny that what I say is true and demand of me a list of their names, I'll tell him, "Here it is, beginning with *alif* and ending with *yā'*.[88] Just think of me as a churchwarden like them."

In addition, I have imposed on the reader the condition that he not skip any of the "synonymous" words in this book of mine, many though they be (for it may happen that, on a single road, a herd of fifty words, all with the same meaning, or with two meanings that are close, may pass him by). If he cannot commit to this, I cannot permit him to peruse it and will not offer him my congratulations if he does so. I have to admit that I cannot support the idea that all "synonyms" have the same meaning, or they would have called them "equi-nyms." They are, in fact, synonymous only in the sense 1.1.7

بعض * والدليل على ذلك ان الجمال مثلاً والطول والبياض والنعومة والفصاحة تختلف انواعها واحوالها بحسب اختلاف المتصف بها فخصّت العرب كل نوع منها باسم ولبُعد عهدهم عنا تظنيناها بمعني واحد * وقس على ذلك انواع الحلى والماكول والمشروب والملبوس والمفروش والمركوب * لا بل عندي ولا اخشى من ان يُقال اوَ لك عندٌ انه اذا كان اسمان مشتقين من مادة واحدة وكانا يدلان على معنى واحد كالخجوج والخجوجاة مثلا للريح الشديدة المرّ فلا بد وان يكون الاسم الزائد فى اللفظ زائداً في المعني ايضا * فان شئت اذعنت او لا فعاند * هذا واني قد الّفته وما عندي من الكتب العربية شى اراجعه واعتمد عليه غير القاموس * فان كتبي كانت قد فركتني فاعتزلتها * غير ان مولفه رحمه لم يغادر وصفاً فى النسآء الّا وذكره * فكانه كان اُلهِم[1] ان سياتى بعده من يغوص فى قاموسه على جمع

هذه اللآلئ فى مولف واحد منتسق لتكون اعلق بالذهن وارسخ فى الذكر * ولولا ٨،١،١

اني خشيت غيظ الحسان عليّ لكنت ذكرت كثيرا من مكايدهن وحيَلهن ومِحالهنّ لكني انما قصدت بتاليفه التقرب اليهن وترضّيهن به * واني آسف كل الاسف على انهنّ غير قادرات على فهمه لجهلهن القرآة لا لعوص العبارة * اذ لا شي يصعب على فهمهن مما يؤول الى ذكر الوصال والحبّ والغرام * فهن يستوعبنه ويتلقفنه من دون تلعثم ولا قصور ولا تَرَج * وحسبى ان يبلغ مسامعهن قول القائل ان فلانا قد الّف فى النسآء كتاباً فضّلهن به على سائر المخلوقات * فقال انهن زخرف الكون * ونعيم الدنيا وزُهاها * وغبطة الحيوة ومناها * وسرور النفس ومشتهاها(١) وعلق القلب * وقرة العين * وانتعاش الفؤاد * ورَوح الروح * وجلآء الخاطر * وتعلل الفكر *

(١) حاشيه قد غلط الفيرزبادي فى اشتقاقها السُرّية من السرّ للجماع بل اشتقاقها من السُرّ بمعنى السرور

[1] ١٨٥٥: الِهم.

that certain of them may take the place of certain others. Proof of this lies in the fact that beauty, length, whiteness, smoothness, and eloquence differ in kind and in collocation, depending on the differences among the objects they describe. The Arabs,[89] therefore, assigned to each type of beauty, length, etc., a specific name, and it is only our distance from their days that makes us think they all mean the same; how much more so, then, in the case of words relating to jewelry, food, drink, dress, household furnishings, and footwear. Indeed, in my opinion—and I am not afraid of anyone saying, "Aren't you being opinionated?"—if two words derive from the same base form and refer to the same object (as is the case for example with *khajūj* and *khajawjāh*, meaning "wind that passes violently"),[90] the longer of the two forms must involve an extension of meaning. Grant me this, if you wish, or be stubborn—it makes no difference to me. Bear in mind, too, that I composed the work at a time when the only book in Arabic I had to refer to or depend on was the *Qāmūs*, for my books had taken against me as a wife does her husband, and I'd decided to have nothing more to do with them—though it must be acknowledged that the author of the work in question, God rest his soul, did not fail to record a single word descriptive of women; it is almost as though he knew by divine inspiration that someone would come along after him and dive into his "ocean"[91] in order to collect such pearls into a single work where they could be so arranged as to lodge more firmly in the mind and become more deeply rooted in the memory.

And, did I not fear the wrath of these beauties against me, I would have made mention of many of their crafty ways, their stratagems, and their artifices too; however, my intention in writing the book has been to approach closer to them and use it to appease, not anger, them. I am indeed extremely sorry that they will be incapable of understanding it—as a result of their ignorance of reading and not of the recondite nature of its language, for nothing that involves the union of souls, love, or passion, is too hard for them to understand; they take it all in and grasp it without hesitation, deficiency, or incomprehension. Enough for me that the rumor should reach their ears that so-and-so has written a book about women in which he gives them precedence over all other creatures, declaring them to be the adornment of the universe, the comfort and pride of this world, the joy and hope of life, the soul's pleasure(1) and its desire, the 1.1.8

(1) Al-Fīrūzābādī is wrong in deriving *surriyya* (concubine) from *sirr* meaning "coition." In reality, the word derives from *surr* meaning "pleasure" (*surūr*).

ولهو البال * وجنّة الجنان * وانس الطبع * وصفآء الدم * ولذة الحواس *
٩،١،١ ونزهة الالباب * وزينة الزمان * وبهجة المكان والباءة * بل اقول غير متحرّج
عَرف الالاهة * اذ لا يكاد الانسان يبصر جميلة الّا ويسبّح الخالق * بذكرهن يلهج
اللسان * ولخدمتهن تسعي القدم * وتحمل الاعبآء * وتجشم المشاق ويهون
الصعب * ويتجرع الصاب * ويقاسى الضرّ * ولرضائهن يذل العزيز * ويبذل
النفيس * ويذال المصون * وان خَلاق الرجل من دونهن حرمان * وفوزه خيبة *
وهنآوه تنغيص * وانسه وحشة * وشبعه جوع * وارتوآه ظما * ورقاده ارق *
١٠،١،١ وعافيته بلآء * وسعادته شقاوة * وطوبى له كالزقوم * والتسنيم كالغسلين * فاذا
قدّر الله بلوغ هذا الخبر المطرب سماع احدى سيداتى هولآء الجميلات وسرت
به وفرحت * ورقصت ومرحت * رجوت منها وانا باسط يد الضراعة ان تبلغه
ايضا مسامع جارتها * واملت من هذه ايضا ان تطالع به صاحبتها حتى لا
يمضى اسبوع واحد الا ويكون خبر الكتاب قد ذاع فى المدينة كلها * وكفاني ذلك
جزآء على تعبى الذى تكلفته من اجلهنّ * اَلَا وَلْيَعْلمن انى لو استطعت ان اكتب
مديحهن بجميع اصابعى وانطق به بكل من جوارحي لما وفّي ذلك بمحاسنهن *
فكم لهن عليّ من الفضل حين بَدَوْن في افخر الحلل * ومِسن وباحسن الحلىّ *
ونظرن الىّ شافنات * حتى ابت الى حفشي وانا اتعثر بافكاري وخواطري * فما
كادت يدي تصل الى القلم الا وقد تدفقت عليه المعانى وساحت على القرطاس *
فاورثننى بين الناس ذكرا وفخرا * ورفعن قدرى على قدر ذوي البطالة والفراغ * نعم
ان من بينهن من نَفِست عليّ بطيفها فى الكرَى * ولكنها معذورة فى كونها لم تكن
تعلم انى اتكلف النوم * بعد ان رات عينى من جمالها ما يبهر العقل ويبلبل البال *

heart's jewel and the eye's apple, the breast's refreshment and spirit's refection, the mind's elucidation and thought's preoccupation, a distraction for the head and paradise for the soul, good cheer for the constitution and limpidity for the blood, pleasure for the senses and diversion for the intellect, the embellishment of the age and the glory of every place and dwelling.

Indeed, I declare unabashedly that they have about them a whiff of the divine, for one can scarce behold a beautiful woman without glorifying the Creator. At their mention, the tongue breaks into praise while the foot runs to serve them, bearing burdens and taking on hardships, and in their service what is difficult seems easy, colocynth may be drunk, injury borne. To please them, what is dear is treated with contempt, what is precious is not spared, what is sacred is trodden underfoot. Without them, a man's lot of what is good in this world is turned into deprivation, his triumphs become disappointments, his happiness displeasure, his sense of companionship loneliness; where once he was full he hungers, and where once he was watered he thirsts; where once he slept he suffers from insomnia, and where once he was strong he is in tribulation; his felicity turns into misery, Paradise to him is become like the fruit of the *zaqqūm* tree[92] and its nectar like pus. 1.1.9

Thus, if God should ordain that this intoxicating news reach the ears of one of these beautiful mistresses of mine and she is pleased and made happy and dances and is merry, I beg of her, extending the hand of supplication, that she communicate it to the ears of her lady neighbor too, who will show it in turn, I hope, to a friend, so that not a week passes before news of the book has spread throughout the whole city. This will be sufficient reward for the trouble that I have gone to for their sakes. Indeed, they must know that, were I able to write their praise with all my fingers and proclaim it with all my limbs, it would still not be equal to their virtues. How much I owe them for appearing in their finest garb, strutting in the best of their jewelry, and casting me such darting looks that I returned to my little house barely able to hold my thoughts and fancies in check! Then, no sooner did my hand touch the pen than the ideas gushed from it and spread themselves over the paper. Thus women have earned me repute and honor among the public and raised my status above that of the unemployed and idle. True, one among them refused to let her specter visit me in sleep, thinking me unworthy, but she is to be excused because she was unaware that I, in fact, was only feigning sleep,[93] after my mind had been dazzled and my brain discombobulated by her beauty. 1.1.10

١١،١،١ فاما اذا تعنّت عليّ احد بكون عبارتي غير بليغة * اي غير متبّلة بتوابل التجنيس والترصيع والاستعارات والكنايات * فاقول له اني لمّا تقيدت بخدمة جنابه في انشآء هذا المولف لم يكن يخطر ببالي التفتازاني والسكاكي والامدي والواحدي والزمخشري والبستي وابن المعتز وابن النبيه وابن نباتة * وانما كانت خواطري كلها مشتغلة بوصف الجمال * ولساني مقيّدا بالاطرآ على من انعم الله تعالى عليه بهذه النعمة الجزيلة * وبغبطة من خوّله عزّ وجلّ عزّة الحسن وبرثآء من حرمه منه * وفي ذلك شاغل عن غيره * على اني ارجوان في مجرد وصف الجمال من الطلاوة والرونق والزخرفة ما يغني عن تلك المحسِّنات استغنآء الحسنآء عن الحليّ ولذلك يقال لها غانية * وبعد فاني قد علمت بالتجربة ان هذه المحسنات البديعية التي يتهوّر فيها المولفون كثيرا ما تشغل القارى بظاهر اللفظ عن النظر في باطن المعنى *

١٢،١،١ ولعمري انه ليس في هذا الكتاب شي يُعاب سوي وجدانك الفارياق فيه تارة يحشر في سرب الغواني * وتارة يدمق عليهن وهن آمنات في مجالهن او في حديقة او في زاوية او على السرير * ولكن لم يكن لي بدّ من ذلك * اذ الكتاب موضوع على قص اخباره وعلم احواله * فقد بلغني ان كثيرا من الناس انكروا وجود هذا المسمى فقالوا انه من قبيل الغول والعنقآء * وبعضهم قال انه كان قد ظهر مرة في الزمان * ثم اختفى عن العيان * وذهب غير واحد الى انه مُسخ بعد ولادته بايام * ولم يُعلَم باي صورة تلبّس والى اي شكل استحال * وزعم قوم انه صار من جنس النسناس * وآخرون من النَسانس * وقال غيرهم انه صار من نوع الجِن * واثبت بعض انه استحال امراة * فانه لما راى ان المراة اسعد حالا من الرجل في هذه الدنيا المسماة دنيا النساكان لا يبيت الا هو جائر الى ربه بالدعآء

If, on the other hand, someone should insist that my language is devoid of rhetorical devices—which is to say, not marinated in the spices of paronomasia[94] and morphological parallelism, of metaphor and metonymy—I'd say to him, "When I undertook to serve His Honor[95] by composing this work, the last persons on my mind were al-Taftazānī,[96] al-Sakkākī,[97] al-Āmidī,[98] al-Wāḥidī,[99] al-Zamakhsharī,[100] al-Bustī,[101] Ibn al-Muʿtazz,[102] Ibn al-Nabīh,[103] and Ibn Nubātah.[104] My thoughts were exercised exclusively by the description of beauty, my tongue tied to the praise of those on whom the Almighty has bestowed this egregious blessing, to the expression of happiness for those to whom He, Great and Glorious, has accorded the glory of comeliness, and to mourning over the fate of those whom He has deprived of it, and this was enough to distract one from everything else. Nevertheless, I hope that the scintillation, the luster, and the decorative nature of the description of beauty will, in and of itself, relieve the book of the need for any such rhetorical embellishments, just as a beautiful woman is relieved of any need for jewelry (which is why she is called a *ghāniyah*[105]). In addition, experience has shown me that these rhetorical embellishments in which authors so freely indulge often draw the reader's attention to the words' outward forms and away from their inner meanings." 1.1.11

I swear that this book contains nothing reprehensible, unless you find the Fāriyāq's[106] sometimes pushing his way through a troupe of *ghāniya*s or forcing himself upon them as they rest safe in their bridal pavilions or in a garden or in the corner of a house or on their beds to be so. This was, however, something I was unable to avoid, for the book has been compiled as an account of his doings and to provide knowledge of the circumstances that influenced him, it having come to my attention that many people have denied that the above named even exists and claimed that he belongs to the same category as the ghoul and the phoenix, while others have asserted that he appeared but once throughout the *age* and thereafter vanished from the *stage*, and more than one has held that he was transmogrified a few days after his birth and that it is not known what shape he adopted or into what form he mutated. Another party has claimed that he joined the race of the monopods and another that of the monopodettes.[107] Still others have said that he joined the *ḥinn*.[108] Some have insisted that he was transformed into a woman, for when he saw that the female enjoys a happier state in this world—this "women's world," as it is known—he let not a night go by without praying to his Lord to 1.1.12

لان يصيره انثى * فتقبّل الله ذلك منه وهو على كل شي قدير * فرايت والحالة هذه من بعض ما يجب عليَّ ان اعرّف هولآء المختلفين فيه بحقيقة وجوده على ما فطر عليه * ما عدا التغيير الذى عرض له عن جهد المعيشة وسوء الحال ومقاساة الاسفار ومخالطة الاجانب والاحتكال * وعلى الخصوص من تلفيع الشيب * والمجاوزة من حد الشباب الى سن الكهولة * فاذ قد علم ذلك فاقول ١٣،١،١
كان مولد الفارياق فى طالع نحس النحوس والعقرب شائلة بذنبها الى الجدي او التيس والسرطان ماشٍ على قرن الثور * وكان والداه من ذوي الوجاهة والنباهة والصلاح (مَرْحَى مرحى) الا ان دينهما كان اوسع من دنياهما وصيتهما اكبر من كيسهما (بَرْحَى برحى) وكان لطبل ذكرهما دويّ يُسمع من بعيد * ولزوابع شانهما عجاج ثنآء يثور فى الجبال والبيد * ولتكرير العفاة عليهما واعتشآء الوفود لديهما * تعطّلت سبل دخلهما * ونزحت بئر فضلهما فلم يبق فيها الّا نزّازات يلقى فيها المخفق المحروم سدادا من عوز * فكانا يجودان به ايضا من عوز السَداد (وهٍ وه) فلذلك لم يعد في طاقتهما ان يبعثاه الى الكوفة او البصرة ليتعلم العربية * وانما
جعلاه عند معلم كتّاب القرية التى سكنا فيها (ويح ويح) وكان المعلم المذكور مثل سائر ١٤،١،١
معلّمى الصبيان فى تلك البلاد فى كونه لم يطالع مدة حياته كلها سوى كتاب الزبور وهو الذى يتعلمه الاولاد هناك لا غير (افّ اف) وليس قولى انهم يتعلمونه موذنا بانهم[١] يفهمونه * معاذ الله * فان هذا الكتاب مع تقادم السنين عليه لم يَعُد فى طاقة بشر ان يفهمه (غُط غط) وقد زاده ابهاما وغموضا فساد ترجمته الى اللغة العربية وركاكة عبارته حتى كاد ان يكون ضربا من الاحاجي والمعمَّى (رُطّ رط) وانما

١ ١٨٥٥: بانه.

turn him into a female and God accepted his prayer (and He is capable of all things). This being the case, it seemed to me that one of my duties should be to acquaint these same people, with their differing opinions, with the fact of his presence in the very form that he bore when he was brought into being, due exception made for the changes wrought on him by the efforts he has expended in the pursuit of a living, his difficult circumstances, the hardships of his travels and of consorting with foreigners and learning their languages, and, especially, the graying of his hair and his passage from the borders of youth to the age of maturity.

This now being known, I declare: the Fāriyāq was born with the misfortune of having misfortune in the ascendant everywhere, the Scorpion raising its tail to strike at the Kid, or Billy Goat, and the Crab set on a collision course with the horn of the Ox. His parents were people of notability, nobility, and righteousness (Bravo! Bravo!) but while their prospects for the world to come were *expansive*, their prospects in the world in which they lived were not with these *co-extensive*, and their reputations were, of their *purse*, the *inverse* (Boo! Boo!). The thunder of their names resounded far and *wide*, while the whirlwinds of their circumstance kicked up a cloud of praise as audible on plain as on *mountainside*, and so frequent were the visits of those seeking solace for their *plight*, so often did petitioners seek out their campfires by *night*, that the fountains of their income had run *dry*, the end of their bounty's wellspring come *nigh*, and all that was left there was a little seepage from which the destitute and deprived might derive provision against want—and still they were generous with this to those who wanted for provisions (Boohoo!). Thus it was that they no longer found themselves with the means to send him to Kufa or Basra[109] to learn the Arabic language, placing him instead with the teacher at the *kuttāb* of the village in which they dwelt (Alas! Alas!). 1.1.13

The teacher in question, like all other teachers of children in that country, had never in his life perused any book but that of the psalms, and it was that and that alone that the children studied there (Faugh! Faugh!) though to say they studied it doesn't imply that they understood it. God forbid! Given its antiquity, it is no longer within anyone's capacity to understand that book (Snore! Snore!), and the inaccuracy of its Arabic translation and the lameness of its language have made it yet more obscure and mysterious, to the point that it has almost come to consist of no more than word puzzles and riddles (Have at it! Have at it!), despite which, the tradition of the people of 1.1.14

جرت عادة اهل تلك البلاد بان يدرّبوا فيه اولادهم على القراة من غير ان يفهموا
معناه * بل فهم معانيه عندهم محظور (تُفّ تف) وكما انهم لا يفهمون معنى حآ
وميم وقاف مثلا * فكذلك لا يفهمون عبارة الكتاب المذكور اذا قراوها (طِيخ طيخ) *
١٥،١،١ والظاهر ان سادتنا رؤسآ الدين والدنيا لا يريدون لرعيتهم المساكين ان يتفقّهوا او
يتفقّوا * بل يحاولون ما امكن ان يغادروهم متسكعين فى مهامه الجهل والغباوة
(أُعْ اع) اذ لو شآوا غير ذلك لاجتهدوا فى ان ينشئوا لهم هناك مطبعة تطبع فيها
الكتب المفيدة سوآء كانت عربية او معرّبة (سُرْسر) فكيف ترضون ياسادتنا الا
عزّة لعبيدكم الاذلة ان تربي اولادهم في الجهل والعَمَه (عزوى عزوى) وان يكون
معلّموهم لا يعرفون العربية ولا الخط والحساب والتاريخ والجغرافية ولا شيا غير
ذلك مما لا بدّ للمعلم من معرفته (تَعْزَى تعزى) فكم لعمري من ملكات براعة وحِذْق
منّ الله تعالى بها على كثير من هولآء الاولاد * غير انه لفقد اسباب العلم وعدم
ذرائع التاديب والتخريج طَفِئَتْ جُذوتها فيهم على صِغَر * بحيث لم يمكن ان يثقبها
بهم نتف التحصيل على كِبَر (أُوْه اوه) هذا وانكم بحمد الله من المتمولين المثرين * لا
١٦،١،١ يعجزكم ان تنفقوا كذا وكذا كيساً على انشآء مدارس وطبع كتب مفيدة (إِيْه ايه) فان
لبطرك الطائفة المارونية دَخْلا له وقع عظيم * وقدر جسيم * بحيث يمكنه ان يحيي
به قلوب طائفته هذه التارزة التى لا همّ لها فى المنافسة والمباراة في شى بين
من سبقوهم الى كل علم وفضل (هَيْس هيس) وانما همّهم ان يتعلموا بعض قواعد
في نحو اللغتين العربية والسريانية لمجرد العلم بها فقط من دون فائدة (آه اه) اذ لم يُعلَمَ
الى الان ان احدا منهم ترجم كتابا او كراسة مفيدة في هاتين اللغتين ولا ان
البطرك امر بطبع كتاب لغة فيهما (تِغْ تغ) ولو انه انفق نصف دخله فى كل سنة
على تحصيل اسباب العلم بدل هذه الولائم والمآدب التى يهيئوها لزوّاره * او لو

the country is to use it to train their children to read, without understanding what it means. Furthermore, in their opinion, it is forbidden to understand its meanings (For shame! For shame!) which makes one think that they don't understand the meaning of the letters *s-t-u-p-i-d*,[110] for example; neither, by the same token, do they understand the purely linguistic components of the book in question when they read it (Belly laugh!).

It seems that our masters, lords of the next world as of this, do not want their wretched subjects either to understand or to open their eyes but instead try as hard as they can to leave them wandering in the labyrinths of ignorance and stupidity (Barf! Barf!). If they wanted otherwise, they would bestir themselves to establish a printing press for them there[111] to print useful books, whether written originally in Arabic or translated into it (Forward! Forward!). How, O mighty masters, can it please you that your abject slaves should raise their children in ignorance and confusion (Too bad! Too bad!) and their teachers not know Arabic or penmanship or arithmetic or history or geography or anything else of the things that a teacher ought to know? (So sad! So sad!) On how many of these children has the Almighty bestowed faculties of capacity and quickwittedness, despite which, for loss of the means to knowledge and lack of the instruments to discipline and raise them, the spark is so thoroughly extinguished in them when young that the tinder of achievement can no longer ignite it in them once grown (Ah! Ah!). What is more, you are, praise God, numbered among the well-heeled and wealthy, and it would not be beyond your means to spend a few purses on the construction of schools and the printing of useful books (Well? What about it?). 1.1.15

The income of the Maronite patriarch is of great *weight* and massive *aggregate*, so much so that with it he could bring life to the hearts of this desiccated sect of his that has lost any interest in competing with or challenging in any area those who, in earlier generations, attained to every science and virtue (On! On!) and whose only concern now is to learn a few rules of the Arabic and Syriac[112] languages simply for the sake of knowing them and not for any benefit (Oh dear! Oh dear!). To date, not one of them has been known to have translated a book or beneficial pamphlet into either of these two languages, nor is the patriarch known to have ordered the printing of a language-teaching book in either (Tee hee! Tee hee!). If he were to spend half his annual income on acquiring the means to knowledge instead of on all those feasts and banquets that they put on for his visitors, or if each emir 1.1.16

كان كلّ من الامرآء والمشايخ الكرام ينفل شيا معلوما في كل سنة لاجل هذه
المصلحة الخيرية * او لو بعث من قِبَله الى البلاد الافرنجية وكلاَء يجمعون من ذوي
الخير والاحسان فيها مبلغا يخصّصه بما نحن بصدده * لاحمد كل من في
الشرق والغرب فعله (جَخ جخ) ولكن اذا تعنّى احد سادتنا هولآء لان يبعث الى ١٧،١،١
اخوانه الافرنج حنّا او متى او لوقا لجمع المال فانما يبعثه لبنآء كنيسة او صومعة
(آحٍ اح) مع ان الانسان مذ يولد الى ان يبلغ اثنتى عشرة سنة لا يمكنه ان يدرك
شيا على حقيقته من جهة الكنيسة والصومعة * ويمكنه في خلال ذلك ان يتعلم
ما يفيده في مدرسة او كتّاب (ثُع ثُع) فهل تَعدِونني ياسادة بانشآء مكاتب وطبع
كتب حتى لا اطيل عليكم هذا الفصل * فان بقلبي منكم لحزازات حاكّة وبصدري ١٨،١،١
عليكم ملامات صاكّة (اَخ اخ) لان خليصى الفارياق في دولتكم السعيدة لم يمكنه
ان يتعلّم فى قريته غير الزبور * وهو كتابٌ حشوه اللحن والخطا والركاكة (اخ اخ)
لانَّ معربه لم يكن يعرف العربية وقس عليه سائر الكتب التى طبعت في بلادكم
وفى رومية العظمي (هُع هع) ومعلوم ان الغلط اذا تاصّل في عقل الصغير ١٩،١،١
شبّ معه ونمى فلم يعد ممكنا بعدُ قلعه * فهل من سبب لهذا الشَين والعيب سوى
اهمالكم وسوء تصرفكم في السياسة المدنية والكنائسية (اَفُوه افوه) * اتحسبون
ان الركاكة من شعائر الدين ومعالمه وفرائضه وعزائمه * وان البلاغة تفضي بكم
الى الكفر والالحاد * والبدعة والفساد (مِطْغ مطغ) ام حسبتم ان تلك الابيات
العاطلة * قد افحمت ذلك المسلم العالم عن المجادلة والمناضلة * (يَع يع) اما بعروقكم
دم يهيجكم الى حبّ الكلام الجزْل الفَخْم * والى البلاغة والبِلّة * ونسق العبارة
على موجب القواعد المقرّرة * والافصاح عمّا يخطر ببالكم دون الحشو المخلّ *
والاعتراض المملّ * والتعقيد المعلّ * والاخلآ المسلّ * وقولكم فى جوز الجملة الخ *

and noble shaykh were to make an annual gift of a certain amount toward this charitable end or were to send agents to the lands of the Franks to collect from the charitable there a sum that could be allocated to such things, everyone, east and west, would praise him for his deed (Hooray! Hooray!).

However, if one of our masters were to go to the trouble of sending Ḥanna 1.1.17
or Mattā or Lūqā to his Frankish brethren[113] to collect money, he would do so only for the building of a church or a hermitage (Ugh! Ugh!) overlooking the fact that, from birth to the age of twelve, no one can properly comprehend anything that comes to him from church or hermitage, though he can, during the same period, be learning useful things in a school or *kuttāb* (Blech! Blech!). Will you then, my masters, promise me to build libraries and print books, so that I don't have to make this chapter too long for you?

My heart with rancor against you *burns*, while my breast with accusations 1.1.18
against you *churns* (Ach! Ach!) because under your auspicious reign, my dear friend the Fāriyāq was unable to learn anything in his village other than the psalms, which is a book that they have stuffed with vulgar usages, mistakes, and lame language (Yech! Yech!) because its translator didn't know chaste Arabic, and you can well imagine what the rest of the books printed in your country and in Great Rome are like (Retch! Retch!).

It is well known that, if error becomes rooted in the mind of the child, 1.1.19
it grows up with him and is thereafter impossible to root out. Is there any other cause for this disgrace and shame than your neglect and mismanagement of civil and clerical affairs? (Ptui! Ptui!) Do you reckon lameness of language to be part of religion's rites and *lineaments*, duties and *requirements*, or that chasteness of language will lead you to unbelief and *heresy*, reprehensible innovation and *errancy*? (Tut-tut!) Or did you reckon that those verses *inastute* might confound the learned Muslim in *dispute*? (Forget it! Forget it!) Is there no blood in your veins to rouse you to a love of eloquent, stately language, of rhetoric and fluency, of the arrangement of the words in accordance with set rules, of the expression of what passes through the mind without grammatically incorrect padding and boring *interpolation*, sickening complexity and phthisic *expatiation*? Without saying "et cetera" in mid-sentence or turning triliteral verbs into quadriliterals and vice versa,[114] without using *fī* instead of *bi-* after a verb and the other way round,[115] without making transitive verbs intransitive and the reverse, or the glottal stop into an elision and the contrary, or failing to distinguish between the active

وجعلكم الفعل الثلاثى رباعيا وبالعكس * واستعمالكم ما يتعدي منه بالبا متعديا بفي وبالعكس * واجرائكم المتعدّي لازما وبالعكس * والمهموز معتلًا وبالعكس وعدم فرقكم بين اسمى الفاعل والمفعول * فتقولون هم محسودون مني اي حاسدون لى وما اشبه ذلك (قَهْ قه) وليس كتابى هذا درّة الثِيْن * في اوهام القسيسين حتى استوعب فيه ذكر اغلاطكم واوهامكم (اَيْحى ايحى) وانما المقصود من ذلك ان ابيّن لكم انّ ادمغتكم قد سُقيت اللحن والركاكة من وقت ذهابكم الى الكتّاب وقراتكم فيه كتاب الزبور الى ان تصيروا كُهّلًا[1] ثم شيوخا (دِحْ دح) وانه ما دمتم على هذه الحال فلن يرجى لكم من اِبْلال (وَيْب ويب) ثم ان الفارياق اقام عند معلمه ريثما ختم الكتاب ٢٠،١،١
المذكور * وبعد ذلك اوجس منه المعلّم ان يربكه في مسائل تصعب عليه فينفضح بها * فاشار على والده بان يخرجه من الكتّاب ويشغله بنسخ الكتب فى البيت (بَه به) فلبث على هذه الحالة مدة طويلة فاستفاد منها ما امكن لمثله ان يستفيد من تجويد الخط وحفظ بعض الالفاظ (بَدْ بد) وكان اهل البلاد يفضلون حسن الخط على كل ما تصنعه اليد * فعندهم ان مَن يكتب خطّا حسنا هو الذى افق بين اقرانه في الفضل * ومع اشتهار ذلك فلم يكن حاكم البلاد يستخدم من الكتّاب الّا من بذأت العين خطّه وعاف الذوق السليم كلامه (عِيطْ عيط) اشعارا بان الحظّ لا يتوقف على الخطّ * وان ادارة الاحكام * لا تفتقر الى تهذيب الكلام * (تُعْ تع) وان كثيرا قد نالوا المراتب السامية والمناصب السنية وهم لا يحسنون توقيع اسمهم الشريف (حسّ حس) غير ان الفارياق لم يكن قرير العين بهذه الحرفة * اذ ٢١،١،١
كان يعتقد ان الرزق الذى ياتى من شقّ كشِقّ القلم لا يكون الا ضيّقا (وَىْ وى) نعم ان كثيرا من الناس قد نالوا العيش الواسع الهنى * والخير المتتابع الوفي *

---

١ ١٨٥٥: كَهْلاً.

and the passive participles—for you say "They are *envied* of me" when you mean "are *envious* of me" and the like? (Ha-ha!) This book of mine is no *Durrat al-thīn fī awhām al-qissīsīn* (*Prize Pearl of the Fishery concerning the Delusions of the Clerisy*)[116] that I have to include in it a mention of every one of your errors and delusions (My! My!). My intention is simply to use it to demonstrate to you that your brains have been fed with incorrect and lame language from the days when you went to the *kuttāb* and read the psalms there until you became grown, and then old, men (Hold your tongue! Hold your tongue!) and that if you remain in this state, no cure is to be hoped for (Woe! Woe!).

Thereafter the Fāriyāq remained with his teacher, where he completed his study of the aforementioned book, after which the teacher became concerned lest the Fāriyāq get him caught up in matters that were beyond him and through them expose him, so he indicated to his father that he should remove him from the *kuttāb* and put him to work copying books at home (Wow! Wow!), which he continued to do for a long while, gaining therefrom as much as the likes of him could by way of improving his hand and memorizing certain words (Good for you! Good for you!). The people of that land gave precedence to good writing over anything else the hand might make, and, to them, one who wrote a good hand had achieved more than any of his peers. Despite this widespread attitude, the country's ruler[117] employed as scribes only those whose writing was ugly to the eye and whose words were disgusting to good taste (Oy! Oy!), this being a kind of public declaration that good fortune is not dependent on good handwriting, that to administer the *law* does not call for language without *flaw* (Abtholutely not![118]), and that they themselves have often attained lofty rank and exalted position though barely able to sign their noble names (Aiee! Aiee!). 1.1.20

The Fāriyāq, however, was not elated at having to practice this craft, believing that any earnings that might reach him through a slit as narrow as that in the nib of a pen must themselves be straitened (Alack! Alack!).[119] True, many a person has obtained a living expansive and *agreeable*, as well as good fortune unabated and *reliable*, from a wellspring that, though broad by comparison with the pen's nib, when measured against their greed and extravagance, was narrow (What a pity!). However, the Fāriyāq was then a greenhorn, with neither practice nor experience, given to judging what is distant by what is close—and nothing is closer to the eye of the scribe 1.1.21

من مورد هو بالنسبة الى شق القلم رحب لكنه بالنسبة الى شرههم وسرفهم ضيّق (واه واه) غير ان الفارياق وقتئذ كان غرًّا لا تجربة له ولا خبرة * فكان يحكم على العبيد بالقريب * ولا شى اقرب الى عين الكاتب من لسان قلمه وعارض قرطاسه * او ادنى الى قلبه من الكلام الذى يكتبه واللبيب من قنع بالحرفة التى يتعاطاها ولم يشق عليه امت الشق ولم يشرئبّ الى ما ليس يحسنه (شُع شع) *

than the nib of his pen and the paper before him, or closer to his heart than the words he is writing. A clever fellow is he who accepts the craft that he practices, to whom the shame of hard work is no burden, and who does not crane his neck to look out for things at which he does not excel (No to the flesh! No to the flesh!).

الفصل الثانى

فى انتكاسة حاقية وعمامة واقية

قدكان من طبع الفارياق كما هو داب جميع الاحداث ايضا ان يحاكى فى الزى ١،٢،١
والاطوار والكلام من كان متميّزا فى عصره بالفضل والدراية * وانه راى ذات
يوم قِرْزاماً معتمّاً بعمامة كبيرة مدورة * وكان هذا القرزام يُحسَب وقتئذ من فحول
الشعرآء * فاحب الفارياق ان يكون له مثل هذه العمامة على صغر راسه * فكان
اذا مشى يميل راسه منها يَمنةً ويَسرةً كالقاضى الذى يخرج فى الاسواق بعد
صلوة الجمعة ويسلّم على الناس * واتفق ان اباه سار مرة الى دار الحاكم واستصحبه ٢،٢،١
معه واركبه مهرة له * وكان هو راكبا حصانا * فمكثا هناك اياما * فعنّ للفارياق
يوما من الايام ان يركض المهرة فى الميدان وكان الحصان مربوطا فى جانب *
فاجرى المهرة نصف شوط حتى اذا قابلت مربط اليفها التفتت اليه كالمشيرة انّ
فارسها غير جدير بركوبها بين جياد الامير * فما كان من الفارياق الا ان سقط
على امّ راسه * واقبلت المهرة تجرى الى الحصان وغادرته مجندلا على الجَدالة *
ولوكان فارساً مُجيدا لما تركته على تلك الحالة بل كانت تنتظره حتى يقوم * ثم انه
قام بعد ذلك يحمد الله على كبر عمامته فانها هى التى وَقَتْ رأسه عن احدى الشجّات
العشر وهى القاشِرة الحارِصَة الباضِعة الدامِية المُتلاحِمة السِمحاق المُوضِحَة الهاشِمة

Chapter 2

A Bruising Fall and a Protecting Shawl

It was in the Fāriyāq's nature, as is normal among the young, to imitate in dress, behavior, and speech those in his time distinguished by merit and knowledge. One day, he saw a wretched poet wearing a large round turban. The said wretched poet then being numbered among the masters, the Fāriyāq set his heart on having just such a turban, small as was his head, and he would walk along nodding under the weight of it to right and left, like a judge passing through the markets on his way home after Friday prayers saluting the people. 1.2.1

Now it happened once, when his father went to the ruler's house, that he took him along with him, mounting him on a filly of his, while he rode a stallion. There they stayed for a number of days, on one of which the Fāriyāq got it into his head to take his filly for a gallop in the square, where the stallion was tied up to one side. He'd raced her one length of the square when his filly, passing the place where her friend was picketed, turned her head toward him as though to indicate that her dashing cavalier was unworthy to ride her past the prince's steeds. The Fāriyāq promptly flew off and landed on his head, while the filly set off running, leaving him flat on the ground, though, had he been an expert horseman, she'd never have left him in such a state but would have waited for him to get up. He then arose, thanking God for the size of his turban, for it was that which had protected his head from receiving any of "the ten head wounds"[120] (to wit, the bloodless abrasion and the bloodless graze, the break in the skin that brings blood but does not make it flow, the one that makes the blood flow, the one that enters the flesh without reaching the periosteum, the one that reaches the periosteum, the one that cuts to the bone, the one that breaks the bone, the one that shifts 1.2.2

المنَقّلة الآمّة الدامِغة * ولكنه قام محقوّا ويومئذ عرف ان لكبر العمامة فضلا ٣،٢،١
ومزيّة * وظن ان اتخاذ العمائم الكبيرة عند اهل بلاده انما هى لوقاية رؤسهم فقط
لا لتحسين وجوههم * فان العمامة الضخمة تخفى محاسن الوجه وتشوه الوجه الصغير
فضلا عن كونها توجع الراس وتمنع صعود الابخرة من مسامّه كما نصّ عليه الساعُور
الاكبر * فان قيل اذا كان سبب اتخاذ العمائم الكبيرة انما هو لوقاية الرؤس لا للزينة ٤،٢،١
والتحسين فما بال الذين يرقدون ليلاً يتعممون * فهل يخافون ان تتدحرج رؤسهم عن
مصادغهم فيسقطوا في مهواة في بيتهم * مع ان فرشهم تكون على الارض *
قلت ان منشا هذه العادة هو ان نسآ تلك البلاد يتخذن في رؤسهن هذه القرون
التى يقال لها هناك طناطير * وهى تكون من فضة او ذهب في طول الذراع
وغلظ الرسغ * فاذا بات الرجل مع امراته حاسر الراس او كان على راسه غطآ
رقيق لم يأمن ان تنطحه بقرنها على قرنه فتمنيه باحدى الشجاج المذكورة * فان ابيت الّا ٥،٢،١
اللجاجة وقلت ما سبب هذه القرون الحسّية * هل هى دليل على التذكير بالقرون
المعنوية عند مخالفة الرجل لامرأته * او عند تقتيره عليها * او اجْفاره عنها * او
هى من قبيل الزينة او من بطر النسآء وشرههن بحيث اذا شممن رائحة الايسار من
ازواجهن رأين ان كل مَجَسّ من اجسامهن قَمِنٌ بالحَلْى والزينة * اذ كنّ يعتقدن ان
المستور منها عن عيون الناس غير مستور عن عيونهن وعيون بعولتهن * وان كان
في المسألة خلاف عظيم * وتحليل وتحريم * وان في التزيّن بحلى غير ظاهر
للذّةً عظيمة * فانّ مجرّد العلم باحراز شى ثمين يسرّ صاحبه * كما لو احرز انسان
كنزا في حرز محجوب فانه يفرح به من غير ان ينظر اليه * قلت اما التذكير بالقرون
المعنوية فغير مظنون في نسآء تلك البلاد لكونهن من ذوات العِرض والتصاون *
ولا سيما نسآء الجبل * وفضلاً عن ذلك فانّ هِراوة الزوج ومقامع اهله واهل

the bone, the one that leaves only a thin layer of skin over the brain, and the one that cuts to the brain).

However, he arose, having taken a blow to his loins, and that day made 1.2.3
the discovery that there are benefits and advantages to a large turban, and he conceived the idea that the people of his country had taken to wearing large turbans simply to protect their heads and not to beautify their faces, for a huge turban hides the good qualities of the face and makes a small face look bad, not to mention that it hurts the head and blocks the ascent of vapors from the pores, something the Great Christian Master Physician[121] prescribes.

If it be said,[122] "If the sole reason for adopting large turbans is to pro- 1.2.4
tect people's heads, not to adorn or beautify them, how do you explain the people who wear their turbans when they go to bed at night? Are they afraid their heads will roll off their pillows and fall into a chasm inside their houses, even though their bedding is placed on the floor?" I reply, "The origin of this custom lies in the fact that the women of that land are given to wearing on their heads those 'horns' that they there call *ṭanāṭīr*.[123] These are made of silver or gold, and are as long as a forearm in height and as wide as a wrist. Now, if a man spends the night with his wife with nothing, or only a thin covering, on his head, he will be in danger of being bashed on his pate by her 'horn' and receiving from her one of the ten head wounds referred to above."

If you were to insist on being argumentative and say, "What is the reason 1.2.5
for these veritable horns? Are they placed there to remind one of the figurative horns that a man acquires when he goes against his wife's wishes or is stingy with her or breaks off relations with her, or as a kind of adornment, or as a sign of women's wantonness and greed, in that, when they catch the smell of riches on their husbands, they think that every inch of their bodies should be decorated and ornamented, believing as they do that, while such things should be concealed from the eyes of others, they should not be concealed from their eyes or those of their husbands (albeit there is many a difference over the matter, with some forbidding it and some taking an attitude of acquiescence), for the mere knowledge that something valuable is safely hidden away may give pleasure to its owner, just as, if a person squirrels away treasure in a concealed hoard, he may revel in it even though he cannot see it?" I would reply, "The idea that they are there to provide a reminder of the figurative horns is not to be entertained, for the women of that country maintain their honor and preserve their chastity, and especially the women

امراته وعيون الجيران ايضا تمنعها عن الاتصاف بالصفة الزوجيّة التامّة * اما
فى المدن فان هذه الصفة اقوى وافشى * وانما كان اتخاذ هذه القرون فى الاصل ٦،٢،١
مناطا للبراقع * وكانت فى مبداها صغيرة قصيرة ثم طالت وكبرت بطول الزمن
وكبر الدينار * وكلّما زاد ايسار الرجل وماله زاد قرن امراته طولا وضخامة *
وهنا فائدة لا بدّ من ذكرها * وهى ان لفظة القرن من الالفاظ التى اشترك فيها
جميع اللغات كالصابون والقطّ والمزج وغيرها * وقد شهرت عند جميع المولفين
بانها كناية عن كذا وكذا من طرف الزوجه فى حق زوجها * الّا عند المولفين من
اليهود فان الصفة القرنيّة فى كتبهم من الصفات الحميدة * ولذلك فكثيرا ما
تسمع فى كتاب الزبور ارتفع قرنى وانت رافع قرنى وانى انطح بقرنى وما اشبه ذلك *
وفى كلا الاستعمالين غموض وابهام * امّا غموض استعمال القرن عند المولفين ٧،٢،١
من غير اليهود كنايةً عن خيانة المراة زوجها فلانَّ هيئة القرن لا تدل على عضو
مخصوص من اعضآ الانسان * وحقيقته ايضا لا تدل على حيوان مخصوص *
فان الثور والوعل والتيس والكركدن فى ذلك سوآء * ولفظه كذلك غير مشتق
من فعل يشير الى خيانة اوضَمْد * فما علّة هذا الاستعمال * وقد استفتيت فى
هذه المسئلة المشكلة كثيرًا من المتزوّجين المجرَّذين * فكلّهم كان يتخيّف الوانا عند
سؤالى له * ويجمجم فى كلامه ويقوم من عندى وقد خجل ووَجَم * فانْ فتح الله
الان على احد ممن يطالع كتابى هذا فى فهم حقيقة ما يراد من هذا الحرف عرفا
واصطلاحاً * وفى بيان سبب استعماله كناية عن الضمد فليتفضّل بالجواب منةً
واحسانا * فاما استعماله من مولفى اليهود كناية عن العزّة والقوّة والمنعة والغلبة فانه
يرد عليه ما ورد على الاوّل من ان كثيرا من الحيوانات قد اشترك فيه * ومنها ما
هو غير ذى قوة ولا باس * فانظر اختلاف الناس فى لفظة واحدة ومعنى واحد *

of the Mountain. In addition, the husband's cudgel, the hooked staffs of his own and his wife's families, and the eyes of the neighbors prevent her from having the full range of marital traits ascribed to her; in the cities, on the other hand, such traits are stronger and more widespread."

In origin, these "horns" were merely a device from which to suspend the face veil and, when first used, were small and short. Then they grew taller and larger as time went by and people got richer, a wife's horns getting taller and larger the richer and better off her husband became. And this brings us to a bit of useful information that we have to mention: the word *qarn* ("horn") is one that is common to all languages,[124] like *ṣābūn* ("soap")[125], *qiṭṭ* ("cat"), [126] *mazj* ("mixing"),[127] and so on and has become famous among writers as a metonym for you-know-what on the part of the wife against the husband, except where Jewish writers are concerned, for in their books the horn has a positive significance, which is why you often hear in the Book of Psalms, "My horn has been exalted" and "You have exalted my horn" and "I shall butt with my horn" and so on.[128] 1.2.6

Both usages contain a certain incomprehensibility and ambiguity. The incomprehensibility of the use of "horn" by non-Jewish writers as a metonym for women's infidelity to their husbands lies in the fact that the shape of the horn does not bring to mind any specific human member and neither do its actual manifestations bring to mind any specific animal, for the ox, the mountain goat, the billy goat, and the rhinoceros all have one. Similarly, the word itself is not derived from any verb that might indicate a woman's being unfaithful or taking a lover.[129] What, then, lies behind this usage? I have asked many married men of lengthy experience about this prickly issue, and all of them changed color on hearing my question and, embarrassed and despondent, stammered, got up, and left me. Should God, then, grant any of those who peruse this book of mine a sudden insight as to the meaning of this word, both in common usage and as a technical term, let him be so good as to respond, out of kindness and charity. As to its usage among the writers of the Jews as a metonym for high rank, power, strength, and victory, what is true of the preceding is true of that too, namely, that it is common to many animals, some of which are possessed of neither power nor might. Observe, then, how people differ with regard to a single word and a single meaning! 1.2.7

امّا العمامة فان اشتقاقها فيما ارى من عمّ بمعنى شَمِل لانها تعمّ الراس وهى على ٨،٢،١
اشكال مختلفة * فمنها الحلزونىّ * والكعكى والاِطارى * والمكوَّرى * والمقوَّرى *
والقُهقُورىّ * والقِرَطلّى والقَبْعَلى * وكلها على اصنافها احسن من هذه الاجران
التى تلبسها رؤسآء المارونية فى الدّين فلينظروا وجوههم فى مرآة جليّة *

As for "turban" (*ʿimāma*), I believe it derives from *ʿamma* meaning "to embrace," for it embraces the head. It comes in various forms, among them the spiral, the cake-shaped, the wheel-shaped, the globular, the coil-shaped, the conical, the basket-shaped, and the cup-shaped, and all of these, whatever the type, are better than the baptismal fonts that the Maronite religious leaders wear. Let them just take a look at their faces in a well-polished mirror! 1.2.8

الفصل الثالث

فى نوادر مختلفة

١،٣،١ كان للفارياق ارتياح غريزى من صغره لقرآة الكلام الفصيح وامعان النظر فيه ولالتقاط الالفاظ الغريبة التى كان يجدها فى الكتب * فان اباه قد احرز كتبا عديدة فى فنون مختلفة * وكان اى الفارياق يتهافت منذ حداثته على النظم من قبل ان يتعلم شيا مما يلزم لهذه الصنعة * فكان مرة يصيب ومرة يخطئ * مع اعتقاده ان الشعرآء افضل الناس وان الشعر اجلّ ما يتعاطاه الانسان *

٢،٣،١ فقرا يوما فى بعض الاخبار عن شاعر كان فى حداثته ابله مغفّلا ثم صار امره الى ان نبغ فى نظم القصائد المطوّلة واجاد * فممّا حُكى عنه انه سكر يوماً فقعد فى نحو ناموس(١) وجعل يخطب منه خطبة ابي العِبَر طرد طبك طلندى بك نك يك من البلوعة * وانه اراد يوما ان يتسوّر حائطا ليتناول من بعض الثمر فوقع فى فخ كان نصبه صاحب البستان للحيوانات * وانه قال يوما لامّه ان عند فلانة خادمة نظيفة غسلت اليوم باب دارها فجآء اسود يلمع * وانه راى يوما صبيًا قد قلع احد اضراسه فسار واقترض

(١) حاشية قد وهَم المطران جرمانوس فرحات فى قوله فى كتابه باب الاعراب التامور الوعآ والنفس والقلب وصومعة الراهب وقانون الرهبنة وعبارة اصله وصومعة الراهب وناموسُه فتوهّم ان الناموس هنا بمعنى القانون او الشرع على ما اشتهر فى عرف النصارى ومراد صاحب القاموس المعنى الاصلى وهو القُتْره والعامّة تقول ناووس وما اشتهر عندهم فهو امّا تجوّز عن صاحب السر او هو يونانى معرّب

Chapter 3

Various Amusing Anecdotes

From childhood, the Fāriyāq had felt an instinctive disposition to read and assiduously study the classical language, picking out the rare words that he came across in books, of which his father had amassed a large number in a variety of disciplines. He, that is, the Fāriyāq, was also, from his youth, wild about poetry, even before he had learned anything about the requirements of that craft; thus sometimes he would hit the mark and other times miss it. He also believed poets were the best people and poetry the most magnificent thing with which a man could occupy himself. 1.3.1

Then one day he read in some chronicle of a poet who in his youth had been stupid and artless but had grown up to excel and to shine at composing lengthy odes. The story is told of him that one day he got drunk and sat down beside a monk's cell(1)[130] from whence he set about delivering the sermon of Abū l-ʿIbar Ṭarad Ṭabak Ṭalandī Bak Nak Yak[131] from the drain.[132] Also that one day, he wanted to scale a wall so that he could reach some dates, and he fell into an animal trap set by the owner of the orchard.[133] And that one day he told his mother that such and such a woman had an excellent maid who had "washed the door of her house today till it was shining black." And that one day he caught sight of 1.3.2

(1) Metropolitan Jirmānūs Farḥāt is misguided in his statement in his *Bāb al-Iʿrāb* (*Gateway to Grammar*) that "*ta'mūr* means 'container' and 'soul' and 'heart' *and 'the monk's cell' and 'the monastic rule'* (*qānūn al-rāhib*)." The wording of the original [from which Farḥāt took this, sc. the *Qāmūs*] is "and the monk's cell *and his hide* (*ṣawmʿat al-rāhib wa-nāmūsuhu*)" and Farḥāt was deluded enough to imagine that *nāmūs* here means "rule" or "path" as is the common usage among Christians. In fact, the author of the *Qāmūs* intends the original meaning, which is "[a hunter's] hide." The common people say *nāwūs* [when they mean *nāmūs*], and this widespread sense in which they use the word is either a figurative extension of the meaning "one who holds a secret" [a further meaning listed in the *Qāmūs*] or an Arabization of the Greek [*naos* ("temple")].

درهما وقال للحجّام اقلع ضرسى انا ايضا فانه غير قاطع فى الأكل * ولعلَّ ينبت لى فى
مكانه ضرس احدّ منه * وقيل له يوما قد دُوّنت عنك حكايات من حمقك كثيرة ٣،٣،١
فقال بودىّ لو ان احدا يقراها علىّ لاضحك * ومرض اخوه يوما فقال ابوه لزوجته
قد اضره الطعام الذى اكله امس * فقال نعم قد اضره الاكل والخادمة معاً * فقال
ابوه ما دخل الخادمة هاهنا * فقال لعلها اعطته ما لم يحبّ * ورات امه على
ثيابه دماً فقالت له ما هذا الدم * قال قد وقعت فجرى دمى وهو احسن * فقد
يقال من وقع وجرى منه دم صحّ وتقوّى * وجرح يده بسكين فرمى بها وقال هذه
السكين لا تساوى شياً * فقال ابوه لو كانت كذلك لما جَرَحت يدك * فقال كل
انسان يجرح يده فى الدنيا سوآء بسكين او غيرها * وقال مرّة قد رايت فى السوق ٤،٣،١
جبنا ابيض كالزفت * وقيل له لمَ لا تغسل يدك قال اغسلها فتعود وسخة فى الحال *
ولست اقدر على تنظيفها لكون دمى وسخا * وراى ذات يوم رجالا مصلوبين
فقال لامّه يا امّ اذا عاشت هولآء الرجال ايضا افيقدر الذين صلبوهم على صلبهم
مرة اخرى * وكان قوم يسالون عن منزل شخص فقال انا اعرف مقره * قيل كيف
عرفته * قال قد رايت الرجل يمشى فى السوق على رجليه * وقال يوما من الثمانية
الى التسعة يمضى الوقت اسرع من الستة الى السبعة * وقيل له اتحب اللحم اكثر
ام السمك قال اظن انى احبّ هذا اكثر * وقال له ابوه اذا كنت تغيب عنا افتحسن ٥،٣،١
ان تكتب لنا كتابا * قال نعم اكتبه واجى به اوصله اليكم * وسمع اباه يثنى على خزّ
اشتراه وكان به فرحا * فقال قد كانت ساعة سعيدة انكم لم تشتروه * وراى اباه
يكتب كتابا فقال له هل تستطيع ياابت ان تقرا ما تكتبه * فقال له كيف لا وانا
الذى كتبته * قال اما انا فلا استطيع * وراى اباه يتاسّف على طير فقده *
فقال له بارك الله فى الساعة التى طار فيها * فقال له يا احمق انا نتاسف على فقده

a boy who had had one of his molars removed, so he went and borrowed a dirham and told the cupper, "Take my molar out too because it doesn't cut my food; maybe another, sharper, molar will grow in its place."

1.3.3 And one day someone said to him, "Many stories have been recorded of your stupidity," to which he replied, "I wish someone would read them to me so I could have a laugh!" And one day his brother fell ill and his father said to his wife, "The food he ate yesterday was bad for him," and the poet said, "Yes, the food was bad for him and so was the maid." "What has the maid got to do with it?" his father asked him, and he said, "Maybe she gave him something he didn't like." And his mother noticed blood on his clothes and asked him, "What's that blood?" and he answered, "I fell over and my blood ran, which is for the good, for it is said, 'If someone falls over and his blood runs, he gets well and is strengthened.'" And he cut his hand with a knife and threw it away, saying, "This knife is worthless"; his father said to him, "If it really were, it wouldn't have cut your hand," to which the man replied, "Everyone in the world cuts his hand, if not with a knife then with something else."

1.3.4 And he said, "Once I saw cheese as white as tar in the market." And someone said to him, "Why don't you wash your hands?" He replied, "I do, but they get dirty again straight away; I can't get them clean because my blood is dirty." And one day he saw some men who had been crucified and he asked his mother, "Mother, if those men survive, can those who crucified them recrucify them?" And a company of people once asked after someone's house and he said, "I know where it is located." "How do you know?" he was asked and he replied, "I saw the man going through the market on foot." And one day he said, "Time moves faster between eight and nine than between six and seven." And someone asked him, "Which do you like better, meat or fish?" and he replied, "Really, I think I like this one better."[134]

1.3.5 And his father said to him, "If you were away from us, would you be able to write us a letter?" and he replied, "Yes. I'd write it and bring it to you, too." And he heard his father singing the praises of some silk-wool he'd bought and with which he was delighted, so the man said, "It would have been a fortunate hour if you hadn't bought it." And he saw his father writing a letter and said to him, "Father, can you read what you write?" and the father replied, "How could I not when I am the one who wrote it?" "For my part," the man said, "I cannot." And he saw that his father was upset over a bird he had lost and told him, "God bless the hour in which it flew away!," so his father said

قال له ولِمَ لم تبنِ له دارا * قال أَوَ يُبنَى للطائر دار * قال انما اعنى عودين يجعلان
من هنا ومن هناك * ووصف مرة حيوانات رآها فقال ورايت ايضا خنزيرا اكبر ١،٣،٦
منى * وشكا وجعاً فى رجله فقال ليت هذى الرّجل تبلَى * وكان ابوه يفسر له
معنى انقذ بان قال له اذا وقع احد فى النار مثلاً وذهبتَ واخرجته منها فذلك هو
الانقاذ * قال ولكنه قد احترق فكيف انقذه * وعلى فرض انى وضعت هذا
السفّود فى النار ثم اخرجته منها افيكون ذلك ايضا انقاذا * وفسر له يوما آخر معنى
يلوم فقال اذا ابطا عليك شخص فى شى وقلت له لمَ ابطأت لمَ تكاسلت فذلك
يكون لوماً * فقال واقول له ايضا لم كبرت لم صغرت لم قَصُرت * ولامته امّه على ١،٣،٧
نخره عند الكلام فقال لها الا لا تلوميني ولكن لومى روحى * واراد ابوه ان يخرج
فى يوم ماطر ثم عدل خوفا من المطر * فقال لامه ياماه من نعم[١] الله انّا لم نخرج
اليوم فان الهوآء كان طيبا * واشترت له امّه ثوبا فصّلته قال لها أَوَ يزول لون
هذا الثوب * قالت لا ادرى * قال ارجو ان يزول فلعله يصير احسن * وقالت
له اوان الشتآء وهو لابس قميصا فقط البس ثوبك فوق القميص * فقال لها لا
لانى ابرد به اكثر * ولامه ابوه علي قرآته بصوت صلق فقال له لمَ هذا الصلق فى ١،٣،٨
القرآة قال لا اقدر ان اصرخ اكثر * وخفى عليه يوما معنى الزيارة فقالت له امّه اذا
سرتُ اليوم الى السيدة فلانة لانظرها فقد زرتها * قال قد فهمت انك تسيرين
اليها كى تخدعيها * وقالت له امه ان فلانة التى تحسن اليك قد ماتت فسكت
ساعة ثم قال * قد حزنت عليها كما حزنت على موت امّى * الله يبعثها الى الجنة
هى وزوجها حالاً * وقال يوما لوالده ان معلمنا اليوم قد اشترى قضيبا ليضرب
به الاولاد ولكنهم يغضبونه عمدا حتى يضربهم به فينكسر فاستريح انا ايضا *

---

١ ١٨٥٥: عمّ.

to him, “You imbecile, I’m upset at its loss.” “So why didn’t you build it a house?” responded the man. “Can one build a house for a bird?” asked the father. “All I mean,” said the man “is two sticks going from here to there.”

And once he described some animals he’d seen, saying, “They included a pig that was larger than me.” And he complained of a pain in his foot and said, “I wish this foot would rot away.” And his father was explaining to him the meaning of “to save” and said to him, “If someone fell into the fire, for example, and you went and pulled him out, that would be saving him,” to which the man replied, “But he would have burned up, so how could I save him? Suppose I stuck this skewer into the fire and pulled him out with it, would that be saving?” And once another was explaining to him the meaning of “to reproach” and said to him, “If someone was slow in doing something for you and you said to him, ‘Why were you so slow? Why were you so slothful?’ that would be reproaching,” and the man said, “And I’d tell him too, ‘Why did you grow large? Why did you grow small? Why did you grow short?’ ”[135] 1.3.6

And his mother reproached him for snorting when he spoke, and he replied, “You should reproach not me but my breath.” And his father wanted to go out one day when it was raining but decided against it because of the rain, so he said to his mother, “Mother, it’s a blessing from God that we didn’t go out today, for the weather was fine.” And his mother bought him a length of cloth and when she had had it made up he said to her, “Will the color of this cloth fade?” “I don’t know,” she replied. “I hope that it does,” he said, “because it might look better.” And once in the winter, when he was wearing only a shift, his mother said to him, “Wear your robe over your shift!” and he told her, “No. It’ll make me colder.” 1.3.7

And his father reproached him for shrieking as he read out loud, and he said, “I can’t shout any louder.” And one day he couldn’t think of the meaning of the word “visit,” so his mother said to him, “If I were to go today to such and such a lady to see her, I would be visiting her.” He responded, “I deduce from this that you’re going to her to play a trick on her.”[136] And his mother said to him, “Such and such a lady who was kind to you has died,” and he was silent for a while and then said, “I have mourned for her as I would for my mother. May God send her and her husband to Heaven this minute!” And one day he told his father, “Today our teacher bought a rod to beat the children, and now they are making him angry in order to make him beat them with it till it breaks, which will be a relief to me too.” 1.3.8

وقال لامه وقد مرضت اذا جئناك بالطبيب ولم يشأ الله ان يشفيك فما الحاجة ٩،٣،١
الى دوآء * وقال لها مرة اخرى استعملى هذا الدوآ فلعلك تمرضين * واراد
يوما ان يوقد النار فقال اردت ان اطفئها فما انطفأت * وقالت له امّه سِرْ الى
فلانة وقل لها لاى شى تخافين من امى انما هى بشر من بنى آدم مثلك * فقال
اقول لها تقول لك امى لاى شى تنفرين منها انما هى من بنى الحيوانات مثلك *
وقال مرة فى شى اعجبه تبارك الله من كل عين * وقيل له يوما ان فلانا يريد ان
ياخذك الى مدرسته ليعلمك * فقال بعثه الله الى الجنة * قال له ابوه اتريد
ان تميته * قال فكيف اقول اذاً * قال قل اطال الله عمره * قال طوّله الله *
وقال لامه اتعطيننى الليلة من تلك الحلوآء * فقالت له ان عشنا الى الليلة *
قال نحن نعيش الى غد فكيف لا نعيش الى الليل- انتهى- فطالع بذلك احد ١٠،٣،١
الالبّا فى بلاده وقال له قد ظهر لى ان هذا كلام ابله ماموه * او مدلّه تُوَه *
او مسمّه مسبوه * او عَمِه مشدوه * او نَمِه معتوه * فكيف صار بعد ذلك
شاعرا * فقال له يحتمل ان كلامه هذا كان قد تعمده ليضحك به ابويه * او انه
كان بليد البادرة ولكنه حديد الفاكرة * فان من الناس من يدهش للسؤال فلا
يكاد يجيب الا خطا * فاذا اعمل فكره فى خلوة احسن كل الاحسان * او انه
قصد بذلك ان يكون نَبَها مشهورا بين الناس ولو بحماقة ورقاعة * فان اكثر الناس
يحاول الشهرة باى وجه كان * فمنهم من يتعاطى الترجمة للكتب والتعليم وهو لا ١١،٣،١
يدرى شيا * ولكنه يفرح بان يضع اسمه فى اول الكتاب * وبان يحشّيه بعبارات
ركيكة واقوال سخيفة من عنده * او بان يُروَى عنه فيقال قال فلان كذا وكذا
ويكون قوله خطا وهذرا * ومنهم من يتربع فى صدر المجلس بين اخوانه واقرانه
ويطفق يحكى لهم حكايات عن بلاد بعيدة ويخلط كلامه ببعض الفاظ تعلمها من

And he told his mother, who had fallen sick, "If we brought you a doctor and God wasn't willing to cure you, what would be the point of the medicine?" And on another occasion he said to her, "Use this medicine. It may make you sick." And one day he wanted to light the fire, so he said, "I wanted to put it out but it wouldn't go out." And his mother told him, "Go to such and such a woman and ask her, 'Why are you afraid of my mother? She's a human being like you,'" so he told her, "I'm going to tell her, 'My mother asks you, "Why will you have nothing to do with her when she's an animal just like you?"'" And once he said of something he admired, "May God be protected from every eye!"[137] And once he was told, "So and so wants to take you to his school to teach you" and he replied, "May God send him to Heaven!" His father asked him, "Do you want to kill him?" "What should I say then?" he asked. His father replied, "Say, 'God prolong his life!'" "He already has," said the man. And he asked his mother, "Will you give me some of that halvah tonight?" and she said to him, "If we live to see the night." He responded, "We're going to live to see the morrow, so how could we not see the night?" End. 1.3.9

An intelligent person of his country came to learn of these things and said to the Fāriyāq, "It appears to me that these sayings are dumb and disturbed, or dotty and deranged, or feather-brained and feeble-minded, or confounded and befuddled, or bedazed and confused, so how could he have gone on to become a poet?" The Fāriyāq told him, "Probably he intended, with these sayings of his, to make his parents laugh, or maybe his first impulses were slow-minded but his more carefully thought-out responses quick-witted. Some people are so put off their stroke by a question that they can only answer wrongly, but if they put their brains to work when they're on their own, they perform excellently. Or maybe his intention in doing so was to become noted and celebrated among men, if only for foolishness and folly, for most people seek fame by any means possible. 1.3.10

"Some practice the translation of books and teaching when they know nothing, despite which they derive pleasure from putting their names at the beginning of the book and stuffing it with feeble phrases and stupid statements that they make up themselves, or in having others report their sayings so that it may be said, 'So and so said thus and such,' the statement itself being erroneous and pointless. Others sit cross-legged at the forefront of the salon among their brethren and peers and suddenly start telling tales of far-away 1.3.11

لغة العجم * فيقول لهم مثلا صان فاصون * وپاردون موسيو * ودنكوى *
وڤارى ول * اشارةً الى انه اطال السياحة فى بلاد فرنسا وايطاليا وانكلترة وتعلم
لغاتهم وهو يجهل لغته التى نشأ عليها * ومنهم من يتخذ له عمامة كبيرة يضاهى ١،٣،١٢
بها بعض العلمآء * فان كبر العمامة يدل على كبر الراس * وكبر الراس يدل على
جودة العقل وصواب الراى * ومنهم من يتكلف محاكاة لهجة مّا ممن عرفوا
بالفصاحة فتراه يتشدّق ويَجْعَم ويستعمل الفاظا فى غير محلها * وبعدُ فلا ينبغى ان ١،٣،١٣
يكون الشاعر عاقلا او فيلسوفا * فان كثيرا من المجانين كانوا شعرآء * اوكثيرا من
الشعرآء كانوا مجانين * وذلك كابى العِبَر وبهلول وعليان وطويس ومزبّد * وقد
قالت الفلاسفة ان اول الهوس الشعر واحسن الشعر ما كان عن هوس وغرام *
فان الشعر العلمآء المتوقّرين لا يكون الا مقرزَماً * فلما سمع الفارياق ذلك زهد فى ١،٣،١٤
الشعر ورغب عنه الى حفظ الالفاظ الغريبة * لكنه لم يلبث ان رجع الى خلقه
الاول * وذلك ان اباه اخذه معه الى بعض القرى البعيدة ليجبى المال المضروب على
سكانها الى خزنة الحاكم * فانزله اهلها منزلا كريما * وكان بالقرب من منزله جارية
بديعة الجمال * فجعل الفارياق على صغره ينظر اليها نظر المحبّ الرانى جريا على عادة
الاغرار من العشاق * من انهم يبتدئون العشق فى جاراتهم استخفافا للطلب
واستشفاعًا بالجاريّة * كما ان عادة الجارات تهنيد جيرانهنّ وتغميزهم[1] اشارة الى انه
لا ينبغى البحث عن الطبيب البعيد اذا امكن التداوى عند القريب * غير ان المحنكين
فى الحب يبعدون فى الطلب ويرودون انزح منتجع * لانهم لما جعلوا دابهم
وديدنهم اشباع النفس من هواها كان عندهم السعى فى ذلك فرضا واجبا *
ووجدوا فى الابعاد والنصب لذة عظيمة * اذ من فتح فاه رجآء ان تتساقط الاثمار

---

١ ١٨٥٥: تغميرهم.

countries, mixing their words with a few phrases from foreign languages that they have learned. Thus they will say to them, for example, *sans façon,* and *pardon, monsieur,* and *dunque,* and *very well* to show that they have spent a lot of time touring France, Italy, and England and have learned their languages, though they are ignorant of the language in which they were brought up.

"Some wear large turbans like those worn by certain scholars of religion, for a large turban is supposed to indicate a large head and a large head is supposed to indicate an excellent mind and sound judgment. Some affect to imitate some nasal intonation of those who are known for the chasteness of their speech, and you find them using high-sounding terms and chewing their words inside their mouths and using words inappropriately. 1.3.12

"But, to return to your original question: the poet does not have to be sensible, or a philosopher. Many madmen were poets. Examples are Abū l-ʿIbar, Buhlūl,[138] ʿUlayyān, Ṭuways,[139] and Muzabbid.[140] The philosophers have stated that poetry is the first product of rapture and that the best of it is that which has its origins in rapture and amorous infatuation, which explains why the poetry of sedate scholars is always feeble." 1.3.13

When the Fāriyāq[141] heard this, he renounced poetry in favor of committing rare words to heart. It wasn't long, however, before he reverted to his first nature, the reason being that his father took him with him to a certain distant village to collect the taxes imposed on its inhabitants and deliver them to the ruler's treasury. The people of the village put his father up in grand style, and, living close to where he was staying, was a girl of surpassing beauty. Despite his tender age, the Fāriyāq began to look on her with the eyes of the star-struck paramour, according to the custom of novices in love of first falling in love with girls who are their neighbors, because they believe the goal is easily reached and because they can make use of their relationship as neighbors to plead their cause. Similarly, the girl neighbors usually sigh over their boy neighbors and wink at them as a way of signaling that there's no need to go looking for a distant physician when the cure is close at hand. Old hands at love, however, look far afield and cruise the most distant grazing grounds, for, having made it their custom and habit to give in to every fancy of their souls, they feel it an obligation and a duty to make things difficult for themselves, and they find enormous pleasure in distancing themselves from the beloved and falling sick over her; any who opens his mouth in the hope that the fruit will fall into it can only be regarded as impotent. 1.3.14

فيه لم يعدّ الّا مع العاجزين * والحاصل ان الفارياق هوى جارته لانه كان غِرّا * ١،٣،١٥
وانها هى استهوته واطعمته لكونها جارة * ولان منزلته من حيث كونه مع ابيه كانت تميل الناس اليه * غير ان مدة اقامته هناك لم تطل * واضطر الى الرجوع مع ابيه وقد بقى كلفا بالجارية * فلما حان الفراق بكى وتحسّر وتنفّس الصُعَدآ * ونخزه الوجد لان ينظم قصيدة يعبّر بها عن غرامه * فقال من جملة ابيات

افارقها على رغمٍ وانى   اغادر عندها والله روحى

وهى اشبه بنفس شعرآء عصره الذين يقسمون ايمانا مغلظة بانهم قد عافوا الطعام والشراب شوقا وغراما * وسهروا الليالى الطويلة وجدا وهياما * وانهم ناسمون وقد ماتوا وكفّنوا وحنّطوا ودفنوا * وهم عند ذلك يتلهّون باىّ لَهْوة كانت * ثم انه لما اطّلع ابوه على تلك الابيات الفراقية لامه عليها ونهاه عن النظم * فكانّما كان قد اغراه به * فان من طبع الاولاد فى الغالب الخلاف لما يريده منهم اباوهم * ثم انه فصل من تلك القرية حزينا كئيبا متيّما مفتونا *

In short, the Fāriyāq fell in love with his neighbor because he was new to the game, and she welcomed his love and gave him hope of success because she was a neighbor and because the prestige that he derived from being with his father disposed people well toward him. His stay did not last long, however, and he was compelled to return with his father. He had fallen very much in love with the girl and, when the time for separation came, he wept and mourned and heaved mighty sighs, and passion prompted him to compose a poem to express his love, one of whose verses went 1.3.15

I part from her against my will and
Leave, I swear, my soul with her

—which is much like the poetry of the rest of the poets of his day, who would swear mighty oaths that they had given up food and drink out of yearning and passion, had spent long nights awake out of love and longing, were dead men, and had died and been put in their shrouds and embalmed and buried, while at the same time indulging themselves in any sport that might be going. When his father took a look at these valedictory verses, he reproached him and forbade him to write poetry anymore, though this seems to have made it the more attractive to him, for it is, generally speaking, in the nature of sons to do the opposite of what their fathers want. Then he left that village sad, *forlorn*, bewitched, *lovelorn*.

الفصل الرابع

في شرور وطنبور

قد كان ابو الفارياق آخذا فى امور ضيّقة المصادر * غير مامونة العواقب ١،٤،١
والمصاير * لما فيها من القآء البغضة بين الرؤس * وشَغْب اهل البلاد ما بين رئيس ومرؤوس * فقد كان ذا ضَلع مع حزب من مشايخ الدروز مشهور بالنجدة والبسالة والكرم * غير انهم كانوا صِفر الايدى والاكياس والصندوق والصوان والهِمْيان والبيوت * ولا يخفى ان الدنيا لمّا كان شكلها كُرَوِيًّا كانت لا تميل الى احد الّا اذا استمالها بالمدوّر مثلها وهو الدينار * فلا يكاد يتمّ فيها امر بدونه * فالسيف والقلم قائمان في خدمته * والعلم والحُسن حاشدان الى طاعته * ومن كان ذا بَسْطة فى الجسم وفضل فى المناقب فلا يفيده طُوله وطَوله بغير الدينار شيا * وهو على صغر حجمه يغلب ما كان كبيرا ثقيلا من الاوطار ولُبانات النفس * فالوجوه المدوّرة المدنّرة خاضعة له أيّانَ بَرَز * والقدود الطويلة منقادة اليه كيفما دار * والجباه العريضة الصليتة مكبّة عليه * والصدور الواسعة تضيق لفقده * فاما ما يقال من ان الدروز ٢،٤،١
هم من ذوى الكسل والتوانى وانهم لا ذمّة لهم ولا ذِمام فالحقّ خلاف ذلك * اما وسمهم بالكسل فاَحْرى ان يكون ذلك مدحًا لهم * فانه ناشى عن القناعة والنزاهة والزهد * غير ان الصفات الحميدة التى يتنافس فيها الناس متى جاوزت الحدّ قليلا التبست بنقيضها * فى الحلم مثلًا يلتبس بالضعف * وفى الكرم يلتبس بالتبذير

Chapter 4

Troubles and a Tambour

The Fāriyāq's father was involved in matters as difficult in point of *extrication* as they were uncertain in terms of outcome and *implication*, given their ability to set people at one another's *throats* and the bad feeling between ruler and ruled that this *promotes*. He had a close relationship with a faction of Druze shaykhs famous for their doughtiness, valor, and generosity, whose hands, money pouches, coffers, cupboards, waist-bands,[142] and houses were, however, empty. It is no secret that the world, being round in shape, favors none unless they lure it with something equally round, namely the golden dinar, without which nothing happens. To serve it, sword and pen stand to *arms*, while knowledge and beauty throng to service its *demands*. Anyone endowed with an ample physique or excellent qualities will find that tallness and talent benefit him nothing without the dinar, which, despite its small size, can bend any large and weighty ambition or care of the soul to its will. Round, well-minted faces thus submit to it when e'er it appears, tall figures are drawn to it no matter where it wanders, shining brows bend o'er it, and the sunniest of dispositions darkens when it's lost. 1.4.1

As to what they say about the Druze being lazy and slow and about their knowing neither covenant nor compact, the truth is entirely otherwise. Their characterization as lazy is more akin to a compliment, for it springs from their moderation, abstention from dishonorable acts, and renunciation of the world. On the other hand, the most praiseworthy characteristics become indistinguishable from their opposites when men compete in making a show of them and they exceed by even a little their proper bounds. Thus, excessive clemency, for example, becomes indistinguishable from weakness, generosity from prodigality, courage from impetuosity and 1.4.2

فالافراط * وفى الشجاعة بالتهور والمغامرة * لا بل الافراط فى العبادة والتديّن
يلتبس بالهوس والخَبال * هذا ولما كانت الدروز مفرطين فى القناعة اذلا ترى من
بينهم احدا يقتحم القفار ويخوض البحار فى طلب الِازآء(١) وفى التانّق في
الملبوس والمطعوم * ولا من يُسفّ للامور الخسيسة ويدنّق فيها * او من
يباشر الصنائع الشاقّة * ظُنّ فيهم الكسل والتوانى * ومعلوم انه كلما كثر
شره الانسان ونَهَمه * كثر نصبه وكدّه وهمّه * فالتجار من الافرنج على ثروتهم
وغناهم اشقى من فلّاحى بلادنا * فترى التاجر منهم يقوم على قدميه من الصباح
١،٤،٣ الى الساعة العاشرة ليلاً * وامّا ان الدروز لا عهد لهم ولا ذمّة فانما هو محض
افترآء وبهتان * اذ لم يُعرَف عنهم انهم عاهدوا بشى ثم نكثوا به دون ان يحسّوا
من المُعاهَد اليه غدرا * او ان اميرا منهم اوشيخا راى امراة جاره النصرانى تغتسل
يوما فاعجبته بضاضتها وبَتيلتها وبُوصها * فبعث اليها من تملّق لها او غصبها *
وانت خبير بان كثيرا من النصارى عائشون فى ظلهم * ومستأمنون فى حماهم *
وانهم لوخيّروا ان يتركوا مستأمنهم هذا ليكونوا تحت اَمْن مشايخ النصارى لَاَبَوا *
وعندى ان من كان يرعى حرمة الجار فى حرمته كان خليقا بكل خير * ولم يكن
ليخونه فى غيرها * فاما ما جرى من التحزّب والتالّب بين طوائف الدروز وغيرهم فانما
هى امور سياسية لا تعلّق لها بالدِّين * فبعض الناس يريدون هذا الامير حاكما
١،٤،٤ عليهم وبعضهم يريد غيره * وكان ابو الفارياق ممن يحاول خلع الامير الذى وقتئذ
واليًا سياسة الجبل * فانحاز الى اعدآئه وهم من ذوى قرابته فجرت بينهم مهاوش
ومناوش غير مرة * وآل الامر بعدها الى فشل اعدآء الامير * ففرّوا الى دمشق
يلتمسون النجدة من وزيرها فوعدهم ومنّاهم * وفى تلك الليلة التى فرّوا فيها هجمت
جنود الامير على وطن الفارياق * ففرّ مع امه الى دار حصينة بالقرب منها لبعض

(١) الاِزآء هو سبب العيش او ما سبّب من رغده

recklessness. Indeed, even excessive worship and religiosity become indistinguishable from obsession and insanity. This being the case, and given that the Druze are excessive in their moderation—so that you will not find any of them braving the desert wastes or setting forth upon the seas to seek their sustenance (*izā'*)(1) or aspiring to elegance in clothing or food or stooping to or becoming deeply involved in any base occupation or practicing the toilsome crafts—they are thought to be lazy and sluggish. It is also well known that as a person's appetites and greed increase, so too do his ill health, his hard work, and his cares. Frankish merchants, for all their wealth and riches, are worse off than the peasants of our country: you find them on their feet from morning until ten at night.

(1) *Izā'* means "means of sustenance, or whatever ease of living has been created through work."

As for the Druze knowing no agreements or covenants, this is mere slan- **1.4.3**
der and falsehood, for they have never been known to undertake to do something and then to break their word, unless they sensed foul play on the other's part. Nor is it known for an emir or shaykh of theirs to see his Christian neighbor's wife bathing one day and, finding her fair-skinned plumpness, her buttocks, and her fine silks pleasing, to send someone to flatter or abduct her. Also, as you are well aware, there are many Christians living under their patronage who have requested and received their promises of protection and who, if given the choice of abandoning their protectors in favor of having their security provided by the Christian shaykhs, would refuse. In my opinion, anyone who takes care to preserve the sanctity of the neighbor who is under his protection deserves every good thing and will not betray him in other matters. As for the factionalism and conspiracies among the Druze and other communities, these are purely political matters, some wanting this emir to rule them and some that, and they have nothing to do with religion.

The Fāriyāq's father was one of those who sought to depose the emir **1.4.4**
who was, at the time, entrusted with the political affairs of the Mountain; he took the side of his enemies, who were the emir's relatives.[143] More than once, commotions and skirmishes broke out. Then the tide turned against the emir's enemies, and they fled to Damascus begging for aid from its governor, who gave them promises and raised their hopes. On the night of their escape, the emir's troops attacked the Fāriyāq's home town, so he fled with his mother to a fortified house nearby belonging to another emir. Looters took all the silver and household possessions that they found in his house,

الامرآء * فنهب الناهبون ما وجدوا فى بيته من فضة وآنية ومن جملة ذلك طنبور كان يعزف به اوقات الفراغ * فلما ان سكنت تلك الزعازع رجع الفارياق مع امه الى البيت فوجداه قاعا صفصفا * ثم رُدّ الطنبور عليه بعد ايام * فان من نهبه لم يجد فى حمله منفعة ولم يقدر ان يبيعه اذ العازفون بالات الطرب فى تلك البلاد قليلون جدا * فاعطاه لقسيس تلك القرية كفّارة عما نهب * فرده القسيس على الفارياق *

١،٤،٥ وكانىّ بمعترض هنا يقول ما فائدة هذا الخبر البارد * قلت ان وجود الطنابير فى الجبل عزيز جدّا كما ذكرنا * فان صنعة الالحان والعزف بالملاهى يَسِمُ صاحبهما بالشَيْن * لما فى ذلك من التطريب والتصبىّ والتشويق * والقوم هناك يَغلُون فى الدّين * ويحذرون من كل ما يلذ الحواسّ * ولذلك لا يشآءون ان يتعلموا الغنآء والعزف باحدى الات الطرب * او يستعملوها فى معابدهم وصلواتهم كما تفعل مشايخهم الافرنج * خشية ان يُفضى بهم ذلك الى الالحاد * فعندهم ان كل فن من الفنون اللطيفة كالشعر والايقاع مثلا والتصوير مكروه * ولكن لوانهم سمعوا ما يتغنّى به فى كنائس مشايخهم المذكورين من الموشّحات * او ما يُعزَف به على الأُرغن من اللحون التى وَلِعَ الناس بها فى الملاعب والمراقص ومحالّ القهوة استجلابا للرجال والنسآ * لما راوا في الطنبور اثما *

١،٤،٦ فان الطنبور بالنسبة الى الارغن كالغصن من الشجرة او كالفخذ من الجسم * اذلا يُسمَع منه الا طنطنة وفى الارغن طنطنة ودندنة وخنخنة ودمدمة وصلصلة ودربلة وجلجلة وقلقلة وزقزقة ووقوقة وبقبقة وفقفقة وطقطقة ودقدقة وقعقعة وفرقعة وشخشخة وخشخشة وجرجرة وغرغرة وخرخرة وقرقرة وبربرة وطبطبة ودبدبة وكهكهة وقهقهة وبعبع وبعبعة وزمزمة وهمهمة وحمحمة وغطمطمة وتاتاة وداداة وضاضاَء ويايآء وقاقاء وصَهصَلق وجَلَنبَلَق وغطيط وجخيف وفحيح وحفيف ونشيش و رنين ونقيق وطنين وعجيج وارير ودوى وخرير وازيز وهرير وصريف وصرير

among them a tambour[144] that he used to play in his spare time. When these convulsions quieted down, the Fāriyāq and his mother returned to their house and found it stripped bare. A few days later, the tambour was returned to him; the person who'd stolen it, seeing no benefit in carrying it about and unable to sell it—for players of musical instruments in those parts were very few—had given it to the village priest to make amends for what he had stolen, and the priest returned it to the Fāriyāq.

Do I hear someone objecting here and asking, "What is the point of 1.4.5
this banal tale?" I respond: as we said, a tambour was a very rare item on the Mountain, for composing tunes and playing musical instruments are regarded as shameful, because they induce ecstatic pleasure and amorousness and incite desire. The natives there are fanatical about religion and warn against anything capable of causing sensual pleasure. Consequently, they do not want to learn to sing or play an instrument or to use the latter in their places of worship and their prayers, as do their Frankish shaykhs,[145] lest this lead them into disbelief. Thus, every one of the gentle arts, such as poetry and harmony, for example, or painting, is an abomination. Could they but hear the hymns sung in the churches of their aforementioned shaykhs or the tunes on the organ that people are so fond of and that are played in places of entertainment, dance halls, and cafés to attract men and women, they'd find no sin in the tambour.

The tambour is to the organ as the branch is to the tree or the thigh to 1.4.6
the body, for the only sound that it makes is a strumming, while the organ produces strumming and humming, mumbling and rumbling, jangling and jingling, squeaking and creaking, chirping and cheeping, burbling and barking, clicking and clacking, gnashing and crashing, chinking and clinking, gurgling and gargling, purring, cooing, and bleating, thrumming and drumming, roaring and guffawing, glugging and gabbling, la-la-ing and lullabying, horses' neighs and the roaring of waves, blubbing of billy goats and cricking of cradles, cries of men at war, call of merlins and raven's caw, old women moaning and heavy doors groaning, snores and stertors, huffing and soughing, water boiling and grief-stricken bawling, frogs ribbiting and ears tinky-tinkling, bulls bellowing and gaming-house reprobates roaring, reverberations and crepitations, pots gently bubbling and chilly dogs whimpering, pulleys squeaking and crickets chirruping, milk flowing, chickens crowing, and cats mewing, not to mention caw-caw and hubble-bubble

وشخب وصيئ ومُوآ وغاق غاق وغِقٍ غق وطاق طاق وشِيْب شيب ومئ مِئ وطِيخ طيخ وقيق قيق وخازِباز وخاق باق * فاين هذا كله هداك الله من طن طن * فان قيل ان الرغبة عن العزف به انما هو لكونه يشبه الاَلَية * قيل فما بال النسآ يدخلن الكنائس وعلى رؤسهن هذه القرون الفضة وهى تشبه فنطيسة الخنزير اجلّك الله عن ذكره * وفنطيسة الخنزير اجلك الله عن ذكره تشبه كذا وكذا * فقد تبيّن لك ان اعتراضك غير وارد * وان ذكر الطنبور كان في محلّه * فان ابيت الّا العناد وتصدّيت لان تخطّئنى وتعقبنى بزلة قلم وبغير زلة * ورمت ان تبدى للناس براعتك في الانتقاد علىّ فانى امسك عن اتمام هذا الكتاب * ولعمرى لو انك علمت سبب شروعى فيه وهو التنفيس عن كربك وتسلية خاطرك لما فتحت فاك علىَّ بالملامة في شى * فقابل الِاحسان اصلحك الله بالاحسان واصبر علىّ حتى افرغ من غزل قصتى * ٧،٤،١

وبعد ذلك فان عنّ لخاطرك ان تلقى بكتابى في النار او المآء فافعل * ولنعُد الان ٨،٤،١ الى الفارياق فنقول انه اقام مع والدته في البيت يتعاطى النساخة * وانه لم يلبث ان ورد عليه نعى والده في دمشق * فتفطر قلبه لهذا الفجع وودّ لو بقى الطنبور عند ناهبه * وكانت امّه تنفرد في كل صباح وتندب زوجها وتتحسّر عليه وتذرف المدامع لفقده * فانها كانت من الصالحات المتحببات لازواجهن عن خلوص وداد وصدق وفآء * وكانت تظنّ ان ابنها لا يراها في انفرادها حتى لا يزيد حزنها برؤيتها اياه يبكى لبكآئها * لكن الفارياق كان ينظرها في خلوتها ويبكى لوحشتها ووحدتها اشدّ البكآء * فاذا رجعت كفكف عبراته وتشاغل بالكتابة او بغيرها * ومذ ذلك الوقت عرف انه لا ملجا له بعد الله غير كدّه فعكف على النساخة * غير ان هذه الحرفة مذ خلق الله القلم لا تكفى المحترف بها ولا سيما في بلاد لوَقْع قرشها طنين ورنين * ولرؤية دينارها تكبير وتعويذ الا ان ذلك جوّد من خطّه ورَقّق من فهمه*

and wham-bam and slurp-slurp and baa-baa and tee-hee and keek-keek and buzz-buzz and schlup-flup[146]—after all of which, what's wrong, God guide you, with plinkety-plink? If it be said that that aversion to playing the organ derives solely from its resemblance to the buttocks, reply may be made, "What do you make then of the fact that their women enter their churches with those silver 'horns' that resemble pigs' snouts (God exalt you above any contamination by their mention!) on their heads, given that pigs' snouts (God exalt you above any contamination by their mention!) resemble you-know-whats?" This should prove to you that your objection is baseless and mention of the tambour appropriate.

If you insist on being obstinate, are bent on catching me out in error and exposing me for slips (and non-slips) of the pen, and want to show people how clever you are by criticizing me, then I won't go through with this book. I swear, if you knew the reason why I embarked on it—namely, to relieve your dudgeon and entertain your mind—you wouldn't utter a word of reproach against me about anything. Meet, then, good deeds with good and be patient with me till I finish my tale. Afterward, if it crosses your mind to throw my book into the fire, or the water, go ahead. 1.4.7

Let us return now to the Fāriyāq. We declare: he lived with his mother in the house and practiced the copyist's trade, but news of his father's demise in Damascus soon reached him. He was heart-broken and wished the tambour were still with the one who stole it. Each morning his mother would go off by herself, utter laments for her husband, and grieve for him, the tears gushing for his loss, for she was one of those righteous women who love their husbands with honest affection and true loyalty. She thought that, if she went off by herself, her son wouldn't see her and her sorrow would not then be compounded by seeing him weep at her grief, but the Fāriyāq would look on her in her private place and weep bitterly over her desolation and loneliness. Then when she returned he would hold back his tears and busy himself with writing or anything else. It was now that he realized that he had nothing he could rely on, after God, but the sweat of his own brow, so he devoted himself to copying. However, since the day that God created the pen, that profession has never been enough to support those who practice it, especially in countries where the appearance of a piaster is cause for rejoicing and the sight of a dinar is greeted with plaudits of "God is great!" and "We seek refuge with God from lapidated Satan!" It did, however, give him a good hand and refine his thinking. 1.4.8

الفصل الخامس

في قسيس وكيس وتحليس وتلحيس

من قرا آخر الفصل المتقدم ثم اتاه خادمه يدعوه للعشآ فترك الكتاب وقام يستقبل ١،٥،١
الكاس والطاس والقدح والكوب مما اختلفت اشكاله وتفاوتت مقاديره *
ثم اقبلت عليه اخوانه يسامرونه فمنهم من قال له انى ضربت اليوم جاريتى ونزلت بها
الى السوق على عزم ان ابيعها ولو بنصف ثمنها * وذلك لانها اجابت سيدتها جواباً
سخيفا * ومنهم من قال له وانا ايضا ضربت ابنى اشد الضرب لانى رايته يلعب مع
اولاد الجيران ثم حبسته في الكنيف وهو باقٍ الى الان فيه * وبعضهم قال وانا
ايضا حرّجت اليوم على زوجتى بان تطلعنى على جميع ما يخطر ببالها ويخلج صدرها
من الافكار والهواجس * وبما تحلمه ايضا في الليل من الاحلام التى تنشا عن
امتلآء الدماغ من بخار الطعام * اومن دخان الغرام قبل النيام * وقلت لها ان لم
تخبرينى باليقين اضربت بك ابانا القسيس فيكفّرك ويحظر عليك ثم يستخرج منك كل
ما تكتمين وتضمرين * ويطّلع على كل ما تسترين وتخفين وتصونين * وعلى ما تحذرين
منه * وتحرصين عليه وترتاحين له وتميلين اليه وتكلفين به * وقد خرجت من دارى
غضبان متنمّرا وجزمت بان لا اصالحها الّا اذا كانت تقصّ عليّ احلامها * وبعضهم
قال ان مصيبتى في بنتى اعظم * وذلك انها بعد ان تمشّطت اليوم وتعصّبت

Chapter 5

A Priest and a Pursie, Dragging Pockets and Dry Grazing[147]

If anyone read the end of the previous chapter and then his servant came and called him to dinner, causing him to leave the book and rise and turn toward glasses and goblets, tumblers and tankards (in all their different shapes and sizes), and then his friends dropped in to pass the evening with him, one saying, "Today I beat my slave girl and went down to the market with her intending to sell her, even at half price, because she'd given my wife a pert answer" and another, "And I too today beat my son because I found him playing with the neighbors' children and then I locked him up in the latrine and he's still there" and another, "And today I insisted to my wife that she make me privy to every thought and worry that goes through her head or troubles her breast and every dream she dreams at night—such dreams coming from the food vapors that fill her brain or from the smoke of passion consummated before sleeping—and I told her, 'If you don't tell me every detail, I'll set the priest on you and he'll declare you a disbeliever and ban you from the church and then he'll get out of you everything you're hiding and harboring and take a good look at everything you're concealing and secreting and holding out on, that you're on guard against, have taken measures to prevent, feel at ease with, have a liking for, and have taken it upon yourself to do,' and I left my house in a rage against my wife, uttering threats, and swore I'd only make up with her if she told me her dreams" and another, "My problem with my 1.5.1

وتعطّرت وتطيّبت وتطوّست وتبرقشت وتزيّنت وتبرّجت وتزيّغت وتضرّجت وتزخّفت وتزبرجت وتشوّفت وتسرجت وتنقشت وترقّشت وتزهنعت وبرّقت وتحفّلت وتزوّقت وتقيّنت وتزلّقت وتزبرقت وتالّقت جلست بالشباك لتنظر الواردين والصادرين * فنهيتها عن ذلك فانصرفت ثم خالفتنى فرجعت الى موضعها * واوهمتنى انها تخيط هناك بعض ملبوس لها * فكانت كلّما غرزت بالابرة غرزة تنظر نظرتين * فقمت اليها مستشيطا غيظا وجبذتها بشعرها الذى مشطته وضفرته وعقصته فطلع بيدى منه خصلة وها هى معى * وهيهات ان تنتهى عن غيّها ولو نتفتُ شعرها كله * فانها كالمهرة الجامحة بغير عنان * لا يردّها لَكْم بالاكف ولا ضرب بعيدان * نعم ان من ملأ اَعْصاله بالوان الطعام * واذنيه بمثل هذا الكلام * فلا بد وان يكون قد نسى ما جرى على الفارياق من الوقوع الحسّى والمعنوى * ومن فجعه بنعى ابيه * ومن اقباله على نسخ الكتب واكتسابه من ذلك جودة الخطّ فمن ثم اضطررت الى الاعادة * وازيد هنا ان اقول * انه لما شاعت براعته ١،٥،٢
في النسخ ارسل اليه من اسمه على وزان بعير بيعر يستدعيه لنسخ دفاتر كان يودعها كل ما كان يحدث في زمانه * وليس الغرض من ذلك افادة احد من العالمين * وانما كان امساكا للحوادث من ان تتفلّت من مدار الايام * او تنفك من سلسلة الاحوال * فانّ كثيرا من الناس يرون ان احضار الماضى وجعله حالا منظورا من الامور العظيمة * ولذلك كانت الافرنج حِراصاً على تقييد كلما يقع عندهم * فخروج عجوز من بيتها صباحا وعودها اليه في الساعة العاشرة وهى تقود كلباً لها * والريح عاصفة والمطر واكف لا يفوت اقلامهم * ولا يَعْدو خواطرهم * ففى مقدَّمة ديوان ١،٥،٣
لامرتين اعظم شعرآء الفرنساوية الموجودين في عصرنا هذا وهو الديوان الذى سمّاه التامّل الشِعرىّ ما ترجمته * وكانت العرب يدخّنون التبغ في قصبات لهم طويلة

eldest daughter is even worse, to wit, today, after she had coiffed, hatted, perfumed, scented, bedecked, painted, made-up, arrayed, displayed, rouged, bedizened, bejeweled, tricked out, beautified, decorated, adorned, dandified, prettified, primped, preened, prinked and pranked herself, donned her saffron-dyed dress and girded her loins for battle, she went and sat by the window to watch the people going in and out. I forbade her to do so, so she left, but then she disobeyed me and returned to her place and tricked me into thinking that she was sitting there to darn some of her clothes, but for every stitch she made, she stole two looks, so I went to her burning with anger and tugged her by the hair that she'd dressed and braided and curled, and a tress came off in my hand (here it is!), and, if she doesn't put an end to her wicked ways, I'll pull it all out, for she's like an unruly filly without reins: boxing her ears doesn't stop her, and nor do beatings with sticks"—if anyone, I say, filled his bowels with all kinds of food and his ears with talk of this sort, he will certainly have forgotten all the physical and moral incidents that have befallen the Fāriyāq (*his grief at hearing of his father's death, his devoting himself to the copying of books, and how he thereby acquired an excellent hand*) which is why I have just been compelled to repeat them.

Though here I would add that, when his excellence as a copyist became bruited abroad, a certain man whose name rhymes with Baʿīr Bayʿar[148] summoned him to copy out the ledgers in which he would enter everything that had happened during his day. His purpose in doing so was not to benefit any scholar but derived from a simple desire to hold onto events lest they escape the orbit of the days or become detached from the chain of circumstance, for many believe that to summon up the past and make it a visible entity is in itself a great thing. This is why the Franks have been keen to record everything that happens in their lands; the exit of an old woman from her house in the morning and her return to it at ten o'clock, leading a dog of hers, with the wind blowing and the rain coming down hard, neither escapes their pens nor is foreign to their thoughts. 1.5.2

There is material of this sort in the introduction to the verse collection *Méditations poétiques* of Lamartine,[149] the greatest French poet of our day, 1.5.3

وهم ساكتون وينظرون الى الدخان متصاعدا كاعمدة زرقآء لطيفة الى ان يضمحل في الهوآء اضمحلالا يشوق الرآى * والهواء اذ ذاك شفّاف لطيف * الى ان قال * ثم ان صحبى من العرب جعلوا الشعير في مخالٍ من شعر المعزى ووضعوها في اعناق الخيل وهى حول خيمتى * وارجلها مربوطة في حلق من حديد وهى غير متحركة * ورؤسها مخفوضة الى الارض مظللة بنواصيها الشَعثة * وشعرها اشهب برّاق يخرج منه دخان تحت اشعة الشمس الحامية * وكانت الرجال قد اجتمعت تحت ظل زيتونة من اعظم ما يكون * وفرشوا تحتهم على الارض حصيرا شاميا واخذوا في الحديث والحكايات عن البادية وهم يدخنون التبغ * وينشدون اشعار عنتر وهو من شعرآء العرب الذين اشتهروا بالحماسة والرعاية (اى رعاية البهائم) والبلاغة وقد بلغت اشعاره منهم مبلغ التنباك في الاركيلة * وحين كان يرد عليهم من الابيات ما يوثر في حسّهم اكثر كانوا يرفعون ايديهم الى اذانهم ويطرقون برؤسهم ويصرخون تارة بعد تارة الله الله الله * الى ان قال في وصف امراة رآها تبكى عند قبر زوجها * وكان شعرها مسدلا من عند راسها ملتفّا عليها ومماسّا للارض * وكان صدرها مكشوفا كله على ما جرت به العادة عند نساء تلك البلاد من بلاد العرب * وحين كانت تتطاطأ للثم صورة العمامة على رِجام القبر او تصغى اذنها اليه كان ثدياها البارزان يمسّان الارض ويرسمان في التراب شكلهما كالقالب * اه صفحة ٢٤ وسائر هذه المقدمة على هذا النمط مع انه سمّاها مقدور الشعر * اى ما قدّره الله تعالى على الشعر والشعرآء * وفى رحلة ٤،٥،١
شاطوبريّان الى اميريكا وهو ايضا من اعظم شعرآء عصره ما صورته * وكان منزل رئيس الدول المتحدة عبارة عن دار صغيرة مبنية على اسلوب الانكليز فى البنآء * من دون خفرة عندها من العسكر ولا حشم داخلها * فلما قرعت الباب فتحت

which I translate as follows: "The Arabs smoked tobacco in their long pipes in silence, watching the smoke rising like graceful blue columns until it dispersed into the air in a way beguiling to the observer, the air at the time being transparent, gentle." Later he goes on: "Then my Arab companions put the barley in goat's hair nosebags and placed these around the necks of the horses that were around my tent, their feet tethered to iron rings, and which stood motionless, their heads lowered to the ground and shaded by their heavy forelocks, their coats a glossy grey and smoking beneath the hot rays of the sun. The men, having gathered in the shade of an enormous olive tree, had spread out beneath them on the ground mats from Damascus, and set about talking and telling tales of the desert as they smoked their tobacco. They recited verses by ʿAntar, one of those Arab poets celebrated for their valor,[150] husbandry"—by which he means, "animal husbandry"—"and eloquence, his verses having as much effect on them as the Persian tobacco in their nargilehs. When a verse cropped up that appealed particularly to their feelings, they would raise their hands to their ears, bow their heads, and cry out over and over again, '*Allah! Allah! Allah!*'"[151] Later, describing a woman whom he saw weeping at the grave of her husband, he says, "Her hair hung down from her head, enveloped her, and brushed the ground. Her entire bosom was exposed, as is the custom among the women of this part of Arabia, and when she bent to kiss the carved turban that topped the gravestone or press her ear against it, her exposed breasts would touch the ground and press their shapes into the dust, as though they were molds" (end; p. 24). The rest of this introduction is of the same character, even though he calls it *Poetry's Destiny*, meaning, "what God Almighty has ordained for poetry and poets."[152]

Similarly, the *Voyage en Amérique* of Chateaubriand,[153] also one of the greatest poets of his day, contains the following: "The residence of the president of the United States was a small house built in the English style, with neither a guard of soldiers round it nor servants inside. When I knocked on the door, a young girl opened to me, so I asked her if the general was at home. She replied that he was. I said I had a letter that I wanted to deliver to him, 1.5.4

لى جارية صغيرة فسالتها هل الجنرال فى البيت * فاجابت نعم * فقلت ان عندى رسالة اريد ان ابلّغه اياها * فسألتنى عن اسمى وصعب عليها حفظه فقالت لى بصوت منخفض ادخل ياسيّدى * (واورد هذه العبارة باللغة الانكليزية وهى (Walk in sir) تنبيها على معرفته لها) ثم مشت امامى فى ممشى طويل كالدهليز * ثم دخلت بى الى مقصورة واشارت الىّ ان اجلس فيها منتظرا الخ صفحة ٢٥ * وفى موضع آخر * انه راى بقرة عجفآء لامرأة من هند اميريكا * فقال لها وهو راثٍ لحالها * ما بال هذه البقرة عجفاء * فقالت له انها تاكل قليلا * واورد هذه العبارة ايضا باللغة الانكليزية وهى (.She eats very little) وفى موضع آخر ذكر انه كان يرى كِسَف السحاب بعضها فى شكل حيوان وبعضها فى شكل جبل او شجرة وما اشبه ذلك * فاذ قد عرفت هذا فاعلم ان اعتراضك علىَّ فى ايراد ما
١،٥،٥ هو غير مفيد لك لكنه مفيد لى لا يكون الّا تعنّتا * فان هذين الشاعرين كتبا ما كتباه ولم يخشيا لومة لائم ولم يعترض عليهما احد من جنسهما * وقد اشتهر فضلهما وصيتهما حتى ان مولانا السلطان ادام الله دولته اقطع لا مرتين فى ارض ازمير اقطاعات عظيمة * ولم يُسمَع عن ملك من ملوك الافرنج انه اقطع شاعرا عربيا او فارسيا او تركيا مقدار جريب واحد فى ارض عامرة * ولا غامرة * فاما كون وزان بعير بيعرقد حاكى الافرنج فى تاريخه وهو عربى وابواه ايضا عربيّان وعمّه وعمته كذلك عربيّان * فمما لم اتيقّنه الى الان * ولعلى اعلمه بعد انجاز هذا الكتاب فاخبر به القارى ان شآ الله * وانما ارجو انه اى القارى الا يقطع قراته لجهله
١،٥،٦ سبب هذه المحاكاة وان يكن العلم به مهمّا * ودونك مثالا مما كان يكتبه الفارياق فى اساطير بعير بيعر * فى هذا اليوم وهو الحادى عشر من شهر اذار[١] سنة ١٨١٨ قصّ فلان ابن فلانة بنت فلانة ذنب حصانه الاشهب بعد ان كان طويلا يكنس

١ ١٨٥٥: ادار.

so she asked me my name, which she found hard to remember. Then she said, *Walk in sir*." (He gives these words in English to show that he knows the language.) "Then she walked in front of me, down a long walkway like a corridor and took me into a private apartment and indicated to me that I should sit down there and wait," etc. (p. 25). Elsewhere he writes that he saw an American Indian woman with a thin cow and said to her, bewailing its state, "Why is this cow so thin?" and the woman answered him, "She eats little," and again he provides these words in English, to wit, *She eats very little*. In yet another place he writes that he observed fragments of clouds, some in the shape of animals and others in that of a mountain or a tree or similar things. Knowing this, you will appreciate that, in objecting to my talking of things that are of no interest to you but are to me, you are simply being stubborn.

These two great poets wrote what they did fearing the censure of none, 1.5.5
and none of their race opposed them. Indeed, the acknowledgment of their worth and their reputations grew to such dimensions that Our Lord the Sultan, may God preserve his rule, awarded Lamartine vast estates in the area of Izmir, even though no one has ever heard of a Frankish king awarding an Arab, Persian, or Turkish poet a single field, sown or barren. As for the person-whose-name-rhymes-with-Baʿīr-Bayʿar imitating the Franks in his history when he was an Arab, both his parents were Arabs, and his paternal uncle and aunt were both Arabs—the reasons remain unclear to me to this day. Maybe I'll find out after finishing this book and then, God willing, let the reader know. All I ask is that no reader stop reading just because he's ignorant of the reasons behind this imitation, important as they may be.

Here now is an example of the sort of thing the Fāriyāq used to write con- 1.5.6
cerning the legends of Baʿīr Bayʿar: "On this day, the eleventh of the month of March 1818, So-and-so, son of Mistress So-and-so daughter of Mistress So-and-so, cut the tail of his grey stallion, which had been so long it swept the ground. That very day, he mounted it and it threw him off." If you ask, "Why does he give the man's ancestry via the female line?" I reply, "Baʿīr Bayʿar was religious, godly, and pious, and it is more proper and precise to trace a man's ancestry via his mother than his father, for there can be only

الارض * وفى ذلك اليوم بعينه ركبه فكَبَا به * فان قلت ما سبب النسبة الى الام دون الاب * قلت ان بعير بيعر كان من المتدينين المتورّعين المتّقين * فنسبة الولد الى امّه اصحّ واصدق من نسبته الى ابيه * فان الامّ لا تكون الا واحدة بخلاف الاب * ولكون الجنين لا يمكنه الخروج الّا من مخرج واحد * ومن ذلك * اليوم نُظرت سفينة فى البحر ماخرة فظُنَّ انها بارجة قدمت من احدى مراسى فرنسا لتحرير اهل البلاد * لكنه عند التحقيق ظهر انها انما كانت زورقا مشحونا ببراميل فارغة * وكان سبب قدومه للاستقآء من عين كذا * فان قيل ان هذا خلاف المعهود * فان من شأن الكبير ان يبدو للعين عن بُعد صغيرا لا عكسه * قيل ان الانسان اذا اعطى نفسه هواها راى الشئ بخلاف ما هو عليه * فمن احبّ مثلا امراة قصيرة لم ير بها قِصرًا * ومن خلا بمحبوبته فى قترة راها اوسع من صرح بلقيس * وبعدُ فانّا نرى النور الصغير عن بُعدٍ كبيرا * فلا غرو ان يبدو الزورق بارجة او شَوْنة * فان القوم هناك ما زالوا يحلمون بان رؤسهم قد تبرطلت ببراطل الفرنساوية ولحموا عِرَضهم بعرضهم حتى يروا نسآهم كما قال الشاعر

تصيد ظبآونا الأُسُد الضوارى بلحظ او بلفظ فى المسالك
وغزلان الفرنج تصيد ايضا بذَيْن معا وبالايدى كذلك

وكان بعير بيعر سُتْهما جَعْظَرًا أُحزُقَّة * لكنه كان حليما يحب السلم والدَّعة * وكان من التغفّل على جانب عظيم * فكان مفوّضا اموره المعاشية الى رجل لئيم شرس الاخلاق عَيَدَهٍ به كِبْر وعُنْجُهيّة وعجرفة وتجّس وغطرسة * وكان تمضى عليه الساعة والساعتان وهو لا يبدى ولا يعيد * فيظن الغِرّ انه معمل فكره فى تدبير الدُوَل * او تلخيص النِحَل * فقد جرت العادة بان الرجل اذا كان ذا منزلة رفيعة فان كان عييّا ٧،٥،١

one mother—which is not the case with the father—because the fetus has only one possible exit point." Further: "Today a ship was seen on the sea, plowing along. It was thought to be a man-o'-war come from one of the ports of France to bring freedom to the people of the land. On investigation, however, it turned out to be just a rowing boat loaded with empty barrels coming to take water from the spring at such-and-such a place." If it be said that this contradicts the normal state of affairs, for large things appear small at a distance and not the opposite, reply may be made that when a person gives himself over to his fancies, he sees things differently from how they really are. Thus, for example, someone in love with a short woman will fail to notice her shortness, and if someone finds himself alone with his beloved in a hunter's hide, he'll think it more spacious than the pavilion of Bilqīs;[154] furthermore, a small light seen from a distance will appear to us as a large one. Small wonder, then, that a rowing boat should look like a man-o'-war or a frigate. The people there still dream that their heads have been crowned with the bonnets of the French and their honor welded to theirs, to the degree that they see their womenfolk to be like those described by the poet when he says:

Our gazelles along the paths
  The raging lions hunt with word and glance.
And the gazelles of the Franks hunt too, with both of those,
  But by adding hands the hunt they enhance.

Baʿīr Bayʿar was a big-buttocked, short-legged, round, waddling little glut- 1.5.7
ton, but he was also mild-mannered and loved peace and self-effacement. To a great extent he was a simpleton. He had delegated his worldly affairs to a base man of vicious morals, conceited, proud, arrogant, uncouth, boastful, and haughty. An hour or two would pass without his uttering a word, so the poor simpleton thought he must be exercising his wits on setting the world to rights or syncretizing the different sects, for it has become a habit to regard the man of elevated status, if he be inarticulate and at a loss to answer questions, as serious and dignified, and if he be a prattler, as a sound counselor.

مخما عُدَّ رزينا وقورا * وان يك مهذارا عدّ فصيحا * فاما اموره المعاديّة فانها كانت ٨،٥،١
تعلو وتسفل وتضوى وتجزل وتُفتَق وترتق بتدبير قسيس ذى دعابة وفكاهة
وبشاشة وهشاشة * قصير سمين * ابيض بدين * وكان هذا القسيس الصالح
قد تمكن من حريمه تمكنًا لا يباريه فيه النسيم * والقى عصاه عند احدى بناته وكانت
ذات وجه وسيم * ومنطق رخيم * وكانت تزوّجت برجل قد جُنّ وتخبَّل فخلّته
وجنونه واعتصمت بعقوة ابيها فكان القسيس آمرًا عليها مطاعا * ناهيا وزّاعا *
فكانت كلما دخل فيها شى او خرج منها شى تطالعه به لانها كانت ممن قَفَط قُطرَى
الدّين والدنيا معاً * وكانت تعترف له بجرائرها في الخلوة * وهو يسالها عن كل
زلة وهفوه * فيقول لها هل تتذبذب اَلياتك ويترجرج ثدياك عند صعودك الدرك
اوعند المشى * وهل يحدث فيك هذا الارتجاج من لذة * فقد ورد في بعض
الاخبار ان بعض الجلامظة كان يرتاح الى اى ارتجاج كان * حتى كان كثيرا ما
يتمنى ان تتزلزل الارض من تحته * وتمور الجبال من فوقه * وهل يُمثَّل لك في
الحلم ضجيع يكالحك * وخليع يصالحك اذ لا فرق عند الله بين اليقظة والمنام *
وان اعظم الحقائق انما بُنى على الاحلام * وهل وسوس اليك الوسواس الخناس
فاشتهيت ان تكونى خُنثَى * اى ذكرا وانثى * لا لا ذكر ولا انثى كما تقول العامة *
٩،٥،١ فان هذا القول لم يرتضه المحققون من الربّانيين الراتين * وغير ذلك من الوسائل
التى يضيق عن تفصيلها هذا الفصل * وكان ابوها لا يسيئ به الظن لما تقرر عنده
من ان كل من لبس السواد فهو من الفاطمين اهوآهم عن اللذات * الخاصين
انفسهم عن الشهوات * حتى انه نظر يوما في بعض الكتب هذا البيت وهو

وذمّوا لنا الدنيا وهم يرضعونها   اَفاويقَ حتى ما تدرّ لنا ثعل

Baʿīr Bayʿar's spiritual affairs, on the other hand, rose and fell, waned and waxed, came apart at the seams and were mended up again through the scheming of a jolly, cheerful, smiling, jovial priest, short and fat, white and plump. This goodly Father had gained an unshakeable control over the man's womenfolk, having found his niche with one of the man's daughters, who was comely of face, dulcet of tongue, and had been married to a man who had gone insane and become a madman; leaving him to his madness, she had sought the sanctuary of her father's household, where the priest had become her master and *commander*, her conscience and *reprimander*. Anything that was delivered to her or that she dispatched she would give him to look at, for she was one of those who made no distinction between the domains of this world and the next. She confessed her transgressions to him in private, and he would question her concerning every slip and lapse, asking her, "Do your buttocks *shake* and your breasts *quake* as you climb the stairs or when walking? And does this shaking produce a pleasurable sensation? I ask only because it is mentioned in a chronicle that a certain sensualist found relief in any shaking whatsoever, even praying many a time that the earth would quake beneath his feet and the mountains above him move from side to side. And did you ever see yourself in your dreams struggling with some *bed-mate*, or shaking the hand of some *profligate* (there being in God's eyes no difference between the waking and the sleeping *state*, the strongest realities being but built upon dreams)? And did the Recoiler ever whisper in your ear and leave you with a desire to be a hermaphrodite (which is to say, both male and female, and not, as the common people say, neither male nor female, the latter being a definition that has found no favor with erudite and learned scholars who make sure of their facts)?" 1.5.8

Thus spoke he, and of other matters that this chapter is not large enough to hold. He could do no wrong in her father's eyes because the latter was so convinced that all who wore black had weaned their appetites off worldly pleasures and cut themselves off from sensual desires, that, when one day he saw the following line of verse in a book[155]— 1.5.9

To us they condemned the world while they themselves on it suckled
Till they'd drained the milk that collects between milkings, so that even the supernumerary teats could yield us nought—

فظن انه تعريض بهم وتلميح اليهم * فامر باحراقه فأُحرق وذُرّى رماده * ورای يوما آخر بيتين في كتاب آخر وهما

ما بال عينى لا ترى من بين مَن   لبس السواد من العباد نحيفا
ماكان من لحم وشئ غيره   فيهم فاصلب ما يكون وقوفا

فامر ايضا باحراق الكتاب * وبعث جواسيس في البلد يتجسّسون عن مولفه ونودى في الروابى والوهاد * الَاَ من دلّ على مولف كتاب كذا فانه يُجزى احسن الجزآ * ويرقى الى رتبة سنية * فلما سمع المولف بذلك اضطر الى الاختتاء مدة حتى نُسِى اسمه * فان قلت ان هذا الفعل خلاف ما وصفته به من الحلم * قلت ان عادة اهل تلك البلاد ان الحلم يكون محمودا في كل شى الّا في امرين حرمة العِرض وحرمة الدين * فان الاخ لَيُبسِل اخاه الى الهلكة من اجلهما * ثم ان الفارياق اقام عند هذا الحليم مدة لم يحصل فيها على طائل * ١٠،٥،١
وكانت نفسه عزيزة عليه فلم يرد ان يسأله * فمن ثمّ جمع ذات ليلة حطبا وتبنا كثيرا واطلق فيهما النار فانبعث اللهيب نحو مقصورة بعير بيعر * فظن ان النار قد سرت في قصره * فاستوشى القيام والقعود فاقبلوا يتسابقون الى موضع النار * فراوا عندها الفارياق يزيدها من الحطب الجزل * فسالوه عن ذلك فقال ان هذه النار من بعض النيران التى تنوب عن اللسان * وان لم يكن لها صورة لسان * ومن فوائدها انها تنبّه الغافلين * وتنذر الباخلين * اَنّ ورآها لقولا شديدا * ولسانا حديدا * فقالوا ويحك انما هى من بدعك اَوَيكلّم احد بالنار * لقد سمعنا ان الانسان يكلم غيره ببوق او بقرع عصا او باشارة اصبع او بغمز عينٍ او برمز حاجب او برفع يد من عند الابط * فاما بالنار فبدعة وضلال *

he imagined that this had been written to run the clergy down and make insinuations against them and ordered that it be burned, which it was, and its ashes scattered. And one day he saw another two verses in a book, which went like this—

How is it that mine eye ne'er sees
A skinny man among those mortals who wear black?
Of what they have by way of flesh or any other thing
The hardest bit is that which stands erect, the rest is slack—

so he ordered that that book be burned too and sent spies out into the town to find out who its author was, the call going out over hill and dale, "Let him who can point out the author of this book come forward, for he will be rewarded with the best of rewards and raised to an elevated state!" When the poet heard this, he was obliged to go into hiding for a while, until his name was forgotten. If you say, "This contradicts your description of him as mild-mannered," I reply, "It is the custom of the people of the country to regard mildness as praiseworthy in all things but two—the sanctity of women's honor and the sanctity of religion, for the sake of which a man will deliver his brother to perdition."

The Fāriyāq resided with this mild-mannered man for a while, during 1.5.10
which he made not a sou. Too proud to complain when asked, he was driven one night to gather large quantities of firewood and straw and set fire to them. The flames leaped toward the private apartments of Baʿīr Bayʿar, who, thinking that the fire had engulfed his palace, roused everyone. They came, each trying to be the first to reach the fire, and there they found the Fāriyāq adding fuel to it by the armful. When they asked him what he thought he was doing, he said, "This is one of those fires that take the place of a tongue, even if it doesn't have the form of one. Among its virtues, it alerts the *slack-twisted* and gives warning to the *tight-fisted* that behind it stand words that are *strong*, and an iron *tongue*!" "Woe unto you!" they said. "This is one of your godless innovations! Who speaks through fire? We've heard of people speaking to one another using a trumpet, or by beating on something with a stick, or by making a sign with a finger, or by winking an eye, or by moving an eyebrow, or by raising a hand in the air, but fire is a godless innovation and a deviation."

وكادوا ان يبدّعوه ويكفّروه وينسبوه الى التمجّس ويطرحوه النار * لولا انّ قال ١،٥،١١
قائل منهم * ردّوا الجواب على مرسلكم * ولا تفعلوا شيا عن تهوّك * فلما
اخبروه بما راوا وسمعوا * استرآه واستنطقه عن ذاك الاجيج * فقال اصلح الله
المولى * وزاده فضلا وطَوْلا * قدكان لى كيس لا ينفعنى ولا انفعه * وللاكياس
ولما جاء على وزنها ورويّها عادة مخالفة لسائر العادات * وهى انها اذا خفّت
ثَقُلت * واذا ثقلت خفّت * فلمّا خفّ كيسى في جوارك السعيد اى ثَقُل
احرقته بهذه النار * وانما جعلتها عظيمة هكذا لانى كنت اتوهمه كَرَضْوَى[1] في
جيبى * حتى انه كثيرا ما منعنى عن النهوض والخروج لحاجة مهمّة * فلما سمع قوله ١،٥،١٢
ضحك من خرافته ورضخ له من كفّه الجامدة شيا يقابل ما كتبه له الفارياق في
اسفاره فى الخساسة * فاقبل يحنبش الى بيته وآلى ان لا يكتب شيا بعد ذلك
الّا ما طاب موقعه * وجل نفعه * رجاء ان تكون الاجرة على قدر العمل *
وهيهات فان اكثر الناس نفعا وشغلا * اقلهم اجرا وجُعلا * ومن لم يحسن
الا التوقيع * اُحلّ المحل الرفيع * ولُقِمت يده وقدمه كما يلقم الثدىَ الرضيع *

١ ١٨٥٥: رُضوىَ.

Just as they were about to declare him a heretic and a disbeliever and call him a Magian[156] and throw him into the fire, one man said to the others, "Before you do anything rash, report his answer to the one who sent you." When they informed Baʿīr Bayʿar of what they had seen and heard, he demanded to see the Fāriyāq and asked him to tell him about the blaze in question, so the latter said to him, "God better Our *Lord* and more blessings and power to him *accord*! Once I had a little pursie that was of no more use to me than I was to it. Now pursies, and other things that have similar-sounding names,[157] have a way with them that goes against all other ways, for, when they're light they're a drag, and when they're heavy, they're delightful. When my pursie grew light while within your Happy Purlieu, which is to say, when it grew to be a drag, I burned it in this fire, which I only made this big because when that pursie was in my pocket it felt as big to me as Mount Raḍwā,[158] to the point that it often prevented me from standing up and going out on some important errand." 1.5.11

When Baʿīr Bayʿar heard his words, he laughed at his fanciful invention and squeezed from his tight fist something equal in its exiguousness to what the Fāriyāq had copied out in his ledgers. The Fāriyāq then hopped and skipped all the way home, swearing he would never again write anything that wasn't worth writing or yielded no profit, with the hope that the fee would be in proportion to the quantity of the work—which is, of course, a ridiculous notion, as those who work hardest and whose work deserves the geatest *consideration* receive the lowest wages and *remuneration*, while for those who can do no more than sign their *names* are reserved the highest *planes*, and the hands and feet of such as these are gobbled at, much as the breast is gobbled at by the suckling child. 1.5.12

الفصل السادس

في طعام والتهام

بينما كان الفارياق راسه ورجلاه فى البيت كان فكره يصعِّد فى الجبال * ويرتقى ١،٦،١
التلال * ويتسوّر الجدران * ويتسنّم القصور ويهبط الاودية والغيران * ويرتطم
فى الاوحال * ويخوض البحار * ويجوب القفار * اذكان اقصى مراده ان يرى
منزلا غير منزله * وناسا غير اهله * وهو اول عناء الانسان فى حياته * فعنّ له
ان يزور اخًا له كان كاتبا عند بعض اعيان الدروز * فسار وحقائبه الامانى *
فلما اجتمع به ورای ماکان علیه القوم من الخشونة والتقشف ومن الاحوال المغايرة
لطباعه * انكر بعضها ووطّن نفسه على تحمل البعض الاخر * ولم يشا وشك ٢،٦،١
الرجوع من دون تقصّى معرفتهم * ولوكان رشيدا لَصرَف نفسه عن هواها من
اول يوم * اذ ليس من المحتمل ان اهل مدينة او قرية يغيّرون اخلاقهم وما ربوا عليه
لاجل غريب دخل فيهم * ولا سيما اذاكانوا شياظمة ذوى بسطة وباس * وكان
هو قميئا * ولكن الانسان كلما قلّ شغله كثر فضوله * فلا يكتفى بمجرد ما يسمع باذنه
حتى يرى بعينه * وكان الفارياق كلما زاد بهولآء القوم خبرة ونقدا * زاد اعراضا ٣،٦،١
عنهم وزهدا * لانهم كانوا غلاظ الطباع * بهم جفاء وافظاع * وسِخى
الوساد والملبوس * ملازمى الضَفَف والبوس * واقذرهم كان طباخ الامير *

Chapter 6

Food and Feeding Frenzies

While the Fāriyāq's head and feet stayed put in his house, his mind was 1.6.1
climbing mountains and hills, scaling walls, conquering castles, descending into valleys and *caves*, plunging into mire, roaming deserts and launching itself upon the *waves*, for his dearest desire was to see a land other than his own and people other than his family, which is everyone's first concern while growing up. It occurred to him therefore to visit one of his brothers who was a scribe working for a Druze notable, and he set forth, with nothing for baggage but his dreams. When he was united with him and beheld how coarse and rough were the people and how at variance with his own nature were the conditions there, he rejected some of those things and resigned himself to putting up with the rest.

At the same time, he didn't want to find himself at some point about 1.6.2
to return without first having got to know them better, albeit had he been wiser, he would have had nothing to do with them from the first day on, for it is not to be expected that the people of a city or a village will change their manners and the ways in which they've been raised for the sake of a stranger who has entered among them, especially if they be hulking fellows of great height and strength while he's a little titch. The less work people have to do, though, the more their curiosity gets the better of them; this being the case, it wasn't enough for him to make do with what his ears had heard: he had to see it with his own eyes.

The better the Fāriyāq got to know these folk through experience and 1.6.3
close examination, the less he liked them and the less he wanted to do with them, for they were coarse-natured, full of boorishness, and horrid to *excess*, their clothes and bedding filthy, they themselves ever prey to shortage of

فان قميصه كان انتن من المِحاة * وقدميه اقلتا من الوسخ ما لا تكاد تكشطه عنه المِسحاة * وكانوا اذا قعدوا للطعام سمعت لهم زمزمة وهمهمة * وقعقعة وطعطعة * فخلتهم وحوشا على جيفه * يثرملون ويرهّطون وينهسون ويتعرقون ويتمشّشون ويتلمّظون ويتمطّقون ويلوسون ويلطعون ويتنطّعون وكل ذلك فى فرشطةٍ خفيفة * فكنت ترى فى جبهة كلٍ منهم مضمون ما قيل مَن لَفْلَف *لم يتقصّف * فاذا قاموا رايت الرُزّ مزروعا فى لحاهم * والوَضَر متقاطرا من كساهم * فكان الفارياق اذا اكلهم قام جوعانا * ومعت عليه امعآؤه فى الليل فبات سهرانا *

١،٦،٤ فكان يقول لاخيه عجبا لمن يعاشر هولآء الناس * من الاكياس * ما الفرق بينهم وبين البهائم * سوى باللحى والعمائم * لا جرم انهم عائشون فى الدنيا لسدّ بصائرهم وافكارهم * ولفتح افواههم وادبارهم * لا يكاد احد منهم يظن ان الله تعالى خلق بشرًا الّا وكان دونه * وما يدرون ان الانسان ليس له بمجرد النطق فضل على العجماوات * ومزية على الجمادات * فان الكلام انما هو مادة لصورة المعانى * ولا تنفع المادة وحدها اذا لم تحلّ فيها الصورة التى هى الوجود الثانى * وقد يقال ان الرقين * تغطّى أَفْن الافين * وهولآء قد حُرِموا من العقل والنَعمة * ورضوا من الكون كله بالنَسَمة * كيف تطيق ان تعاشر

١،٦،٥ هولآء الهَمَج * وفضلك بين الناس قد بلج * فقال له اخوه ان كثيرا يحسدوننى على مكانتى عند الامير * وانى لكيد حسّادى اصبر على العسير * كما قيل

provisions and *distress*. The filthiest of all was the emir's cook: his shirt was fouler than a *cum-rag*, and his feet bore more dirt than one could scrape into a *vomit bag*. When they sat down to eat, such rumbling and mumbling and teeth-gnashing and lip-smacking was to be heard you would have thought they were wild beasts at a carcass. They ate like animals, taking huge bites, burying their front teeth in the food, stripping off the meat down to the bone, sucking out the marrow, licking their lips and smacking them, polishing off the desserts, licking the plates with their tongues, and throwing half-eaten food down on the table, all the while seated on the ground with their legs crossed under them at their ease. You might think that on each one's brow was inscribed the proverb "Eat your fill and you'll never be ill." When they stood up, one beheld their beards strewn with *rice*, their clothes dripping with *grease*. When the Fāriyāq ate with them, he'd get up hungry from the *table* and his guts would rise against him, so that till late at night to sleep he'd be *unable*.

To his brother he'd say, amazed at how any with *wits* could live in the **1.6.4**
company of these barbarous *twits*, "What distinguishes the Druze from the beasts save their beards and their turbans? For sure, their very way of life leads to the closing of their eyes and *minds*, the opening of their mouths and *behinds*. Scarce one of them can credit that God Almighty has created a race of men to which they are not superior. They're unaware that a man isn't better than a dumb *animal* or distinguishable from an inanimate *mineral* simply because he has the power of speech. Words are but the Matter pertaining to the Form in which various meanings may be *expressed*, and this Matter alone is of no use if the Form, which is the second stage of existence, has not within it been *impressed*.[159] It has been said that 'a silver coin covers the fool's shortcomings,' but these people have been deprived of both brains and *ease* and are content to take from this whole world nought but the *breeze*. How can you bear to live alongside such *kine*, and at a time when your own gifts have just begun to *shine*?"

His brother replied, "They often envy me for my standing with the *emir*, **1.6.5**
but I bear the wiles of my enviers with patience, however hard they be *to bear*. As it is said:

وكم اشآء يحسبها اناس لفاعلها نعيما وهى بوسُ
ولولا اَن يكيد بها حسودا لانكر ذكرها وبه عبوسُ

وفضلاً عن ذلك فان القوم ذوو نخوة ومروة * وشهامة وفتوّة * وانهم وان يكونوا سيّئى الادب على الطعام * فهم متادبون فى الفعال والكلام * لا ينطقون بالخنَى * ولا يُعرَف بينهم لواط ولا زنا * غير ان الفارياق كان يرى ١،٦،٦
الاَدَب كله في المأدبة * فكاّنه كان قد تخرّج على بعض الافرنج او كان فيهم نسبة * فمن ثم استدعى بقريحته على هجوهم فلبَّته * ونادى القوافى لوصفهم فاجابته * فنظم فيهم قصيدة بيّن فيها سوء حالهم * وخشونة بالهم * من جملتها

فى ثغر كلٍ منهم سكّينة وسلاحه الماضى فاَيْن المُطْعِمُ

ثم عرضها على اخيه وكان مشهودا له بالادب * وعلم لغة العرب * فاستحسنها ١،٦،٧
منه على صغر سنّه * واعجب ببراعة فنّه * ثم لم يلبث ان اشتهر امرها * وشاع ذكرها * وذلك لان اخاه من شدة اعجابه بها تلاها على كثير من معارفه فبلّغها بعض الحسّاد * الى امير الناد * وكان هذا المبلّغ نصرانيا فان الحسد لا يكون الا عند النصارى * مع ان كثيرا ممن تليت عليهم من الدروز كانوا داخلين في
عداد المهجوّين * فلما سمع الامير بذلك استآء جدّا وقال لاخيه * تالله لقد ١،٦،٨
جآء اخوك امرا فريّا * كيف يهجونا وهو ضيفنا وقد انزلناه منزلا كريما * وسقنا اليه رزقا عميما * لعمر الله لئن لم يتدارك هجوه بقصيدة مدح لأَغيظنّه * وكان هذا الامير متصفا بصفات العرب في الفروسة والنجده * وفى شرآء الحمد جَهده[١] * غير انه كان يَكِل الامور الى المقدور * ولا يهمه ترتيب حاله *

١ ١٨٥٥: جهَده.

Many things men think a blessing
To those who have them, when in fact they bring them down.
Did not the envious plot to take them from them,
They'd disavow them with a frown.

"In addition, these people are endowed with pride and *chivalry*, courage and *gallantry*, and though ill-mannered at the *board*, they're well-mannered in deed and *word*. They never utter a word *obscene*, and among them sodomy and adultery are nowhere to be *seen*."

The Fāriyāq, however, could appreciate no manners but those of the dining table, as though he'd been gently raised by *Franks* or belonged somehow to their *ranks*. Summoning, then, his native wit to mock them and being *obeyed*, calling for rhymes to describe them and being not *gainsaid*, he composed on them an ode in which he exposed the wretchedness of their daily *grind* and their coarseness of *mind*, one line of which went: 1.6.6

When each one holds knife and cutter
In his mouth, what's left for him to eat with?

He showed this to his brother (to whose knowledge of literature all bore *witness*, as they did to his grammatical *fitness*) and the latter thought it well done—even though the Fāriyāq's age was still *tender*—and was impressed by the skill with which his art he did *render*. In no time, however, the ode became *celebrated*, and much *debated*, the reason being that his brother, so proud, recited it to many of those whom he *knew*, at which one of the envious communicated it to the emir of the *crew*. This informer was a Christian—envy being a quality found only among Christians—even though many of those to whom it had been read out were among the Druze who were the object of the satire. 1.6.7

When the emir heard about it, he was greatly offended and told his brother, "*Forsooth*, your brother's committed an act *uncouth*! How can he satirize us when he's our guest whom we've dealt with as one of high *station*, and to whom we've alloted generous *compensation*? I swear to God, if he doesn't cancel out his attack with a poem of praise, I shall vex him greatly." This emir was, of the Arab qualities of chivalry and courage, the *epitome*, and would do anything in his power to attract a *eulogy*, though he submitted his affairs to *fate*, giving little thought to his current or future *state*. Now, however, he feared this threat might invite further *attacks*, should the Fāriyāq 1.6.8

والنظر فى مآله * ثم خشى من ان يكون هذا الوعيد ادعى الى زيادة الهجو اذا فصل عنه الفارياق وهو مغيظ * فرای ان الاغضآء اجلب للارضآء * وان التملّق * اوفق للتلفّق * فمن ثم سارَّ صديقا له من علمآء ملته * وفُضَلا نحلته * ان يصنع مادبة ويدعوه اليها والفارياق واخاه * فلما جمعهم النادى * ٩،٦،١
وجِئَ بالحلوآء على اطباق كالهوادى * اقسم الامير قائلا والله لا اذوقن من هذا شيا او ينظم ابو دلامة يعنى الفارياق بيتَى مديح ارتجالا * فابتدر وقال بديها

قد كان طبع ابى دلامة انه يهجو لان الهجو وفق جنانهِ
لكنّما هذا الخبيص نهاه اذ مُزِجَت حلاوته بمرّ لسانهِ

فجُنّ الحاضرون استحسانا لهما * حتى الامير لم يتمالك ان صافح الفارياق وقبّله بين عينيه فانعقدت بذلك الموادعة ورجع كلّ راضيا * وقفل صاحبنا الى بيته * وآلى ان لا يعقد فيما بعد ناصيته بذنب احد من كبرآء الناس * وان يسدّ اذنيه عن صوت صيتهم وان غلب على الاجراس *

leave his service while in a *wax*, and thus decided that to disregard the slight was the best path to *placation*, flattery the surest route to *reconciliation*. As a consequence, he discreetly asked a friend of his, a scholar of his *sect*, a member of the community's *elect*, to put on a feast, to which he was to invite him, the Fāriyāq, and his brother.

When all had been gathered by the public crier in one *place*, the sweets brought in on dishes like a herd of camels heading up a *race*, the emir made an oath and swore, "I shall not taste of these, till Abū Dulāmah"[160] (meaning the Fāriyāq) "has composed two lines of praise *impromptu*!" The Fāriyāq, not slow to respond, came up with the following, *in situ*: 1.6.9

Abū Dulāmah by nature can scarce forbear to mock
For mockery's in his nature fixed.
But this date-and-butter pudding stopped him in his tracks
When his sour tongue with its sweetness mixed.

The company went into transports over the lines, to the point that the emir couldn't restrain himself from shaking the Fāriyāq's hand and kissing him between the eyes. This sealed their mutual *conciliation* and all returned home in *jubilation*, though our friend went to his house and swore he'd never again tie his forelock to any great man's skirts and would block his ears to

the reverberations of their *reputations*,
though they rang louder
than any church bells' *tintinnabulations*.

الفصل السابع

في حمار نهّاق وسفر واخفاق

ثم لبث الفارياق يتعاطى حرفته الاولى وملّ منها ملل العليل من الفراش * وكان ١،٧،١
له صديق صدوق يراقب احواله * فاجتمع به مرة وخاضا في حديث افضى الى ذكر المعاش * والتظاهر بين الناس باحسن الرياش * فقرّ راى كلّ منهما على ان الانسان في عصرهما لا يُعدّ انسانا بفضله ومزيّته * بل بِبِزّته وزينته * وان الناس المولودين من الخزّ والحرير والقطن والكتّان المعلقين فى اوتاد حوانيت التجار اعظم قدرا من الناس الماشين العارين عنها * وان المرء اذا كان ضيّق الصدر والراس * بحيث يكون واسع السراويلات واللباس * كان هو النبِه[1] الآفق المشار اليه بالبنان * المحمود بكل لسان * فاجمعا رايهما على ان يستبضعا بضاعة ويقصدا ترويجها فى بعض البلاد استطلاعا لحال اهلها وتفرّجاً من كرب بالهما *
٢،٧،١ فاكتريا حمارا لحمل البضاعة وهو لا يستطيع حمل جثته من الهُزال والضَوَى فضلاً عن عِلاوته * ولم يكن قد بقى فيه شى شديد سوى نُهاقه و زُقاعه * فالاول للاستعلاف * والثانى لمن ينخسه او يلقى عليه الاكاف * ثم سارا وهما يفصّلان ثوب النجاح على قامة الآمال * ويقدّران بساط الفوز على نُدحة الاجال * فما بلغا طِيّتهما الا والحمار على شفا جُرف هارٍ من رَمَقه * والفارياق ايضا زاهق الروح من

[1] ١٨٥٥: النبَه.

Chapter 7

A Donkey that Brayed, a Journey Made, a Hope Delayed

Thereafter the Fāriyāq continued to practice his first profession, becoming, in the process, as sick of it as the invalid of his *bed*. He had a true friend who kept an eye on how he was; once they met and embarked on a discussion of how a person might keep himself *fed* and cut a dash before others by dint of wearing the best *thread*, both concluding that the people of their day judged others not by their virtue and *discrimination* but by their attire and its *decoration*, that those who were born to the wearing of the silk-wool, silk, cotton, and linen that are hung on the pegs of merchants' stores were of greater account than those who were without of such things, and that a person, be he petty and *dumb*, so long as his pantaloons and drawers were baggy, was the one man all would point to as noble and learned and who'd be praised by every *tongue*. They ended up agreeing that they'd acquire some goods for trade and try to sell them in certain towns, as a way to observe how their inhabitants lived and to dispel the rancor from their minds. 1.7.1

They hired a donkey to carry their wares, though the donkey was so thin and emaciated he could barely carry his own carcass, let alone whatever might be put on top of him. Nothing of any force was left him but his bray and his fart. The first of these was an appeal for *fodder*, the second directed at any who threw a pack-saddle on him and at any *prodder*. Then they set off, cutting the cloth of success to fit the figure of *hope*, measuring out the carpet of triumph to fit fate's *scope*. By the time they reached their destination, however, the donkey was at the edge of a crumbling dike of *prostration*, while the Fāriyāq too was about to give up the ghost from fatigue and *vexation*, remorseful at having abandoned his pen, however *ungiving*, along with the little it spat out by way of a *living*. 1.7.2

تعبه وقلقه * نادم على ترك القلم الضئيل * مما كان ينفث به من الرزق القليل *
ويومئذ عرف عاقبة الجَشَع * وتَبِعة الرَّغَع * وظهر له سَفاه رايه فى الشراهة الى ٣،٧،١
ما يوجب نَصَب الابدان * وبَلْبال الجَنان * غير ان اللبيب من استخرج من كل
مضرة منفعة * ومن كل مفسدة مصلحة * حتى ان فى فقد الصحة لنفعاً لمن رشد *
وخيرا لمن قصد * اذ العليل وهو ممدود على وساده * تقصر نفسه عن التمادى فى
فساده * وفى شهواته المنكرة واهوائه الموبقة * فتقوى بصيرته والمرض ناهكه *
ويملك سداده والالم مالكه * ويُرضى الله والناس بما هو سالكه * وهكذا كانت
حال الفارياق * بعد مقاساته تلك المشاقّ * فانه لما احسّ بضنك السفر * ولقى
منه ما لقى من الضرر * تبيّن له ان شق القلم اوسع من حقائب البياعه * وان
سواد المداد ابهى من الوان البضاعه * وان فى ترويج السّلعة لمَعرّةً دونها معرّة
الغُدّة والسِّلعة فجزم بانه عند الاياب الى وطنه يرضى بليّن العيش وخشنه * ولا
يبالى ان لم يكن ذا شارة رائعة * او طَلالة رافعة * او معيشة واسعة * بحيث لا
يجوب امصارا * ولا يتلوا حمارا * اما وصف الحمار على اسلوبنا معاشرَ العرب ٤،٧،١
فانه كان زبونا بليدا * حرونا عنيدا * تارزا قديدا * لا يكاد يخطوا الا بالهراوه *
واذا راى نقطة مآء فى الارض ظنّها بحرًا ذا طُفاوه * فاجفل منها اجفال النعام *
ووَجِل كما يُوجَل من الحِمام * واما على الطريقة الافرنجية فانه كان حماراً ولد حمار ٥،٧،١
وامّه اَتان من جيل كلهم حمير * وكان لونه يضرب الى السواد * ومسّ شعره
كمسّ القَتاد * مصلّم الاذنين ولا نشاط * اعسم الرجلين بادى الامِّعاط * ادرم
اَفْوَه * اَدْلم اقره * يفرك فى بسّه * ويرفس عند نخسه * ويكرف ويتمرّغ * ويشغّ
ويَبْدع لا تحيك فيه العصا * ولا يعمل فيه الزجر اذا عصى * ولا يتحرّك الا اذا
احسّ بالعَلَف وان يكون زؤانا * ولا تظهر فيه الحيوانية الا اذا راى اتانا * فيريك

That day he discovered the consequence of *greed* and where cupidity can *lead*. He realized how foolish he'd been to lust after that which brings with it physical *contusion* and mental *confusion*. It is also true, though, that the wise man is he who extracts some benefit from each *reverse*, some advantage from each circumstance *adverse*. Even in loss of health there's benefit to him whose path is *straight*, good fortune for him who doesn't *deviate*, for the soul of the sick man stretched out head upon pillow is too constrained to pursue *depravity*, forbidden lusts, or mortal *iniquity*. As the disease makes him weaker, his insight becomes *stronger*, and he sees things more plainly as the pain lasts *longer*, thus pleasing both God and men with his behavior. This was how things stood with the Fāriyāq, after he had suffered through these *travails*, for when he became sensible of the hardships of *travel*, and saw what it had to offer by way of *trials*, it became clear to him that the slit of the pen nib was more capacious than the salesman's *sack*, colored wares less gay than ink, however *black*, while to the marketing of goods there pertained a *stigma* no less great than that of buboes or of *goiter*. He determined, therefore, that, on returning to his hometown, he'd rest content with whatever ease or discomfort life might *bring*, not caring if he were a man of *note*, wore an elegant *coat* or lived like a *king*, and that never again through the world's cities would he *pass*, walking behind an *ass*. 1.7.3

Now, were I to describe the donkey after our *fashion*, my dear Arab *nation*, I'd say he was a slow-witted beast with a vicious *kick*, balky, stubborn, and shaggy, with a hide that was *thick*, scarce willing to move without the *stick*. Catching sight of a drop of water on the ground, he'd think it a flotsam-covered *ocean* and, as scared as though it promised death, shy from it like an ostrich and make a *commotion*. 1.7.4

Were I, though, to describe him in the Frankish way, I'd say he was a donkey son of a donkey, born of a she-ass all of whose ancestors were donkeys. His color tended toward the *black* and his hair felt like thorns when you touched his *back*; his ears were cropped and *listless*, his legs stiff, his coat starting to fall, and he was *toothless*; wide-mouthed, slack-lipped, and with hide discolored, he kicked out when goaded and when driven walked with buttocks *splayed*, not to mention that he sniffed at she-asses' pee, rolled on the ground, smeared his dung everywhere and *sprayed*. The stick on him had no effect, nor did rebuke, when he *disobeyed* and he never *moved* unless he sensed *food*, be it only darnel. No trace of animal nature would he show until 1.7.5

ح سَموهاً واستنانا * ونشاطا وصَميَانا * حتى كثيرا ما كان يقلب حمله * ويفسد عِدله * وفيه خَلّة اخرى وهى انه كان دائم الِاحداث على قلة اِعمال ضرسه * مواصل الغَفَق فى النجوة والخفض زيادة على نحسه * فان منشأه كان فى بلاد يكثر فيها الكرنب والفجل والسلجم * واللفت والقنبيط كبعض بلاد العجم * فلهذا اعتاد على اخراج هذه الرائحة من صغَره * وزادت فيه بازدياد عمره * فكان لا بدّ للماشى خلفه من سدّ انفه * والاكثار من أُفّه * وفى كلا الوصفين فان رفقة هذا البهيم *
لم تكن اقلّ اذىً من السفر الاليم * وانه بعد جولان عدة قُرى * ليس فيها من ١،٧،٦
ماوى ولا قِرى * وبعد مجادلات مع الشارين طويلة * ومحاولات ومصاولات وبيلة * قنع الفارياق وشريكه من الغنيمة بالاياب * ورضيا باللّفآ والعود الى المآب * وعلما ان البئر الفارغة لا تمتلى من الندى * وان التعب في تجارتهما يذهب سُدى * فتسبّبا في بيع البضاعة بقيمتها * كيلا يشمت بهما من ينظرهما راجعين بماهيتها * وباتا تلك الليلة خاليى البال * من القيل والقال * فان من الناس من لا يعجبه شرآء شى الّا بعد تقليبه * وبعد تحميق بائعه وتكذيبه * فلا بدّ للبائع من ان يكون عن مثل هولا متصامّا متغافلا * متعامياً متساهلا * وتلك خلّة لم تكن فى الفارياق ولا فى صاحبه * فان كلّا منهما كان يحاول استمالة الكون الى جانبه *
ثم انهما رجعا بثمن البضاعة وبالحمار وسلّما المال لصاحبه * فعرض عليهما سلعة ١،٧،٧
اخرى فأبَيا * وتواعدا ان يجتمعا مرة اخرى للشَّركة فى مصلحة اهمّ * وآثرا ان تكون في البيع والشراء * وقد جرت العادة بين الناس بانه اذا تعاطى احد عملا ولم ينجح به اَوّل مرّة لجّ به الشَرَه الى معاطاته مرة اخرى * اذ ليس احد يرضى لنفسه نحس الطالع وشُؤم الجَدّ * وانما ينسب حُرَفَه فيما احترف به الى بعض عوارض وطوارئ حدثت له * فيقول في نفسه لعلّ هذه العوارض لا تقع هذه المرّة * وعلّة ذلك

a she-ass he *espied*; then you'd see him frisk and gambol, show vigor and pull the bridle to one *side*, so that he often overturned his load or sent it *askew*; and another peculiarity he had *too*, which was that, rarely though his molars were put to work, everywhere he *defecated* and incessantly over hill and dale he *flatulated*, making him seem yet more *ill-fated*. He'd been raised in lands where there was an abundance of cabbage, radish, rape, turnip, and cauliflower, as there is in certain foreign *parts*, and was therefore accustomed from his youth to producing *farts*, and this condition had only grown worse as he'd grown older. Thus any who walked behind him had, *perforce*, to hold his nose and keep saying "*How coarse!*" In any case, whichever of the two descriptive modes you choose, of all the pains of the journey and its injuries, keeping company with this *beast* was by no means the *least*.

After touring a number of villages offering neither bed nor *board*, and 1.7.6
after long debates with customers and hagglings and chafferings they could ill *afford*, the Fāriyāq and his partner returned with *nowt*, deciding to cut their losses and return to whence they'd set *out*, well aware that "the empty well cannot be filled by *rain*," that any further toil at this affair would be in *vain*. They were thus compelled to sell their goods for the price they'd *paid* to forestall from gloating any who might see them returning with the very stuff they'd taken to *trade*, and spent the night as though stunned from all the *rout*, for there are people who'll buy a thing only after they've turned it inside *out* and called the seller a fool and a *gyp*, leaving him no choice but to bite his *lip*, to the likes of these paying no *attention* but turning, rather, a blind eye and offering no *contention*. This talent, though, was not one possessed by either the Fāriyāq or his *friend*, each of whom sought to bend the world to his own *end*.

Thus they returned with the cost of the goods and the donkey and handed 1.7.7
the money over to his owner, who offered them other goods, which they refused. They did, however, agree to meet again to work as partners on some business of greater import, preferring that this be in selling and buying too, for it is usual, when someone does a job and does not at first succeed, that his avarice insist he try again, since no one will accept that he was born to be unlucky or suffer dire fortune; rather, he attributes his bad luck in his chosen profession to certain accidents and unexpected incidents that have befallen him, telling himself, "The same will not occur this time around." The root of all this is man's dependence on his own intelligence, his confidence in his

كله اعتماد الانسان على رشد نفسه * وثقته بسعيه والركونُ الى حدسه * وقد تهّور في ذلك كثير من الخلق * واكثرهم جنى على نفسه في التهافت على الرزق *

own efforts, and his reliance on his own intuitions. Many of God's creation have done so *fecklessly*, most hurting themselves in the process and destroying their livelihoods *recklessly*.

الفصل الثامن

في خان واخوان وخِوان

١،٨،١ ثم انه بعد مذاكرة طويلة بين الفارياق وصاحبه قرّ رايهما على ان يستاجرا خانا على طريق مدينة الكعيكات * حيث ترد القافلة منها الى مدينة الركاكات * فاستبضعا ما يلزم لهما من المِيَرة والاَدَوات ولبثا فيه يبيعان ويشتريان بما تيسَّر لهما من راس المال وذنبه * فلم تمضِ عليهما برهة وجيزة حتى انتشر صيتهما عند الواردين والصادرين * وعرف رشدهما جميع المسافرين * فكان الناس يقصدونهما لاقتصادهما * وكثيرا ما انتاب خانهما اهل الفضل والبراعة * والوجاهة والاستطاعة * حتى كأنّه كان حديقة يتفرّج فيها المكروب *
٢،٨،١ وعادة اهل ذلك الصقع انهم لا يكادون يجتمعون في محل الّا ويتنازعون كاس البحث والمناظرة * ويخوضون فى امور الدنيا والاخرة * فان اثبت احد شيا نفاه الآخر * وان استحسنه استهجنه وزعم انه من المُنكَر * فيتحزب القوم احزابا قِدَدا * ويمتلئ المكان صخبا واِدَدا * وربما انتهى البحث الى التفاخر بالنسب * والتكاثر بالحسب * فيقول احدهم مثلاً لقرينه * اتردّ عليّ واَبى نديم الامير وسميره واكيله وشريبه وجليسه وانيسه وخصيصه ونجيّه * لا يقضى ليلة من الليالى الّا ويستدعى به لمسامرته * ولا يحكم بشى الا بعد مشاورته * وقد عُرِف اهلى من قديم الزمان بانهم سُفرآ البلاد * ونواميس الامجاد * وما احد من الناس ماجَدَهُم ولا شارفهم ولا كاثرهم ولا فاخرهم ولا فاضلهم الا وعاد مجودا

Chapter 8

Bodega, Brethren, and Board

After a long discussion between the Fāriyāq and his companion, they settled on renting an inn on the road to the city of al-Kuʿaykāt, where are to be found the caravans that leave for the city of al-Rukākāt.[161] They stocked up on what they needed by way of provisions and equipment and settled there, doing business with whatever *cap*ital (and *ass*ets)[162] they'd been able to muster. It wasn't long before their renown spread among all who came and went *thence*, all travelers learned of their good *sense*, and people started seeking them out for their reasonable prices, so that their inn was so much frequented by the better and more skilful class of *men*, those possessed of means and *gravamen*, that it became as a garden where the distressed could find relief. 1.8.1

Now, it is typical of the people of that district that they can hardly meet together in any place without passing back and forth among them the chalice of discussion and *debate*, plunging into matters that both to this world and the next *relate*. If one asserts a *proof*, the next denies its *truth*, and if the first believes that it is *well*, the other condemns it and claims it'll send you to *Hell*. The people thus divide into opposing *factions*, the place filling with clamor and disastrous *actions*. Sometimes the discussion ends with boasting over noble *extraction* and high degree of influential *connection*, one saying, for example, to his fellow, "Would you answer me back, when my father's the companion of the *emir*, sits with him of an evening to maintain his good *cheer*, is his partner at *board* and at *bar*, the frequenter of his salon and his *mate*, his special friend and *intimate*? Not a night goes by without him summoning him to *socialize*, and he makes no decisions without first asking his *advice*. Plus, my people have been known since time immemorial as ambassadors to many a *land* and confidential advisors to the *grand*. Never has any man vied with him in glory, honor, plenty, pride, or virtue without being 1.8.2

ومشروفا ومكثورا ومفخورا ومفضولا * وربما أُعمِلت بعد ذلك الهراوات * وقامت مقام البيّنات * فيتنمَّر منهم من لم يكن يتنمّر * ويعربد من سكر ومن لم يسكر * فينتهي الامر الى امير الصُقع * فيبعث عليهم مصادرين ذوي صَقع * وويل لمن يكون قد ذكر اسم الامير وقت الجدال * فان عفوه حينئذ من المحال * فاما فى الحوادث العظيمة فان المتعدّى اذا فرّ من القِصاص أُخِذ بذنبه احد اهله او جيرانه *
او ماشيته او ماعونه وقُطع شجره وأُحرق منزله * غير ان زمرتنا هذه لم تكن تعدَّى ٣،٨،١
حدَّ الجدال الى القتال * فان الفارياق وصاحبه كانا يقومان فيهم مقام فَيْصَل * فمن هذه الحيثية كثرت الوفود عليهما * وكثيرا ما بات عندهما اصحاب العيال والراح عليهم دائرة * والاغانى متواترة * والوجوه ناضرة والعمائم متطايرة * فكان ذلك داعيا الى خصام النسآء مع بعولتهن * ومن طبع النسآء عموما انهن اذا علمن اَنَّ احداً يعوق ازواجهن عنهن اضمرن ان يتقربن الى ذلك العائق ببعض حيلهن * فان كان ممن يُعْشَق صفقن له حالا على المقايضة والمبادلة اَخْذاً بثارهنّ * فجعلن من كل عضو منه بعلا * ومن كل شعرة خِلّا * وان كان ممَّن تبذأه العين رَمَيْنه
بداهية وتحيَّلْن فى خلاص بعولتهن منه وردّ بضاعتهن اليهن * غير ان نسآ تلك ٤،٨،١
البلاد لا يخاصمن بعولتهن وهن مضمرات خيانتهم او مستحلّات استبدالهم * فانهن رَبَيْن على محبة ابآئهن وعلى طاعة بعولتهنَّ * وما خصامهنّ لهم الّا عتاب * وكم فى العتاب من لذَّة * ولم يُسمَع عن واحدة منهن الى الان انها خاصمت زوجها لدى حاكم شرعىّ او امير او مطران * مع ان كثيرا من هولآء الاصناف الثلثة يتمنّون ذلك في بعض الاحوال * اما للافتخار باجرآء العدل والانصاف فى رعيتهم اولعلّة اخرى * ومن طبع هولآء المخلوقات المباركات سلامة النيّة وصفآء العقيدة والتقرب الى الرجال لا عن فجور * فترى المراة منهن متزوّجة كانت او ثيّبة تجلس الى

beaten, thrashed, trashed, outdone and undone." At this, cudgels might be set to work and take the place of arguments, he who hadn't lost his temper losing it, and *all*, drunk and sober alike, setting down to *brawl*. In the end, news of the affair would come to the ear of the emir of the local *lands*, who would send men to exact punishment by dealing out to them slaps with their *hands*, and woe betide any who dragged the name of the emir into the *discussion*: pardon for him was out of the *question*. Where grave matters were concerned and the aggressor fled in fear of retribution, a member of his family or a neighbor, or his cattle and stores, would be taken to pay for his crime, his trees would be felled, and his house burned.

Our company, however, never crossed the line between debate and donnybrook, for the Fāriyāq and his companion took on the role of arbiter, and, this being the case, the number of those who frequented them became great. Many a time, family men would spend the night with them, each the other with wine *plying*, songs succeeding one another, faces radiant,[163] turbans *flying*—which led to conflict between the women and their husbands. It is in the nature of women generally, should anyone keep their husbands from them, to scheme till, by one of their wiles, they can get close to that person. If the man is *handsome*, they promptly make a deal of barter and exchange with him, to exact revenge, taking every limb of his as their husband, every hair as their boon *companion*; should he be of the type to which the eye's *averse*, they get him into trouble, plotting to wrest their husbands from him and thus their loss of goods *reverse*. 1.8.3

The women of those lands,[164] however, do not oppose their husbands, keeping the latter's infidelities to themselves and regarding it as permitted for their husbands to replace them. They have been raised to feel affection for their fathers and be obedient to their husbands, and their disputes with them go no further than reprimands—and how pleasurable a reprimand can often be! To this day no one has heard of any of them taking a dispute with her husband to the legal authorities or an emir or a bishop, though many members of these three groups would like that to happen in certain circumstances, either so that they could boast of their imposition of justice and fair dealing upon their subjects, or for some other reason. Also part of the nature of these blessed creatures is the purity of their intentions, the sincerity of their belief, and their capacity to create intimate relationships with men without hint of debauchery. One may observe one of these 1.8.4

جانب الرجل وتاخذ بيده * وتلقى يدها على كتفه وتسند راسها على صدره وتبسم له وتؤانسه فى الحديث * وتتحفه ببعض ما تصل اليه يدها * كل ذلك عن صفآء نية وخلوص مودة * واحسن ما يرى فيهن البلاهة والغِرّية فانهما فى النسآء خير من النُكر والدَّهاء * هذا اذا كان فى غير ما يشين العرض وينتهك الحرمة * فاما فى

١،٨،٥ وقت الجِدّ فلا تصح البلاهة * هذا ولما كان من دابهن ان يكشفن عن صدورهن ولا يرفعن اثدآهن من صغرهن بشى * كان اكثرهن هُضلاً اى ذوات اثدآء طويلة * واكثرهن يعتقد ان فى طول رضاع الولد زيادة صحّة له * فمنهن من ترضع ولدها عامين تامّين * ومنهن من تزيد على ذلك * فامّا محبتهن لا ولادهن ورفقهنّ بهم وشوقهن اليهم فيجلّ عن الوصف * واعرف كثيرا من البنات كنّ يبكين يوم زواجهن على فراق ابآئهن وامهاتهن واخوتهن كما يبكى غيرهن فى المأتم او اشدّ * فاما ما يقال من ان البعولة ياكلون وحدهم دون نسآئهم فكلام لا اصل له * وانما يكون ذلك اذا كان عند الرجل ضيف غريب حتى لو اراد حينئذ ان تقعد امراته مع الضيف لتاكل معه لأبَت ورات ان ذلك يكون استخفافا بها وانتهاكا لحرمتها *

١،٨،٦ وفى الجملة فانهن لا يُعبَن بشى الا بالجهل وهنَّ فى ذلك معذورات * فاما الجاهلات من الافرنج فانهن يُضفن الى الجهل مَكرًا وخُبثا * وناهيك بذلك من سُبَّة * وانى ليحزننى جدّا ان اسمع اَنَّ هولآء المحبوبات قد مللن من هذه الفضائل وتخلّقن باخلاق اخرى * فيجب علىّ والحالة هذه ان اغيّر ما وصفتهن به من المحامد * او اَن اذن للقارى فى ان يكتب على الحاشية كذب كذب او هذين البيتين *

ان النسآء حيثما كنّ سوى   يملن من حيث اتاهنَّ الهَوَى
لا يغرُرَنَّ الغِرَّ منهنَّ تُقًى   ولا هُدًى ولا نُهًى ولا حَيا

women, married or a widow, sitting beside a man and taking his hand, or putting her hand on his shoulder and resting her head on his chest, smiling at him, holding friendly converse with him, and making him a present of something that has come her way, and all that with sincere intent and uncomplicated affection. The best qualities to be observed in them are their simplemindedness and naiveté, which, in women, are to be preferred to guile and cunning, so long as they do nothing to bring them dishonor or destroy their sanctity as women. When things get serious, however, simplemindedness will not do.

In addition, given their habit of exposing their chests and their use of 1.8.5
nothing, from childhood on, to support their breasts, theirs are mostly pendulous. Most of them think that the longer they breastfeed their children, the healthier it is for them, and some breastfeed them for two whole years, or even longer. Their affection for their children and their kindness to them and tenderness toward them are too great to describe. I have known many girls who, on their wedding days, wept at being separated from their fathers, mothers, and siblings as other women do at funerals, or more. The claim that their husbands eat on their own, without their wives, is completely without basis; this happens only if the husband has a guest who is not a member of the family, on which occasion, even if he should wish to have his wife sit down with the guest, she would refuse, believing that such a thing would indicate lack of respect for her and a violation of her sanctity.

Overall, there is nothing for which they can be blamed save ignorance, 1.8.6
and in that they are to be excused. Ignorant Frankish women add to their ignorance cunning and baseness, so how much the worse is their shame! It pains me greatly to hear of the beloved women of Lebanon growing discontented with these virtues and adopting other ways. If this is indeed the case, I shall be obliged to change my description of their virtues, or give the reader permission to write in the margin either "Lies, lies, lies!" or the following lines of verse:

Women, where'er they be, are all the same—
  They incline to love from wherever it may appear.
Let not piety, right guidance, reason, or shame on their part
  Take the gullible unaware!

او هذين

سِرْ مَضْرِبَ الارض فى طول وفى عَرْضِ   ترَ النسآء يبعن العِرْضَ كالعَرْضِ
بالرِجل يصفقن عند البيع لا بِيَد   وكلُّ قاضٍ على تسجيله يُمضى

او هذين

واذا رأيت من الخرائد غادةً   تبدو وتخفَى فارجعونّ وصالها
واذا دعتك لحاجة عنَّت لها   لتكون قاضيها فرجّ مبا . . . . . .

او ما قاله دعبل

لا يُوْئِسنَّك من مخدَّرة   قولٌ تغلّظه وإنْ جرَحا
عُسر النسآء الى مُياسرةٍ   والصَعْبُ يمكن بعد ما جمحا

واعلم ان البلاد التى يُتَّجر فيها بعرض النسآء بغير مانع الّا بمكس عليه قليل يدفع ١،٨،٧
لبيت المال لبنآء معابد وغيرها دون اعتبار لقول من قال اَمُطْعمة الايتام الخ يقلّ
فيها التغزل بهن * فانّ الرجل هناك ايّان خطر بباله ان رؤية الوجه الصبيح تنفى
همَّه وتزيل بلباله * وتخفف اثقاله * وتنفّس عنه كربه وتجلو صدا قلبه وتصفى
دمه * خرج فوجد ضالَّته تنتظره ورآء الباب * فلا يحتاج عند ذلك الى
شكوى وعتاب وتواجُد * والى قوله اَرَق على ارق ومثلى يارق * وكفى بجسمى
نحولاً اننى رجل * وذبت وجدا وغراما ونحو ذلك * فاما البلاد التى يُحظَر فيها ١،٨،٨
هذا الاتّجار فتجد الكلام فى النسآء متجاوزا به ورآء الحدّ * ولذلك كان فى شعر
الافرنج الاقدمين من المجون ما تجده فى كتب العرب * وما الّا لانّ هذه البياعة

Or these:

Walk the length of the world and its breadth—
You'll see women selling their honor like market wares.
They clap with feet, not hands, once the sale is made,
And every judge[165] "It's legal!" declares.

Or these:

Beg a young maiden, a virgin, to let you love her
If you see her prowling on the hunt
And if she invites you to satisfy some urgent need she feels,
Comply with her and shake up her c . . . .[166]

Or the words of Diʿbil:[167]

Let not the harsh words of a chaste lady,
Though wounding, make you refrain.
Women's recalcitrance leads to complaisance:
After bolting once, the prancing steed submits to the rein.

You should know too that in those countries where their honor is traded without constraint, apart from a small levy paid to the treasury for the building of temples and so forth, without regard to the words of him who said, "O feeder of the orphans . . ." etc.,[168] women are rarely courted with words of love, for it would never occur to a man in such a place that the sight of a charming face could dispel his worry and put paid to his *unrest*, alleviate his burdens and relieve his *distress*, from his heart polish the *rust*, from his blood remove the *dust*. Since he leaves the house and finds what he's looking for waiting for him right there on the other side of the door, he has no need of a lover's complaints, reproaches, and passionate protestations, or of saying, "Sleepless night after sleepless night!" or "Such as I can never sleep!" or "I have lost enough weight! I am a man and have melted away with burning desire and love!" and so on. 1.8.7

In countries, however, in which this trade is forbidden, you'll find that talk of women exceeds all bounds, which is why you find the same bawdiness in the poetry of the ancient Franks as in the works of the Arabs, the sole reason being that this commerce was, in their day, banned. Once it became common, bawdiness became rare among them. On the Mountain, 1.8.8

كانت وقتئذ ممنوعة * فلما كثرت قلّ عندهم المجون * اما فى الجبل فانك لا تجد لهم بياعة ولا مجونا * وحكى عن الفارياق انه هوى واحدة من اولئك اللاى كن يترددن عليه ولم يكن يحظى منها الا بلثم اخمصها فكان اذا اصبح يقول لصاحبه

ان المقبِّلَ رجلها يَجِلُّ عن   تقبيل راحة قسّه واميرِهِ
هنّ الفواتن للخلىّ فشعرة   منهنّ خيرٌ من كنوز غَروره

however, you'll find neither commerce of this sort nor bawdiness. It is said of the Fāriyāq that he once fell in love with one of the women who used to visit him, and all she granted him was a kiss on the hollow of her foot. When he got up the next morning, he recited to his companion

Any who's kissed her foot thenceforth's too good
To kiss the hands of priests or of emirs,
Such women are the bachelors' charmers, and all the treasures of this world
Are worth less than one of their hairs.

الفصل التاسع

في محاورات خانية * ومناقشات حانية

لا باس فى ان نذكر هنا مثالا لما كان يقع بين تلك الزمرة من المحاورات فنقول * ١،٩،١
اجتمعت زمرتنا هذه مرة والكاس تدار عليهم * والسرور يرقص بين يديهم *
فقال افصحهم مقالا * والَدُّهم جدالا * ایّ الناس فيما علمتم انعم بالاً * واحسن
حالا * فقال مَن بيده الكاس هو من كان على مثل هذه الحالة * وفى راحته ذى
الآلة * فقال له ليس ذلك على الاطلاق * ولم يقع عليه اتفاق * فان هذه الحالة
لا يمكن كونها دائمة * فتكون غبطتها غير تامّة * وانما هى بعض من كل * وجز
من جُلّ * وبقى النظر فى الباقى * ولا خفا ان مداومة المدام * تورث السقام *
وتُقْهِى عن الطعام * ولذلك سمّيت القهوة * ولا يعتادها انسان الّا حلّت به
الشقوة * فقال آخر ان انعم الناس بالاً امير يجلس على اريكته * وتحفّه جماعة من ٢،٩،١
حشمته وحفدته * ياتيه رزقه رغدا * ويكفيه رازقه فى المعيشة جهدا * فاذا اوى
الى حريمه خلا بازهر امراة على اوطأ فراش * فصدق فيه قولهم * اعجب الاشيآء
وَثْر على وِثْر * هذا وانّ اكْلَه المُرازَمة * وثيابه الناعمة * وامره مطاع * وحكمه
مقابل بالاتّباع * فقال بعضهم ليس الامر كذلك * وما الحقّ فيما هنالك * فان
الامير لا يخلو بامراته الا وهو مشغول الخاطر * مكدّر السرائر * اذ لا يزال يفكر
فى كونه مخونا بماله * مغشوشا من عمّاله * ياكل رهطه رزقه ويذمونه * ويأتمنهم

Chapter 9

Unseemly Conversations and Crooked Contestations[169]

It would be well to provide here an example of the kind of conversations that used to take place among this company. Thus we declare: Once, when this company of ours had gathered, the cup was on its rounds, joy *unconfined*, the chastest among them in speech and most dogged in debate posed the following question: "Which person, in your opinions, is the best-off and has the greatest peace of *mind*?" Replied the one with cup in hand, "He who's in this same state as *I*, holding his vessel *high*." The first told him, "It is not so at all, nor is it *he* on whom men may *agree*, for his condition's one that will not *last* and his joy, it follows, will soon be *past*. Moreover, it rests on but a partial *proof*, is but a part of a greater *truth*, of which the rest remains to be considered—namely there's no denying that imbibing wine can make a man *ill* and stop him from eating his *fill*, which is why it's called *qahwah*;[170] no man can use it regularly without *disaster*." 1.9.1

Another now declared, "He who enjoys the greatest peace of mind is the emir when on his sofa he sits at *ease*, a party of servants and scions at his *knees*. His living comes to him without a *care*, for his Provider relieves him of any effort regarding daily *fare*. When he takes himself off to his harem, he closets himself with the most gorgeous of women on the softest of beds (and how true the words of him who said, 'There's nothing more wonderful than to bed on a comfortable bed'!). What's more, with a different dish each day his table's *laid*, in soft garments he's *arrayed*, his orders are *obeyed*, his judgment never *gainsaid*." Another then declared, "That's not how things *are*. The truth from that is *far*. The emir never sees his *wife* but his head's full of *strife*, his heart with worries *rife*, for he's always thinking how he's 1.9.2

فيخونونه * ويعطيهم فيخلونه * وهو مع ذلك مرصود منهم فيما يفعله * منتقد
عليه بما يتعمّله * وانه لَيودّ السفر ولا يتاح له * ويتمنّى رؤية غير بلاده ولا يدرك
امله * فهو يحسد من يمشى فى الارض سَبَهْللا * ويغبط من يعتسف الطريق
ضَلَلا * فقام بعض النقّاد وقال سمعا يااهل الرشاد * ان اسعد خلق الله راهب ٣،٩،١
لزم كنّابه فى صومعته * وتفرّغ عن الشغل بعقاره وضيعته * فهو ياكل من ارزاق
الناس * ويعوضهم عنه دعآء يطفح من اَصمار الكاس * ويغنيهم في الدياجى
عن النبراس * ويركب ما لديهم من النجائب * فهو كما قيل آكل شارب راكب * ثم
ما عليه بعد ذلك ان خرب الكون او عُمر * وان مات الخلق او نُشر * فقال بعض
ذوى الرشاد * ما هذا القول من السداد * فان الراهب وامثاله اذا راى الناس
مقبلين على اعمالهم * مشتغلين باشغالهم * لم يرضَ الدنآءة لنفسه ان يعيش من
كدّهم * ويستريح على تعبهم وجهدهم * ويتحيّن اوان رفدهم * بل يود لوكان شريكا
لهم في اتعابهم * احرى من ان يكون شريكا في مصوناتهم * هذا اذا كان نزيه
النفس * كريم القنس * صادق السعى * ضابط الوعى * ثم ان له عند رؤية
الرجال مع نسائهم واولادهم لَغُصّات * وحَسَرات واَىّ حسرات * ولا سيما اذا
خلا فى الصومعة * وراى ان ِسمَنه ذاهب سدًى من غير منفعه * وان غيره ممن
اضواهم الكدّ والنصب * واجاعهم الجهد والتعب * اقدر منه على بلوغ الارب *
مما اصطلح عليه سائر خلق الله من عجم وعرب * فقال من استوصب مقاله * ٤،٩،١
وارتاح لما قاله * هذا لعمرى هو الحق المبين * فان الراهب ومن اشبهه حرىّ بان
يُعدّ مع الشقيين * وانما يظهر لى ان اسعد الناس عيشاً هو التاجر يقعد في
حانوته بعض ساعات من يومه * فيكسب باَيمانه المُغلّظة فى ساعة واحدة ما
ينفقه فى شهره * يجعل الكاسد من سلعته بتكرير كلامه نافقا * والمكروه شائقا *

been betrayed over his *wealth*, cheated by his agents of his *pelf*. His income's consumed by his *court*, which yet finds *fault*. He places his affairs under their *sway* and yet they *betray*. He treats them with *generosity* and yet they accuse him of *illiberality*. In addition, they watch every step he *takes*, criticize him for every move he *makes*. He'd love to travel, but has to *stay*, longs to see new lands but can never have his *way*. He's jealous of those who walk aimlessly hither and *yonder* and looks with envy on all who whimsically *wander*."

Now rose another to *criticize*, saying, "Listen now, all you who're *wise*. 1.9.3
The happiest of God's creation is the monk who remains in his cell to *read*, who from work on his land or in his village is *freed*; he eats of what others labor to *earn*, providing prayers in overflowing measure in *return* (so relieving them of any need for *light*, in the darkness of the *night*), and he takes his steed from among whatever beasts to their lot may be *counted*, so that he is, as the saying has it, 'Fed, watered, and *mounted*.' Thus equipped, it matters not to him whether the world flourish or go to *pot*, mankind be resurrected or left to *rot*." One of those wise men then said, "These words are far from true. The monk and his like, should they see men setting forth on their *labors*, occupied in their *endeavors*, are far from happy to be reduced to living off their *toil*, taking their ease at the expense of others' exhausting labor on the *soil*, idly waiting till they bring him their gifts. On the contrary, he'd rather take on a part of their *chores* than be a partner in what they've set aside as *stores* (this if he be of blameless soul and noble *stock*, honest in his striving, his conscience not *ad hoc*). Nay more—on seeing men with their wives and children he suffers agonies and sorrows too great to *tell*, especially when, alone in his *cell*, he sees his plumpness going to waste and doing him no *good* while others, weakened by toil and fatigue, enfeebled by effort, sickness, and lack of *food*, are more capable than him of realizing the *desires* to which all mankind, Arab and non-Arab alike, *aspires*."

Another, who the last man's opinion *shared* and was at ease with his view, 1.9.4
declared, "This, I swear, is the revealed *truth*! The monk and those like him are better counted among those who live in *ruth*. However, it seems to me that the happiest of men where livelihood's concerned is the merchant. He sits in his store for a few hours of his day and earns in one hour, with his mighty oaths, enough to pay his expenses for a month. By means of constant

والدون فائقا * ثم هو ان اَوى الى منزله ليلا * اصاب في خدمته دعد وليلى *
فهو في نهاره كسّاب للمال * وفى ليلته منفقه على رَبّات الحِجال * فقال من
انتقد كلامه * وتبيّن ذامه ان * التاجر لا تمكن له هذه العيشة الراضية * ولا
تهنؤه هذه النعمة الوافية * الا اذا كان قازبا ذا معاملات فى البلاد القاصية *
وركوب للاخطار * واقتحام للاوطار * ومتى كان كذلك نقص من رغده * وِافرُ
تجشمه وكدّه * ونغّص من لذّاته * تعدّدُ بَغيّاته * وملأ خاطره اشجانا * ما حاوله
ليرضى به زبونا واخوانا * فكلما هبت ريح خشى على سلعته في البحر * وكلما
جَشَرَ صبحٌ اوجس من ورود قادم يخبره بِشَر * او مألكة تنبى عن تلَف وخُسْر *
٥،٩،١ وكَساد وحظر * فهو لا يزال فى اعمال نظر * وتجرّع اسف وكدر * فقال بعض
السامعين * انك لمن الصادقين * اما انا فلا اودّ ان اكون ذا اتّجار * ولو ربحت
في كل يوم مئة دينار * لما يعقب هذه الحرفة من القيل والقال * والتكذيب
والمحال * والمحاولة والمكر * والمداهاة والنُكر * فضلا عن اقتصارى فى الحانوت
ربع عمرى * ولا علم لى بما يجرى في وكرى * فلعلّ رقيباً يخالفنى الى دارى *
وانا اذ ذاك اكذب على الشارى واماري * واجامل وادارى * ففى عنقى حبل الاثم
بما افعل فى مُحْتَرَفى * وبكونى صرت وسيلة لارتكاب الحرام فى مألفى * وانما
اظن ان احق الناس بان يغبط على عيشته * ويبارك له فى حرفته ومهنته * انما
هو الحارث الذى يسعى لنفع نفسه ولغيره فيما يحرثه * فيكسب به صحة بدنه ومؤنة
عياله وذلك خير ما يبرّثه * وان زوجه تراوحه على عمله * وترفق به في عُسْره
وعَطَله * انْ مرض مرّضَتْه بنفسها وقامت بامر مربعه * وان غاب رعت له ذمّة
وباتت تنتظر وشك مرجعه * هذا والتَعِبُ يستطيب طعامه * ويستحلى نيامه *
الا ترى ان اولاد ذوى السعى والكدّ * اصح ابدانا واذكى فهما من اولاد ذوى

hype, he converts loss to gain, the unwanted into things desired, the shoddy into goods of superior *stripe*. Plus, when he goes home at *night*, Daʿd and Laylā[171] are waiting there to treat him *right*; thus by day he earns his *monies*, and by night he spends it on his ankleted *honies*."[172] One who the truth of these words *denied* and wished to prove that the man before had *lied* now said, "The merchant can attain this pleasant life, enjoy this ample ease, only if he be ambitious, a rolling *stone*, with dealings in lands far from his *own*, a master of risks, one who boldly seizes what he wants. This being so, the realization of the results of his greed and toil must put paid to his *leisure*, the burgeoning of his ambitions must spoil his *pleasure*; what he must do to please customers and *family* must fill his soul with *anomie*. He fears for his goods at sea whenever the wind *blows* and, when dawn breaks, worries that someone will come to inform him of *woes*, some letter arrive to inform him of damage or loss, of stagnant markets or *embargoes*. Thus in thought his brow he ever *furrows*, gulping down regret and *sorrows*."

One of his audience now said, "Verily, your words are true. As for me, 1.9.5
I'd have no desire to engage in *trade*, even if each day a hundred golden dinars I *made*. Any who engages in that profession spreads gossip, tells lies and absurdities, schemes, practices craft and deception, and *betrays*, not to mention that I'd be stuck there in the store for a quarter of my *days*. I'd have no idea of what was afoot in my nest: perhaps some watcher would go there and make *hay* while I was *away*, while I was lying to a buyer and *wangling*, flattering, and *wrangling*. Sin's rope would then be round my neck both for what I did in the *store* and for being a means to the commission of forbidden acts behind my very own *door*. For my part, I believe the man who most deserves to be envied for his way of life, whose craft and profession most deserve our *praises*, is none other than the cultivator, who labors to do good to both himself and others with what he *raises*, thus gaining both health for his body and provender for his dependants, which is the best of the many blessings by him *enjoyed*, though in addition his wife goes back and forth with him to work and keeps him company when times are hard and he's *unemployed*. If he falls sick, she nurses him herself and looks after his *mead*; if he's absent, she watches out for his interests and waits, hoping he'll return with *speed*. What's more, the tired man savors his *meat* and finds his slumbers

الترفّه والجدّ * وما ذلك الا لانهم يرقدون عن نُعاس وياكلون عن جوع ويشربون عن ظما * فاجابه اقرب مَنْ وَلِيَه * انَّ فيما قلت لَنظرا * فانك لم ترَ الصورة الّا من جهة واحدة وفاتتك الجهة الاخرى * فلعمرى ان الحارث مع كدّ بدنه * اسير همه وشجنه * وضجيع قلقه وحزنه * اذ هو عبد العناصر * ورقيق الحوادث والاكابر * ان عصفت ريح خشى على ثمره ان يتساقط فيسقط قلبه معه * وان كثر المطر او قل وجل من ان يتلف ما زرعه * وان مات كبير فى بلده * اشفق من كساد ما تحت يده * وان يكن ذا بصيرة وحِجى * سآءه ما يرى اهله فيه من العُرى والوَجَى * والذُلّ والاستكانة * والابتئاس والمَهانة * وتحسرهم على الطيِّب من الماكول * والناعم من الملبوس * وعلى كونه لا يحسن تربية ولده كما يشا * ولا يمكنه رؤية بلد غير الذى فيه نشا * فهو مهده وقبره * وسجنه وحُجْره * ومع ذلك فهو غرض لاغراض امامه فى الدين * وعصا يتوكأ عليها من هو فوقه من المثرين * والسائدين والمُسَيطرين * فما يكاد يتخلص من ورطة احدهما الا ويقع فى شرك الآخر * ولا يفوته شرّ الا واستقبله شر اكبر * وهو مع اِصْرِه وجهله * لا يجد مَخْلَصاً له ولا لاهله * ولوانه رام ان ينهج لاهله منهجا ارتضاه لنفسه واستصوبه * ولم يك على وفق مرام اِمامه واميره او آخر ذى مرتبة * لم يامن غَرامة منهما او حسم عَرْتَبة * او قصم رقبة * ولم يلبث ان يرى اصحابه له اعدآ * واخدانه اَلِدّآ * فهو على هذا رهين الخضوع * واسير القنوع * فقال قرين له * وقد صدق على ما فصّله * ٦،٩،١
نعم ان هذا لهو الحق الواضح * وما بعد الرقّ ذل فاضح * وانى ارى بعد امعان النظر والتروى * والتحقق والتحرّى * ان اسعد الناس حالا * رجل رزقه الله مالا * واصلح له بالا * فجعل دابه السفر في البلاد الغريبه * والمشاهدة للكائنات العجيبة * فهو كل يوم في شان * وله فى كل مَعان * اوطان واخوان * فقال قائل

sweet. Do you not observe that the children of those who strive and toil have healthier bodies and are quicker *witted* than the children of those who live a life of ease and are better *outfitted*? The sole reason for this is that they go to sleep when tired, eat when hungry, and drink when thirsty." The one closest to him now answered, "I must take issue with what you *say*, for you look at the picture in only one *way*, while the other side escapes you. The cultivator, I swear, over and above his body's hard work, is captive to care and *woe*, bedfellow to anxiety and *sorrow*, for he's a slave to the *elements*, at the bidding of the great families and of *accidents*. If a storm blow, he fears his fruit will *fall* and he feel *gall*; if the rain's too little or too *savage*, he fears lest what he's sown be *ravaged*; if a great man in his town *dies*, he worries he won't be able to market his *supplies*. If he be a man of insight and sensibility, it hurts him that his family should see him poorly clothed and *shod*, abject and submissive, wretched and *downtrod*, as does their grief at having nothing by way of food that's *tasty* nor by way of clothes that's *comfy*, at being unable to raise his son as he would have *desired*, unable to visit any town but the one in which he was *sired*, for that is his cradle and his *tomb*, his prison and sole dwelling *room*. In addition, he is the object of the designs of his leader in religion, and a stick on which any may lean who has more money than *he*, or any ruler or wielder of *authority*. He barely escapes the snare set for him by the one before he falls into the trap set by the other, and should one evil pass him *by*, he'll find another, yet greater, *nigh*. Given his burdens and lack of *education*, he finds no escape for himself or for any *relation*. Should he ever desire to follow a path for his family that's of his own choosing and he believes *correct*, but which is not what his imam, emir, or other high-ranking person would *elect*, he may not be spared a fine, or the lopping of his *nose*, or the breaking of his neck, and in no time his friends will be his enemies, his boon companions his dogged *foes*. In short, he's a pawn to *subjection*, a prisoner to *supplication*."

Said a companion, who held that what the former had outlined was correct, "Indeed, we may say with *certitude* that there is no abjection worse than *servitude*. Now, after all this scrutiny and *reflection*, interrogation and *investigation*, I see that the happiest of men in *kind* is he to whom God has allotted wealth, and a good *mind*, and who makes it his habit to travel to foreign *places* and observe new *races*. Each day some fresh matter he *discovers*[173] new **1.9.6**

قد استوعب فحوى مقاله * واعتقد ما ذهب اليه انه من فَنَده وضلاله * لقد زغت قصدا * ولم تقل رشدا * اوليس المتعرّض للسفر * بَلْوَ عناّء وخطر * اذ كثيرًا ما يمنيه بامراض شديدة * تغييرُ الهوآء عليه والاحوال غير المعهودة * واضطرارُه اَن يطعم ما يعافه * ويشرب ما به ادنافه * فيكون آكلا لما ياكل بدنه * ويُذْهب وَسَنه * هذه الافرنج تاتى الى بلادنا فينغّصهم عدم وجود الخنزير فيها * وخلوها عن السلاحف والارانب وما يضاهيها * اذ يزعمون انهم يخلطون شحم الخنزير ودمه فى كل صُبة وحَسُوّ وحَلْوآ * ويتخذون من لحم السلاحف مرقا به شفآ من كل دآء * ويعيبون علينا ان لبننا غير ضَيِحٌ ولا ممذوق * وخبزنا مملوح وطعامنا غير مزعوق * وان مآنا غير ممزوج بالجير * وخمرنا غير مصبوغة بالعقاقير * وانّا نذبح الحيوانات ذبحا وناكل لحمها غريضا * وهم يخنقونها خنقا وياكلونه دائدا انيضا * وان جوّنا غير ذي دَجْن * ومطرنا غير دائم الهَتن * وان سمآءنا غير مُحْلِسة * وارضنا غير مطليّ وجهها بالرجيع والروث وسائر الاشيآ المنجّسة * فَبُقولُنا غير مسيخة * واثمارنا غير مليخة * وان شتآنا لا يدوم ثلثى العام * وصيفنا لا يُسمَع فيه رعد ذو اِرزام * فاذا جآء احدهم الى بلادنا ليتعلم لغتنا ومكث بين اظهرنا عشر سنين * ثم رجع وهو من اجهل الجاهلين * احال الذنب على الهوا * فقال انه مُنى منه بالحمّى والجَوَى * او بالاسهال المفرط * والسعال المقنط * هذا وان من جهل لسان قوم وهو فيهم * لم يمكنه ان يعرف عاداتهم واخلاقهم واستوى عنده ظاهرهم وخافيهم * فيرى عندهم ما يرى دون علم * ويسمع ما يسمع من غير فهم * فلم يكن لذى السياحة بُدٌّ من اتخاذ ترجمان * واعتماده عليه فى كل خطب وشان * ولا يلبث ان يسيئ به الظن * ويرى ان له عليه المَنّ * ولو انه حاول ان يستغنى عنه لفاته معرفة الاحوال * وبات بين القوم ذا وحشة وبلبال *

homelands of every sort and new *brothers*." Said one who'd understood his *tenor*, and attributed his views to dotage and *error*, "You've gone off track as you well *know*, and what you say is not thought *through*. The *lot* of any exposed to travel is suffering and danger, is it *not*? With the change of air and strange surroundings, awful diseases often *strike*, not to mention that he's forced to drink things that bring chronic sickness and to eat what he doesn't *like*. Thus he consumes what eats his body *away* and drives any wink of slumber from his *eye*. When these Franks come to our lands, their mood is ruined by the absence of *swine*, as by their innocence of turtle, rabbit, and other creatures of this sort to which they *incline*, for they claim to mix the grease and blood of the pig into each dish, every soup, and all their *sweets*, and make from turtle flesh a broth that all ills *treats*. They fault us because our milk's neither watered nor thinned, our bread too salty, our food not with salt *saturated*, our water not mixed with chalk, our wine not *adulterated*, because we slaughter our animals by cutting their throats and eat the meat fresh, while they strangle theirs and eat it wormy and almost *raw*, because our weather's never overcast, our rain's not always pelting down and it doesn't always *pour*, because our land's not covered with a *tilth* of excrement, dung, and other *filth*. Our legumes they say are *tasteless*, our fruits *flavorless*. They blame us that our winter doesn't last two-thirds of the *year* and in our summers no booming thunder fills the *ear*. Having made their way to our land to learn our *tongue* and after living among us a decade only to return as ignorant of it as they *come*, they blame the *weather* and say, 'It gave me consumption and *fever*, or terrible *diarrhea*, or a cough that drove me to *despair*.' Moreover, because of the foreigner's ignorance of the language of those among whom he *dwells*, he cannot learn their customs and ways and one and the same to him are their outer and their inner *selves*. He sees what he sees and learns nothing, hears what he hears and understands *nought*; thus the traveler has no choice but to hire a dragoman, depending on him for business of every *sort*. Soon, however, he develops an unappreciative *attitude* and decides the man seeks to burden him with a debt of *gratitude*. Should he try to dispense with him, however, he can no longer the meaning of events *discern*, and he lives on among the people, a victim of loneliness and *concern*. He may yearn to see his family, to be reunited with his *kin*, in which case longing will make him sick, separation

وربما حن الى رؤية اهله * والاجتماع بشمله * فأذنفه الحنين * واضناه بَيْنُ
الخَدِين * وانما يطيب السفر ما اذا اتفق انسان مع نِدٍّ له نَوِىّ * وصديق نِجىّ *
وكانا عارفين بلغات كثيرة * وقلوبهما خالية من علاقة الحبّ بالقلب والبصيرة *
وهيهات ان يتفق اثنان على راى واحد * وان تتمّ لذة من دون مانع جاهد *
وهمّ عاصد * فقال اقل الحاضرين رشدا وفضلا * واكثرهم هزلا * ياقوم * ١،٩،٧
انى قائل قولا ولا لوم * ان اسعد الناس واحظاهم * واترفهم وارضاهم *
البغىّ الجميلة التى تفتح بابها لقاصدها * وتبيح نفسها لمراودها * فانها تغتنم انس
زائرها وماله * وتتبلُه بحبّها حتى يرى ذلّه فيها عِزًّا له * ومتى تمكنت من نفر
يبذلون لها العَيْن * ويكفونها موئنة الاطيبين * فلا تحتاج بعدها الى البحث عن
مراود في المسالك * والتعرّض للمكاره والمهالك * فاذا هى شاخت وجدت
مما ادّخرته فى صبائها ما تنفق منه عن سعة * وما تكفّر به عن سيّئاتها السالفة
فتعيش فى دعة * ويثنى عليها الناس بالتوبة الناصعة * والمعيشة الواسعة *
والانسان * مطبوع على النسيان * لا يبالي الّا بما هو كائن لا بما كان * ولا
سيما اذا كان الحاضر يجدى نفعا جزيلا * ويُسرًا مأمولا * وكفى بائمّة الدين اذا
نالوا منها العطايا الوافره * والصلات المتواترة * ان ينشروا عليها احسن الثنا *
ويبرّؤها من كل فحش وخنى * فلها منهم على كلّ صلة صلوات * وعلى كل
دعوة دعوات * فمن مارانى في ذلك فليسال قرينته * ويكظم ضغينته * ريثما
اقيم له على ذلك البراهين * ممن غبر وبقى من العالمين * فلما سمعت الجماعة ١،٩،٨
دعواه * ولحنت مغزاه * ضحكوا من هَذَيانه * وراوا ان الجواب على بُهتانه *
على طريقة الجدال انما هو من وضع الشى فى غير صِوانه * فاضربوا عنه صفحا *
وقالوا له قبحا لرايك وشقحا * فلو كان اهل صقع على رايك لفسدت الارض *

from the beloved *thin*. One can only have fun being *peripatetic* if one travels with a companion *sympathetic*, a confidant with whom one can share a *lot*—especially if each is *polyglot*, fancy-free, preconceptions quite *forgot*. How difficult it is, though, for *two* to agree on any one *view*, or for there to be any pleasure without strenuous *objection* or constraining *reflection*!"

Now spoke the least of those present in terms of good sense and scholarly *renown*, the one most likely to play the *clown*. "Dear *friends*!" said he. "I have something to say—forgive me if it *offends*. The happiest and most favored of persons, the best-off among them and most *content*, is the beautiful whore who opens her door to visitors and makes herself available to any who accosts her, for *rent*. She wins her visitor's companionship as well as his *wealth* and drives him so wild with love he thinks groveling before her an honor to *himself*. Once she has a *band* of men who'd sell their eyes for her in *hand*, they provide her with all she needs of 'the two best things,'[174] and she's no longer obliged to look for custom on the *roads* or be exposed to anything that harms or *discommodes*. When she grows old, she finds she'd saved a lot when young, and so, with open hand, she *spends* and, with the money, for her earlier misdeeds she makes *amends*, living blamelessly the *while*, all praising her for her radiant repentance and large *style*. *Man* is by nature *amn*esiac. He thinks only of what's present, not what's passed, especially if the current situation yield a mighty *dividend* and the good life on which all hopes *depend*. The clergy have only to praise her high and low, to exonerate her of all debaucheries and *abominations*, to be given non-stop gifts and abundant *donations*. With each *present* she gets from them *prayers*, with each *banquet blessings*. Let any who doesn't believe me, ask his consort and master his *irritation*, till such time as I can furnish proofs from both this and any earlier *generation*." 1.9.7

When the company had heard his *claim* and seen through to his hidden *aim*, they laughed at his raving and decided that the correct response to his misleading words, simply for the sake of the *wrangle*, should be to address the matter from a different *angle*, so they snubbed him, saying, "Shame on your opinion and God damn you! If all the people of a place sang the same *refrain*, the land would become corrupted, honor be blighted, and no vestige or smidgen of decent behavior *remain*. But the fault is the cup's, which has 1.9.8

وبار العِرض ولم يبق من الصلاح اثر ولا بَرَض * وانما اللوم على الكاس التى ذهبت بلبّك * وكشفت عن فساد مذهبك * وقبح اِرْبك * ولعلك تهتدى الى الرشاد اذا افقت من خمارك * وتبيّن لك فظاعة هترك واستهتارك * فراى ان السكوت له اسلم عاقبة من المحاورة والمجاوبة * والمناقرة والمغاضبة * وان الجمهور يغلب الفرد * وان كانوا على ضلال وكان هو على هُدًى وقصد * فاستف تفنيدهم * وخشى وعيدهم * وتفرقوا ولم يجمعوا رايهم على اىّ الناس اسعد * واىّ عيش ارغد * اذ راوا دون كل حرفه نَغَصا * ومع كل حالة غَنَصا * وفى كل اكلة مَغَصا * وقد فاتهم من احوال الناس كثير مما ضاق وقتهم عن ذكره * كما ضاق هذا الفصل عن احصا كل ما اوردوه وعن حصره * فقف على هذا القدر الذى ذكرته * وسرمعى الى استئناف قصة مَن غادرته * وعليكم السلام *

made off with your *brain* and revealed the corrupt thinking of your *kind*, the ignominy of your mischief-ridden *mind*. Perhaps, when you sober up, you'll be guided to what's *right*, and, after your gross falsehood and irresponsibility, see the *light*." The man decided then that silence was a safer *course* for him than discussion and back-and-*forth*, or bickering and getting cross, and that the mass outranks the *one*, even if the latter's well-guided and full of wisdom, the former in the *wrong*. He swallowed therefore their rebuttals and took fearful account of their *monitions* and the company dispersed without having come to a consensus as to who is the happiest of men or which the most easeful of *conditions*, finding that for each trade there was a fly in the *ointment*, for every state a *disappointment*, and every dish was accompanied by its own form of *indigestion*, albeit to many a condition of men they'd paid no *attention*, the time being too short to allow its *mention*, just as this chapter has been too short to allow a *computation* of all the arguments they made or their *enumeration*. Halt with me, then, at this portion that I've *outlined*, and let us return together to the story of the one I've *left behind*. Farewell.

الفصل العاشر

في اغضاب شوافن * وانشاب براثن

السجع للمولف كالرِجل من خشب للماشى * فينبغى لى ان لا اتوكا عليه فى ١،١٠،١
جميع طرق التعبير لئلا تضيق بى مذاهبه * او يرمينى فى ورطة لا مناص لى منها * ولقد رايت ان كلفة السجع اشق من كلفة النظم * فانه لا يشترط فى ابيات القصيدة من الارتباط والمناسبة ما يشترط فى الفقر المسجعة * وكثيرا ما ترى الساجع قد دارت به القافية عن طريقه التى سلك فيها حتى تبلغه الى ما لم يكن يرتضيه لوكان غير متقيد بها * والغرض هنا ان نغزل قصتنا على وجه سائغ لاى قارى كان * ومن احب ان يسمع الكلام كله مسجعا مقفى ومرشحا بالاستعارات ومحسنا بالكنايات فعليه بمقامات الحريرى او بالنوابغ للزمخشرى *

فنقول ان صاحبنا الفارياق بعد اقامته مدة على الحالة التى ذكرناها * جرى بينه ٢،١٠،١
وبين جده من النزاع والمناقشات ما اوجب عليه ترك ماكان فيه واقتفاء طريق آخر من طرق المعاش * فتاح له ان يكون معلما لاحدى بنات الامرا وكانت ذات طلعة بهية * وشمائل مرضية * تامة الظرف * ناعسة الطرف * ولكن ليس المراد بذلك انها كانت لا تبصر من يحبها كما يكون من به نعاس * وانما المعنى انها ذابلته * حتى ولا هذه العبارة مفصحة بما[1] اريد ان اقوله * فانها توهم إنها[2] كانت

١ ١٨٥٥: ثما [كذا]. ٢ ١٨٥٥: إانها [كذا].

Chapter 10

Angering Women Who Dart Sideways Looks, and Claws like Hooks

Rhymed prose is to the writer as a wooden leg to the walker. I must be careful therefore not to rest all my weight on it every time I go for a stroll down the highways of literary expression lest its vagaries end up cramping my style or it toss me into a pothole from which I cannot crawl. Indeed, it seems to me that the difficulties of rhymed prose are greater than those of poetry, for the requirements regarding linking and correspondence set for lines of verse are fewer than those for the periods of rhymed prose. In rhymed prose, the rhyme often leads the writer from his original path to a place he would never have wanted to reach had he not been subjected to its constraints. Here our aim is to weave our story in a way acceptable to every reader. Anyone who likes to listen to language that's entirely *rhymed* and *chimed*, with metaphors and metonymies adorned and *primed*, should go to the *Maqāmāt* of al-Ḥarīrī[175] or the *Nawābigh*[176] of al-Zamakhsharī. 1.10.1

Thus we declare: after our friend the Fāriyāq had lived for a while in the state that we've described, he was obliged by the conflicts and quarrels that occurred between him and his grandfather[177] to abandon what he was at and adopt another means of making a living. Fate ordained he should become tutor to the daughter of an emir, and a bonny lass was *she*, her features pleasing to a *degree*, with a body in which naught was *awry*, and a sleepy *eye*[178] (which doesn't mean that she was unable to see anyone who loved her, as would be the case with one who was actually sleepy; it means that she had an eye that was "dried up."[179] And even that doesn't fully express what I'm trying to say, because it gives the false impression that *she* was dried up, when, in fact, she was tender and full of sap. No, what I'm trying to get at is 1.10.2

ذابلة مع انها كانت غضة بضة * بل المقصود ان نقول انها كانت كانها تنظر عن تحشيف * ولكن مادة حشف لا تعجبني * فان فيها معاني اليبوسة والخساسة والرداءة وشي اخر تجل الملاح عن ذكره * بل المراد انها كانت تكسر جفنيها عند النظر * ولا الكسر ايضا لائق بها * فلا ادرى كيف الحن للقارى ما اردت *

١،١٠،٣ ولعل الاوفق ان يقال انها كانت ترمي بسهام عن عينيها * ولم يكن صغر سنها مانعا من تتبيل من ينظرها * فان القلب يعلق بهوى الصغيرة الجدّاء * كما يعلق بهوى الكبيرة الوطباء * اذ ليس كل عشق مودّيا الى الدَّعارة * فقد عشق الناس الرسوم والاطلال والاثار * والاشكال والديار * ومنهم من عشق لرؤيته كفّا مخضّبا او عقيصة شعر او ثوبا او سراويلات او تكة او نحو ذلك * واعرف من احب هرة امراة فكان يلاعبها ويخيّل له الغرام انه ملاعب صاحبتها * وكثيرا ما كانت تنشب فيه اظفارها وتدميه * وهو يستعذب ذلك ويستحليه * اما لاستعذاب العذاب في هوى المحبوب * او لاعتقاده ان مداعبة النسآء ايضا لا تخلو من خدش و ادمآء * فكون الجرح منهن اصالة او وكالة انما هو شي واحد * وقد سئل احد العشّاق عن مبلغ الوجد منه فقال كنت ارتاح للريح اذا مرّت على نتن مقبلة من صوب المحبوب * هذا وان عشق اهل تلك البلاد اكثره على هذا النمط * اى ان العاشق منهم يكلف باثر من محبوبه كمنديل او زهرة او رسالة وخصوصا بنصّة شعر فيشمّه ويضمه ويقبله ويعانقه كما قيل

الشِعر مثل الشَّعر داعية الهوى   والشَّعر مثل الشِعر ذُخر يُذخَرُ
من غاب عنك فلست تنظره سوى   بالشِعر او بالشَّعر وهو الاكثر

١،١٠،٤ فان قيل انهم انما عشقوا ذلك طمعا فى وصال الحبيب الذى تفضّل بهذه النعم لا

that she would seem to be, as we say, "given to looking through half-closed eyes [*taḥshīf*]"—but the whole entry for *ḥ-sh-f* in the dictionary is repugnant to me: it contains the senses "dryness," "baseness," and "mediocrity," plus something else that pretty girls are too dignified to speak of.[180] What I really mean is that, when looking, she would open her eyelids a crack—but even "crack" isn't the right thing here. In the end, I don't know how to to convey to the reader what I'm trying to get at. Perhaps the most appropriate way of saying it would be "she shot arrows from her eyes.")

Her youth was no impediment to her "tenderizing" a man's heart with her glance, for the heart attaches itself as easily to the small-breasted girl as to the big-busted grown woman, not every passion being a prelude to prostitution. Men have fallen in love with pictures, with the remains of the beloved's campfire, with her footprints in the *sand*, with outward forms, with a beloved *land*. Some have fallen in love at the sight of a hennaed hand, a lock of hair, a dress, a pair of drawers, a drawstring, or whatever. I know a man who fell in love with a woman's cat and would play with it, led by passion to imagine that he was playing with its owner; often it would fasten its claws in him and draw blood, which pleased and delighted him, either because he took pleasure in being tormented as part of his love for the beloved or because of his belief that toying with a woman was likely to lead to scratches and blood-letting so in the end it would come to the same thing, whether the wound was inflicted personally or by proxy. One who had loved was asked to what lengths his ardor had gone and he said, "I used to find pleasure in the wind if, coming to me from the direction of the beloved, it carried with it the smell of carrion." Most loves of the people of these lands are of this sort: when one of them is in love he goes into ecstasies over anything associated with the beloved, such as a handkerchief, a flower, a letter, or, especially, a lock of hair, which he will sniff and hug, kiss, turn over in his hands, and hold to his chest, in accordance with the words of the poet who said, 1.10.3

Verses, like hair, are summoners to love,
A lock of hair, like a line of verse, a relic to be hoarded.
The only way to feel him close when he's not there
Is through a verse or through a lock (the latter the less oft accorded).

If it be said that they only love such relics out of hope of union with the beloved who has been so generous as to give them these favors, not because 1.10.4

كلفا بها من حيث هى هى * قلت ما المانع من ان تعشق الصغيرة طمعا فى ان تصير كبيرة * ما اضيق العيشَ لولا فُسحة الامل * ورُبَّ اَمَل احلى من فوز * وقد علم اهل الدراية اَنّ مَن حَرَمَه الله من الجمال لغاية لا يعلمها الا هو عوّضه عنه زيادةَ قصاص له بحدّة الفكر والبصيرة وشدة التصوّر والتخيّل ودقة الحَدَس فيكون اسرع الى العشق واكثر حرصا على اهل الجمال * اذ الانسان كلّما بعد عن الشى المقصود كان توقانه اليه اكثر وتولّعه به اشدّ * والمراد من ذلك كله ان نقول ان الفارياق كان يعلم من صغره انه بمعزل عن الجمال * وانه من صبآئه كان يعظّم اهله ويمزّيهنّ على غيرهنّ وان القبيح معذور على عشق المليح كما قال الشاعر *

وقـالوا ياقبيح الوجـه تهوى　　مليحـا دونـه السُمْر الرقـاقُ
فقـلت وهـل انا الا اديب　　فكيـف يفوتنى هـذا الطباقُ

قالوا * او اقول انا عنهم * وقد يكون عشق الصغير كبيرا كما يكون عشق الكبير صغيرا * فان الصغير لما كان غير ذى رشد يردّه عن الاسترسال والتمادى فى هواه كان هذا الاسترسال معقبا للجموح دون حد * الا ترى ان الصغير اذا ولع بشى من اللعب واللهو فانه يتهتّك فيه وينهمك غاية ما يكون * فكيف به اذا جنح الى شئ هو اقوى من كلّ ما يستميل الطبع ويشوق النفس * نعم ان الكبير يُقدّر[1] منافع ما يقصده من معشوقه اكثر من الصغير ولذلك يكون حرصه عليه ابلغ وطلبه له اكثر * غير ان عزّة نفسه وسَوْرة طباعه ونُهيته قد تمنعه من ان يسلّم عنان مشيئته للهوى * فيكون فى طريق ميله وتوقانه تارة مقدّماً رجلا وتارة موخرا اخرى * والصغير متى ما استرسل استسهل * ١،١٠،٥

١ ١٨٥٥: يَقدر.

they feel any fondness for them in and of themselves, I reply, "There's nothing wrong in loving a young girl in the hope and expectation that she will grow into a mature woman. Without hope's broad horizon, how narrow life would be, and many a hope is sweeter than a triumph. People of experience know that he to whom God has denied beauty for a purpose of which he is unaware is more than equally recompensed by Him with sharpness of intellect and insight, powers of visualization and imagination, and acuity of intuition, and as a result is quicker to fall in love and more solicitous of those who possess beauty, for the further a person finds himself from the desired object, the greater his longing for it and the more powerful his infatuation with it." The point of all of this is to provide an opportunity to say that the Fāriyāq was aware, from an early age, that he was himself far removed from beauty, that from his childhood he venerated those who possessed it and favored them above all others, and that the ugly man is to be excused for loving pretty girls. As the poet says,

"Ugly fellow," they asked, "wouldst thou love
  A pretty girl, access to whom dusky slaves will stymie?"
"Am I not a literary man?" I replied.
  "Never could I let such a 'contrast' get by me!"[181]

("They asked"—or I do on their behalf.)[182]

Young love can be big, too, just as grown-up love can be little. A young 1.10.5
person, being still without the emotional and intellectual maturity that might inhibit him from the unaffected and extreme expression of his affections, may be led by such unaffectedness to a wildness of passion that knows no restraint. Have you not observed how, when a child becomes infatuated with some toy or game, he may become intemperate in its pursuit and abandon himself to it entirely? How much more so, then, if he inclines to that thing that is stronger than anything else to which temper may incline or for which soul may yearn? True, the adult calculates the benefits of what he wants from his lover more carefully than the child and is therefore more solicitous of him and demands more from him; however, self-esteem, strength of character, and the instinct for self-preservation may prevent him from surrendering the reins of his will to love; thus on the road of his longing and desire he takes one step forward, one back. The child, having once abandoned himself to his natural spontaneity, believes that everything will be easy.

وبعد فقد نذرت على نفسى ان اكتب كتابا * وان اودعه كل ما راق لخاطرى من القول سديدا كان او غير سديد * فانى اعتقدت ان غير السديد عندى قد يكون عند غيرى سديدا كما تحقّق لدى عكسه * فان شئت فَاذْعن او لا فليس هذا الوقت وقت العناد والخلاف * والحاصل ان الفارياق لبث يعلم سيّدته الصغيرة وجعل من دأبه ان يتودّد اليها باغضآء النظر على اصلاح غلطها * بل لم يكن يرى ان صاحبة هذا الجمال يجوز ردّها فتاخَّرت هى فى العلم وتقدم هو فى الهوس * فمما قال فيها * ١،١٠،٦

بروحى مَن اعلّمه وقلبى　　اسير هواه لن يسطيع صبرا
اغار عليه وجدا من حروف　　يفوه بها فتلثم منه ثغرا

والحمد لله على كون اللغة العربية خالية عن اليآء الفارسية والقا الافرنجية والا لزادت غَيْرَة صاحبنا وربما كان ذلك سببا فى جنونه * فان الغيرة والجنون يخرجان من مخرج واحد كما افاده المشايخ الراسخون فى الزواج * وهنا دقيقة وهى ان بعض ١،١٠،٧
العتاول جمع عِتْول وهو من لا خير عنده للنسآء يستثقل المونث فى الغزل والنسيب فيجعله مذكرا وبعضهم يضمره * وعليه قول الفارياق اعلّمه * والظاهر ان المقدَّر فى ذلك لفظة شخص * فياليت هذا الحرف كان فى لغتنا مونّثا كما هو فى الفرنساوية والطليانية حتى لا يجد الناسب مَحِيْدا عن التانيث * فاما تعليم نسآء بلادنا القرآة ١،١٠،٨
والكتابة فعندى انه محمدة بشرط استعماله على شروطه * وهو مطالعة الكتب التى تهذّب الاخلاق وتحسن الاملآء * فان المراة اذا اشتغلت بالعلم كان لها به شاغل عن استنباط المكايد واختراع الحيل كما سياتى ذكر ذلك * ولا باس بالمتزوّجات بقرآة كتابى هذا وامثاله * لانه كما ان من الوان الطعام ما يباح للمتزوجين دون

To return to our topic: I committed myself to writing a book that would be a repository for every idea that appealed to me, relevant or irrelevant, for it seemed to me that what was irrelevant to me might be relevant to someone else, and vice versa. If you're of a mind, submit—if not, so be it: this is no time for quibbling and quarreling. The long and the short of it is that the Fāriyāq continued to tutor his young mistress, making a habit of gaining her affection by forbearing to correct her mistakes. In fact, he couldn't see how anyone so beautiful could be refused anything, as a result of which she fell behind in her education while he progressed in his obsession. One poem he wrote about her went as follows: **1.10.6**

My soul I'd give, and heart, for him I teach!
    The prisoner of his love ne'er can patience know.
Passion makes me jealous of every letter
    He mouths and that kisses his lips as he does so.

Thank God the Arabic language lacks the Persian *p* and Frankish *v,*[183] or our friend's jealousy would have been even greater and might have driven him insane: jealousy and madness issue from the same place, as learned scholars familiar with marriage tell us.

This brings us to a nice point, to wit, that certain of the people known as *ʿatāwil* (plural of *ʿitwal* and meaning "men who can see no good in women") find it irksome to use the feminine gender in amorous and erotic poetry and so turn it into the masculine instead, and others invoke it only implicitly. The words of the Fāriyāq "for him I teach" conform to this practice.[184] It seems likely that the implicit referent of such masculine pronouns is the word *shakhṣ* (person). Would that the word referred to in our language by the pronoun were feminine, as it is in French and Italian, so that the erotic poet would find no impediment to using that gender![185] **1.10.7**

On the question of whether the women of our country should be taught reading and writing, in my opinion, it's a good idea, provided it be according to certain conditions, namely that reading be confined to the perusal of books that refine their moral conduct and improve their writing skills, for if women are kept busy learning, they will find no time to work up schemes and concoct stratagems, as we shall see below. There would be nothing wrong with married women reading this book of mine or its like, for, just as certain sorts of food are reserved for married people only, so it is with ideas. **1.10.8**

غيرهم فكذلك هى الوان الكلام * والظاهر ان اللغة العربية شَرَك للهوى اذ يوجد
فيها من العبارات الشائقة المتصبّية ما لا يوجد فى غيرها * فمن قرأت مثلا فى شرح ٩،١٠،١
المشارق لابن مالك ان مراتب العشق ثمانية ادناها الاستحسان وينشأ عن النظر والسماع ثم يقوى بالتفكّر فيصير مودّة وهى الميل للمحبوب (اى المحبوبة) * ثم يقوى فيصير محبة وهى ائتلاف الارواح * ثم يقوى فيصير خُلّة وهى تمكّن المحبة فى القلب حتى تسقط بينهما السرائر * ثم يقوى فيصير هوى بحيث لا يخالطه تلوّن ولا يداخله تغيّر * ثم يقوى فيصير عشقا وهو الافراط فى المحبة حتى لا يخلو فكر العاشق عن المعشوق (اى المعشوقة) * وانه يقوى فيصير تتيّما * وفى هذه الحالة لا ترضى نفسه سوى صورة معشوقه (اى معشوقته) * ثم يقوى فيصير ولهاً وهو الخروج عن الحدّ حتى لا يدرى ما يقول ولا اين يذهب وحينئذ تعجز الاطبآء عن مداواته * قلت وان من انواعه ايضا الصبابة وهى رقّة الهوى والشوق * والغَرام وهو الحب المستأسِر * والهُيام وهو الجنون من العشق * والجَوَى وهو الهوى الباطن * والشوق وهو نزاع النفس * والتَوَقان وهو بمعناه * والوجد وهو ما يجده المحبّ من هوى المحبوب (اى المحبوبة) * والكَلَف وهو الولوع * والشَغَف وهو اصابة الحُب الشَغاف اى غلاف القلب او حجابه او حبّته او سُوَيدآءه * والشَغَف وهو ان يغشى الحبُّ شَعَفة القلب وهو راسه عند معلَّق النِياط منه * والشَعَف وهو بمعناه * والتدليه وهو ذهاب الفواد عشقا * لم تمالك ان تحس بهذه المراتب السنية كلها حالا بعد حال * بخلاف لغات العجم فانها لا يوجد فيها الّا لفظة واحدة بمعنى المحبّة يطلقونها على الخالق والمخلوق *

It seems that the Arabic language is a snare for love, for it contains words of passion and amorousness found in no other.

Any woman who reads, in Ibn Mālik's *Sharḥ al-mashāriq*,[186] for example, that the stages of love are eight—the lowest of which is liking, which has its starting point in seeing and hearing and is then strengthened through cogitation, which turns into friendly regard, which is an inclination toward the beloved person (meaning the beloved *woman*), which in turn becomes stronger and turns into affection, which is the congenial intercourse of spirits, which grows stronger and turns into intimate companionship, which is affection's taking control within the heart to the point at which the couple start to share secrets, and then grows stronger until it turns into full-blown love unmixed with shifts of mood and not subject to change, which then grows stronger until it turns into passion, which is an affection so extreme that the passionate lover's mind is never empty of thoughts of the passionately loved person (meaning the passionately loved *woman*), which then grows stronger until it turns into lovesickness, in which condition the only thing that can satisfy the lover's soul is the image of the person whom he passionately loves (by whom I mean, of course, the *woman* he passionately loves), which then grows stronger until it turns into love-crazed distractedness, which is when he goes so far over the edge that he no longer knows what he's saying or where he's going, at which point the doctors are powerless to treat him—and noting in addition, as I do, that there are also different varieties of love, such as *ṣabābah*, which is love and longing in their most delicate form; *gharām*, which is love as surrender; *huyām*, which is insanity born of passion; *jawā*, which is the love one holds inside oneself; *shawq*, which is the struggle with the self; *tawaqān*, which means the same; *wajd*, which is the affection that the lover receives from the beloved person (by which I mean, again, of course, the beloved *woman*); *kalaf*, which is craving; *shaghaf*, which is what happens when love reaches the pericardium, which is to say the tissue that enwraps the heart or the fat that surrounds it or the kernel or core of it; *shaʿaf*, which is when love coats the *shaʿafah* of the heart, which is the top of it, where the aorta is attached, or *shaʿf*, which means the same; and *tadlīh*, which is when one loses one's mind from love—will be able to refrain from experiencing all these sublime stages one condition after the other. This contrasts with the languages of the non-Arabs, in which there is only one word meaning love, which they apply to Creator and created alike. 1.10.9

وقد يظهر لى ان كثيرا من الصفات المحمودة فى الرجال تكون مذمومة فى النسآء ١٠،١٠،١
كالكرم مثلا فان كرم الرجل يغطى جميع عيوبه وهو مذموم فى المراة * وقس
على ذلك النُكر والدهآ والاطرآ والفروسة والشجاعة والحماسة والصلابة والخشونة
والهمّة الى المراتب السامية والامور الشاقة والاسفار البعيدة والنيّات النائية
والمطامع المتعذرة وغير ذلك * والعلّة فى ذلك كون المراة تميل بالطبع الى الشطط
ومجاوزة الحدّ * ودليله فى من تميل الى العبادة والنسك فانها لا تقف فى ذلك
على اَمَد بل تتمادى فيه حتى تتهوّس وتتخبّل فتدّعى المعجزات والكرامات وتعمد الى
الرُؤى والاحلام وتُخيَّل لها انّ ملكا يناجيها * وهاتفا يناغيها * وانها تقيم
بدعائها الاموات * وتحيى الرُفات * وربما قتلت اولادها على صِغَر ابتغآء دخولهم
الجنة بغير حساب * او ولدت توأمين فادّعت انهما من غير اب * وفى من
مالت الى الهوى فانها تترك اباها وامها اللذين ولداها وربّياها وتقبل تجرى فى
اثر رجل لا تعرف من صفاته شيا سوى كونه ذكَرا * فكل ما كلفت به المراة
كانت فيه اكثر تماديا من الرجل * فكلفهن بالقرآة لا ادرى اين يكون مصيره *
والحامل لها على هذا الغلو والشطط انما هو معرفتها من نفسها انها اقوى على
اللذّات من الرجل * فزيادة اطاقتها لذلك زادت فى تماديها فيه * ومنه سرى فى
غيره من الاطوار والشؤون والاحوال الطارئة وفى بعض الغريزية ايضاً * وذلك
كالكلام والضحك والسَبح والحركة * وما قلّ منه فيها فى بعض الاحوال فانك
تراه زائدا فى البعض الاخر زيادة فوق القياس * ولعل كلامى هذا يسوء النسآء
اذا سمعن به وهنّ بين الرجال * لكنى اعلم عين اليقين انهن يضحكن له فى اكمامهنّ
استحسانا وتعجّبا * حتى كانى بهن يحسبن انى عشت برهة من الدهر امراة حتى ١١،١٠،١
امكن لى معرفة سرائرهن ثم مسخنى الله تبارك وتعالى رجلا * او انى علمت ذلك

It seems to me that many qualities considered praiseworthy in men are considered blameworthy in women. Take liberality, for example. Liberality in a man covers all faults, but the same quality is considered blameworthy in a woman, and the same applies to truculence, craftiness, praising people hypocritically, horsemanship, bravery, heroism on the field of battle, callousness, and coarseness, as well as zeal in the pursuit of high office, difficult affairs, distant journeys, hard-to-achieve purposes, impossible ambitions, and so on. The reason for this is that the woman inclines by nature to deviation and excess, as evidenced by those of them who develop a taste for worship and self-abnegation. Such women never know where to draw the line; on the contrary, they go to such lengths that they become obsessed and demented, claiming miracles and supernatural gifts, getting caught up in visions and dreams and imagining that angels are speaking to them and voices whispering in their *ears*, or that they can bring mortal remains back to life and raise the dead with their *prayers*. Sometimes they kill their children when they're still young, in the hope that they will enter Heaven without being held to *account*, or give birth to twins and claim they were conceived with no father *about*. Some have a weakness for love and leave their mothers and fathers who bore them and raised them and run off after a man of whose qualities they know nothing except that he's a male. Everything, then, that women set their hearts on they go to greater lengths over than men, and if they set their hearts on reading, who knows where it will end? What drives them to such exaggeration and excess is their innate awareness that they are stronger in resisting sensual pleasures than men; having extra capacity in this area, they go to excess in it, and from there it has spread to other states, affairs, and contingent conditions, as also to certain instinctual matters. These states and so forth include talking and laughing, bustling about and physical exercise. What one of them lacks in a particular area you'll find immeasurably compensated for in another. What I say may displease women if they come to hear of it when they're among men, but I'm certain they'll laugh behind their hands at it in approbation and amazement. **1.10.10**

It even seems to me that they'll decide that I must have lived for a while as a woman and learned their secrets, until such time as God, blessed and almighty, turned me into a man, or that I learned these things from Hind and Suʿād, Mayyah and Zaynab,[187] when, as a youth, I would write them love sonnets and lie to them that I'd gone without sleep all *night* and, complaining **1.10.11**

من هند وسعاد وزينب وميّة حين كنت اشبّب بهنّ وانا فتًى واكذب عليهنّ بقولى لهن انى حُرمت الكرى * واجريت على نواهنّ عِبَرا * وانى قد فُتن لبى * وفارقنى قلبى * لا جرم انه لم يفارقنى قط * ولو فارقنى مرة لما رجع الىّ ابدا * لانى طالما ادخلت عليه هموما واحزانا لم تكن لِتَهمَّ احدا من الناس فى بلادى * اذكنت احزن لتعصّى معنى من المعانى علىّ واحاول اختراع شى من البديع لم يكن احد سبقنى اليه * ظانّا انه يقوم للناس مقام هذه المخترعات التى يُزهَى بها الكون عصرنا هذا فلم يتهيّا لى فكنت ابيت الليل فى ياس وكرب * معاذ الله لم تكلّمنى وما كلّمت هند وانما عرفت ما عرفت من الاحلام الصادقة اذكنت ابيّت وانا مخلص لله الانابة والقنوت * فان لم يصدّقنى فليبتن ليلة او ليلتين تائبات قانتات مثلى وانا ضامن لهن انه يهبط عليهن من الاحلام الصادقة ما يوقفهن على امور الرجال *

of our separation, make up maxims about my *plight*, saying my soul had been *bewitched*, my heart from its moorings become *unhitched*. In fact, we can be sure that it never left me, for if it had, it would never have returned, so often had I burdened it with cares and sorrows of a kind that had never previously bothered anyone in my country. These included mourning if a trope proved uncooperative when I tried to compose in the "novel" style[188] something that no one had ever said before, believing it would be accorded the same status as those inventions on which everyone prides himself so much these days, and it wouldn't come out right for me, causing me to spend the night in torment and despair. I swear before God, "Hind" never spoke to me and I never spoke to her. I just learned what I did from truth-telling dreams, for I spent the nights in sincere repentance and obedience to God, and if they don't believe me, let them spend a night or two in repentance and obedience as I did and I guarantee them that He'll send them down enough truth-telling dreams to provide them with a complete overview of men's affairs.

الفصل الحادى عشر

في الطويل العريض

فلنرجع الان الى الفارياق فانه هو ايضا رجع الى حرفته وهى النساخة وان كان ذلك على غير مراده * واتفق اذ ذاك ان فتيَيْن * من امرآء ذلك الصقع ارادا ان يقراا النحو على بعض النحاة وكان الفارياق يحضر الدرس وهو مكبّ على النسخ * وكان احد التلميذين بطيئا عن الفهم سريعا الى الجواب * يتثآب ويتمطّى * ويَغْرَض ويَحْطا * ويتناعس ويتقاعس * ويتفاسأ ويتعاطس * واذا خُيِّل له انه فَهِمَ مسئلة حكّ تحت ابطه * وشمّ رائحتها وكرف ثمّ تمطّق كما يتمطّق من اقْطه * ثم عربد من افتتانه * وسلق مَن وَلِيَه بلسانه * وقال اَلَا قُبحًا لذوى الخواطر البليدة * والفطن البعيدة * كيف لا يتعلم الناس كلهم فن النحو * وهو اسهل من حكّ ما تحت الحَقْو * اما والله لو كانت العلوم كلها مثله * لما غادرت منها كبيرا ولا صغيرا الا واستوعبته كله * لكنى سمعت ان النحو انما هو مفتاح للعلوم ولا يعدّ منها فلا بدّ وان يكون ١،١١،١

غيره اصعب منه * فقال معلمه لا تقل هكذا بل النحو اساس العلوم وكل العلوم مفتقرة اليه افتقار البنآء الى الاساس * الا ترى انّ اهل بلادنا لا يتعلّمون سواه ولا يعرّجون على غيره * وعندهم ان من تمكّن منه فقد تمكّن من معرفة خصائص الموجودات كلها * ولذلك لا يولّفون الا فيه * وانما يحصل الخلاف بينهم في تقديم بعض الابواب على بعض * وفى توضيح ما كان مبهما منه بادلّة وشواهد * ٢،١١،١

Chapter 11

That Which Is Long and Broad[189]

Let us now return to the Fāriyāq, just as he returned to his profession—namely, the copying of manuscripts—albeit against his will. It happened that at that time two young emirs of the region had decided to study works of grammar at the feet of a grammarian, and the Fāriyāq was present at these classes, bent over his copying. One of the two pupils was slow to understand, quick to answer. He'd yawn and stretch, fidget and fart, slack off and snore, stick out his bum and sneeze. If he thought he'd understood a point, he'd scratch himself under his armpit and smell the scent, sniffing at it with bared teeth and smacking his lips like someone savoring a piece of cottage cheese. Then, out of delight at his own cleverness, he'd kick up a rumpus and tongue-lash the one next to him, saying, "Shame indeed on those of slow *comprehension* and dim *apprehension*! How is it that not all men can master grammar's *rules*, which is easier than scratching your *balls*? If all the sciences were like *that*, I swear I'd have them down *pat*. I've heard, though, that grammar, while being 'a key to the sciences' is not regarded as one of them, so the others must be harder." 1.11.1

Then his tutor would tell him, "Say not so! Say rather, 'Grammar is the basis of the sciences' and all the rest are as much in need of it as a building is of a foundation. Have you not observed that the people of our land learn only this and do not stray from it to any other? They think that he who has a command of grammar commands a knowledge of all aspects of the universe. That's why it's the only thing they write books about and why the only disputes that arise among them are about which chapters to put before others and the clarification of the ambiguities of that science with proofs and citations. They also disagree over the latter, some saying that they're fabricated, 1.11.2

واختلفوا ايضا فى الشواهد فمن قائل انها مفتعلة ومن قائل انها ضرورة او شاذّة بيد ان المآل واحد * وهو ان العالم لا يسمَّى عالما الا اذا كان متمكّنا من النحو مستقصيا لجميع دقائقه * ولا يكاد يستتبّ امر الا به * ولو قلت مثلا ضرب زيد عمر من غير رفع زيد ونصب عمرو فما يكون ضَربه حقّا ولا يصح الاعتماد على هذا الاخبار * فان حقيقة فعل الضرب متوقفة على علم كون زيد مرفوعا * وجميع اللغات التى ليس فيها علامات الرفع فهى خالية عن الافادة التامة * وانما يفهم بعض الناس بعضا من دون هذه العلامات عن دربة او اتّفاق * فلا معوّل على كتبهم وان كثرت ولا على علومهم وان جلّت * وانى وان كنت قد لقيت منه عَرَق القربة وكثيرا ما بت وبالى مشغول بِعُقْلة من عُقَله وبداهية من عراقيله * فكنت آرق ليلي كله ولا اهتدى الى وجه الصواب فيما عوص عليّ من ذلك * الّا انى استفدت منه فائدة عظيمة جعلتنى ممنونا لبنت ابى الاسود الدُئَلِي اَبد الدهر فانها هى التى كانت سببا فى استنباطه * (قلت وكذا سائر البدائع كان اصل استنباطها مسبَّباً عن النسآ)

١،١١،٣ فقال له التلميذ ما هذه الفائدة ياإستاذى * قال قد طالما كان يخامرنى الريب فى قضية خلود النفس * فكنت اميل الى ما قالته الفلاسفة من انه كل ما كان له ابتدآء فهو متناهٍ * فلما رايت النحو له ابتدآء وليس له انتهآء قست النفس عليه فزال عنى والحمد لله ذلك الابهام * ومثله او اكثر منه فى الصعوبة فنّ المعانى والبيان * فقال له التلميذ لم اسمع بذكر ذلك قطّ * قال اما انا فقد سمعت به واعرف ما يشتمل عليه * وهو المجاز والكناية والاستعارة والتورية والترصيع وغير ذلك مما ينيف على مئة نوع * وبيان ذلك مفصّلا * يستفرغ اَجَلا * وربما قضى الانسان عمره كله فى علم الاستعارات وحدها ثم يموت وهو جاهلها * او يكون قد نسى فى

١،١١،٤ آخر الكتاب او الكتب ما عرفه فى اوله * وذلك انّ من اخترع هذا العلم الجليل لم

others that they are determined by the meter or anomalous, though it all comes to the same in the end, namely that a scholar cannot be considered such unless he has acquired a command of grammar and gone deeply into all its finer points, and that almost no business can go smoothly without it. If you were to say, for example, 'Zayd struck 'Amr'[190] without putting Zayd in the nominative and 'Amr in the accusative, he would not in fact have struck him, and it would be wrong to depend on the information thus conveyed, for a true understanding of the nature of the act of striking is dependent in this instance on knowing that Zayd is in the nominative. Any language that has no markers for the nominative is utterly worthless, people understanding one another in the absence of these only by virtue of custom or convention; their books cannot therefore be relied on, however they may *multiply*, and neither can their sciences, however they *ramify*. Even though I might toil over this science by day and would often go to bed racking my brains over one of its knotty points or fiendish difficulties, I'd have to spend the whole night awake, unable to find my way to the proper solution to whatever was giving me such trouble. I did, however, derive one great benefit from it that made me eternally grateful to the daughter of Abū l-Aswad al-Du'alī (since she was one of the reasons for its invention)."[191] (To which I would add that all the other rhetorical sciences owe their existence to women, too.)

"And what was that benefit, master?" asked his pupil. Replied the tutor, 1.11.3
"I had long harbored doubts over the question of the immortality of the soul and inclined toward the dictum of the philosophers to the effect that whatever has a beginning must have an end. But when I found that grammar has an 'inchoative' but no 'terminative,' I drew an analogy between that and the soul and ceased to be confused, praise God. Similar to grammar or greater in difficulty is the science of topoi and rhetoric." "That I have never ever heard of before," said the pupil. "I, however, have," said his teacher, "and I know what it covers, which is metaphor, metonymy, figurative usage, punning, morphological parallelism, and more than a hundred other things. Laying all that out in detail takes an age, and one could spend his whole life just on the science of figurative usages and then die and still know little about it, or forget by the end of the book or books what he'd learned at the beginning.

"The reason for this is that the inventor of this magnificent science was no 1.11.4
sultan with the authority to force everyone to follow up on it and unceasingly pursue it. On the contrary, he was a just poor man who fell in love with the

يكن سلطانا حتى يمكنه اجبار الناس جميعا على متابعته ومشايعته * بل كان فقيرا فأُولع بهذا الشى وشرح الله صدره لتقرير قواعد له فكان لا يقع بصره على شى الّا وخطر بباله طريقة من طرقه * فاذا نظر الشمس مثلاً طالعةً قال كيف ينبغى ان يفهم هنا طلوع الشمس هل هو حقيقيّ او مجازيّ وهل المجاز هنا عُرفى او لُغويّ * وكذا لو راى البقل نابتاً فى زمن الربيع قال كيف تأويل قول القائل انبت الربيع البقل * فهل يصح اسناد ذلك الى الربيع وهو انما نشأ عن دوران الارض حول الشمس فهو ولا شكّ مسبّب عنها * ولا ريب ان مدير الارض انما هو الله عزّ وجلّ * فيكون قوله انبت الربيع البقل مجازا بدرجتين * لانّ الربيع مسبب عن دوران الارض ودوران الارض مسبب عن تقدير البارى تعالى * وكذا قولهم جرت السفينة او الجِرّ * ومن المجاز ما له ايضا ثلث درجات ومنه ما له اربع * ومنه ما تفوق درجاته درج المأذنة * ومن هذا الدرج ما شكله قِرقيّ ومنه حَلَزونىّ ومنه لولبىّ * ومنه غير ذلك ثم ما زال المستنبط يفكّر فى هذه البدائع حتى ادركه الاجل فمات وبقى 5.11.1
عليه اشيآء كثيرة لم يحكمها * فقام من بعده مَن اُولع مثله بهذا الفنّ فاستدرك على سلفه مواضع كثيرة * وظل يباحثه ويعارضه الى ان قضى نحبه وقد ترك مجالا لغيره * فجآء من بعده مَن اصلح بينهما فى عدّة مواطن وعاب على كلّ منهما ايضا اموراً * ثم مات ولم يُنهِ ما قصده * فخلفه من صنع به ما صنعه هو بغيره * وهكذا بقيت ابواب النقد مفتوحة الى عصرنا هذا * فمن قائل ان هذه العبارة من الاستعارة التبعية * ومن قائل انها من الترشيحية * قال بعض العلمآ الاستعارة تنقسم الى مصرَّح بها ومكنىّ عنها * والمصرح بها تنقسم الى قطعية واحتمالية * والقطعية تنقسم الى تخييلية وتحقيقية * وتنقسم ثانيا الى اصلية وتبعية * وثالثا الى مجردة ومرشحة * وقال بعضهم وهذه تنقسم ايضا الى عِقْيَوِنيّة ومُكائيّة

subject and whose heart God had made receptive to the laying out of its principles. Thus his eyes had only to fall on a particular thing for his mind to come up with a way of dealing with it. If, for example, he saw the sun rising, he'd say, 'How are we to understand the "rising" of the sun here? Is it "literal" or "metaphorical," and would the metaphor here be "conventional" or "linguistic"?' Likewise, if he were to see green plants sprouting in the spring, he'd say, 'How should we analyze the words of the one who said, "The spring caused the plants to sprout"? Can we correctly trace the sprouting back to the spring, which itself is born of the revolution of the earth around the sun, this revolution being without doubt a contributing factor? At the same time, however, there can be no doubt that the one who makes the earth revolve is God, Mighty and Majestic, in which case his words "the spring caused the plants to sprout" would be a two-step metaphor, for the spring is caused by the revolution of the earth and the revolution of the earth is caused by the ordinances of the Almighty Creator. The same applies to the expressions "the ship sails" or "the mare runs."[192]' There are also three- and four-step metaphors and some with more steps than the stairway of a minaret. Some of these stairways are smooth, some spiral, some winding, and others something else.

"The originator of this science went on thinking about these rhetorical figures until he came to the end of his life, and he died leaving much undecided. 1.11.5 After him, another, similarly enamored, arose and fleshed out many areas left by his predecessor, continuing to debate with and contradict him until he too passed away, making room for others. Next came someone who reconciled the two with regard to a number of cases, while declaring them both at fault with regard to others, but he died without finishing what he'd set out to do, and after him another came along, who did to him what he'd done to the rest, and thus it is that the doors of criticism have remained open down to these days of ours. One will say, 'This expression belongs to the category of "subordinate metaphorization,"' while another will claim that it is 'propositional.' Certain scholars have said that metaphors may be divided into the literal and the analogical, the literal into the categorical and the presumptive, and the categorical firstly into the make-believe and the factual, secondly into the primary and the subordinate, and thirdly into the abstracted and the presumed, with some claiming that this last may be sub-divided into the aeolian,[193] the ornitho-sibilant,[194] the feebly chirping, the tongue-smacking,[195] the faintly tinkling, the bone-snapping, the emptily thunderous, and the phasmic,

ونَبيصيَّة وطَعْطَعيّة وغَميْسيَّة ولَعْلعيّة ويَلمعيّة وعَسْعاسية * والعقيونيّة تنقسم ايضا الى فرقعية وقرقعية ومقامقية * والفرقعية الى جَخْلَنْجَعية وشُنْظَفيَّة وعُطْروسيَّة ودمْحالية وشينقورية وكِربرية * والقرقعية الى خخعية وعُهْعخية وعهخغية وكشعثجية وكشَعَظجية * والمكائية الى مَعويّة وعنتريّة وصَفَرية وعَصَلية وبُلُكيّة وصَفّاريّة وضَغيْليّة وطَرْطبيّة وانقاضية * الى غير ذلك من التنقسم * ويشترط فى خطبة الكتاب ان تكون جامعة لجميع هذه الانواع * وان يراعى فيها وفى الكتاب كله نوع الطباق * مثال ذلك اذ قال القائل فى فقرة طلع * فلا بدّ ان يقول فيها او فى الثانية نزل * واذا قال اكل يقول بعده من غير تراخ تقيأ او – وفى الجملة فينبغى ان تكون الخطبة عويصة ما امكن * واية خطبة لم تكن كذلك كانت عنوانا على ركاكة الكتاب
كله فلم يكن جديرا بالمطالعة * فقال له التلميذ وقد امتُقع لونه وهل النحاة ايضا ٦،١١،١
ماتوا ولم ينهوا قواعد هذا العلم * وهل قرآتى له عليك تغنى عن اعادته عند غيرك هنا * وهل يجب على الطالب فى كل بلد سافر اليه ان يتعلم نحو اهله ام هو علم مرة واحدة * فقال له شيخ اما عن المسالة الاولى فاجيب انه ما جرى على البيانيّين فقد جرى ايضا على النحاة * فقد قال الفرآء اموت وفى قلبى شى من حتى * وقد مات سيبويه وبقى فى قلبه من فتح همزة ان وكسرها اشيآ * ومات الكسائىّ وفى صدره من الفآ العاطفة والسببية والفصيحة والتفريعية والتعقيبية والرابطة حزازات * ومات اليزيدىّ وفى راسه من الواو العاطفة والاستئنافية والقسمية والزائدة والانكارية صداع واى صداع * ومات الزمخشرى وفى كبده من لام الاستحقاق والاختصاص والتمليك وشبه التمليك والتعليل وتوكيد النفى وغير ذلك قروح واى قروح * ومات الاصمعى وفى عنقه من رسم كتابة الهمزة غُدَّة * وفى الجملة فان معرفة حرف واحد من هذه الحروف اذا تعمد الطالب استقصاها وجب عليه

while the aeolian itself may be sub-divided into the stridulaceous, the crepitaceous, and the oropharyngeal, the crepitaceous may be sub-sub-divided into the absquiliferous, the vulgaritissimous, the exquipilifabulous, the seborrhaceous, the squapalidaceous, and the kalipaceous, the crepitaceous into the panthero-dyspneaceous,[196] the skrowlaceous[197] and the skraaagh-halaceous,[198] as well as the transtextual and the intertextual,[199] and the oropharyngeal into the enteric, the dipteric, the vermiculo-epigastric, the intestinal, the audio-zygo-amatory, the anal-resonatory, the oro-phlebo-evacuative, the capro-audio-lactative, the ovo- (or assino-) audio-lactative, and other 'may-be-sub-divideds.' A book's prologue[200] is required to bring together all of these kinds of metaphor, just as attention should be paid, there and throughout, to the specific kind known as 'opposition.'[201] For example, if someone writes in a certain paragraph 'he went up,' in the next he has to write 'he went down,' and if he says 'he ate' he has to say afterward, without let up, 'he vomited' or '** ****.' Over all, the prologue should be as difficult as possible to understand; a prologue that isn't serves notice that the book as a whole is poorly written and not worth the reading."

The pupil, who by now had turned pale, asked his teacher, "Did all the 1.11.6
grammarians too die before completing the rules for that science? And does the fact that I've studied it at your hands relieve me of the need to go over it all again with someone else here? And is the student obliged to learn grammar as it is understood by the people of every country he travels to, or is it a science that has to be learned only once?" The shaykh told him, "As far as the first's concerned, my response would be that the story of the rhetoricians is that of the grammarians. Al-Farrā'[202] said, 'I shall die still pondering the meaning of *ḥattā*,'[203] and Sībawayhi died still unsure as to certain questions relating to when **nna* should be realized as *anna* and when as *inna*.[204] Al-Kisā'ī died of tetters he was so exercised over the difference between connective *fā'*, causative *fā'*, clarifying or deductive *fā'*, consequential *fā'*, and binding *fā'*,[205] while al-Yazīdī[206] died of a headache (and what a headache!) caused by connective *wāw*, resumptive *wāw*, affirmative *wāw*, supplemental *wāw*, and negative *wāw*.[207] Al-Zamakhsharī died with ulcers on his liver from the differences between the right-related, ascriptive, proprietorial and semi-proprietorial, purposive, emphatic-negative, and other uses of *lām*,[208] and al-Aṣma'ī[209] died with a goiter on his neck from worrying about the glottal stop. In sum, if a student wants to acquire an in-depth knowledge

ان يترك جميع اشغاله ومصالحه ويعكف على ما قيل فيه واجيب عنه * وما قيل من
الامثال اعطِ العلمَ كلّك يُعْطك جزأَه الا لاجل ذلك * واما قولك هل يلزم ان تقرا ١،١١،٧
النحو ايضا على غيرى هنا اى فى بلادنا فذلك غير لازم * فان اهل بلادنا كلهم لا
يطالعون غير هذا الكتاب الذى تطالعه انت * بل قلّ من يطالعه ويفهمه او يعمل
بمقتضى قواعده * واما عن سؤالك الثالث فاقول انه لا ينبغى اعادة هذا العلم فى كل
بلد ولكنك حيثما سرت وايّان توجهت وجدت اناسا ينتقدون عليك كلامك * فان
عبّرت بالواو مثلا قالوا الافصح هنا الفآء * او باو وقالوا الاولى ام * وفى بعض
البلاد اذا عُلم انك تنقط يآء قائل وبائع سقط اعتبارك من عيون الناس * فقد قرات
فى بعض كتب الادب ان بعض العلمآء عاد صديقاً له فى حال مرضه فراى عنده
كرّاسة قد كتب فيها لفظة قائل بنقطتين تحت اليآء فرجع فى الحال على عقبه وقال
لمن سار معه لقد اضعنا خطواتنا فى زيارته * وهذا هو سبب قلّة التاليف فى ١،١١،٨
عصرنا * فان المولّف والحالة هذه يعرّض نفسه للطعن والقدح والبلآء * ولا
يراعى الناس ما فى كتابه من الفوائد والحِكَم * الّا اذا كان مشتملا على جميع المحسّنات
البديعية والدقائق اللغوية * ومَثَلُ ذلك مثل رجل فاضل يدخل على قوم بهيئة
رثة ورعابيل شماطيط * فالناس لا تنظر الى ادبه الباطنى بل الى بزّته وزيّه *
والحمد لله على قلة المولفين اليوم فى بلادنا اذ لو كثروا وكثر نقدهم وتخطئتهم لكثرت
اسباب البغض والمشاحنة بينهم * وقد استغنى الناس عن ذلك بتلفيق بعض
فِقَر مسجّعة فى رسائل ونحوها كقولك السلام والاكرام * والسنيّة والبهية *
فاخفّه ما كان ساكنا * فاما الشعر فى عصرنا هذا فانه عبارة عن وصف ممدوح
بالكرم والشجاعة او وصف امراة بكون خصرها نحيلا * وردفها ثقيلا * وطرفها
كحيلا * ومن تعمّد قصيدة جعل جلّ ابياتها غزلاً ونسيبا وعتابا وشكوى وترك

of just one of these particles, he will have to give up all other concerns and interests and devote himself to what has been said about it and the refutations thereof, which is why we have such proverbs as 'You may give all of yourself to scholarship but it will give only part of itself to you.'

"As to your question whether you should study grammar with others 1.11.7
than myself here, meaning in this country of ours, that will not be necessary. None of our countrymen have read any books other than the very one you are reading. Indeed, few are those who have read that and understood it or can apply its rules. As for your third question, I'd say that it is not necessary for you to go over the same science in every country. However, wherever you go and in whichever direction you head, you will find people who will criticize you for your way of speaking. Thus, if you use *wāw*, for example, they will say that *fā'* is the more correct, and if you use *aw*, they will say that *am*[210] is preferable, while in some countries, if you put dots below the letter *yā'* in the words *qā'il* or *bā'iʿ*,[211] you will lose all respect in people's eyes. I read in some work of *belles lettres* that a certain scholar paid a visit to a friend of his who was sick in bed and caught sight of a notebook in which the word *qā'il* was written with two dots below the *yā'*, so he turned on his heel and said to his companion, 'We have wasted our steps in coming to see him.'

"This is why so few people write works on grammar in this day and age: 1.11.8
under such circumstances, the writer exposes himself to criticism, vilification, and tribulation and no one will pay any attention to the useful information and maxims in his book, unless it be replete with every kind of stylistic embellishment and linguistic nicety. It's as though a virtuous man were to go into a gathering dressed in rags and tatters; they wouldn't see his inner refinement, only his outer clothing and attire. Thank God there are so few writers in our country these days: if they were to increase—and, along with them, their criticism and fault-finding—the occasions for their mutual hatred and quarrelsomeness would increase in proportion. People have substituted for serious writing the concoction of a few paragraphs in rhymed prose that they put in letters and the like, as when they say 'salutation and veneration' or 'the splendid and resplendent,' these being easiest to take when pronounced without vowels at the end.[212] As far as poetry in this day and age is concerned, it consists merely of describing a man who is the subject of a eulogy as generous and brave or of a woman as having a slender *waist*, heavy *nates*, and an eye with collyrium *laced*. Anyone who sets out to

الباقى للمدح * ثم ان التلميذ النجيب استمر يقرا على شيخه الاديب فى النحو حتى ٩،١١،١
وصل الى باب الفاعل والمفعول فاعترض على ان الفاعل يكون مرفوعا والمفعول
منصوبا * وقال هذا الاصطلاح فاسد لان الفاعل اذا كان مرفوعا كان الذى
عمل فيه الرفع آخر * والحال انه هو العامل * وبيانه انّا نرى الفاعل فى البنآ يرفع
الحجر وغيره على كتفه فالحجر هو المرفوع والفاعل رافع وكذلك فاعل ال . . . .
فانه هو الذى يرفع الساق * فقال له المعلم مه مه لقد افحشت، فكان ينبغى لك
التادّب فى مجلس العلم فانه غير مجلس الامارة * ثم ختم التلميذان قراة الكتاب ولم
يستفيدا شيا وكانّ الشرح كله كان موجّها الى الفارياق * ومذ ذلك الوقت اخذ
فى تجويد عبارته بمقتضى القواعد النحوية *

فصار يهوّل بها على رعاع الناس

كما يظهر فى

الفصل الاتى *

compose a poem fills up most of its lines with amatory and erotic or plaintive and querulous material and keeps the rest for eulogy."

This brilliant pupil continued to read grammar with his shaykh until he got to the chapter on the "doer" and the "done,"[213] when he objected to the fact that the doer was "raised" while the done was "laid,"[214] claiming that the terminology was corrupt, for if the doer was raised then someone else must have raised him, whereas in fact it was the doer who did the work, the evidence being that we may observe a man working on a building raising a stone or the like on his shoulder, in which case the stone is the thing raised and the doer is the raiser, and likewise the doer of the . . .[215] is the one who raises his leg. At this point, the tutor told him, "Steady on! Steady on! You're being foul-mouthed. In the scholarly gathering—which is quite different from the princely—you're supposed to demonstrate good manners." Then the two pupils concluded the reading of the book, neither having benefited in any way, and the commentary might as well have been directed entirely at the Fāriyāq who, from then on, took to 1.11.9

improving his speech by following the rules of grammar
till he came to scare the pants off the rabble
as will become clear
in the following
chapter.

الفصل الثاني عشر

في اكلة وأُكال

لا بدّ لى من ان اطيل الكلام فى هذا الفصل امتحانا لصبر القارى * فان اتى على اخره دفعة واحدة من غير ان تحترق اسنانه غيظا * او تصطك رجلاه غيرة وحميّة * او ينزوى ما بين عينيه اَنَفةً وحشمة * او تنتفخ اوداجه وَغْرا وهَوَجا * افردتُ له فصلاً على حدته مدحا فيه وعددته من القرآء الصابرين * ولكون الفارياق فى هذا الوقت قد طال لسانه وان يكن فكره قد بقى قصيرا ورأسه صغيرا ناقصا من عند قَمَحْدُوَته * وقد نذرت على نفسى ان امشى وراه خطوة خطوة واحاكيه فى سيرته * فان رايت منه حمقة جئت بمثلها * اوغواية غويت مثله * او رشدا قابلته بنظيره * والا فانى اكون خصمه لا كاتب سيرته او ناقل كلامه * وينبغى ان يعلّق هذا الحكم فى اعناق جميع المولفين * ولكن هيهات فانى ارى اكثرهم قد زاغ عن هذه المحجّة * اذ المولف منهم بينا هو يذكر مصيبة احد من العباد فى عقله او امرأته او ماله اذا به تكلّف لا يراد الفِقَر المسجّعة والعبارات المرصعة وحشّى قصّته بجميع ضروب الاستعارات والكنايات * وتشاغل عن همّ صاحبه بما يدل على انه غير مكترث به * فترى المُصابَ ينتحب ويُولول ويشكو ويتظلم * والمولف يسجّع ويجنّس ويرصّع ويروّى ويستطرد ويلتفت ويتناول المعانى البعيدة * فيمدّ يده تارة الى الشمس وتارة الى النجوم * ويحاول انزالها من اوج سمائها الى سافل قوله * ١،١٢،١

Chapter 12

A Dish and an Itch

I must go on at some length in this chapter, just to test the reader's endurance. If he gets to the end of it at one go without his teeth smoking with rage, his knees knocking together from frustration and fury, the place between his eyes knitting in disgust and shame, or his jugulars swelling in wrath and ire, I shall devote a separate chapter to his praise and count him among those readers "who are steadfast."[216] And because the Fāriyāq had become prone in those days to making a long tongue at people—even though his brains remained quite short and his head quite small and exiguous at the occiput—and I had taken a vow to follow along behind him step by step, mimicking the way he walked, if I saw him doing something stupid I would do the same, wandering off the path if he did, and matching too anything sensible he did, for otherwise I'd be his foe, not the writer of his life story or the reporter of his sayings. An injunction to do the same should be hung around the necks of all writers, who, in fact, are very far from obeying it. I observe that most of them depart from this approach, and you suddenly find such a writer, in the middle of describing a disaster that has affected some mortal's sanity, wife, or wealth, going to the trouble of inserting paragraphs in rhymed prose and expressions full of parallelisms, padding his story with all sorts of metaphors and metonymies, and forgetting all about his subject's worries, thus indicating that he doesn't care about them. As a result you find the victim moaning and wailing, objecting and complaining, while the author is rhyming and using paronomasia, making parallel constructions and puns, going off on tangents, switching persons,[217] and playing with unlikely topoi, as when he reaches out his hand now to the sun, now to the stars, trying to bring them from the zenith of the heavens down to the lowly level of his words, 1.12.1

ومرة يقتحم البحار * واخرى يقتطف الازهار * ويطفر فى الحدائق والغياض من اصل الى فرع ومن غوطة الى ربوة * ما ذلك دابى فانى اذا اوردت كلاما عن احمق انتقيت فيه له جميع الالفاظ السخيفة * واذا نقلت عن امير تادبت معه فى النقل ما امكن فكانى جالس بمجلسه * اوعن قسّيس مثلا او مطران اتحفته بجميع اللفظ الركيك والكلام المختلّ * لئلاّ يصعب عليه المعنى فيفوت الغرض من تاليف
هذا الكتاب * فاعلم اذاً ان الفارياق بعد ان فار دماغه بحرارة النحو زيادة على ما ٢،١٢،١
كان له من الرغبة فى النظم سار ذات يوم لقضآء مصلحة له * فمرّ فى طريقه على دير للرهبان * وكان الوقت مسآء * فراى ان يبيت ليلته تلك فى الدير فعرج عليه وطرق الباب فبرز له رويهب * فقال له الفارياق هل من مبيت عندكم لضيف * فقال له الرويهب * اهلاً به ان لم يكن ذا سيف * ففرح الفارياق بهذا الجواب وعجب من انه يوجد فى الدير من يحسن المساجلة * وانما قال له الرويهب ما قال لان الدير كان ينتابه كثير من اتباع الامير ليبيتوا فيه من كلّ سِرْطِمٍ قِهقَمٍّ لَهِمٍ نَهِمٍ وَحِمٍ وَخِمٍ هَقِمٍ يُسمَع له هَيْقَم * فكان احدهم اذا بات ثمّ ليلة يكلّف الرهبان من المطاعم الفاخرة ما لم يعهدوه * لان هولآء الخلق يعيشونَ عيشة المتقشفين المقتّرين المتبلّغين بادنى القوت * اذهم ينظرون الى الدنيا والى لذاتها نظر العدو * فهى عندهم ضرّة الآخرة * كلما تباعد عنها الانسان المخلوق فيها تقرّب الى الجنة * حتى ان الخبز الذى كثيرا ما ياكلونه بغير اِدام ليس كخبز الناس * فانهم بعد ان يخبزوه رقيقا يشمّسونه ايّاما متوالية حتى يجفّ وييبس * بحيث يمكن للانسان اذا اخذ بكلتا يديه رغيفين وضرب احدهما بالآخر ان يخيف بقرفعتهما جميع جرذان الدير * او ان يتخذهما متخذ الناقوس الذى يُضرب به لاوقات الصلوة * ولا يقدرون على اكله الا منقوعا بالمآء حتى يعود عجينا * فاما تقلّد تابع الامير بالسيف فانما هو تهويل

or, on some occasions, plows across *oceans* and at others plucks *orchids* while bounding around in garden and thicket from trunk to branch and from hollow to hill. Such, though, is not my way of doing things, for if I introduce the words of an idiot, I put every kind of silly expression in his mouth, and if I report something said by an emir, I use, to the extent possible, polite language, as though I were sitting with him in this salon; or by a priest, for example, or a bishop, I make him a gift of every variety of lame and defective phrase so that it isn't too difficult for him to express himself, which, should it happen, would undermine the purpose of writing this book.

Know, then, that after the Fāriyāq's brains had boiled over following the **1.12.2**
application of the heat of grammar, which came on top of his desire to be a poet, he set off one day to take care of some business. On the road he passed a monastery and, it being evening, thought it would be a good idea to spend the night there. Turning off to it, he knocked on the door, at which a young monk appeared before him. "Can you provide a guest with bed and *board*?" the Fāriyāq asked, to which the young monk replied, "He'd be most welcome so long as he has no *sword*." The Fāriyāq was delighted with this response and amazed to find in the monastery someone who was good at repartee. The young monk had only said what he did because numbers of the large-gulleted, omnivorous, gluttonous, voracious, craving, dyspeptic, ravenous, loudly swallowing followers of the emir afflicted the monastery with their demands for lodging, and, whenever one of them spent the night there, he would charge the monks with providing fine dishes that they knew nothing of, for these folk live a life of short commons and *abnegation*, surviving on the most meager *ration*, regarding, as they do, this world and its pleasures as their foe; it is to them the arch-rival of the life to come, and the further mortal man distances himself from it, the closer he approaches Paradise. Even their bread, which they often eat plain, is unlike other people's, for after they've baked it in thin layers, they expose it to the sun for several days in rows until it dries and gets so hard that if one were to take a loaf in each hand and strike them against each other, the din would panic all the rats in the monastery, or they could use them in place of the wooden plank they strike to mark the times of prayer, and they can eat it only after it's been soaked in water so long it has turned back to dough. The emir's followers wear swords to terrify those who pay them less than total respect and to warn them of the consequences, in just the same manner as the Fāriyāq terrified

واندار بنكال المتهاون به * كتهويل الفارياق على الرويهب بسواله * ومن لم يكن
له سيف استعار سيف صاحبه * او اتخذ له خشبة رقيقة فى غمد سيف *
وليس فى استعارة الماعون وغيره عند اهل الجبل من عار بل كثيرا ما يستعيرون
حليّا ومِعْرضا للعروس يزفونها به وللرجل ثيابا وعمامة يزينونه بها * ثم انه لما حان ٣،١٢،١
وقت العشآء جآء ذلك الرويهب بصحفة من العدس المطبوخ بالزيت وبثلثة اَصْنُجُ
من ذلك الخبز وجعلها بين يدى الفارياق *فجلس للعشآ وتناول رغيفا ودقّه بالاخر
حتى انكسر * فلما التقم اول لقمة نشبت شَظِيّة من الخبز فى سنّه وكادت ان
تذهب بها *فجعل يسندها ويسدّ مواضع الخلل منها بالعدس * ولم يكد يتم العشآ
حتى اشتدت حرارة العدس فى بدنه فجعل يحكّ باظفاره وبعض قصَد الرغيف
حتى تهشّم جلده * فساءه ذلك جدا وقال لقد خلخلت هذه الكسرة سنّى فلاقلعنّ
سنّا من اسنان هذا الدير * ثم انه اعمل فكره فى نظم بيتين فى العدس تشفيّا مما
ناله منه جريا على عادة الشعرآء من انهم يتشفّون بعتابهم الدهر مما هم فيه من النحس
والقهر * والشقاوة والضرّ * فالتبست عليه لفظة فقام فى طلب القاموس * ٤،١٢،١
فطرق باب جاره وكان من المتحمّسين فى الدين * فقال له هل عندك ياسيدى
القاموس * قال ما عندنا بالدير جاموس بل ثيران فما حاجتك به الان * فطرق
باب آخر وكان اشدّ منه خشونة * فقال له هل لك فى ان تعيرنى القاموس ساعة
قال اصبر علىّ الى نصف الليل فان الكابوس لا ياتينى الا فى هذا الوقت * فمضى
الى غيره واعاد عليه السؤال * فقال له اى شى هو هذا القاموص ياماغوص فرجع
الى صومعته وقال * لا بدّ من نظم البيتين * وساترك محلاً فارغا للّفظة فقال *

the young monk with his question. If one of them doesn't have a sword, he borrows his friend's or takes a thin stick and puts it in a scabbard. The people of the Mountain find nothing shameful about borrowing provisions or other things; on the contrary, they often borrow jewelry and apparel for the bride for her procession and borrow clothes and a turban for the groom to make him look smart.

When dinnertime came, the same young monk brought a dish of lentils cooked in oil and three "cymbals" of that bread and placed them before the Fāriyāq, who then sat down to eat, taking a piece of bread and whacking it against another until it broke. When he took the first mouthful a sliver of the bread caught against a tooth and almost carried it off. The Fāriyāq tried to prop it up and fill the holes in the tooth with lentils but hardly had he finished his meal before the heat of the lentils started to grow in his body and he took to scratching with his fingernails and fragments of the loaf until his skin was in shreds. This upset him greatly and he said to himself, "That crust almost dislodged my tooth, so I'm going to dislodge one of the monastery's," and he cudgeled his brains to compose a couple of lines of verse on lentils to avenge himself for what it had done to him, in imitation of the custom of poets of getting their own back by rebuking fate for any ill-fortune or depression, wretchedness or oppression they may have suffered. 1.12.3

Searching for a certain word, he rose and went looking for a copy of the *Qāmūs* and knocked on the door of his neighbor, who was one of those particularly zealous in religion, and asked him, "Do you have, sir, a *Qāmūs*?" to which the other replied, "In the monastery we have neither *qāmūs* nor *jāmūs* ('buffaloes') nor oxen, and what would you be needing them for at this hour, anyway?" So he knocked on the door of another who was even coarser and asked him, "Would you mind lending me the *Qāmūs* for an hour?" to which he replied, "Hang on till midnight, for the *kābūs* ('nightmare') never comes at any other time." So he went to another and asked him the same question and the man replied, "What *qāmūṣ*, you *māghūṣ*?[218]" So he returned to his cell, saying, "I'll have to compose the lines and leave a space for the missing word," and he wrote, 1.12.4

اكلتُ العدس فى ديرِ مسآء   فبتُّ وبى أُكال لا يطاقُ
فلولا اننى اعملتُ ظفرى   لقال الناس ــــ الفارياقُ

فلما كان نصف الليل والفارياق نائم اذ باحد الرهبان يقرع عليه الباب * فظن انه ١،١٢،٥
اتاه بالكتاب المطلوب * ففتح له وهو مستبشر بوجدان ضالته * فقال له الراهب قم الى الصلوة واقفل الباب واتبعنى * فتذكر عند ذلك ما قاله له جاره من ان الكابوس لا ياتيه الا فى نصف الليل * فقال فى نفسه لقد صدق الرجل فان هذا الداعى اشدّ على النائم من الكابوس * قبحًا لها من ليلة شوئمى لقد كاد الخبز يقلع سنّى والعدس منانى بالحكّة * وماكدت الان اغفى حتى اتانى هذا القارع الاقرع النحس يدعونى الى الصلوة أكان ابى راهبا وامّى راهبة ام وجب علىّ الشكر والصلوة من
اجل اكلة عدس * ولكن ساصبر الى الصباح * فلما كان الغد جآء ذلك الرويهب ١،١٢،٦
ليساله عن حاله اذ كان قد دخل الدير مذ عهد غير بعيد فكان فيه بقيّة رقة ولطف * فقال له الفارياق سألتك بالله ان تجلس عندى قليلا * فلما جلس قال له قل لى فديتك افى كل يوم انتم تفعلون هذا * فوجم الرويهب وظنّ به سوءا ثم قال اىَّ فعل تعنى * قال اكلكم العدس مسآء وقيامكم فى نصف الليل للصلوة * قال نعم ذلك دأبنا فى كلّ يوم * قال ما الذى اوجبه عليكم * قال التعبّد لله والتقرب اليه * قال ان الله تبارك وتعالى لا يهمه ان كان الانسان ياكل عدسا اولحما * ولم يامر بذلك فى كتبه * اذ ليس فيه مصلحة لنفس الآكل او للماكول * قال هذا دأب النسّاك العُبّاد اذ التقشف فى المعيشة ونهك الجسم بالردىّ من الطعام وبقلّة النوم ينفى
الشهوات * قال لا بل هو مناف لما شآءه الله * اذ لو شآء ان ينهك بدنك ويخليه ١،١٢،٧
من الشهوات لخلقك ضاويا دَنِفا * ما قولك فى من خلقه الله جميلا * ايجوز له ان

I ate lentils in a monastery of an evening,
Then spent the night with an itch that my mind did almost derange.
Had I not set my nails to working,
Men would have said, "The Fāriyāq's got *****!"

When it was midnight and the Fāriyāq was sleeping, one of the monks suddenly knocked on his door. Thinking that he'd brought the book he wanted, he opened the door in expectation of finding what he'd been looking for, only for the monk to tell him, "Get up and come to prayers. Lock your door and follow me." Then the Fāriyāq recalled what his neighbor had said about the nightmare not coming till midnight and said to himself, "The man spoke truly, for this summoner is harder on the sleeper than a nightmare. Damn this for a wretched night for me: the bread almost pulled out my tooth and the lentils made me scratch, and now I'd barely started to doze off when this miserable scald-headed door-striker comes and summons me to prayer. Was my father a monk or my mother a nun, or have I incurred some other obligation, to have to give thanks and perform prayers for the sake of a dish of lentils? All the same, I shall endure until morning." 1.12.5

Next day, the same young monk came to ask him how he was, for he had joined the monastery only a little while before and still retained some traces of finer feeling and kindness. "I beg you," said the Fāriyāq, "do sit with me a little," and when the man had taken his seat, he asked him, "Tell me, if you'd be so kind, do you do that every day?" The young monk frowned at him and thought his question odd. Then he said, "What are you alluding to?" The Fāriyāq replied, "Eat lentils in the evening and get up at midnight to pray." "Yes indeed," he answered. "Such is our custom every day." "What imposed this duty upon you?" said the Fāriyāq. "The need to worship God and become closer to him," he replied. The Fāriyāq responded, "God, Blessed and Mighty, doesn't care whether a person eats lentils or meat, and he didn't command any such thing in His Book, as there is no benefit therein, for the soul of the eater or for the eaten." "This is the way of the contemplative ascetics," said the other, "for a life of abnegation and chastisement of the body through eating the worst foods and reduction of sleep drives away the appetites." 1.12.6

"On the contrary," said the Fāriyāq, "it is inconsistent with God's will, for had He wanted to chastise your body and free it of its appetites, He would have created you emaciated and sickly. What say you about those whom God has created beautiful? Is such a person allowed to disfigure his face, 1.12.7

يشوّه وجهه بان يخق عينه او يخرم انفه او يشرم شفته او يقلع اسنانه كما اردتم قلع اسنانى البارحة بخبزكم هذا اليابس * او ان يسخّم سحنته * قال فى ظنى انه لا يجوز * قال اليس البدن كلّه على قياس الوجه * لعمرى ما خلق الله الساعد الفعم الا وهو يريد بقآه فعما * ولا الساق المجدولة الّا وشآء لها ان تكون كذلك دائما * ولا حلّل الطيّبات من المآكل للناس الا وهو يريد ان ياكلوها هنيئا مريئا * نعم قد حرّم هذه الطيّبات بعض الاديان المشطة * غير ان دين النصارى يحللها * وانما جآء التحريم من بعض شهارب طعنوا فى السنّ فلم يكن بهم قَطَم الى اللحم ولا الى غيره *
ما المانع تناوله كل يوم * قال لا ادري وانما سمعت علمآنا يقولون ذلك فقلّدتهم * ١،١٢،٨
وانى اقول لك الحقّ انى مللت من هذه العيشة * فانى ارى جسمى كل يوم فى ذبول ونفسى فى انقباض * ولوكنت عرفت من قبل ما اصير اليه لما سلكت هذه الطريقة * غير ان ابى وامى فقيران وخشيا ان اكون من ذوى البطالة والتعطّل * اذلا صنائع نافعة فى بلادنا يمكن للانسان ان يتعلّمها ويعيش منها فزيّنا لى الرهبانية * وقالا لى اذا واظبت على طريقة فى الدير بضع سنين فربما ترتقى الى رتبة عالية فتنفع نفسك وايانا * وما زالا بى حتى اجبتهما ولولم اجبهما طوعا لاكرهانى على ذلك *
فقال له الفارياق نعم ان الرهبانية هى ملجا من البطالة فكل من كان عطلا عن علم ١،١٢،٩
او صنعة يقصدها * الا انك ما زلت مثلى حدثا فيمكن لك ان تقصد احدا من اهل الخير والشفقة فيدلّك على ما ينفعك * والله تعالى خلق الاشداق * وتكفّل لها بالارزاق * وقد جعل فى الحركة بركة * هذا وانت تعلم ان الرهبانية مشتقة من الرهبة وهى خوف الله تعالى * فاذا تعاطيت حرفةً وعشت بها بين الناس وتزوجت ورزقت ولدا وخشيت الله فانت ح راهب * ليست الرهبانية باكل

gouge out an eye, pierce his nose, slit his lip, or pull out his teeth—as you wanted to pull out my teeth yesterday with that hard bread of yours—or to blacken his appearance?" Said the other, "In my opinion, that would not be allowed." Said the Fāriyāq, "Isn't the body as a whole analogous to the face? I swear, God cannot have created a well-muscled forearm without wanting it to remain a well-muscled forearm, or a leg rippling with muscles without wanting it to stay that way for ever. Nor would he have made it permissible to people to eat good foods unless he had wanted them to eat them in blooming good health. True, some eccentric religions have forbidden these good foods, but the Christian religion permits them and they only came to be prohibited because of a few aging dodderers who didn't care for meat or anything else. What is your objection to eating them every day?"

"I don't know," said the other, "but I heard our scholars say it was so, so **1.12.8**
I imitated them, and to tell you the truth, I've grown sick of this life. I see my body wasting away day by day and my spirit becoming dejected, and if I'd known beforehand how I'd end up, I never would have taken this path. My father and mother, though, are poor and were afraid I'd end up unemployed and idle, for there are no useful crafts in our land for a person to learn and live by, so they painted me a pretty picture of the monk's life. They told me that if I stuck to the path in the monastery for a few years, I might be promoted to a high rank, 'and do yourself some good and us too.' They kept on at me until I agreed, and if I hadn't done so of my own free will, they would have forced me into it."

The Fāriyāq told him, "It's true: the monastic life is a refuge from un- **1.12.9**
employment, for anyone who's too idle to have acquired any knowledge or a craft makes a beeline for it. But you're still a young man like me, so you can go to any person of good will and charity and he will direct you to something that will help you. The Almighty created the *jaws* and He's guaranteed the daily bread to fill those *maws*, just as He's made *action* the key to *benefaction*. Moreover, you will be aware that the word *rahbāniyyah* ('monasticism') derives from *rahbah* ('fear'), meaning fear of Almighty God. It you adopt a profession, make your living from it among your fellow men, marry, and are blessed with a child, you will have manifested fear of God and will then be *rāhib* ('god-fearing/a monk'). True *rahbāniyyah* doesn't depend on eating lentils and dry bread. Isn't it the case that there's more quarreling, name-calling, and grudge-bearing among the monks of your monastery

العدس والخبز اليابس * اليس ان رهبان ديرك بينهم من الخصام والطعن والحقد ما لا يوجد عند غيرهم * فان رئيسهم لا يزال يحاول اذلالهم واخضاعهم له * وهم لا يزالون مدمدمين عليه شاكين منه * وبينه وبين روسآء الاديار الاخرى من الحسد والمنافسة ما بين وزرآء الدول * واكثرهم ينال الرئاسة بالتملق للامير الحاكم او للبطرك * فاذا احس بوشك انقضآء مدته وخشى العزل رايته يجود بالهدايا والتحف لذوى الامر والنهى بما لا يجود به اكرم اهل بلادنا * وذلك حتى يقرّوه على
رئاسته * وهولآء الرهبان المكرَهون على التبلّغ بالعدس وعلى التنحس اذا دعاهم ١٠،١٢،١
احد لمادبة سمعت لاستراطهم دويّا * فيلفلفون ويلعمظون ويلتمظون ويتكظكظون ويشتفّون حتى تجحظ عيونهم * واضرَّما يكون عليّ منهم انك لا تكاد تسلّم على احد منهم الا ويمدّ لك يده لتبوسها * ربما كانت نجسة قذرة * فكيف الثم يد من هو اجهل منى ولا غناء[1] عنده فى شى * انظرِكم عندنا فى بلادنا من دير وعلى كم تشتمل هذه الاديار من الرهبان * ولم ارَ احدا منهم نبغ فى علم ولا من
أُثِرت عنه مكرمة * بل لا تسمع عنهم الا ما يشين الانسان فى عقله وعرضه * ١١،١٢،١
قدكنت فى خدمة بعير بيعرمدة فرايت احد هولآء الكارزين قد تمكّن من ابنته تمكن الزوج من امراته * فكان يقول لها فيما يسالها عنه هل تجمجم اَلْيَتاك ويترجرج ثدياك * فما للراهب ولترعّد الالايا النسوان ورجرجة اثدآئهن * وآخركان رئيسا فى دير فعلق بنتا فى قرية بالقرب من الدير فلم تلبث ان علقت منه * غير انه لمّا كان اخوه وجيها عند الحاكم خاف ابو البنت من ان يخاصمه ويفضحه * بل قد تقرر فى عقول الجهلآء من اهل بلادنا ان افشآء امرمثل هذا مما يفتضح به عرض احد هولآء النسّاك حرام * ايم الله ان الستر عليه حرام فان فضيحته تردع غيره *

---

١ ١٨٥٥: ولآ غناء.

than among other people, that their chief never stops trying to humiliate them and force them to submit to him, that they never stop grumbling and complaining about him, and that there's as much envy and competitiveness between him and the other heads of monasteries as there is among the ministers of the world's countries? Most of them obtain their posts by flattering the ruling emir or the patriarch, and when they feel their terms are approaching their end and fear dismissal, you find them showering people of influence with gifts and presents such as the ordinary people of our land would never give and continuing to do so until they are confirmed in their positions as heads of their monasteries.

"If anyone invites their monks—who have to put up with lentils and abstain from meat—to a feast, you can hear the roar as they swallow, for they dive into their food, gnaw on the bones using their whole mouths, lick their lips by sticking out their tongues like snakes, fill their waterskins to the brim, and drink them dry until their eyes start from their sockets. The thing that I hold most against them, though, is that you can hardly say hello to one of them without his stretching his hand out for you to kiss, and often enough it's defiled and filthy—how am I to kiss the hand of one who is more ignorant than me and good for nothing? See how many monasteries there are in our land and how many monks each monastery holds—and yet I haven't come across a single one of them who excels in scholarship or has left behind him anything to boast of. **1.12.10**

"On the contrary, all you hear of them are things that are a disgrace to the mind and morals of mankind. I was in the service of Baʿīr Bayʿar for a time and discovered that one of these preachers had acquired as much control over his daughter as a husband over a wife. Among the things he'd ask her were, 'Do your buttocks shake and your breasts quake?' What has a monk got to do with the quivering of women's buttocks and the jiggling of their breasts? Another was head of a monastery. He conceived an affection for a girl in a village near to the monastery and it wasn't long before she conceived a child by him. Because his brother was highly regarded by the ruler, the girl's father was afraid to stand up to him and expose him; indeed, it has become an accepted fact in the minds of the ignorant people of our land that it's a sin to disclose a matter of this sort that might expose one of these so-called ascetics to scandal. I swear by God, concealing such things is a sin, for exposure would deter others! **1.12.11**

١٢،١٢،١ واعرف آخر جآء الى قريتنا متماوتا وقد طوّل كمّيه واسبل قلنسوته حتى لم يكد يظهر من تحتها الّا فمه ولحيته تظاهراً بالصلاح والتقوى * ثم انزل نفسه منزلة خطيب فى القوم * فجعل يخطب ويعظ وينذر بصوت جهير * وكان يبكى عند ذلك اشد البكآ ويذرف المدامع اذ كان جعل فى منديله الذى يمسح به وجهه شيا ذا حُرّتة لا ادرى ما هو * ثم آل امره الى انه يقضى ايّاما وليالى مع ارملة حسنآ شابّة من نسآء الامرآ فى خلوة استذراعاً بانها تعترف له اعترافا عامّا * اى من يوم انتخ ثديها ونبت شعرها الى ذلك اليوم * واعرف آخر كان قد ذهب الى رومية

١٣،١٢،١ وكان مغفّلا فكان ينام فى فراشه بثيابه الرهبانية على طريقته فى الدير ويوسخ المُلآة * فكان صاحب المنزل ينهاه عن ذلك * ثم لما راى ان جميع قسّيسي رومية واعيان ائمتها من البابا الى الكردينال الى الراهب ينامون عريانين لا شى يستر سوءاتهم غير مُلآء الكتّان الرفيع كفر بهم وصار يستحلّ الحلال والحرام معا * فانظر الى هولآ العُبّاد من العباد فانك لا ترى فيهم الا خبيثاً منافقا * او جاهلا

١٤،١٢،١ مائقا * وندر وجود الصالح بينهم * اما العلم فهو محرّم عليهم كلّهم * لا باس فى الرّهبانية تطوعا لا باس انما هى طريقة محمودة * ولكن بشرط مجاوزة الخمسين سنة * وان يكون الداخلون فيها من اهل الفضائل والمعارف * يشتغلون بالعلم وبتهذيب املآء اخوانهم ومعارفهم * ويحضّون على مكارم الاخلاق والاتصاف بالمزايا الحميدة * ويولفون الكتب المفيدة وينهجون لقومهم المناهج المودّية الى الخير والفلاح والفوز والنجاح * لا مثل هولآء الجهال الذين لا يعرفون شيا من الدنيا سوى التقشّف والرّثاثة * وناهيك دليلا على جهلهم انى سالت اشدهم تحمّسا ان يعيرنى القاموس فظنّه الجاموس * واخرظنه الكابوس * وآخر القاموص * فبادر ياصاحِ وتخلّص منهم هداك الله والّا فتكون لا من اهل الدنيا ولا من

"I know another, too, who came to our village pretending to be at death's door. To show how righteous and pious he was, he wore his sleeves long and had pulled his cowl down till almost nothing could be seen but his mouth and beard. The first thing he did was to set himself up as a preacher to the local laity, and he took to preaching and sermonizing and uttering warnings of coming judgment in a basso profundo, weeping as hard as he could the while, tear ducts overflowing, for he had put something pungent, I know not what, on the handkerchief with which he wiped his face. Eventually he ended up spending days and nights in seclusion with a pretty young widow of the princely class, justifying himself by saying that she was making plenary confession to him, meaning starting from the time when her breasts swelled and her hair sprouted and going all the way up to that very day. **1.12.12**

"And I know of another who went to Rome. Being a simpleton, he would go to bed in his monk's habit just as he did at his monastery and thus dirty the sheets, so the owner of the house forbade him to do so. When the monk discovered that all the priests of Rome, from the cardinals to the monks, slept naked, with nothing to cover their shame but a thin linen sheet, he renounced his faith and started declaring that everything, sinful or not, was permitted. Observe, then, how none of these 'contemplative' worshippers of God turns out to be anything but base and *hypocritical* or ignorant and *hysterical*. A righteous man among them is rarely to be *descried* and with regard to scholarship they're all equally *deprived*. **1.12.13**

"There's nothing, nothing at all, wrong with becoming a monk of one's own free will; it is a praiseworthy path—on condition that one is over fifty and that those who join the monastic ranks be people of virtue and knowledge who occupy themselves with scholarship and improving the writing skills of their brethren and acquaintance, spurring them to noble morals and the adoption of praiseworthy qualities, writing useful books and laying down for their people the roads that lead to good fortune and *salvation*, triumph and a happy *termination*, unlike those ignoramuses who know nothing but mortification of the flesh and ragged clothes. To demonstrate their ignorance it's enough to say that I asked the most zealous of them to lend me the *Qāmūs* and he thought I said *jāmūs*, while another thought I said *kābūs*, and a third *qāmūṣ*. Set to, then, my friend, and have done with them: God guide you right, or you'll end up as a man of neither this world nor the next, for **1.12.14**

اهل الآخرة * فان دين الجاهل عند الله ليس بشى * واذا بلغت الستين سنة
فها هى الرهبانية بين يديك * فقال له كيف التخلّص * قال اَلَك فى الدير متاع ١،١٢،١٥
فاساعدك على حمله * قال مالى سوى ما تراه علىّ * قال فامضِ بنا اذاً فان
الرهبان الان عاكفون على الصلوة * فخرجا من باب الدير ولم يعلم بهما احد *
فلما بعدا قليلا هنّأ الفارياق صاحبه بخروجه من ربقة الجهل وقال له * لعمرى
لو كنت كلّما اكلت اكلة عدس خلّصت راهبا او رُوَيهبا او بالحرى راهبة او
رُوَيهبة لوددت ان لا آكل الدهر غيره وان اكّل بدنى * فجزى الله الدير خيرا *

God doesn't give a fig for the religion of the ignorant. Then, when you reach sixty, you'll find the monastic life awaiting you."

"How am I to get free?" the man asked him. "If you have belongings in the 1.12.15
monastery," said the Fāriyāq, "I'll help you carry them." "I have nothing but what you see upon me," said the other. "Let's be off, then," said the Fāriyāq, "for the monks are presently occupied with their prayers," and they set off through the door of the monastery, and no one noticed. When they had gone a little way, the Fāriyāq congratulated his friend on his escape from the noose of ignorance and told him, "I swear, if I were to free a monk or a novice, or at least a nun or a novice nun, every time I ate lentils, I'd want to eat nothing else so long as I should live, even if the lentils consumed my body. May God reward the monastery well!"

الفصل الثالث عشر

في مقامة
او مقامة في الفصل الثالث عشر

قد مضت عليّ برهة من الدهر من غير ان اتكلف السجع والتجنيس واحسبني نسيت ١٫١٣٫١
ذلك * فلا بدّ من ان اختبر قريحتي في هذا الفصل فانه اولى به من غيره * اذ هو
اكثر من الثاني عشر واقل من الرابع عشر * وهكذا افعل في كل فصل يُوسَم بهذا
العدد حتى افرغ من كتبي الاربعة * فتكون جملة المقامات فيما اظن اربعا * فاقول
حدَّس الهارس بن هشام قال اَرِقت في ليلة خافية الكوكب * بادية الهَيْدَب * ٢٫١٣٫١
طويلة الذنب * مَلْاَى من الكُرَب * الى الكَرَب *فجعلت انام على ظهري مرة وعلى
جنبي اخرى * واتصوّر شخصا ناعسا امامي يتثآب وآخر ينخر نخرا * واخر يتهوّم
سكرا * فان التصوّر فيما قالوا يبعث على فعل ما ترغب النفس فيه * وينشط الى ما
تصبو اليه وتشتهيه * ومع ذلك فما اكتحلت غُمضا * ولا فتح فمي تثاؤب طولا ولا
عرضا * وكان يُخيَّل لي ان اهل الارض كلهم رقود وانا وحدي من بينهم اَرِق *
وان جميع جيراني في سكون وانا دونهم قَلِق * فقمت الى الشراب فحسوت[1] منه
حسوة * فلم تك الّا غفوه * كانّما كانت هفوه * فافقت في اسوأ حال * وشرّ
بلبال * والهموم قد انثالت عليّ من كل جانب * والافكار متطايرة على كل مقارب

١ ١٨٥٥: حسوة.

Chapter 13

A *Maqāmah*, or, a *Maqāmah* on "Chapter 13"

A while has passed now since I tasked myself with writing in rhymed prose and patterned period, and I think I've forgotten how to do so. I must therefore put my faculties to the test in this chapter, which is worthier than the rest—because it's higher in number than the twelfth and lower than the fourteenth—and I shall continue to do so in every chapter branded with this number till I've finished my four books. The total number of *maqāmah*s in it will therefore, I believe, be four. Thus I declare: 1.13.1

Faid al-Hāwif ibn Hifām in lifping tones:[219] "Sleepless I lay on a night on which the stars were *concealed*, the clouds *revealed*, a night never-*ending*, full of worries to anguish *trending*. Now on my back to sleep I *tried*, now on any other *side*, placing before my eyes the image of a person drowsing or yawning or *snoring*, or of another into a drunken stupor *falling*. Imagination, they say, is conducive to the doing of the thing for which you *burn*, and stimulates the achievement of that for which you *yearn*, despite which sleep to my eyes not a drop of salve *applied*, not a yawn spread wide my mouth, from top to bottom or from side to *side*. Meseemed the people of the earth, without exception, were fast *asleep*, while I alone among them all no repose could *reap*, that all my neighbors were at *rest*, while I alone remained *distressed*. So I arose to take a *nip* and took indeed a *sip*, but all this brought was an *oscitation*, something barely more than a lapse of *attention*, after which I awoke once more quite *overwrought*, in a desperate agony of *thought*, cares thronging toward me from every *side*, my worries ranging far and *wide*. 1.13.2

ومجانب * فكان يخطر ببالى كل ممكن ومحال * ويعاودنى ما كنت فكّرت فيه من
الاحوال * مرة منذ احوال * فلما علمت ان النوم قد ندّ عنى وان تناومت * وانه ٣،١٣،١
لا بد من ترقب الفجران اذعنت وان قاومت * مددت يدى الى كتاب اطالع فيه *
وقلت ان لم يُمنى فينبّهنى ببعض معانيه * فتناولت اقرب ما وصلت اليه يدى *
وانا غير موثر احد الكتب على غيره فى خَلَدى * واذا به كتاب موازنة الحالتين *
ومرازنة الآلتين * للشيخ الامام العالم العامل * الفاضل الكامل * ابى رُشْد نُهَية
بن حزم * المشهور بالبلاغة فى النثر والنظم * وهو كتاب لم يسبقه اليه احد من
المولفين * ولم يجاره فيه كاتب من المجلّين * فقد وازن فيه بين حالتى بوس المرء ونعيمه *
ورَوحه وهمومه * ومنافعه ومضارّه * واحزانه ومسارّه * منذ كونه طفلا * الى
ان يصير كهلا * ثم شيخا محلا * وقد جعل ذلك فى جدولين متقابلين * واسلوبين
متفاضلين * الا انه لما كان الشيخ قدس الله سرّه * ورفع فى اعلى عليّين مقامه
وقدره * على ما يظهر لى ذا عيشة راضية * وسعادة وافية * وهمة ماضية *
رجّح طرف اللذات على غيرها * واستقلّ شرّ الحيوة بالنسبة الى خيرها * حتى
انه زعم ان اللذة تكون عن الفعل والتصوّر معا * بخلاف الالم فان الفكر لا يقع منه
موقعا * وانه كان اذا امتثل خَوْدا يداعبها وتداعبه * هزّته نشوة طرب مال بها
سريره ومركبه * وكلكله ومنكبه * بيدَ انى ارتبت فى كلامه فى هذا المحلّ * وقلت
سبحان الله لا بدّ لكل مولف من هفوة وان جلّ * وذلك انى لما تصورت الشخص
المتهوّم * والناعس والمتثائب وانا متناوم * لم يُغْننى التصوّر عن الفعل نقيرا *
ولا وجدت فيه لذة لا قليلا ولا كثيرا * على انى اذهب الى ما ذهب اليه بعض
المجانين * من ان لذة النوم لا تكون قبله ولا معه ولا بعده للنائمين * وهى عقدة
للطبائعيين * لا يمكنهم حلّها بلسانهم وافكارهم * ولا باسنانهم واظفارهم *

All things possible and impossible to my mind *occurred*, every situation over which I'd ever worried (if only once and many years before) *recurred*.

"When I grasped that slumber had escaped me, even though sleep I *feigned*, and that I'd have to witness dawn whether I resisted or was *resigned*, I stretched out my hand for a book to read, with the following *hope*, that, 'If it doesn't make me sleep, it may at least engage my attention with some *trope*.' I picked up the first thing to come to hand, feeling no preference for any particular work, and what should it be but *Kitāb Muwāzanat al-ḥālatayn wa-murāzanat al-ālatayn* (*The Book of Balancing the Two States and Comparing the Two Straits*)[220] by the Honored Shaykh and Productive Scholar of Perfect Virtue, Abū Rushd 'Brains' ibn *Ḥazm*,[221] whose rhetorical skills in both prose and verse have provoked widespread *enthusiasm*. This is a book such as no author before him ever *hatched* nor any writer, however distinguished, ever *matched*, for in it he compares man's two states of wretchedness and *leisure*, of joy and care, of gain and loss, of sorrow and *pleasure*, from childhood till he arrives at *maturity*, then desiccated *senility*, all set out in facing *tables* using a columnar system that comparison *enables*. However, the shaykh (God sanctify his soul and elevate his rank and *worth* to the highest point above the *earth*) living, as it seems to me, a life of goodly *weal*, with abundant fortune and energetic *zeal*, gave undue weight to *pleasure* and failed to treat life's evils in equal *measure*. He even asserts that pleasure is to be had from both deed and *thought*—unlike pain, in which thinking is of no *import*—claiming that were he to picture himself cavorting with a ripe young *wench*, and she with him, he'd be so shaken by ecstasy he'd be entirely carried away, chest and flank, bed and *bench*. However, I doubted his words upon this *point*, thinking to myself, 'Glory be! Every writer, however great, must on occasion be out of *joint*': in my case, when I pictured the drunkard, the drowser, and the yawner, as I lay there trying to sleep, all that picturing didn't compensate for the actual thing by even a *jot*,[222] and I found no pleasure in it, either a little or *a lot*. I tend to the belief of a certain madman that the pleasure of sleep is not felt by the sleeper, either while, after, or before it *prevails*—a knot those who hold to the humoral theory[223] remain incapable of untying by talking or thinking, or even with their teeth and their *nails*. 1.13.3

غير ان عبارة المصنف كانت من العلم والحكمة بحيث تخلب عقل الناقد الخبير * وتربك فى تحرّى احد القولين كل نحرير * فلما اطلقت النظر فيهما وعاد الىّ كليلا * واعملت حدّ النقد ورجع مفلولا * عزمت على ان استجلى هذا الاشكال * من بعض ذوى الدراية والجدال * فقلت في نفسى كما ان يدى نالت ادنى الاسفار * كذلك يكون مراوحى عليه ادنى الجار * وكان يسكن بالقرب منى مطران يطرئ قومه على حِلْيته * ويُعَظِّمون فضله وادبه على طول لحيته * فقصدته ضحوة النهار * باديَ الاستبشار * فرايته ذا بكّلة تروق * وبِزّة تشوق * فعرضت عليه الجدولين وقلت افتنى فى هذه القضية * ولك الاجر من رب البرية * فنظر فيهما ثم حرّك راسه * وجعل يرمش ثم يشكو نُعاسه * وقال لى ما ترجمته * اذ لم يكن ممن تسمو الى السجع همّته * ما لحنت مغزاهما * ولا دريت فحواهما * ولوكانا ٤،١٣،١

بعبارة ركيكة * كان ذلك علىّ اسهل من الجلوس على هذه الاريكة * فقلت قد اخّره في العلم والثّقْف * تقدمه فى الصف * ونقص من عقله وفهمه ما زاد فى لحيته وكمه * فلاستعملنّ بعده اكثر الناس حمقا وهَوَجا * وما ذلك الا معلم الصبيان الهجا * وكان في البلد مَنِ اتّصف بهذه الصفة * وهو مع ذلك ذو كبر وعجرفة * فقصدت محلّه * والقيت عليه المسئله * فاذا به قام يصفّق بيديه * ويرارئ بعينيه * ويقول لقد سقطت على الخبير * واهتديت براى بصير * ان شئت ان تعرف اىّ القولين ارجح * واصدق واصح * فَزِنِ الجدولين دون جلد الكتاب في ميزان * فما رجح منهما فهو الراجح ما اختلف في ذا اثنان * فقمت من عنده غضبانا[1] نادما * ولعنت الارق الذى كان السبب في ان اكون لمعلمى الصبيان مكالما * بعد ان قرات في غير كتاب * وسمعت من ذوى الالباب * ٥،١٣،١

---

[1] ١٨٥٥: غضبان.

"This said, the words of the compiler of these tables are of so full of knowledge and *wisdom* as to bemuse the expert critic, and reduce any maven, in the investigation of either argument, to *confusion*. After, then, I'd turned on them my eye's *gaze*, and it had returned *aglaze*, and I'd applied to them the blade of careful *examination*, only for it to come back full of *indentation*, I determined to throw light on this *problematique* by consulting one known for his skill in debate and insightful *critique*, saying to myself, 'Just as my hand fell upon the nearest *tome*, so let my next choice be the neighbor closest to *home*.' Living near me was a metropolitan whose adornments, worth, and culture by his congregation were lauded and *cheered* at a length equal to his *beard*. I went to see him at midday, all ready to rejoice, and found him wearing a buckle to *amaze*, a habit to set the heart *ablaze*. Setting before him the two tables, I said, 'Rule for me on this *case*, and may you be rewarded by God, Lord of the Human *Race*.' He looked at them, then nodded off and started *blinking*, complaining he was too sleepy to do much *thinking*, and telling me something to the effect that since he wasn't one of those whose ambitions ever *rose* to rhyming in *prose*, he 'hadn't caught their *implication* or grasped their *signification*, though, had they been penned in hackneyed terms, I *vouch*, I'd have got them as easy as sitting on this *couch*!' 1.13.4

"I thought, 'His advancement up the ranks of the clergy has retarded his scholarship and *erudition*, and the longer his beard and sleeves have grown the shorter have become his intellect and *intuition*. Let me enquire *then* of the silliest and least intelligent of *men*, and who other should that *be* but the one who teaches children their *ABC*?' In the *town* was one who, despite his pride and arrogance, had, for these qualities, won *renown*. Off I set, then, to where he was and put to him the *case*, and he stood up, clapped his hands, rolled his eyes, and said, 'Guided by sound judgment, you've arrived at the right *place*. If you wish to know which of the two arguments carries the greater *weight*, is the more correct and *accurate*, place the two columns (minus the binding) in a *scale*. The one that dips will be the weightier; on that all men will agree without *fail*.' I left him, then, in fury and regret, cursing the sleeplessness that had driven me to ask a teacher of young boys, even after I'd read in books on more than one *occasion*, and heard from men of *perspication*, that they were the most feeble of *mind* among God's *creation*, the most to 1.13.5

انهم اسخف خلق الله عقلا * واكثرهم جهلا * وابعدهم عن الفهم * واسفههم
٦،١٣،١ الى الوهم * فسرت في ذلك اليوم * الى فقيه من جلّة القوم * قد كبر عمامته
وكوّرها * ووسّع جبّته وزوّرها * فقلت افتنى ايها الفاضل الاحذق * اى
القولين عندك احقّ واصدق * فقال امّا اذ جئتنى مستفتيا * ورمت ان تكون
برأيى مستهديا * وبطريقى مقتديا * فانى اقول لك بعد التروّى * في هذا المذهب
المتحوّى * انّا معاشرَ الفقهآ من اهل الكلام * القائمين بِاحكام الاَحكام * وتبيين
المتشابه بين الانام * وانّ من دأبنا اظهاراً للحق ان نسهب في التعليل * ونكثر من
قال وقيل * اذ لا بدّ من انتشآء عَرف الصواب * من الاسهاب * ومن الاهتدآء
الى بعض المذاهب * بفرض المستحيل وجعل المعدوم كالموجود الواجب * فعندى
انه لا بدّ من عدّ الفاظ القولين * واحصآء حروف الجدولين * فما كان منهما اكثر
حروفا * فهو ارجح واحسن تاليفا * والله اعلم * ففصلت من عند الفقيه * كما
٧،١٣،١ فصلت من عند صاحبه السفيه * وقلت انما اللوم على مستفتيه * ثم قصدت
شاعرا كنت اعهده يتلهوق ويتشدّق * ويتفصّح ويتمدّح * ويتبجّح ويترنّح * وقلت
له هاك ما تحرز عليه اجرا * ويكسبك بين الناس فخرا * فاَبِنّ لى اىّ الاهلوبين
اَبدع * وبالحق فاَصدع * قال اما انا فما لى من خَلاق[1] في الدنيا ولا نصيب *
غير المدح والنسيب * ففى الاولى غُصّتى وفي الثانى لذّتى * فاصبر علىّ ريثما
اطالع ديوانى كلّه * واتصفحه جُملَه * فان وجدت المديح فيه اكثر من الغزَل *
كان الخير في الدنيا اقل * فالحقته بصاحبيه الفقيه والمعلّم * وقلت كم من متكلّم
٨،١٣،١ مُكلِم * ثم سرت الى كاتب الامير * وكان مشهودا له بالتحرّى والتحرير * فاثنيت
عليه قبل السؤال مطرئا * وقلت لم يكن غيرك في ذا مجزئا * فقال انّ سعادتى

١ ١٨٥٥: خلاق [كذا].

ignorance *inclined*, the furthest from *ratiocination* and most given to foolishness and *hallucination*.

"On that day then I betook myself to a *jurisprudent*, of all that people the most *resplendent*, who had inflated his turban and coiled it round and *round*, using extra cloth, and decorations on his *gown*, and to him I said, 'Give me a ruling, most virtuous and sagacious man, as to which of the two arguments in your opinion is the closer to the *truth*, which most *sooth*.' Answered he, 'If you've come to me seeking a ruling, by my opinion to be guided and my path to *emulate*, allow me to tell you (due deliberation having been *devoted* to this school of law so *convoluted*) that we—we noble company of jurists, that is—are men of *debate*, makers of the rules that govern the rules that govern the *game*, revealers of fine distinctions among things that might otherwise seem the *same*; likewise that it is our way, to make clear the truth, to analyze in depth and go to great lengths in *argumentation*, since there's no escape, if you'd sniff the aroma of veracity, from *expatiation*, and from seeking the guidance of one of the *schools*, which, by insisting on the impossible and making from the nonexistent something necessarily existent,[224] imposes its *rules*. In my opinion, then, you must add up the words of the two arguments and calculate the number of letters that in each column are *disposed*, and whichever has more will then be the weightier and better *composed* (though God alone truly *knows*).' So I parted ways with that jurisprudent as I had from his foolish *friend*, telling myself that any who asked him for a ruling had none to blame but himself, in the *end*. 1.13.6

"Next I proceeded to a poet whom I knew to be a great *flatterer*, a mouth-twisting faux-Arabic *patterer*, a would-be master of classical *lays* and spouter of *praise*, a *gusher* and self-*pusher*, and I said to him, 'Here's something off which you can make some money and that may make you *renowned*. Show me which of the two forms is the more brilliant in style, and let the truth *resound*!' Said he, 'Eulogies and poems of love are all I *write*; in the first I express my pain, in the second my *delight*. Be patient while I review my *Collected Works*, leafing through it from cover to *cover*; if I find the panegyrics there more numerous than the sonnets, the good things of this world must be the *fewer*.' I added him then to his friends the jurisprudent and the *teacher*, remarking, 'How many a wound from how many a *speaker*!' 1.13.7

"Then I set off for the scribe of the *emir*, one whose skills of discernment and careful accounting were acknowledged far and *near*, but before putting 1.13.8

في الكون هى ان ارضى عن اميرى ويرضى عنى * وشقاوتى هى ان اغضب منه ويغضب منى * وقد نسيت كل ما جرى علىّ من الغضب والرضى * لكثرة المشاده والمقتضَى * فان صبرت علىَّ في المستانف شهرا * لاقيّد في دفترى ما القاه منه حلوا ومرّا * ونفعا وضُرّا * افدتك الجواب فاقبل عذرا * فصيّرته رابع الثلثة * وقلت لا ستشيرن ذا حَداثة * فان اهل المراتب والمناصب قد ذهبت صدارتهم

٩،١٣،١ بالبابهم * فلم يبقَ فيهم خير لقارع بابهم *فجئت الفارياق وهو مكبّ على النسخ * وفى طلعته مبادئ المسخ * فقد رايت عينيه غائرتين * ويديه ذاويتين * وعظم خديه ناتئا * وجلده كالظل زائنا * حتى رثيت لحالته * وكدت امسك عن الكلام اشفاقا من بطالته * لكنه لما رآنى قام الىّ * ثم اقبل علىّ * وقال هل من خدمة اقتضت سَعْيِى * او نجوَى اوجبت وعيى * فقلت قد اقدمنى كذا وكذا * فاكفنى ذل السؤال كُفِيتَ الاذى * فاخذ رقعة من تحت اسمال * وكتب فيها في الحال *

١٠،١٣،١ اتيتني مستفتياً فى امرِ يعلمه كل امرءٍ ذى حِجْرِ
الخيرَ ان قابلته بالشرّ فى العمركان قطرةً من بحر
الا تَرَى الاَجْرب كيف تَسْرى عَدْواه فى جميع اهل المصر
وليس من ذى صحّـَة ويُسْر عدوى لمن داناه طول العمر
والطفل اذ يُثغركم من ضُرّ يَلْقىَ ويُلْقَى عنده فى قبر
وعند اِشعارٍ ونبت ظُفرِ ليس له من لذَّةٍ وسُرّ
وكلّ عُضولقبول الكسر اقرب منه لقبول الجبر

the question, I praised him to his *face* and said, 'None but you could possibly *suffice*.' Said he, 'Happiness for me lies in being content with my emir and his *contentment*, unhappiness in resenting him and feeling his *resentment*. At this point, given the fighting and all that goes with it that there's *been*, I've forgotten both any anger and any content that I may have *seen*. If you can wait for a month into the *future*, so I may inscribe in my ledger all that I meet with from him that is sweet and all that is sour, all that is gold and all that is *pewter*, I'll inform you of the answer in due *time*; till then, I must *decline*.' I added him then to the three, making him number *four*,[225] and thought, 'I really must consult someone who's still young, for pride of *place* has left of the brains of those who hold high rank and office not a *trace*, and there's nothing left for those who knock at their *door*.'

"To the Fāriyāq then I *went*, to find him o'er his copying *bent*, on his visage 1.13.9
the first signs of *transmogrification*, eyes, as I beheld, deeply sunken, hands suffering from *desiccation*, cheekbones as though from the face's surface *hewn*, skin as tight as the shade at *noon*, so that I deplored his *state* and came close to staying silent for pity at his *plight*. When he saw me, though, he rose and came toward me, saying, 'Is there some service you require me to perform, or private word you need to *convey*?' 'Thus and so,' I said, 'have come my *way*, so settle this question, God save you from *harm*,' at which he pulled from inside his tattered coat a scrap of paper and on it wrote without a *qualm*:

You came to me seeking an answer— 1.13.10
　One to mindful men[226] already known—to a question.
Good, compared to evil,
　Is, over a life span, as a drop to an ocean.
See you not how, if one man has the mange,
　To a whole city he spreads his disease,
Yet no one infects his fellows, no matter how close,
　Who's healthy and lives a life of ease?
How many a sickness afflicts the child from the day he cuts his teeth,
　And with him to the grave's consigned?
How he, from the first sprouting of his hair and nails,
　No pleasure and no joy can find?
Any limb's more easy broken
　Than it is mended

وما فساده سريعا يُزرى   كالعين لن تصلحه فى دهر
ونعى طفل لابيه يفرى   فؤاده وكلَّ عظم يبرى
وليس فى مولده من بِشر   ندٍ لحزنٍ موته الاضرّ
وما تكون لذة عن فكر   اذا تحققتَ ولا عن ذِكر
وانما ذا هوَس قد يجرى   فى خاطر المغفَّل المغترّ
فهل تصوُّر الشفآء يبري   ذا مرض أُمرِض منذ شهر
وهل لمن يبرد وقت القُرّ   دِفء بتذكار اوان الحرّ
فليس دُنيانا لاهل الخِبر   سوى بلآء دائم وخُسر
يُولَد فيها العبد غير حُرّ   وهكذا يموت رغما فادرِ

قال فلما اخذت الرقعة وتاملت فيها * وتحققت معانيها * علمت ان ١١،١٣،١
قوله هو الاسدّ * وان قول غيره هذيان وفَنَد * فقلت له بورك فى زمن جاد بمثلك * وهدى المستفيدين الى رشدك وفضلك * وقبحا لاهل الثَرا * اذ لم يُحلّوك ارفع الذرى * ثم انصرفت من عنده داعيا * ولما قاله واعيا *

And that, like the eye, whose corruption will fast destroy you,
  You'll ne'er fix, till time is ended.
Mourning for a child rends his father's heart
  Wears through his every bone,
And in his birth there is no joy
  Equal to the sorrow of his death, by which the greater harm is done.
Pleasure cannot come from thinking,
  Nor from recollection; that's naught but an illusion
When you think upon it well—one that may occur
  To the dimwit or victim of delusion.
Can a patient who for the past month's been sick,
  By picturing a cure, his illness treat?
Can one who in winter's depth grows cold
  Feel warm by recalling the days of heat?
This world of ours, to those who know,
  Is naught but loss and tribulation that we must endure.
Man's born enslaved, not free,
  And so he dies, of that you may be sure.

"Thus his words, and as I took the scrap, my gaze upon it *bent*, and started **1.13.11** thinking what it *meant*, I realized that these words of his were the most *wise*, those of the others mere drivel and *lies*, and I told him, 'Blessed be the Lord for an age that has brought us the likes of *you*, and guided seekers after knowledge to your good sense and superior *view*, and shame upon the people of this *earth*, should they fail to recognize your *worth*!' Then I departed from where he was, calling blessings down upon his *head*, and heedful of everything he'd *said*."

الفصل الرابع عشر

في سرّ

هجع هجع الحمد لله * الحمد لله * قد تخلصت من انشآء هذه المقامة ومن رقمها ايضا ١،١٤،١
فانها كانت باهظة * ولم يبقَ لى همّ منها سوى حث القارئ على مطالعتها *
وهى وان تكن خشنة غير مهلهلة كسجع الحريرى الا انها تُلبَس على علّاتها * وتحمد
لا فاداتها * وفى ظنى ان الثانية تكون احسن منها * والثالثة احسن من الثانية *
والرابعة احسن من الثالثة * والخمسين احسن من التاسعة والاربعين * لا تخف
من هذا التهويل والتوهيل لا تخف * انما هى اربع لا غير كما وعدتك * والان ينبغى ٢،١٤،١
ان اعصر يافوخى لاستقطر منه افكارا ومعانى حسنة والفاظا رائقة مع تجنب
الثرثرة * فان العلمآء يسمون ذلك فيما اظنّ اِخلآء * ولكن قف هنا حتى اسألهم *
ماذا تسمّون الكلام الذى يتدفق بالمعانى ويبلّ قارئه حتى آتيكم به * فان لم تسمّوه لى
حالا فلا تلومونى على نقيضه * فانى انا من الموجود ودابى ان ابحث عنه لا عن
المعدوم * ولما كان اسم الاخلآ موجودا ونقيضه معدوما ناسب ان اعدل اليه
عن غيره * الى ان تتواطئوا على اسم ولكن لا بالخناق والتناوش * والنقار والتهاوش *
وبالجلاد والجدال * وبالتماسك بالجيوب والاذيال * بل بالرزانة والوقار * والاَوْن
والاستبصار * فان الرزين اذا وضع اسمًا لشى جآء ذلك الاسم رزينا مثله *

Chapter 14

A Sacrament[227]

Ahahahah! Ahahahah! Thank God! Thank God I'm done with the composition of that *maqāmah,* and with its number too,[228] for it was weighing on my mind. Now all that remains for me to do is to urge the reader to read it. Though more coarsely woven than the finely knit rhymed prose of al-Ḥarīrī and despite its prosodic *irregularities,* it may, for all that, be worn, and commended for its beneficial *verities.* I believe the second will be better than it was, the third better than the second, the fourth better than the third, and the fiftieth better than the forty-ninth. (Don't panic! Don't panic at these attempts to shock and scare! There are in fact, as promised, only four.) 1.14.1

Now I have to squeeze my sconce to extract some more nice thoughts, figures, and choice words, at the same time avoiding chatter, a process that scholars refer to, I believe, as "voiding verbiage." But hang on a moment, and I'll ask them! What do you call words that are so bursting with meaning that they drench the reader, so that I can fetch them for you? If you don't tell me their name right away, don't blame me if I use their opposite. I exist, and it is my custom to look for what exists, not for what doesn't. Given that the term "voiding verbiage" exists and its opposite doesn't, it is perfectly appropriate for me to turn to it in preference to some other term. You may if you wish put your heads together and come up with a word—but instead of flying at each other's throats and *fighting,* pecking out each other's eyes and *biting,* or striking with *swords* and swiping with *words,* or grabbing each other by your pockets and *skirts,* do so sedately and *soberly,* serenely and *rationally,* for when someone sedate bestows a name on something, it comes out as sedate as he is and cannot thereafter be converted into something different. In fact, the thing named may even acquire dignity from the name given it, 1.14.2

فلا يمكن بعدُ انتقاله الى آخر * بل ربّما وَقُرَ بالاسم المسمّى وان يكن مما اتصف بالخفّة
والطيش * الا ترى ان كلام الشاعر الرقيق ياتى رقيقا * وكلام الضخم ياتى ضخما *
كما قيل كلام الملوك ملوك الكلام * وشعر المرأة ياتى خالبا للعقول لاعبا بالالباب
مثلها * ويستثنى من هذه القاعدة وضع الولد من قبل ابيه اى مادة توزيغ الولد * ١،١٤،٣
لا ان الاب يحبل ويلد * وذلك ان الوالد قد يكون قبيحا وياتى ولده صبيحا *
وسببه ان الايلاد لما كان من الافعال التى لا تتمّ الا بمشاركة اثنين اعنى رجلا
وامراة اذ التغليب هنا لا يخلو ايضا من الابهام * لم يكن للوالد مطلق التصرف فى
تهيئته ولده كما شآء * فقد يكون هو عند ذلك مقدّرا له شكلا ارتضاه وتكون امّه
حرسها الله مقدّرة له شكلا آخر بحسبما استحسنته وخلج صدرها اذ ذاك * فياتى
الولد خنفشاريّا * لا يقال ان الرجل لا يستحضر عند ذلك صورة معلومة لذهوله
بشاغل المادة * فان ذلك لا يصدق على من اَلِفَ شيا واحدا بخصوصه * فان
طول الفة الانسان لشى تعدّل هواه فيه * فيباشره برشد ورويّة * فَمَثَله كَمَثَل
الطبّاخ الشبعان يطبخ خضض الطعام باتقان واحكام بخلاف الجائع فانه يلهوج
عمله ويلهوقه * فاعلم اذاً بعد هذا الاستطراد البديع * والعضال المُجيع * ان ١،١٤،٤
الفارياق ذهب ذات يوم الى بعض القسيسين ليعترف له بما فعل وفكر * وقال
من المُنكَر * فقال له القسيس فيما ساله به * قد سمعت عنك انك كَلِف بالنظم
وبالالحان وهما من اعظم اسباب الفساد والغرام * فهل سوّل اليك الخناس ان
تتغزل فى الشعر بامراة قاعدة النهد * مورّدة الخدّ * بيّنة الكَحَل * مرتجّة الكفل *
نحيلة الخصر * مفلّجة الثغر * عَثِلة الساقين * مجدولة الساعدين * سودآ الشعر
والحَلَمتين * نجلآء العينين * مخضّبة الكفين * رقيقة الشفتين * مزججة الحاجبين *

even when it is innately insignificant and frivolous. Have you not noticed how the words of a slim poet come out slim, and those of a big poet come out big? As the saying goes, "The words of kings are the kings of words." By the same token, poetry written by a woman is as bewitching to the mind and teasing to the heart as a woman.

An exception to this principle is the donation of the child by the father, meaning the donation by the father of the material used to form the child. By making an exception of this I don't mean to say that the father becomes pregnant and gives birth but that the father may be ugly and the child turn out good-looking. The reason is that, because conception requires the collaboration of two persons, i.e., a man and a woman, it is unclear which contribution is determinative. The father does not have absolute sway to shape the child as he wishes. He may have in mind at that instant a certain form that he finds attractive, while the mother, God protect her, may have another, depending on her preferences and whatever is then uppermost in her mind; as a result the child may come out a bit of this and bit of that. By the way, it cannot be said that the man is incapable of summoning up a familiar form at that moment just because he's all in a tizzy over the business of that formative material. That's not credible in the case of one who's become used to what is always the same old thing where he's concerned, for long acquaintance modifies a person's attitude to a thing, and, as a result, he deals with it with good sense and deliberation. Take for example the well-fed cook, who prepares all the various dishes with perfect skill and mastery, unlike the hungry cook, who hurries his work and botches it. 1.14.3

Know then (after this polished *excursion* and prolonged and stimulating *insertion*) that the Fāriyāq went one day to a priest to make confession to him of all he had done, said, and *thought* that he didn't *ought*. The priest asked, among other questions, "I hear you're fond of poetry and tunes, which are among the worst causes of evil and passion. Has the Recoiler ever put it into your mind to court in verse a woman firm of breast, rosy of cheek, the kohl on her eyes clear to *see*, her buttocks wobbling *free*, slender of *waist*, her teeth widely *spaced*, her legs with thickness and splendor *graced*, her forearms muscled and without *slack*, her hair and nipples *black*, her eyes startling in the contrast of black and *white*, her hands with henna *bright*, her lips *fine*, her eyebrows a thin, arched *line*, her belly-button *round*, her belly folds *unbound*, her smile *sweet*, her figure *svelte*, with saliva like *honey*, 1.14.4

مدورة السرّة * ذات عُكَن مفترّة * حلوة الابتسام * مهفهفة القوام * لها رُضاب عذب * ونكهة تسكر الصبّ * قال قد فعلت ذلك لكنى اِنْ اراك الّا
حريفى فى هذه الصنعة * فقد رايتك تحسن وصف الحسان اىَّ احسان * قال ٥،١٤،١
ليست حرفتى تلفيق الكلام * وانما هو شئ عرفته بالقياس والالهام * فان كلّ مَن تعاطى النظم يملأ دماغه بهذا الوصف المحرّم * وكيف كان فلا بدّ من ان تحرق غَزَلك كله * بالتفصيل والجملة * فانه يبعث الاَغرار على المعاصى * فتُجزَى به يوم يُؤخَذ بالنواصى * وتعزّ التفاصِى * قال كيف احرق فى ساعة واحدة ما سهرت فيه ليالى متعدّدة حرمت فيها من الكرى * وكابدت بها جهدا ولا جهد الشَرَى * او السُرَى * فكنت اذا نظمت البيت من القصيدة يخيّل الىّ انى قطعت مرحلة الى محلّ المتغزّل بها * وعند تمام القصيدة اتصوّر انى وصلت اليها ولم يبقَ بينى وبينها سوى فتح الباب * فكان الختام عندى افتتاحا خلافا لجميع الشعرآء * ولذلك لم اكن اقصد القصائد الطويلة خشيةَ اَن تطول علىّ المسافة بطولها * فهل من الراى السديد ان يحبط عملى كله من اجل الاغرار * وبعدُ فانى لا اريد انهم يقراون كلامى * لانهم ان لم يفهموه سألوا عنه اهل العلم فيذمه هولآء ويخطّئوننى ويفنّدوننى * اذ لا يرون فى كلام الصغير الوضيع حسنا * وان استحسنوه لم يكن جزآى منهم الا قولهم اخزاه الله وقاتله الله وثكلته امه ولا ابَ له ولا امَّ له * قال ان ابيتَ الا الاِصرار على العناد * والزيغ عن جادّة الرشاد * امسكت
عنك مغفرة ذنوبك * ونددت فى الكنيسة بعيوبك * قال لا تعجّل فان العجلة ٦،١٤،١
من الشيطان * ارايتك لو مدحتك بقصيدة طويلة تجعلها كفّارة عن الذنب * وان شئت ان امدح فيها ايضا جميع الرهبان والراهبات والعابدين والعابدات والزاهدين والزاهدات والناسكين والناسكات والقانتين والقانتات والمفرّدين

sweet enough to turn iron into *candy*?" Said the Fāriyāq, "I have indeed done so, but I see that you are my fellow in this craft, for I note how well you can describe a beautiful woman."

Said the other, "It isn't my job to produce such verbal *fabrication*, just something I've learned by analogy and spontaneous *inspiration*, for all who listen to *verse* find their brains filled with such descriptions *perverse*. But, be that as it may, you must burn your love poems, *each one*, singly and in *sum*, for they incite the heedless to *err* and you'll be punished for them on that day when men are 'seized by their forelocks,'[229] and you hold extrication *dear*." "How," said the Fāriyāq, "can you expect me to burn in a single moment things I stayed up working on for many a night, during which I knew no slumber and on which I worked as hard as a horse in a *race*, or cameleers who, from dusk to dawn, maintain their *pace*? When I finished a line of the poem, it would seem to me as though I'd covered a stage on the road to her whom I was wooing, and, when the poem was done, I'd imagine I'd reached her and all that stood between us was for me to open the door, which made the conclusion in my case an inauguration, in contrast with all other poets. That is why I didn't attempt long poems—lest the time it took to write them should be as long as the time it took me to cover the distance to my beloved. Does it make sense that all that effort of mine should be thwarted for the sake of the heedless? Not to mention that I don't want them to read what I write anyway, because if they don't understand it, they'll ask the scholars, who will proceed to hold it up to scorn, accusing me of mistakes and pointing out shortcomings. They never see merit in the writings of the young and humble, and even if they do, my only reward will be, 'God shame him! God destroy him! May his mother be bereaved of him! May he have no father and no mother!'" Said the priest, "If on stubbornness you *insist*, and in divergence from the road of right guidance you *persist*, I'll withhold *absolution* and expose your dirty laundry in open church for *ablution*." 1.14.5

"Don't be so hasty," said the Fāriyāq, "for 'haste is of the Devil'! Do you suppose, if I praised you in a long ode, you could take that as expiation for my sin? And if you'd like me to laud therein each monk and nun, each contemplative (male and female), each ascetic (male and female), each recluse (male and female), each person who stands long in prayer (male and female), each hermit (male and female), each ecstatic reciter (male and female), each preacher (male and female), each caller on God's name (male and female), 1.14.6

والمفرّدات والمغبّرين والمغبّرات والمذكّرين والمذكرات والذاكرين والذاكرات والمتقين
والمتّقيات والمتبتلين والمتبتلات والمتهجدين والمتهجّدات والساجدين والساجدات
والمُخْبتين والمخبتات والمسبّحين والمسبّحات فعلتُ * ففكّر ساعة وكانّه رأى ان ليس
فى التغزل كبير اثم * فان وصف المراة مثلا بِضخَم الكفل وفعومة الذراع وتدملك
الثدى اذا كانت فى الواقع كذلك انما هو من قبيل قول القائل البدر طالع عند طلوعه
او السحاب منقشع عند انقشاعه * وانما يكون افترآءً واثما ما اذا وُصِفت بذلك
وكانت مسحآء مردآ * وكانت تتَّخذ الحشايا لتُحسَب عجزآء فصدّقها ناظرها فى ذلك
وقال فيها ما قال مجازفة * فلما تدبّر الامر ورازه بعقله قال * لا ينبغى ان تتَّخذ ٧،١٤،١
مدحى كفارة فانى اخشى ان تمسك بى ولا تعود تطلقنى * اذ ارى من قوافيك فى
الفاعلين والفاعلات انك مُسَكة عُلَقة نُشَبة لُزَمة * وانما تمدح اوليآء الله والربّانيين
الصالحين الذين زهدوا فى الدنيا رغبة فى الاخرة لوجه الله ولبسوا المسوح ولزموا
السهر فى طاعة الله وداوموا على التقشف حبا بالله * فمنهم من لم ياكل مدّة
حياته كلها الا العدس والخبز جافّا صلبا * فقال الفارياق واعقبه ايضا كسرسن ٨،١٤،١
وحكة * قف قف * قد نسيت ان اذكر لك شيا اخطره الان ببالى العدس *
وذلك انى تسبّبت مرة فى اخراج رويهب من ديره وتركه الطريقه * وانما الذى
اغرانى بذلك ما قاسيته فيه ففعلت ما فعلت تشفّيا * فقال ذنبك فى التشفى وهو
ضرب من الانتقام اكبر من ذنبك فى اخراج الرويهب * فان اكثر الرهبان لا فائدة
من اقامتهم فى الدير لا لهم ولا لغيرهم * وما عدا ذلك فقد يحتمل ان هذا الرويهب
يتزوّج ويجعل من ولده رهبانا كثيرين * ولكن اذا مدحت الراهبات فاحذر من
ان تذكر لهن اثدآء واعجازا اذ لا شى لهنَّ من ذلك * فان طول الاعتكاف
والاحتجاب قد صيّرهنّ مخالفات لسائر النسآء * ونحن معاشر العبّاد اعلم بهن *

each God-fearer (male and female), each celibate (male and female), each one who arises from sleep to pray (male and female), each one who prostrates him- (or her-)self in prayer, each one who humbles him- (or her-)self before God, and each teller (male or female) of the rosary, I could do so." The priest thought for a moment and apparently discovered that love poetry wasn't such a great sin, for if it described a woman as having huge buttocks, fat arms, and round breasts, and she really did, then it would be just like someone saying "the moon has risen" when it really had, or "the clouds are parting" when they really were. It would be a lie and a sin only if the woman so characterized was in fact flat-chested and flat-buttocked or used stuffing to make people think she had a large backside, and the one who saw her took what she'd done for real and said what he did without exercising due caution.

When the priest had thought the matter through and weighed it in his 1.14.7
mind, he said, "It won't do for you to use your praise of me as expiation, for I'm afraid that, once you get hold of me, you'll never let me go, seeing as I do from your rhymes about those who do this and that (male and female) that you're stubborn, leech-like, dogged, and assiduous. You may praise only those close to God and the righteous divines who deny themselves in this world out of desire to see God's face in the next, who wear hair shirts and spend their nights in constant prayer out of obedience to God, and who subject themselves to perpetual mortification out of love for Him, some eating nothing all their lives but lentils and hardtack."

"Followed," said the Fāriyāq, "by the breaking of a tooth and pruritis. 1.14.8
Wait! Wait! I forgot to mention something that the lentils have just now brought to mind. Once I was responsible for persuading a young monk to leave his monastery and abandon the path. The reason was the sufferings I'd undergone there, and I did what I did so that I could gloat over the monastery's discomforture." Said the priest, "Your sin in gloating, which is a type of revenge-taking, was greater than your sin in persuading the young monk to leave, for there is no benefit to be had from the residence of most of the monks, or anyone else, in the monastery. In addition, it may be supposed that this young monk will marry and create lots of monks from his children. If, however, you go praising nuns, be careful you don't talk of them as though they had breasts and buttocks, since they know nothing of such things. Their prolonged devotion and seclusion have made them into something different from other women. We, as contemplatives, are the best authorities on them."

٩،١٤،١ فقال له الفارياق سالتك بالله معبود اهل السماوات والارض هل جميع القسيسن مثلك
فی الظرافة والدعابة * قال لا ادری وانما ادری انی انا وحدی شقيت بما عرفت *
وانی لو بقيت جاهلا مثلهم لكان خيرًا لی * انَّ من الجهل لراحة * فقال له وكيف
ذلك * قال اعندك للسرّ مكان حريز * قال ان سرّی من دمی فلا ابوح به * (قلت
بل باح به الان) قال اتريد ان اقصّ عليك قصتی * قال اكرم بها قال اَصِخ سمعا *

The Fāriyāq then asked him, "In the name of Him who's worshipped in Heaven and in Earth, are all priests like you, so witty and funny?" "I have no idea," the other replied. "I do know, though, that I have suffered for what I've learned and would have done better to remain ignorant like them. Indeed, 'in ignorance lies ease.'" "How can that be?" asked the Fāriyāq. The man replied, "Have you a place well guarded where a secret may be kept?" Said the Fāriyāq, "Secrets to me are like my own blood: I never let them out!" (though I say, he's let it out now). "Would you like me," asked the priest, "to tell you my story?" "It would be an honor," said the other. "Listen well, then," said he. 1.14.9

الفصل الخامس عشر

في قصة القسيس

١،١٥،١ ثم طفق يقول * اعلم انى كنت فى مبدأ امرى حائكا * ولما شآء الله تعالى من الازل ان يخلقنى قبيحا وقصيرا * حتى ان امى عند نظرها الىّ كانت تحمد الله على انه لم يخلقنى بنتا لم اكن اصلح للحياكة * لانّ قصرى الفاحش منانى غير مرة فى حفرة النول بالبُهر والخُناق * اذكان جسمى كله يغيب فيها فينقطع نَفَسى * مع ان منخرىّ بحمد الله يسعان من الهوآء ما يكفى خمسين رئة وخمسين كرشا * وكثيرا ما كان يُغشَى علىّ فيها واوخذ منها على آخر رمق * فلما قاسيت من هذه الحرفة كل جهد وعنآء رايت ان
٢،١٥،١ التسبّب ببعض ما يرغب فيه النسآء اصلح * فاكتريت لى حانوتا صغيرا وقعدت فيه فكانت النسآء يمررن علىّ وينظرن الىّ ثم يتضاحكن * وسمعت مرة منهنّ مَن تقول * لوكان الظاهر عنوانا صادقا على الباطن لكان خرطوم هذا التاجر يشفع له فى جثّته ويروّج سلعته * فاعتمدت على كلامها وقلت لعلّ من القبح سعادة * فقد قيل فى الامثال انَّ من الحسن لشقوة * ومكثت مدة على هذه الحال من غير طائل * فان انفى وقف بينى وبين رزقى * وبلغ كبره من الفحش بحيث انه لم يدع لغير الإِبآء والاعراض عنى موضعا * فقعدت يوما افكّر فى خلق الله تعالى هذا الكون * واقول
٣،١٥،١ يالحكمة الله كيف تخلق فى الدنيا انسانا ثم تخلق فيه شيا يمنع رزقه وقوام معيشته * ما الفائدة من هذا الانف الضخم الذى لا يصلح لشى الا لان تضمّن فيه اعجاز

Chapter 15

The Priest's Tale

Without further ado, he spoke. "Know that when I started out in life I was a weaver. However—given that Almighty God had decided, in His sempiternal wisdom, to make me so ugly and short that even my mother, when she looked at me, would thank God that He hadn't made me a girl—I was no good for weaving. The reason for this was that my terrible shortness often caused me to pant and choke in the loom pit, because my whole body would disappear inside it, and I'd find it impossible to breathe, despite which my nostrils, praise God, could take in enough air to fill fifty lungs and fifty bellies. Often I'd faint down there and have to be pulled out at my last gasp. 1.15.1

"When I'd suffered from that craft as much toil and trouble as I could stand, I decided it would be better to set up shop selling a few things that women crave, so I rented me a little store and sat there, and the women would pass by, look at me, and then laugh to one another. Once I heard one of them say, 'If the outside is a true guide to the inside, that shopkeeper's hose will intercede for his body and sell his goods for him.' I put my trust in her words and said, 'Maybe from ugliness will come good fortune, for, as the proverb has it, "from good comes evil."' I went on for a while that way but to no avail, for my nose stood between me and my living, and it grew so monstrous that it left room for nothing but rejection and aversion. 1.15.2

"One day I was sitting thinking about the Almighty's creation of this universe, when I said to myself, 'My, my! What a wise God! How could He make an individual a part of this world and at the same time make a part of that individual an impediment to his earning a living or making his way in it? What use is this huge nose except for having the "buttocks" of "Halt and weep"[230] 1.15.3

قفا نبك * ولِمَ لم يقوَّر منه شي ويكوَّر فى جثتى * ومالى ارى بعض الناس جميلا
كالمَلَك وبعضهم قبيحا كالشيطان * السنا جميعا خلق الله * اليس سبحانه يعمّهم
كلّهم بعنايته على حد سوى * اليس الصانع الارضىّ اذا اراد ان يصنع شيا فانه
يتانّق فيه ويتقنه عند استطاعته وياتى به من احسن ما يكون * هل يصوّر المصوّر
صورة قبيحة الا لكى يضحك الناس من المصوّر عنه * العلّ فى ضِخَم الانف حُسنا
او خيرًا او نفعا ونحن معاشر المخلوقين لا نعلمه * ثم اقوم الى المرآة واتامّل وجهى ٤،١٥،١
فيها فانكره ولا اجد فيه موضعا للاستحسان * فاعود الى مذهبى الاول واقول *
ان كنت انا لم استحسن وجهى فهل يستحسنه آخر غيرى * على ان الانسان يرى
ذأم غيره فيه حسنا ورذيلته فضيلة * اترى فى الناس مَن يروق لعينه القبح *
فقد يقال ان السود لا يرون فى الابيض منا حسنا * غير ان لون السواد عندهم
عامّ فلذلك يستحسنونه * وما ارى غيرى مَن اقلّ انفا كانفى حتى اطمع فى انه يكون
مستحسنا * اما اللون فانى لست من البيض ولا من السود فانا بين اللاعنَين * الا
ليت اهل بلدتى كانوا كلهم مثلى قُنافيّين فاتسلّى واتاسّى بهم * من اين ورثت هذا
الجلمود وانف ابى كان كانوف الناس * ليت شعرى اين كان عقل ابى حين نقر فى
راسه فكر انشاى فى هذا الكون وفى اىّ طود او طربال او منارة كانت امّى تفكر
ليلة راوحَته على هذا العمل * اَلَا ليتما غُشى عليهما تلك الليلة فما افاقا * او فَدَرا فما
اطاقا * او سُحرا فما تاقا * او سَكرا فما فاقا * وجعلت اجيل هذه الافكار فى راسى ٥،١٥،١
واصوغها فى قوالب مختلفة وافانين متنوّعة * واذا بامراة متنقّبة اقبلت علىّ وقد نتأ
من تحت نقابها شى شبيه بالقُلّة * فظننت انها جعلت حنجور عطر عند انفها لتشمّه
عند مرورها على الجيف فى اسواق المدينة * فسالتنى عن شى تريد شراه فسَعّرته
لها فكانها استغلته فقالت لى اقصدْ فان تسعيرك هذا تسعير * فقلت لها وانّ

stuffed up it? And why shouldn't a part of it be cored out and curled about my body? How is it I see that some people have been created as beautiful as angels and others as ugly as the Devil? Are we not all God's creatures? Has not He, glory be to Him, taken them all into His care, on the same footing? Does not the earthly craftsman, when he wants to make something, work on it meticulously and make it as nearly perfect as he can, bringing it to the best state possible? Does a painter paint an ugly picture, unless he wants to make people laugh at the thing portrayed? Could it be that, in a nose of huge size, there is some comeliness, value, or benefit of which we ordinary mortals are unaware?'

"Then I would get up and go to the mirror and contemplate my face and 1.15.4
reject it, finding nothing in it to like, and say, returning to my first line of thought, 'If I cannot find anything to like about my face, how can anyone else find it attractive?' People will, however, find good in the faults of others and in their vices virtues. Do you not observe how, to some people's eyes, ugliness is attractive? It is said that blacks find nothing attractive in the fair-complexioned among us, while blackness, being general among them, is something they appreciate. Never do I see anyone carrying around a nose like mine without hoping that he'll find mine attractive. As for color, I belong neither to the blacks nor the whites and am cursed by both their houses. Would that the people of my town were all like me, with big noses; then I could share in their joys and sorrows. From whom did I inherit this boulder, when my father's nose was just like other people's? I wish I knew what my father was thinking about when the idea of bringing me into this universe came knocking at his head, and about what lofty mountain peak, craggy landmark, or minaret my mother was thinking on the night when she collaborated with him in that deed! Would they'd swooned that night and not *awoken*, or gone off the boil and found their appetites *broken*, or been bewitched and lost all *feeling*, or got drunk and and gone about *reeling*!

"I was turning these ideas over in my head and fashioning them into 1.15.5
different forms and varying shapes, when behold, a woman with covered face approached, with something that might have been a water pitcher forming a bump beneath her veil; I thought she must have placed a flask of scent by her nose to sniff at when passing the carrion in the city's markets. She asked me about something she wanted to buy, and I told her its price, which

شِرآءك لَشَرى * فضحكت وقالت لقد احسنت فى الجواب ولكنك اسأت فى الطلب * فراعِ حقوق الشركة والجنسيّة فانى شريكك و رفيقتك * فكان ينبغى لك ان تحابينى * قلت اىّ شركة بيننا اصلحك الله وهذه اول خطرة شرفتنى فيها بالزيارة * فرفعت النقاب واذا بانفها الناتئ يضيق عنه وجهها * وكانه واجهَ انفى ليحيّيه * فخطر ببالى ح ما قيل عن ذلك الغراب الذى كان يخمع والِفَ غرابا مهيض الجناح * وان احد الشعرآء لما ابصرهما قال ما كنت ادرى ما اراده بعضهم بقوله ان الطيور على الآفها تقع حتى رايت هذين الغرابين * ثم انى بعتها اخيرا ما ارادت ان تشتريه * وحاولتُ ان اقبّلها قُبلة واحدة تعويضا عما خسرته معها فما امكن لى * لان انفينا حالا ما بيننا * ثم ذهبَتْ ومكثت انا على تلك الحال مدة *
فلمّا تحققت انى لا اصلح للتجارة لان النسآء لا يشترين الا ممّن كان فرهدا غَيْسانيّا ٦،١٥،١
تبركا بجمال طلعته فى انهن يتمتّعن بما اشترين من عنده * وتذكّرًا لذلك النهار السعيد الذى عرفنه فيه * وانى مذ فتحت الدكان لم ابع الا لتلك الكَرْنيفيّة وكان ذلك بخسارة * عزمت على الرّهبانية فذهبت الى دير ما وقلت للرئيس * وقد اقدمنى الزهد فى الدنيا والرغبة فى الاخرة * فان الدنيا لا تغنى عن الآخرة شيا * وان اللبيب من اتخذ دنياه هذه مجازا الى تلك * اذ لوكانت هذه وطننا الذى شآءه لنا خالقنا لكنّا نعمِّر فيها طويلا * على انّا نرى ان من الناس مَن يولد فيها ويعيش يوما واحدا فهذا دليل على انّا لم نخلق لها * واشباه ذلك من الكلام الذى جرى على السنة العبّاد * فقبلنى الرئيس واعتقد فىّ الفضل * واتّفق فى اليوم القابل انه حاول التسوّر على حائط لينفذ منه الى بعض بيوت الشركآء * فدخلت فى احدى عينيه قِصدة من غصن شجرة فذهبت بها * فرجع غضبان وقد تشآم بقدومى الى الدير * اذ كان قد اَلِف التسوّر قبل مجيئى بمدّة طويلة ولم يعرض له شى قط *

she seemed to find high, so she told me, 'Bring it down. Your price is pyretic,' to which I responded 'And your proposal's pruritic.' She laughed and said, 'You did well on the response but you made a mess of the request. Make allowance for the rights of partnership and commonality, for I'm your partner and comrade, which means you should make me a gift for friendship's sake.' 'What partnership can there be between us, God set you to rights,' I asked, 'when this is the first time you have honored me with a visit?' At this she raised her veil, and I beheld that her nose bulged out so far it left almost no room for her face and seemed to stand face to face with mine as though to salute it. It made me think of the story of the lame crow that made friends with a crow with a broken wing, on seeing which a certain poet declared, 'I never knew what people meant by the saying "Birds of a feather flock together" until I saw these two crows.' In the end I sold her what she wanted to buy, trying to get one kiss as a compensation for my loss, but I couldn't because our noses got in the way. Then she departed and I continued for a while as before.

"When I realized that I wasn't cut out for trade (for women buy only from young men who are well-built and supple as a branch, taking the beauty of their faces as a good omen that they will enjoy whatever they buy from them and as as a memento of the happy day on which they made their acquaintance), and that since I'd opened the store the only thing I'd sold had been to the woman with the bulbous beezer (and that at a loss!), I decided to become a monk. I found my way to a monastery and said to its abbot, 'I come to you disillusioned with this world and eager for the next, for this world can never assume that other's place. The wise man is he who takes this as a metaphor for that, for were this the home that our Creator desired for us, we would live in it for eons, though in fact we see that some people are born into it and live a single day, which is evidence that it's not what we were created for' and similar stuff of the sort that trips off the tongues of contemplatives. The abbot saw virtue in me and accepted me, but the next day he happened to try to climb over the wall to get to the houses of certain partners and the broken end of a tree branch entered his eye and blinded him, so he returned in a fury, saying that my arrival at the monastery had brought bad luck, because for ages before I came he'd climbed that wall all the time and nothing had ever happened to him. 1.15.6

٧،١٥،١ فمن ثمّ طردني من الدير فدخلت ديرا آخر واعدت الكلام الاول * فقبلني رئيسه
فاقمت ثمّ اياما اقاسى فيها من قشف المعيشة والوسخ ما لا يرضى الله ولا احدا
من العالمين * هذا ما عدا ما كنت ارى من عناد الرهبان وتفرق آرائهم * وطعن
بعضهم فى بعض وشكواهم الدائمة للرئيس من امور باطلة * وتكبّر هذا عليهم
وأثَرَته باشياء استخصّها لنفسه من دونهم * وتنافسهم فيما يهدى اليهم النسآء
٨،١٥،١ من نحو منديل وكيس وتكّة * وزد على ذلك كله جهل الجميع اذ لم يكن فى الدير كله
مَن يحسن كَتْب رسالة فى معنى من المعانى * حتى ان الرئيس نفسه ادام الله
عزّه لم يكن يعرف ان يكتب سطرا واحدا بالعربية * وانما كان يخط هذه الحروف
السريانية المعروفة عندهم باسم كرشونى * وكان هذا الجاهل يتبجّح بمعرفته لها ويحمل
كل من دخل صومعته على اعظامها *حتى انه كان يدعو ايّاً ما كان لزيارته *
فكانت الاغرار من الرهبان تعتقد ان ذلك من حسن اخلاقه وكرم طباعه *
وكان قد كتب بها على بابه سطرا وعلى الحائط سطرا آخر * فكنت حين انظر
ذلك اضحك * وهو من غفلته يظن انى اضحك اعجابا بها * ومن كان خبّاً مخاتلا
من الرهبان على جهله (فان كثيرا من الناس قد جمعوا بين الجهل والختل) كان
يتقرّب اليه استجلابا لرضاه بان يقول له وهو حاسر الراس تواضعا وخشوعا اكرم
علىّ ياسيدى بنسخة من خطّك اصلح عليها خطّى * فكان ذلك من احسن ما
٩،١٥،١ يُدلّ به عليه * فلما اشتدّ علىّ الخطب من عشرتهم وخصوصاً من ردآءة الطعام
طفقت ادمدم واتضجّر * فسمعنى يوما طباخ الدير اشكو من قلّة السمن فى الارزّ
الذى كان يطبخه فى بعض الاعياد العظيمة * وكان عُتُلّا زنيما * فاستشاط منى
غيظا وحملنى على كتفه كما يحمل الرجل ولده ولكن بلا شفقة * ثم ذهب بى الى مَمار
الدير وغطّسنى فى خابية السمن وهو يقول * هذا السمن الذى اطبخ به الارز

"As a result, he threw me out of the monastery, so I entered another and repeated what I'd said the first time. Its abbot accepted me, and I resided there for a few days, suffering such squalor and dirt as neither God nor man could put up with, in addition to the obduracy of the monks, the divergence of their opinions, their accusations against one another, and their constant complaints to the abbot over matters of no importance, as well as the way the latter lorded it over them, his selfishness over things that he kept for himself alone, allowing them no share in them, and their rivalry over things that women would give them, such as a handkerchief, a purse, or the drawstring from a pair of bloomers. 1.15.7

"To this you have to add the ignorance of them all, for in the whole monastery there wasn't one who could pen an epistle on any topic. Even the abbot himself, God preserve his high degree, was incapable of writing a single line in proper Arabic, using instead the Syriac letters known as *karshūnī*,[231] of his knowledge of which the ignoramus was so inordinately proud that he'd force everyone who entered his cell to say how wonderful they were, and even invite all and sundry to visit him, which the gullible monks thought he did out of noble morals and generosity of character. He had written a line in these letters above his door and another on his wall, and when I looked at it, I'd smile, which he, in his simplemindedness, believed was because I admired them. Other monks who, for all their ignorance, were wily swindlers (and how many a man combines ignorance and dishonesty!) would, in hope of gaining his favor, cozy up to him by telling him, as he sat there with his head lowered in modesty and submissiveness, 'Would you be so generous, Master, as to let me have a sample of your handwriting to use as a model for my own?' and this was one of the best ways for them to get things out of him. 1.15.8

"When, then, their company, and, above all, the awfulness of the food, became too much for me to bear, I took to grumbling and muttering. One day the monastery cook heard me complaining about how little clarified butter there was in the rice he was cooking for a high holiday. He was a ruffian and a knave and he exploded at me in anger, picking me up and putting me over his shoulder as a man might his child, though without the tenderness. Then he carried me through the passageways of the monastery and plunged me into the vat of butter, saying, 'This is the butter with which I cook the rice that 1.15.9

الذى لم يعجبك ياصاحب الخرطوم * ياسليل البوم * يانصيب المحروم *
يابن اللوم * ياابا الكبائر والجروم * يارائحة الثوم * ياريح السَّموم * ياعُلُجوم *
يامَنْهوم * يالَهوم * ياوخوم * وصبَّ علىَّ قوافى كثيرة غير هذه * فبلغ منى
تعطيسه عرضى فى السبّ اكثر من تعطيسه راسى فى السمن * فتملّصت منه بعد
جهد ودخلت صومعتى حتى اغتسل واذا به يطرق الباب ويعجّ ويقول * لا بدّ من
ان اعصر انفك فقد دخل فيه من السمن ما يكفى الرهبان ايّاماً * ثم اهوى بيديه
على منخرى كانهما كلبتا حدّاد وجعل يعصرهما اشد العصر * حتى ظننت ان قد
زهقت نفسى منهما * فان الانف وحده دون سائر ثقوب الجسد محل دخول
النفس وخروجها خلافا لقوم * ولذلك يقال تنفّس الانسان * فلما شقّ علىّ ما ١،١٥،١٠
قاسيته ولم اجد فى الدير من اشكو اليه * اذ الرهبان كلهم يتملّقون ويتودّدون
اليه حتى يشبعهم ولو من الثُرتُم * (وهو ما فضل من الطعام او الإدام فى الانآء)
خرجت من الدير مبتئسا حزينا قانطا وقد ضاقت الدنيا علىَّ برُحْبها * وقلت اين
اذهب بانفى هذا الذى سد علىّ مذاهب الرزق * ام اين يذهب بى هو * فخطر
ببالى ان اقصد ديرا بعيدا كنت اسمع عن رهبانه انهم صُلّاح * وان بعضهم
يحسن الخط العربىّ ويحبّ الغريب ويكرم الضيف * فتوجّهت اليه فلما سلّمت
على رئيسه وطالعته بما عزمت عليه احمد رأيى وهشّ بى * لكنه لم يتمالك ان
نظر الىّ نظر المتعجب منى المستعيذ من

شؤم تبعة تلحقه من انفى *

فمكثت فى ديره ما

شآء الله ان

امكث *

you don't like, you schnozzle-*chik*, owl-*chick*, poor man's *portion*, rascal's *scion*, committer of sins great and *small*, emitter of a garlicky *pall*, poisonous wind *anabatic*, blood-sucking tic *parasitic, insatiate, crapulate, indigestate*'—and poured over me many more rhymes of this sort, the dunking in insults received by my good name exceeding the dunking my head got in the butter. After some effort, I contrived to slip out of his clutches and entered my cell to wash, and suddenly there he was again, knocking on the door and bellowing, 'I have to squeeze your nose out, for enough butter's got into it to keep the monks going for days!' Then he reached for my nostrils with hands like iron pincers and set about squeezing them as hard as he could till I thought the soul (*nafs*) was about to about to depart, for the nose alone among the body's orifices (and I say this in knowing contradiction of the beliefs of a certain school) is the point of entry and exit for the breath (*nafas*), which is why one says that a person *yatanaffas* ('breathes').[232]

"As my sufferings were too much to bear, and I could find no one in the monastery to complain to, because the monks all flattered him and made up to him so that he'd give them enough to eat, even if it were only the *thurtum* (which is the food or condiments left on a dish), I left the monastery, in parlous state, saddened and discouraged, the world in all its expansiveness seeming me a narrow space, and said, 'Where am I to take this nose of mine that has blocked every avenue by which I might make a living, or where is it to take me?' It occurred to me to head for a monastery far away, of which I had heard that its monks were righteous men and that some wrote a good Arabic hand, loved strangers, and honored their guests. So I made my way to it, and when I saluted its abbot and acquainted him with what I had resolved, 1.15.10

he praised my opinion highly and welcomed me warmly,
though he couldn't prevent himself from gazing at me in surprise
and praying for God's protection from any ill consequences
that might befall him because of my nose.
So I stayed in his monastery
for as long as it was God's will
that I should stay."

الفصل السادس عشر

فى تمام قصة القسيس

وجعلت من همّى مدة مكثى هناك بادى بَدْيٍ مداراة الطباخ ومساحنته والثناَ ١٫١٦٫١
عليه * فكان لا يحوجنى الى شى مما يمكن نيله فى الدير * حتى انى جعلت جُلّ مقامى فى المطبخ * وكنت احسن ايضا طبخ الوان من الطعام لا يعرفها هو فعلّمته اياها فكلف بى * فكان رئيس الدير اذا استضافه احد عزيز عليه او اشتهى لونا من الطعام بخصوصه كلّفنى به * فكنت اتانّق له فى عمله ما امكن حتى حظيت عنده * اعنى انى كنت اسامره واجلس بين يديه * ثم انى تلبّست بالصلاح والتقوى بين الرهبان * فكنت اسدل قلنسوتى حتى تبلغ قصبة انفى * وياليت العادة جرت بان يُستَر الانف بها كلّه * وكنت اذا مشيت اخفض راسى الى الارض ولا انظر يمينا ولا شمالا الا لمحا * واذا اكلت او شربت او رقدت او مشيت او غسلت وجهى اخبر عن ذلك كله حامداً لله ومثنياً عليه * فاقول مثلا * قد خرجت اليوم من صومعتى ولله الحمد او ولله المجد وهى احبّ الى الرهبان * او تناولت فى هذا الصباح مُسْهلا ان كان الله تقبّل وما اشبه ذلك مما عُرف عند المتظاهرين بالتقوى * حتى اعتقد الرهبان فىّ جميعا الصلاح والفضيلة * وكنت ايضا قد كتبت بعض صلوات ركيكة للرئيس فاعجب بخطّى ومدحنى على ذلك * ووعدنى بان يرقّينى الى درجة تليق بى * اذ رآنى متميزا عن الرهبان بالعلم وجودة الرأى * واخصّ ذلك بكونى غَيْداراً

Chapter 16

The Priest's Tale Continued

"From the outset and for as long as I was there, I made it my concern to humor the cook, get on his good side, and praise him. He, in return, let me want for nothing that could be had in the monastery. In fact, I spent the greater part of my time in the kitchen. I was also good at cooking dishes he knew nothing of, so I taught him these, and he became exceedingly fond of me. Thus it came to pass that, when the abbot invited someone dear to him to eat with him, or had an urge to eat a certain kind of food on his own, the cook would charge me with preparing it. Because I was as meticulous as possible in doing so, I ended up in his good graces, meaning that I'd sit with him in the evenings and keep him company, acquiring in this way a reputation for righteousness and piety among the monks. I pulled my hood down till it reached the bridge of my nose—and would that custom had allowed it to cover the nose entirely!—and when I walked I kept my head bent toward the ground and cast only brief glances to right and left, and when I ate, drank, slept, walked, or washed my face, I made mention of all of those things, thanking and praising God as I did so. Thus I would say, for example, 'Today I left my cell, praise be to God!' or 'To God be glory!' (the latter being the monks' preferred form), or 'This morning I took a laxative, may this find favor in God's eyes!' and other stuff that those who make a show of piety are known to say. Thus the monks ended up believing that I was full of righteousness and virtue. I'd also written out a few hymns in bad Arabic for the abbot, who admired and praised me for my hand, promising to promote me to a rank worthy of me, for he believed I was distinguished from the rest of the monks by my learning and excellence of judgment, a faculty he attributed to my being *ghaydār* (meaning 'a suspicious person who ponders a matter and then comes up with a correct interpretation'). 1.16.1

(الغيدار هو السيئ الظن يظن فيصيب) * ثم قدّر الله رب الموت والحيوة انْ مات ١،١٦،٢
فى بعض البلدان البعيدة بعض القسيسين الذين يباشرون خدمة الرعية * اى الذين
ياكلون ويشربون فى بيوت الناس لا فى الدير * والذين يختلطون برعيتهم خلافا
لعادة الرهبان * فان هولاء لا يخالطون الناس الا عند الضرورة * فتسبّب رئيس
الدير فى ان بعثنى الى ذلك البلد فى مكان القسيس المتوفَّى اى بدلًا منه لا انى دفنت
معه * فلما وصلت تلقانى اهل كنيستى بالاكرام والترحيب * فابديت فيهم الورع
والعفة فشاع فضلى بينهم * حتى ان بعض التجار ممن كان حرمه الله من لذة البنين
دعانى الى منزله لاقيم عنده رجآء ان يفتح الله رحم امراته بسببى كما تقول التوراة فتلد
له البنين * وكانت جميلة رشيقة القد * قاعدة النهد * تحب الخلاعة واللهو *
والقصف والزهو * (سبحان الله ما احد يذكر النسآء الا ويهيج خاطره للسجع) فاقمت
عنده مدة فى انعم عيش وجِدَة * ثم عنَّ لى ان اغازل زوجته واناغيها * واعاشرها ١،١٦،٣
واراضيها * فاجابت الى مُراودتى * ولم تبالِ بارنبتى * فان من طبع النساء الميل
الى الولىّ * والاستغناء عنه بالقَصى * وما ادراك ما اعتذرت به احدى النسآء
بقولها قرب الوِساد * وطول السِواد * فبرزت الدنيا لعينى ح فى احسن صورة *
ونسيت ما لاقيت فى الدير من المشاقّ الكثيرة * وقلت لاعوضنّ علىّ ما دامت
فرصة الحظ لى ممكنة * وشوارده مذعنة * كل ما فاتنى منه ايام كنت حائكا *
وطبّاخا وناسكا * ثم فرضت على نفسى ان تُقسَم لذّاتى معها على كل يوم غَبَر مرة *
كدأب المتزوج بحرّة * وعلى الحاضر * وهو الان ايضا فى حيّز الغابر * بحسب
البواعث والبوادر * فبدأت بالعدد * حتى بلغت الامد * وكان الرجل ذا نية
سليمة * وشيمة مستقيمة * فلم يكن يسئ بى الظن * ولا يعوقه عن شغله امر
عنّ * فترك لنا قُطوف اللذّات دانيه * وكؤس المسرّات صافيه * ومن العجب * ١،١٦،٤

"Then God, Lord of Death and Life, decreed that one of those priests who service the laity in certain far-off parts (meaning that they eat and drink in people's houses instead of at the monastery and mingle with their congregants, against the custom of monks, who mix with people only when they have to) should die, causing the abbot to send me to that country to adopt the same position as the deceased (meaning to substitute for him, not to be buried along with him). On my arrival, my congregation received me generously and with open arms, while I demonstrated god-fearingness and chastity to them and my virtues became well known among them. A merchant, one to whom God had denied the pleasure of children, even invited me into his home and asked me to lodge with him, in the hope that, by virtue of my presence, God would 'open his wife's womb,' as it says in the Old Testament,[233] and children be born to him. This wife was beautiful, slender of figure, and well-endowed of *chest*, fond of dissolute pleasure, revelry, and *zest* (God be praised—the mere thought of women produces the urge to write in rhymed prose!), so I stayed with him a *while*, living in the most luxurious *style*. 1.16.2

"Then it occurred to me to flirt with his wife and to *pursue her*, be her close companion and *woo her*. She responded to my enticements, paying no attention to the tip of my *nose*, for it is in women's nature to incline to what's *close*, ignoring what's far away (and I'm sure you're aware of what one woman *said*, concerning 'long converse and closeness in *bed*.')[234] The world now appeared to my eyes at its *best*, I forgot the many hardships that, at the monastery, I'd had to *digest*, and I said to myself, 'So long as my good fortune persists and its currents serve, I shall make up to myself for all the good things of which I saw no *use* when I was a weaver, a cook, and a *recluse*,' and I made it a rule that my pleasures with her be *measured*—taking care that I be *pleasured* once for each day *past* (like any man with his lawful wedded wife) and then once again for the present (which of course didn't *last*), as incitement and impulse might take me—and kept *count*, soon reaching a huge *amount*. The husband, having no ill thoughts and being of a trusting disposition, was quite *unperturbed*, and, with no suspicions to distract him from his work, pleasure's fruits were there for the plucking, the cups of our joy *undisturbed*. 1.16.3

"Now here's an amazing thing that deserves to be recorded in books—she'd pick quarrels with the *maid*, both in her husband's presence and when he was *delayed*, and abuse her in front of him in the nastiest *way*, thus forestalling any suspicions of his that might come into *play*—she fearing no consequences 1.16.4

الذى ينبغى ان يدوّن فى الكتب * انها كانت تخاصم الخادمة فى حضرته وغيابه * وتشتمها بين يديه افحش الشتم منعا لارتيابه * ولم تخشَ منها تبِعة * ولا كانت من طردها جَزِعة * وقد طردت كثيرا من الخوادم لسبب ولغير سبب * بعد سبّهن كل السبّ * وحملهن على الحقد والغضب * وذلك من معجزات النسآ وبِدْعهن الغريب الذى يعمى الرجال عن كُنه سرّه العجيب * والحاصل انى كنت أُعجَب بحسنها * كما كنت اَعجب من فنّها * وانى اقمت معها على هذه الحالة فى
غاية السُرّ * مُفْنقا راتعا ولا حَظر(١) ومتزوّجا ولا مَهر * ثم استانفت ١،١٦،٥
عدداً آخر * اطول من ذاك واكثر * فلما ابطرتنى النعمة * وامنت من الدهر كل نقمة * نقر فى راسى ان اجمع بين الكافين * فان بكثرة العين قُرّة العين * وقلّما رايت من انهمك فى الاول * الا وتعاطى الثانى وما اشبه من العُقَل * وذلك كالقمار والجَنْخ والفَشْخ والحَدْج والمَجْر والإمجار والنَدب والخَطَر والرَشق والقَرَع والنَجْش والصَبْن والضَغْو والغذمرة والمحارضة والمناحبة والمراهنة والمجازفة والمحاقلة والمزابنة والاجبآء والمُداحلة والمعارضة والمنابذة والمبادّة والمباخسة والمغابنة والموالسة والتدليس والتَطويش والمقاطرة والمعاومة والمراوضة والمواصفة * فطهبل وطهفل * ومحل وتطهمل * ودجّل وزعفل * وابطل وتخبّل * وعرقل وتبهلص * وتبلهص وبَهْصَل(٢) فاجتمعت برجل كنت اسمع عنه انه يتعاطى هذه الصنعة * وقد تفرّغ لها بجِدّ وبذل فيها وُسعه * واوسع فيها بذله * وعقل بها عقله * وفى الجملة والتفصيل * من دون قافية
وسجع طويل * تعاطيتها معه (انتهى سجع القسيس) قال فجعلت انفق فيها ما اجمعه ١،١٦،٦
من العجائز والاغرار برسم النفوس والارواح * وانا مع ذلك مواظب على الصنعة الاولى * بل كان ذلك داعيا لزيادة هيام كلّ منى ومن بزيعتى * فانها طمعت ح فى

(١) افنق الرجل تنعّم بعد البؤس

(٢) تبهلص الرجل وتبلهص خرج من ثيابه وبهصل خلع ثيابه فقامر بها*

from *this*, nor being concerned at what might happen should she the said maid *dismiss*, for she'd fired many a maid *before*, for good reasons and for *poor*, after subjecting them to every kind of insult, and making them to hatred and anger *inclined*; and this is one of the miracles of women and their strange uniqueness, to the essence of whose extraordinary secret we men are *blind*. In sum, I was entranced by her beauty, just as I marveled at her art, and I dwelt with her in this state in extreme *delight*, like one married without having to pay a bride-price, coddled after calamities, indulging without restraint my every *appetite*.(1)

(1) "*afnaqa l-rajul*: 'to live a life of luxury after destitution.' [The author's gloss refers to the word *mufniqan* 'coddled after calamities.' Translator.]

"Then I started another count, longer and more extended than the first, for, as the easy life made me reckless and I felt safe from any blow that fate might *deal*, I couldn't stop thinking I should combine the two *c*s,[235] for 'much prosperity brings much *weal*' and rarely have I seen one truckle with the first who does not also indulge in the second and similar worldly attachments—such as shuffling gaming arrows and twirling bones,[236] cheating at games and accusing others of the same, trading in livestock as yet unborn and usury, shooting arrows and brandishing spears, arrow-shooting contests and casting lots, flushing game and picking up the dice before a throw, cheating and selling things at arbitrary prices, inciting others to shuffle the gaming arrows and inciting them to lay bets, betting and laying stakes, dealing in grain futures and selling dates while still on the tree, selling seed before it has matured and other fast practice, swapping commodities and making bargains, bartering and defrauding, swindling and misrepresenting, concealing defects and delaying payment of debts, selling grain on the basis of the weight of a single sample and deferring (while at the same time increasing the amount of) a debt, offering blandishments and contracting to buy things on the basis of a description only—at which point [i.e., when he has lost], he wanders, making do with nothing to eat but bread made of sorghum, and he cheats and plots, swindles and lies, jokes around, behaves like a lunatic, and tries to con people, taking his clothes off, stripping naked, and using them as stakes for his bets.(2) So I met with a man of whom I'd heard it said he practiced this *profession* and devoted himself to it seriously and without *digression*, devoting to it great *pains* and expending on it much of his *gains*, while confining his thoughts to that alone. To cut things *short*, and without 1.16.5

(2) *abahlaṣa* and *tabalhaṣa* both mean "to take off one's clothes," and *bahṣala* means "to remove one's clothes and gamble with them."

الهدايا والصلات كما هو دأب النسآء فى كل امر يحدث لازواجهنّ وعشّاقهن * فبلغ خبر صنعتى هذه الحديثة للجاثليق * فارسل يطلب منى المال الذى جمعته * فتعلّلت له بعلل اباها ولم يرضَها * فتسبّب فى احضارى اليه وضبط ماكان عندى من متاع وغيره * ولم يشقّ عليّ فَقْد ذلك كله قدر ما شق عليّ انقطاع العدد الذى كنت شرعت فيه فى بيت التاجر الصالح * ثم انى تفلّتّ من عِكال الجاثليق بعد مدّة كادت ان تنسينى لذّات الايام الغابرة * وخرجت فى طلب آخر نكاية لذاك فصرت الى جاثليق من اشدّ الناس عداوة لجاثليقى القديم * اذ العداوة توجد بين الجثالقة * كما توجد بين الزنادقة * فاقمت عنده مدة ثم خشى عليّ ان يرهقنى من
ذاك سوء فسفّرنى الى بلاد بعيدة فى سفينة حرب * فما سرنا بعض ساعات حتى ٧،١٦،١
تعطّل بعض ادوات السفينة وخشى رُبّانها ان تغرق بهم * فرجع وقد تشآم بى وقال لبعض الركّاب انه انما جرى عليه ما جرى من شَمْخَتَرِيّتى فتعجّبت اذ بلغنى كلامه جدًّا * لان اولئك القوم لا يرتسمون ولا يتشآمون * ولا يتطيّرون ولا يتفآلون * ولا يتحمّون ولا يتيمّنون * ولا يتسعّدون ولا يتمسّحون * ولا يُقلّدون بعُود الشبارق ولا يستعملون نَبْت العَطَف * وما عندهم هَقْعة ولا لُجام * ولا عاطُوس ولا عاطس * ولا كابح ولا كادس * ولا قعيد ولا داكس * ولا بارح ولا سانح * ولا زَجْر ولا تحزّى * ولا عَيْثَرة ولا عِيافة * ولا طَرْق ولا عرافة * ولا هَجِيج ولا كهانة * ولا ابنا عِيان ولا تنجّى * ولا لَمّة ولا حُفُوف * ولا لُعْطة ولا انتجآء * ولا تشوّه ولا تعيّد * ولا طلاسم ولا تشهّق * ولا عزائم * ولا رُقَى ولا تمائم * ولا اليَنْجَلَب ولا تُوَلَة * ولا حَوْط ولا غَزّ * ولا تدسيم النونة ولا شَدّ الحِقاب * ولا رَسْع ولا صَخَبْة * ولا قُلَيب ولا كَبْدة * ولا وَجِيه ولا سُلْوانة * ولا سُلْوان ولا عُقَرة * ولا مِجْوَل ولا مُهْرة * ولا أُخْذة ولا عُوذة * ولا هَبْرة

having to further lengthy rhyme *resort*, I went into the same trade with him." (Here ends the priest's rhymed prose.)

"I started funding it from what I gathered from the old women and greenhorns by way of fees for welcoming new souls and seeing off old, as I continued to ply my first profession. Indeed, all the preceding was a stimulus to extra passion from both my side and that of my little cutie, for she now grew greedy for presents and gifts, as women do every time there is some occasion in the lives of their husbands and lovers. The news of my new profession reached my abbot, who sent to demand from me the money that I'd made. I made excuses that he refused and didn't accept, and he found a reason to recall me, seizing the baggage and everything else I had with me, though the loss of all of that didn't upset me as much as the interruption of the first count (the one I'd initiated at the house of the righteous merchant). After a period almost long enough to make me forget the pleasures of those by-gone days, I slipped from that abbot's bonds and set off in search of another, to spite the former. I thus made my way to an abbot who was one of those most hostile to the abbot I'd been with before—for hostility is to be found as much among abbots as among atheists—and the former, fearing that I might come to harm from the latter, sent me off to distant lands in a ship of war. 1.16.6

"Before we'd been at sea for more than a few hours, some of the ship's instruments failed, causing its captain to fear that it would take us down, so he turned back, having decided that I was the cause of his misfortune and telling one of the passengers that what happened had occurred because of my ugly mug. I was greatly amazed to hear his words, for such people[237] are not given to *irtisām*,[238] to *tashāʾum*,[239] to *taṭayyur*,[240] to *tafāʾul*,[241] to *taḥattum*,[242] to *tayammun*,[243] to *tasaʿʿud*,[244] to *tamassuḥ*,[245] or to hanging necklaces of *shubāriq* wood or making use of *ʿaṭaf*; nor do they place any faith in *haqʿah* or *lujām*, *ʿāṭūs* or *ʿāṭis*,[246] *kābiḥ* or *kādis*, *qaʿīd* or *dākis*,[247] *bāriḥ* or *sāniḥ*, *zajr* or *taḥazzī*, *ʿiyāfah* or *ʿaytharah*, *ṭarq* or *ʿirāfah*, *hajīj*, or *kahānah*,[248] *ibnā ʿiyān* or *tanajjī*, *lammah* or *ḥufūf*, *luʿṭah* or *intijāʾ*,[249] *tashawwuh* or *taʿayyud*, *ṭalāsim*[250] or *tashahhuq* or *ʿazāʾim*,[251] *ruqā*[252] or *tamāʾim*,[253] *yanjalib* or *tuwalah*, *ḥawṭ* or *ghazz*, *tadsīm al-nūnah* or *shadd al-ḥiqāb*, *rasʿ* or *ṣakhbah*, *qulayb* or *kabdah*, *wajīh* or *sulwānah*, *sulwān* or *ʿuqarah*, *mijwal* or *muhrah*, *ukhdhah* or *ʿūdhah*,[254] *habrah* or *raʾamah*, *kaḥlah* or *hinnamah*, *julbah* or *ṣarrah*, *qablah* or *nushzah*, *qublah* or *nufrah*, *ṣudḥah* or *hamrah*, 1.16.7

ولا رأمة * ولا كَحْلة ولا هِنَّمة * ولا جُلْبة ولا صَرّة * ولا قَبْلة ولا نُشْرة * ولا قُبْلة ولا نُقْرة * ولا صَدْحة ولا هَمْرة * ولا زَرْقة ولا عَطْفة * ولا فَطْسة ولا صَرْفة * ولا غضار ولا كَرار * ولا بَرِيم ولا حِرْز * ولا خَصْمة ولا رَتِيمة * ولا أسْحَمَ ولا صِهْميم * ولا تذعّب ولا صوت اللُّوف * ولا هامة ولا صفر * ولا أُخْذة النار ولا تنجيس * ولا لَجّ ولا اِنكيس * ولا أُسّ ولا شَحِيثا * ولا طبّ ولا تَوّل * ولا سحر ولا ماقِط * ولا عاضه ولا مستنشئة * ولا نفّاثات فى العُقَد ولا صدى * ولا شعبذة ولا نِيْرَنْج * ولا شعوذة ولا حابل ولا حاوٍ *
ويومئذ ايقنت ان القنافيّ مكروه عند جميع الامم * وان اوقية لحم زائدة فى وجه ٨،١٦،١
الرجل تشقيه وتحرمه * ورطلين فى بتيلة المرأة يسعدانها ويفيزانها * فزاد تعجبى من هذه الدنيا المبنيّة على رطلين واوقية اللحم * ومع ذلك فلم يمكن لى الزهد فيها * ثم انى سافرت بعد ذلك الى تلك البلاد وامنت فيها من مكر اعدآى * واستاجرت بيتا واتخذت لى امرأة تخدمنى * وقد جرت العادة فى تلك البلاد وفى بلاد الافرنج ايضا بان يتخذ القسيسون نسآء للخدمة * فاتى المراة احدهم صباحا وهو فى فراشه الوثير وتقضى له ما يروم منها * فلما ذقت طيب العيش وسوس الىّ الوسواس ان اتزوج بنتا فقيرة لكنها كانت جميلة * غير انى لم اكن على يقين من نهود ثدييها ومع ذلك فقد كلفت بها * فطلبت من الجاثليق ان يزيد وظيفتى فأبَى * فالحت عليه وهو مصرّ على المنع وانا مصرّ على الاستزادة * ثم ناقشته وراغمته فراى ان يردّنى من حيث جئت * فسرت الى جاثليق محب للجاثليق الاول فسرّ برؤيتى وانزلنى عنده * فرجعتُ الى ما كنت عليه سابقا * وها انا مترقّب فرصة اخرى تمكّنى من المقايضة على هذا النحس الآخر ايضا فانه جاهل جدّا * وعندى ان مبادلة الجثالقة فى هذا الزمان العَسُوف انفع من حجر الفيلسوف * انتهت قصة القسيس

zarqah or *ʿaṭfah, faṭsah* or *ṣarfah, ghaḍār* or *karār, barīm* or *ḥirz, khaṣmah* or *ratīmah, asḥam* or *ṣihmīm, tadhaʿʿaba* or *ṣawt al-lūf, hāmah* or *ṣafar, ukhdhat al-nār* or *tanjīs, laḥj* or *inkīs, us* or *shahīthā, ṭibb* or *tawl, siḥr*[255] or *māqiṭ, ʿāḍih* or *mustanshiʾah, naffāthāt fi l-ʿuqad* or *ṣadā,*[256] *shaʿbadhah* or *nīranj, shaʿwadhah* or *ḥābil* or *ḥāwī.*

"On that day I learned for sure that a man with a big nose is hated in every country and that half a pound of extra flesh on a man's face will bring him woe and privation, while two pounds on a woman's rump will bring her fortune and success, and my wonder at this world that's built on two-and-a-half pounds of flesh increased, despite which I couldn't bring myself to renounce it. Then I traveled to those lands[257] and found safety in them from the intrigues of my enemies, and rented a house and brought a woman to serve me. It has become customary for priests, in those lands and in the lands of the Franks too, to take a woman to serve them, who comes to him in the morning, while he is still in his comfortable bed, and provides him with whatever he wants from her. Having tasted the sweetness of that life, the Tempter whispered in my ear that I should marry a girl who was poor but beautiful. I wasn't quite certain that her breasts had completely rounded out but had taken a fancy to her all the same. I therefore asked the abbot to increase my stipend, but he refused. I insisted, but he was adamant in saying no, while I was adamant in asking for more. Then, when I argued with him and ended our discussion on an angry note, he decided to send me back to whence I'd come, so I went to an abbot who was friendly with the first abbot, and he was delighted to see me and put me up with him, and I found myself back where I'd begun. Now I'm waiting for an opportunity to exchange this other no-hoper too, for he is very ignorant, and, in my opinion, swapping abbots in these days of oppression brings more benefit than the philosopher's stone." Here ends the priest's tale. 1.16.8

وهذا تفسير ما اشار اليه آنفاً من الالفاظ الغريبة * ٩،١٦،١

ابنا عيان طائران أو خطّان يخطهما العائف فى الارض ثم يقول ابنا عيان اَسرعا البيان الخ *

أُخذة النار بُعَيد صلاة المغرب يزعمون انها شرّساعة يُقتَدح فيها *

الأُخذة رُقية كالسحر او خرزة يوخَّذ بها *

الارتسام التكبير والتعوّذ والتختّم التفاؤل *

الاَسْحِم الدم تغمس فيه ايدى المتحالفين *

اُسْ كلمة تقال للحيّة فتخضع *

الانكيس فى اشكال الرمل كالمنكوس *

البارح من الصيد ما مرّ من ميامنك إلى مياسرك *

البِرِيم خيطان مختلافان احمر وابيض تشده المراة على وسطها وعضدها . . . . . . والعوذة *

التحزّى حزا حزواً وتحزى زجر وتكهّن وحزّى الطير ساقها وزجرها * ١٠،١٦،١

تدسيم النونة تدسيم نونة الصبىّ تسويدها يكلا تصيبها العين *

التذعُب تذعَّبَتْهُ الجن افزعته *

التشهّق شهقت عين الناظر عليه أصابته بعين *

التشوّه يقال لا تشوّه علىّ اى لا تصبني بعين *

التعيّد تعيَّد العاينُ على المعيون تشهّق عليه وتشدد ليبالغ فى اصابته بعينه * ذكره الفيروزابادى فى ع و د *

Here are the meanings of the rare words mentioned above: 1.16.9

ibnā ʿiyān,	[literally, "the Sons of Sight"] "Two birds, or two lines; the augur would draw lines on the ground and say, 'Sons of Sight, tell us quickly what you see!'," etc.
ukhdhat al-nār,	[literally, "the fire spell"] "Shortly after the sunset prayer; they claim that this is the worst time at which to strike [a flint]."
ukhdhah,	"An incantation, like sorcery, or a bead with which spells are made"
irtisām,	"Saying, 'God is great!' or 'I take refuge with God!' or believing that certain things are inevitable or believing in omens"
asḥam,	"The blood in which the hands of those swearing oaths are dipped"
us,	"A word said to the serpent, on hearing which it obeys"
inkīs,	"A shape made in the sand [by a geomancer]; some call it the *mankūs*"[258]
bāriḥ,	"Game that passes from one's right to one's left"
barīm,	"Two separate threads, red and white, tied by a woman around her waist and her forearm . . . and incantation"
taḥazzī,	*ḥazā/ḥazwan,* and *taḥazzā* are synonymous with *zajr* [see below] and *takahhana* ("to divine")[259] 1.16.10
tadsīm al-nūnah,	To perform *tadsīm* on a child's chin-dimple is "to blacken it with soot so that 'the eye' does not afflict it"
tadhaʿʿub,	[One says,] "he suffered *tadhaʿʿub* from the jinn," meaning "they gave him a scare"
tashahhuq,	[One says,] "the observer's eye performed *tashahhuq* upon him," meaning "it afflicted him with 'the eye'"
tashawwuh,	One says, "Do not perform *tashawwuh* upon me!" meaning "Do not afflict me with 'the eye'!"
taʿayyud,	"'The beholder performed *taʿayyud* on the beheld' means he afflicted him with 'the eye' and did so forcefully so as to intensify the injury done to him"; mentioned by al-Fīrūzābādī under *ʿ-w-d*

التنجيس	اسم شى من القذر او عظام الموتى او خرقة الحائض كان يعلّق على من يخاف عليه من ولوع الجن به *
تنجّى	تنجّى لفلان تشوّه له ليصيبه بالعين كنجا له ونجأه بالهمز اصابه بالعين *
التِوَل	تال يتول عالج السحر *
التُوَلَة	السحر او شبهه وخرز تحبَّب معها المراة الى زوجها كالتِوَلَة * ١،١٦،١١
الجُلْبَة	العوذة تخرز عليها جلدة *
الحابل	الساحر *
الحِرْز	العُوذة *
الحُفُوف	شدة الاصابة بالعين *
الحَوْط	خرزات وهلال من فضة تشده المراة فى وسطها لئلاّ تصيبها العين *
الخَصْمة	من حروز الرجال تلبس عند المنازعة او الدخول على السلطان *
الرأمة	خرزة المحبة *
الرَتِيمة	كان من اراد سفرا يعمد إلى شجرة فيعقد غصنين منها فان رجع وكانا على حالهما قال ان اهله لم تخنه والاّ فقد خانته وذلك الرَتَم والرَتيمة *
الرسع	رسع الصبىّ شد فى يده او رجله خرزا لدفع العين *
الزجر	العيافة والتكهّن * ١،١٦،١٢
الزَرْقة	خرزة للتاخيذ *

tanjīs, [literally, "defilement"] "The name given something dirty, or bones from the dead, or a menstrual rag that they used to hang on anyone whom it was feared might have been afflicted with madness by the jinn"

tanajjā, "To perform *tanajjī* on (*li-*) someone means to perform *tashahhuq* [q.v.] on him in order to afflict him with 'the eye,' as also *najā*"; *naja'a* with the glottal stop means "to afflict with 'the eye'"

tawl, "[The verb] *tāla, yatūlu* means 'to practice sorcery'"

tuwalah, "Sorcery, or anything like it, or beads used to make a woman love her husband"; also *tiwalah* **1.16.11**

julbah, "An amulet strung on a leather string"

ḥābil, "Sorcerer"

ḥirz, "Amulet"

ḥufūf, "Severe affliction with 'the eye'"

ḥawṭ, "Beads and a silver crescent that a woman ties around her waist so that 'the eye' will not afflict her"

khaṣmah, "An amulet used by men, worn in battle or when going into the presence of the sultan"

ra'amah, "A love bead"

ratīmah, "One intending to make a journey would go to a tree[260] and tie two branches together. If he returned and they were still tied, he would say that his wife had not betrayed him; otherwise she had betrayed him. This was called *ratm* or *ratīmah*"

rasʿ, "'He performed *rasʿ* on the child' means he tied a bead onto his hand or foot against 'the eye'"

zajr, "Divination through *ʿiyāfah* [q.v.] or the taking of auguries" **1.16.12**

zarqah, "A bead for casting spells"

السانح ضد البارح *

السُلوان ما يُشرَب ليسلّى ما هو ان يوخذ تراب قبر ميت فيجعل فى مآ فيسقى العاشق فيموت حبّه الخ *

السُلوانة خرزة للتاخيذ وخرزة تدفن في الرمل فتسودّ فيبحث عنها ويسقاها الإنسان فتسلّيه *

شد الحِقاب الحقاب خيط يشدّ فى حِقو الصبى لدفع العين *

الشَعْبَذة الشعوذة *

الشَعْوَذة أُخَذ كالسحر يُرى الشى بغير ما عليه اصله فى راى العين *

شحيثا كلمة سريانية تنفتح بها الاغاليق بلا مفاتيح *

الصَخْبَة خرزة تستعمل فى الحبّ والبغض * ١،١٦،١٣

الصَدْحة وبالضم والتحريك خرزة للتاخيذ *

الصَرَّة خرزة للتاخيذ *

الصَرْفة خرزة للتاخيذ *

الصِهْمِيم حُلوان الكاهن *

صوت اللوف نبات له بصلة تسمّىَ الصرّاخة لان له فى يوم المهرجان صوتا يزعمون ان من سمعه يموت فى يومه *

الصَفَر حيّة في البطن تلزق بالضلوع فتعضها او الخ *

الطِبّ مثلثة الرفق والسحر *

الطَرق ان يخلط الكاهن القطن بالصوف اذا تكهّن *

العاضه الساحر والعِضَه[1] الكذب والبهتان والسحر * ١،١٦،١٤

---

[1] ١٨٥٥: العضة.

sāniḥ,	Opposite of *bāriḥ* [q.v.]
sulwān,	[literally, "consolation"] "Something that is drunk to bring consolation, or the taking of dust from the grave of a dead man and making it into something that is given to the lover to drink so that his love-sickness dies, etc."
sulwānah,	"A bead used for working magic, and a bead that is buried in the sand and which then turns black, is sought for, [is pulverized], and is drunk by someone, to whom it then brings consolation"
shadd al-ḥiqāb,	[literally, "the tying of the *ḥiqāb*"] "The *ḥiqāb* is a thread that is tied around the loins of a child to ward off 'the eye'"
shaʿbadhah,	*shaʿwadhah* [q.v.]
shaʿwadhah,	"Spells, a form of sorcery: things are seen in a shape different from their original shape as seen by the eye"
shaḥīthā,	"A Syriac word by which what is locked may be opened without keys"
ṣakhbah,	"A bead used for love and for hatred" 1.16.13
ṣadḥah,	"(also *ṣudḥah* or *ṣadaḥah*) a bead used for casting spells"
ṣarrah,	"A bead used for casting spells"
ṣarfah,	"A bead used for casting spells"
ṣihmīm,	"The sooth-sayer's fee"
ṣawt al-lūf,	[literally, "the cry of the loofah"] "A plant with a bulb that is called 'the shrieker' because on the day of the festival it emits a cry which, they claim, causes any who hears it to die within the day"
ṣafar,	"A serpent in the belly that clings to the ribs and bites them," or etc.[261]
ṭibb,	"Also *ṭabb* and *ṭubb*; gentleness, and magic"
ṭarq,	"The soothsayer's mixing of cotton with wool when he prognosticates"
ʿāḍih,	"Magician"; *ʿiḍah* means lying, falsehood, and magic 1.16.14

العاطوس	ما يُعطس منه ودابّة يتشآم بها والعاطس ما استقبلك من امامك من الظبآ *
االعِرافة	العَرّاف الكاهن والطبيب وصنعته العرافة وقد عرف ككتب *
العَطف	نبت يوخذ بعض عروقه ويُلوَى ويطرح على الفارك فتحبّ زوجها *
العَطَفة	خرزة للتايذ *
العُقَرة	خرزة تحملها المراة لئلآ تلد *
عود الشُبارق	الشبارق شجر عال ويقلّد الخيل وغيره بعوده للعين *
العيافة	عفتُ الطير اعيفها عِيافة زجرتها وهو ان تعتبر باسمآئها ومساقطها وانوآئها فتتسعّد أو تتشآم *
العَيْثَرة	عيثر الطيرَ رآها جارية فزجرها *
الغزّ	غز الابلَ والصبىَّ علّق عليها العهون من العين * ١٥،١٦،١
غَضار وكَرار	الغضار خَزَف يحمل لدفع العين وكرار خرزة للتاخيذ تقول الساحرة ياكَرار كُرِّيه وياهمرة اهمريه ان اقبل فسرّيه وان ادبر فضرّيه *
الفَطسة	خرزة لهم للتاخيذ يقلن اخذته بالفَطسة بالثُوَّآ والعَطسة *
القَبَلة	ضرب من الخرز يوخَذ بها *
القُبلة	ما تتخذه الساحرة لتُقبل به وجه الانسان على صاحبه *
القُلَيب	خرزة للتاخيذ *
الكابح	ما استقبلك مما يتطيّر منه *

ʿāṭūs, "Something that is sneezed at and a beast from which an evil omen is taken"; the *ʿāṭis* is "a gazelle that approaches head-on"

ʿirāfah, A *ʿarrāf* is a soothsayer, or a physician, and his profession is called *ʿirāfah*; the verb ["to practise soothsaying"] is *ʿarafa*, on the pattern of *kataba*[262]

ʿaṭaf, "A plant some of whose roots are twisted and . . . thrown over a misogynist to make him love his wife"

ʿaṭfah, "A bead used for casting spells"

ʿuqarah, "A bead worn by women in order not to give birth"

ʿūd al-shubāriq, "[The wood of] a tall tree, necklaces made of which are hung around the necks of horses and other beasts to protect them from 'the eye'"

ʿiyāfah, "[The verb] *ʿiftu* [first person singular perfect], *uʿīfu* [first person singular imperfect], *ʿiyāfatan* [verbal noun]) *al-ṭayr* is synonymous with 'I took an augury from the birds,' meaning that one takes into consideration their names and their descents and ascents and then draws a happy or an unhappy omen"

ʿaytharah, *ʿaythara l-ṭayr* means, he saw the birds flying and took an augury from them

1.16.15 *ghazz*, "To perform *ghazz* upon camels or a child is to hang colored threads on them against 'the eye'"

ghaḍār and *karār*, "The *ghaḍār* is a piece of pottery worn to ward off 'the eye'; a *karār* is a bead for casting spells. The witch says, 'O *karār*, turn him back! O *hamrah* [q.v.], knock him flat! If he come this way, give him joy! If he turn his back, give him pain!'"

faṭsah, "Beads they use for casting spells; women say, 'I take him with the sudden death, the yawn, and the sneeze!'"

qablah, "A kind of bead used for casting spells"

qublah, "What the magician uses to summon up a person's face for his friend"

qulayb, "A bead used for casting spells"

kābiḥ, "Things [i.e., animals] used for taking auguries that approach one head-on"

الكادِس	ما يتطيّر به من الفال والعطاس وغيرهما والقعيد من الظبآء وهو الذى يجى من خلفك ويتشآم به ونحوه الداكس *	
الكَبْدة	خرزة للحبّ *	
الكَحْلة	خرزة للتاخيذ او للعين *	
اللُجام	ما يتطيّر منه *	١٦،١٦،١
اللّجْ	لجه بعينه اصابه بها *	
اللُعطة	اسم من لعطه بسهم او بعين اصابه *	
اللَمّة	يقال اصابته من الجنّ لمّة اى مسّ او قليل والعين اللامّة المصيبة بالسو *	
الماقِط	الحازى المتكهن الطارق بالحصى *	
المِجْول	العُوذة *	
المستنشئة	الكاهنة *	
المُهْرة	خرزة كان النسآء يتحبّبن بها *	
النُشْرة	رقية يعالج بها المجنون او المريض *	
النفّاثات فى العقد	السواحر *	١٧،١٦،١
النُفْرة	شى يعلّق على الصبى لخوف النظرة *	
النِيرَنْج	أَخْذٌ[١] كالسحر وليس به *	
الهامة	الصَدَى وهو طائر يخرج من راس المقتول بزعم الجاهلية *	
الهَبْرة	خرزة يوخّذ بها الرجال *	
الهجيج	الخطّ يُخط فى الارض للكهانة *	

١ كذا في القاموس وفي ١٨٥٥: أُخَذ.

kādis,	"Things used in divining, such as a good omen, a sneeze, or the like; the *qaʿīd,* said of gazelles, is the one that comes up behind you, and from it a bad omen is drawn, and the *dākis* is the same"
kabdah,	"A bead for love"
kaḥlah,	"A bead used for casting spells, or against 'the eye'"
lujām,	"Things from which omens are drawn" 1.16.16
laḥj,	"'He performed *laḥj* on him with his eye' means 'he afflicted him with it'"
luʿṭah,	"The noun formed from [the expression] *laʿaṭahu bi-sahm* ('he struck him with an arrow') or *bi-ʿayn* ('with "the eye"'), meaning 'he afflicted him'"
lammah,	"One says, 'He was afflicted by a *lammah,* or fit, or a touch [of madness] from the jinn' . . . and *al-ʿayn al-lāmmah* (literally, 'the gathering eye') is that which afflicts with evil"
māqiṭ,	"The minor magician who claims powers of divination and knocks small stones together"[263]
mijwal,	"Cantrip"
mustanshiʾah,	"The woman soothsayer"
muhrah,	"A bead women used to attract love"
nushrah,	"A spell with which the insane or the sick are treated"
naffāthāt fī l-ʿuqad,	"Witches"[264] 1.16.17
nufrah,	"Something hung on a child for fear of 'the eye'"
nīranj,	"Charms that look like magic but are not"
hāmah,	"The *ṣadā,* which is a bird that emerges from the head of a murdered man, according to the Arabs of the Days of Barbarism"
habrah,	"Beads by which men are bewitched"
hajīj,	"A line drawn on the ground for purposes of divination"

الهَقْعة دائرة فى الفرس يتشآم بها *

الهَمْرة خرزة للتاخيذ

الهِنَّمة خرزة للتاخيذ *

الوجيه خرزة م كالوجيهة * قلت الظاهر انها للوجاهة * ١،١٦،١٨

الينجلب خرزة للتاخيذ او للرجوع بعد الفرار *

الحاوى رجل حَوّآء وحاوٍ يجمع الحيات * قلت هذا غاية ما ذكره صاحب القاموس فى ح ى ى والظاهر انه واوىّ ولكن ضعّفه فى الواو بقوله قيل ومنه الحية لتحوّيها الخ وقوله يجمع الحيّات كانه لحظ فيه معنى حوى لا يناسب ما قاله فى تفسير الخِنْفش وعبارته * او حية عظيمة ضخمة الراس رقشآء ركدآء اذا حويتها انتفخ وريدها * فهو صريح هنا فى الرقية وقد ذكرت ذلك وما اشبه فى كتاب مفرد *

haqʿah, "A ring on a horse that is regarded as ill-omened"

hamrah, "A bead used for casting spells"

hinnamah, "A bead used for casting spells"

wajīh, "A bead, too well-known to require definition,[265] as is *wajīhah*"; it seems to me they must be [worn] to impress with "high-standing" (*wajāhah*) 1.16.18

yanjalib, "A bead for casting spells, or for return after flight"

ḥāwī. "The man called a *ḥawwāʾ* or a *ḥāwī* collects snakes."

I declare: This is all that the author of the *Qāmūs* says under the root *ḥ-y-y*, though it appears that the root is really *ḥ-w-y*; however, the *Qāmūs* relates the word to the root *ḥ-w-y* when he doubles the *w* and says, "It is claimed that *ḥayyah* ('snake') is from this root because of its coiling upon itself (*taḥawwī*)," etc. His statement that the *ḥāwī* "collects snakes" (*yajmaʿu ḥayyāt*)—as if the word was derived from *ḥawā* ("to gather")—is inconsistent with his definition of the word *ḥinfish*, namely, "[the viper] or a great serpent with a huge head, variegated black and white, given to lying still; if you charm it (*ḥawwaytahā*), its jugular swells." Here he relates it unambiguously to the casting of spells, as I state, along with other things, in a separate book.[266]

الفصل السابع عشر

في الثلج

لا غرو ان يجد بعض القارئين كلامى فى هذا الفصل باردا لانى كتبته فى يوم عبوس ١،١٧،١
قمطرير * ذى زمهرير * والثلج اذ ذاك ساقط على السطوح * وقد سدّ الطرق
ودخل فى البيوت والصروح * وكاد يطفى النار * ويذهب بالاصطبار * ويمنى
بالقَمَر والقِمار * غير انه لا ينكر احد ان شارب الثلج او آكله او اللاعب به يحسّ ٢،١٧،١
منه بحرارة * وكذلك قارى كلامى فانه وان وجده باردا فلا بدّ وان يحتمى علىَّ من
هذه البرودة * فيكون قد حصل الغرض وهو تسخين دماغه * ولا سيما اذ كان قد
بقيت فيه بقية غيظ وحدّة من الفصل المتقدم * ولكنى لم اقصد فيما حكيته الا
الصدق * ولو خطر ببالى ان آتى افكا وعضيهة لاوعيت ذلك فى قصيدة وختمتها
بدعآ ومدح لاحد البخلآ * ومن مارانى فى ذلك فليسال القسيس نفسه * الا ان
الثلج يخالف كلامى من جهة انه يسقط على الاسود فيبيّضه وكلامى قد سقط على
القرطاس فسوّده * وكلاهما فى ظنى يروق العين وكلاهما يجتمعان فى هذه الجهة *
وهى ان الثلج لا تطلع عليه الشمس اياماً الّا ويذوب * وكذا كلامى فانه لا يكاد يبقى
منه شى فى راس القارى بعد تقمّره اوعند ظهور بُوح عليه * وهناك جهة اخرى
تضمّهما * وهو ان الثلج بعد سقوطه ينشا عنه الصحو وانجلآ الجو * وكذلك كلامى
فانه بعد تساقطه من راسى ينشا عنه انجلآ جوّ فكرى وصحو بالى واستعداده الى

Chapter 17

Snow

No doubt, some readers will find what I have to say in this chapter hard to warm to as I wrote it on a "frowning day, *inauspicious*,"[267] a day of cold that was *vicious*. Snow at the time o'er the rooftops was *sifting*, had blocked the highways, and into house and palace was *drifting*. It was almost enough to extinguish any *fire*, put an end to any patience, and thoughts of moon and of money-wagering *inspire*.[268] 1.17.1

Be that as it may, no one can deny that anyone who drinks, eats, or plays with snow derives from it a feeling of heat. The same goes for the reader of my words: if he finds himself getting chilly, all he has to do is seek protection with me from the cold, in which case the goal, which is to put his brain through some warm-up exercises, will have been achieved. This will be especially true if the said brain still carries some traces of anger and indignation left over from the preceding chapter, though I meant nothing by telling the tale but to speak the truth, and, had it crossed my mind to lie or fib, I would have done so in a poem concluding with prayers and praise for some miser; if anyone doesn't believe me, let him ask the priest himself. All the same, snow differs from my words in one thing: snow falls on what is black and makes it white, while my words fall on paper and make it black. Both, in my opinion, are a delight to the eye, and the two share the following feature: a few days after the sun rises over the snow, it melts, and the same is true of my words, for almost nothing will remain of them in the reader's head after the passing of one moonlit night or the rising over him of one Shining Orb. And here's a further point of resemblance: the falling of the snow gives rise to a clearing and brightening of the weather; so too the descent of my words from my head brings about a brightening of the weather of my thoughts, 1.17.2

ما يروق ويروع * فعلى كل حال تجد المشابهة هنا فى موقعها وعذرى فى محله *
وبعدُ فانى ارى الاغنيآء المثرين يتخذون فى ديارهم الفسيحة مساكن للصيف واخرى ٣،١٧،١
للشتآء وكنّاً للمبيت واخر للاستحمام * ومن لم يكن له من غيرهم الّا بيت واحد فغير
جدير بان يزار فيه الّا حين يكون بيته موافقا لوقت الزيارة * او يكون وقت الزيارة
موافقا لبيته * فبنآء على ذلك ينبغى للعلمآء اقتدآء باكابرهم الاغنيآ ان يتخذوا لهم
فى رؤسهم الفيحآ مواطن متعددة مختلفة لما ياتى عليهم من الكلام البارد والفاتر
والحميم * ففى وقت ثوران الدم وهيجان الطبع يقراون البارد تقليلا مما حركهم من
بواعث الحرارة * وفى وقت السكون يتلون الحميم * او بالعكس على مذهب من
يداوى الشى بجنسه لا بضده * لا يقال ان القارى يضيع وقته فى تمييز البارد
والحميم من هذه الفصول * اذ لا يستوعب مضمونها الا اذا اتى على آخرها *
بخلاف سائر الكتب فانه لا يتعمّد فيها الكلام البارد فهى على منهاج واحد *
فانى اقول ان كل فصل من تلك الفصول له عنوان يدل عليه دلالة قطعية كدلالة
الدخان على النار * فمن درى العنوان فقد درى الفصل كله * مثال ذلك اذا مرّ
بك فى احد الفصول ترجمة البالوعة او البلّوعة او البلّاعة او البَرْبَخ او الارْدَبة فلا بدّ
لك من ان تفطن الى ان حمارا من حُمُر الدير قد غطس فيها للتعريب او الترجمة *
الا انه لا ينبغى للقارى اذا درى مَغْزَى الفصل من العنوان ان يضرب عن قراته * ٤،١٧،١
ثم يقول متبجّحا بين اقرانه واخوانه قد قرات كتاب الساق على الساق وفهمت معانيه
كلها * فان ذلك يكون كقول مُقنس(١) قد رايت اليوم
الامير اعزه الله وكلمته مع انه لم يكن راى منه الّا قذاله
عن بُعد * ولم يتح له تقبيل يده الشريفة * او كان ذلك

(١) اقنس الرجل ادّعى الى قَنس شريف (اى اصل) وهو خسيس[1]

[1] ١٨٥٥: حنسيس.

a clearing of my mind, and a readiness on its part to delight and please. In any case, I'm sure you'll agree that the comparison is appropriate here and my excuse to the point.

To proceed. I see that the well-off and well-to-do, in their spacious homes, use one set of living quarters for the summer and another for the winter, one nook for passing the night and another for taking a bath. Others, who have only one house, aren't worth the visiting, unless that house happens to be close by at the time for visits or the time for visits happens to coincide with closeness to their houses. It follows that, in emulation of their better-off betters, scholars should assign themselves, in their roomy heads, numerous and varied locations for the cold, tepid, and hot words that come to them. That way, when their blood is hot and their natural tempers are aroused, they'll be able to read something cold and so reduce the underlying causes of the heat that has exercised them, and when things are quiet they'll be able to recite out loud from the hot, or pursue the opposite strategy, in keeping with the school of those who treat things with their like and not with their opposite. Let no one say that the reader will be wasting his time if he spends it distinguishing between the cold and the hot among these chapters, for the only way to thoroughly digest their contents is to read them through to the end, unlike other books, in which the sin of "cold talk"[269] isn't committed and which follow one set curriculum. Every one of these chapters, I declare, has a title that points to its contents as unambiguously as smoke does to fire; anyone who knows what the title is knows what the whole chapter is about. If, for example, you happen to come across some chapter with the word *bālūʿah* or *ballūʿah* or *ballāʿah* ("drain") or *barbakh* ("drainpipe") or *irdabbah* ("sewer") as a heading, you can assume that one of the donkeys at the monastery must have dived into something of the sort looking for help with their Arabizations and translations. 1.17.3

On the other hand, of course, just because the reader has got to know the gist of the chapter from its title doesn't mean he can decide not to read it and then boast to his friends and brethren, "I read *Leg over Leg* and understood it all!" That would be like someone who claims to be of noble origin(1) saying, "Today I saw the emir, God strengthen him, and spoke to him," when all he saw of him was the back of his head, and that from a distance, and it wasn't granted to him to kiss the noble hand; or 1.17.4

(1) *muqnis* ["claiming to be of noble origin"]: *aqnasa l-rajul* means "he laid claim to a *qans sharīf*, i.e., a noble origin, when he was a low-born upstart."

الامير قد ساله عن شى فتلعثم فى الجواب او تروّى فيه فسبّ اباه واجداده ولعنه وتهدّده بالصلب او بسَمْل عينيه * او كقول هَبَنْقَع (لمزهوّ الاحمق المحبّ لمحادثة النسآء) قد رايت اليوم فلانة * ولما ان واجهتنى وقفتْ وتنفّست الصعدآ * مع انها تكون قد وقفت لتبصق او انها تنفسّت الصعدآ بُهْرا * بل الاولى ان ينوى القارى عند افتتاحه هذا الكتاب ان يتصفحه كله من اوله الى آخره حتى حواشيه وعدد صفحاته * ويعتقد ان لكل مولف اسلوبا * وانه لا يمكن لاحد ان يعجب ١،١٧،٥
الناس كلهم * اذ الاهوآ متفاوتة والآرآ مختلفة * ومن الاسرار التى بقيت مكتومة عنى انك تجد بعض المولفين فاتر الحركة غير ذى نشاط ولا مرح * قليل الارتياح الى ما يبعث على التهاوش والتناوش * متقاعس الهمة عن السَبْح والحركة * ناظر الى الحوادث كلها نظر المتوقع لها * وهو مع ذلك اذا اخذ القلم انبض كل عرق فى القارى وحرك كل ساكن * ومنهم من تراه نَزِقا حركا ذا تترّع وتسرع وحفد وصَمَيان واقبال وادبار وسعى وتهافت * ومعاجلة ومبادرة ومزاحمة ومزاهمة ومسابقة ومحاشرة * ثم هو ان قال شيا سقط من راسه على ذهن القارى سقوط الثلج حتى يكاد ان يجمد منه ذكآه * فلما تاملت فى ذلك وتحققته ارتبت فى كون سقوط ١،١٧،٦
الثلج ناشئا عن فرط برودة متكونة فى الهوآ وقلت بل لعل سببه فرط حرارة حزّت فى صدر الجو على سكان هذه الارض * ووافر وغر تكوّن فى حشاه فلفظه عليهم ثلجا انتقاماً منهم عما ياتونه فى الليالى الباردة من المنكرات * وذلك ان بعضهم يحاول عكس الطبيعة فيسخّن فراشه باداة فيها نار * وبعضهم باداة فيها مآ حميم * وبعضهم باداة فيها شراب * واخرون باخرى فيها لحم * وربما كان من ذلك اللحم لحم خنزير اجلّك الله * فمن اجل ذلك اسقط الجوّ عليهم الثلج المتراكم منعاً لهم من الخروج من ديارهم لاستعمال هذه الادوات لكى يستريح من فسادهم ولو يومين *

the same emir asked him about something and he stammered over his reply or had to think about it, so the emir insulted his father and forefathers and cursed him out, threatening to have him crucified or to have his eyes put out with hot irons; or like some *habanqaʿ* (one who puts on airs, is stupid, and loves talking to women) saying, "I saw such and such a woman today, and, when she was face to face with me, she stopped and sighed deeply," when she probably stopped to spit, or she sighed a deeply malodorous sigh. The reader should, preferably, on opening this book, go through it page by page, from the beginning to the end, including the footnotes and page numbers.

It is believed that each author has his own style and no one can please everybody, for people's likes are diverse, their opinions various. One mystery I've never been able to get to the bottom of is that a certain author will appear slothful, with neither energy or good cheer, ill at ease with anything that might stir up commotion or conflict, tepid in both inaction and action, viewing everything that happens as though it was just what he'd expected—and yet set every vein of the reader's throbbing and every muscle aquiver the moment he takes up the pen; and there are some whom you'll find lively and brisk, always in a hurry and a rush, quick and agile, coming and going, running around and falling over himself, chasing and speeding, ducking and weaving, shoving and jostling—and then, when he composes something, it falls out of his head onto the reader's brain like snow and almost douses the fires of his intelligence. 1.17.5

When I thought about the matter and looked into it in depth, I started to doubt that snow could be created by an excess of cold formed in the air. I decided that, on the contrary, it may well, in fact, be caused by the creation by excessive heat of an irritated patch on the air's breast above the inhabitants of the Earth plus a superabundance of ire inside its guts, followed by the precipation of the latter onto the said inhabitants in the form of snow, to pay them back for the abominations they practice on cold nights, meaning the way that some of them try to turn nature upside down and heat their beds with an instrument containing fire or, in the case of others, one containing piping hot water or, of others, by using an instrument containing drink, or of others, one containing meat.[270] Such meat might even include pork, God save your dignity, and the air would therefore drop accumulations of snow upon them to prevent them from leaving their houses to make use of these instruments, and thus be relieved of their corruption, be it but for a couple of days. 1.17.6

الا انه قد فاته ان كثيرا من هولاء الناس يتخذون اداة للاداة او اداة لاداة ٧،١٧،١
الادوات * مثال الاول ما اذا تربّع الغنى فى دسته وتدثّر بفروته وقال لغلامه سرّ
ياغلام الى محل كذا وائتنى منه باداة لتسخين فراشى هذه الليلة * فيذهب الغلام
يطأ الوحول والثلوج ورجل سيده نظيفة * ومثال الثانى ما اذا كان السيد
جوادًا سخيًا فيبعث غلامه فى مركب له او فى آخر مما يستاجر من الطرق * او
اذا كان ذا سيادة وامارة ويريد ان يكتم سره عن غلامه * لان لذة الخادم انما
هى الثلب فى عرض مخدومه وجعل نفسه اولى بالخدومية منه * فيستعمل ذلك
السيد آخر او اخرين او أُخَر فى مكان غلامه * ويكون قد بعث اليهم من قبل
بهدية على يد خادمه اظهارا لمكارمه * او انه اعطاهم اياها من يده * فيكون
سقوط الثلج على اى حال كان سببا فى التسخين والحرارة * لانه اذا اعتُبر فى
حق المخدوم كان سببا فى اتخاذه الاداة * وان اعتُبر فى حق الخادم وغيره ممن
سدّ مسدّه كان موجبا للحسد * وهو من اعظم الموثّرات تسخينا واحماء * ومع ٨،١٧،١
كونه اى الثلج يرى ساقطا على كل موضع فى المدينة دون تمييز دار عن دار فان
لفظه فى الحقيقة لا يصيب الا رؤس بعض الناس * وكان الاولى ان يطرد حكمه
فيعمّ لا مثل احكام اللفظ الارضى فانها تجرى على قوم دون قوم * والفرق بين
اللفظين هو ان الثلج لما كان سقوطه او لفظه من علو الى سفل كان المظنون به انه
يتصوب على جميع الروس بشدة * فيشمل الكبير منها والصغير والمسفَّط منها
والمسمرَط * فاما الاحكام والقوانين الارضية فمن حيث كان لفظها من سفل الى
علو اى من روس ناس مسودين الى روس ناس سائدين * لم يكن من المحتمل ان
يكون تبعّثها قويا حتى يبلغ ذوى الرفعة والعلآ الذين يمرّ السحاب من تحت قُذُلهم *

What would have escaped its notice, however, is that many of these same people make use of one instrument to instrumentalize another, or several others. An example of the first would be the rich man who sits cross-legged in his tub, wraps himself in his fur mantle, and says to his servant, "You there! Off with you to such and such a store and bring me an instrument with which to heat my bed tonight!" so that the servant treads the mire and snow while his master's foot stays clean. An example of the second would be if the master is open-handed and liberal and sends his servant in a vehicle either belonging to him or hired off the street, or, if he's a sovereign emir and wants to keep his secret from his servant (it being ever the pleasure of servants to slander their master's good name and pretend that they are worthier to be served than he), in which case the master will make use of another, or a couple of others, or of several others, in place of his servant, he having sent them, ahead of time, via his servant, a gift as a way of showing his generosity or perhaps having given it to them with his own hand. Whatever the case may be, the falling of snow will have been the cause of heating and warmth, for, if the latter be regarded as due to the action of the master, it would be the cause of his having made use of the instrument, and if it is regarded as being due to the action of the servant or others who might take his place, it would be attributable to envy, which is one of the most effective stimulators of warmth and heat. 1.17.7

Despite the fact that it (the snow, that is) appears to fall everywhere in the city without favoring one house over another, in reality this precipitation (by the sky, of its anger) targets only the heads of certain people, though it would be more proper if its sentence were inclusive and thus felt equally by all, unlike sentences of earthly precipitation, which are applied to some groups and not others. The difference between the two precipitations is that it might have been supposed that the snow, given that its falling, or precipitation, is top down, would be deposited on all heads with equal force and thus include old and young, fat-headed and long-headed. Earthly sentences and laws, on the other hand, given that their precipitation is bottom up, or in other words from the heads of people who are themselves ruled to the heads of those who rule,[271] are unlikely to carry strongly enough to reach those who are possessed of high status and elevated station, whose heads are so high that the clouds pass beneath them. 1.17.8

ثم ان الثلج معما يتبعه في الواقع من الضنك والمشقة لمن الفه فقد يروق لعين من ١،١٧،٩
لم يكن رآه * فقد بلغنا ان بعض الصعاليك كان مرة ضيفا عند اناس لم يكرموه ولم
يحتفلوا به اذ كان دونهم في المعارف والنباهة * وكان بلدهم لا يسقط فيه الثلج
البتة * فلما فصل من عندهم الى بلاد اخرى راى فيها الرزق وعاين بها الثلج كبّر
لرؤيته وهلّل واعجب به غاية الاعجاب * حتى زعم انه منة من الله خصّ بها ذلك
الصقع تمزية له على غيره * كما انه تعالى حرم منها بلد مضيفه الاول * وكذلك ١،١٧،١٠
كلامى ههنا * فانه معما فيه من الاستطراد والحشو والالفاظ المضغوطة بين
المعانى ومن المغازى المعقودة بالتلميح والتلويح * والتحويل والتمليح * فقد يروق لخاطر
من لم يكن قد الف هذا التخليط بل ربما يجعله الاعجاب به على تحديه ومحاكاته *
ولكن هيهات فان الباب قد اغلق في وجوه المتحدّين * على انى لست ازعم انى
اول كاتب في الدنيا نهج هذه الطريقة واسعطها المتناعسين * الا انى رايت
جميع المولفين فى سَهْوة كَبى قد قيدوا انفسهم بسلسلة نَفَس من التاليف واحدة *
لكنى لا اعلم الان هل غيّروا اسلوبهم اَوْ لا * اذ قد مضى علىّ بعد فراقهم اكثر
من خمس سنين * فكانّ العارف بحلقة واحدة من تلك السلسلة قد عرف سائر
الحَلَق حتى ان كل واحد منهم يصدق عليه ان يسمّى حلقيّا * بنآء على انه مشى
ورآ القوم وحذا حذوهم * فاذ قد تقرر ذلك فاعلم انى قد خرجت من السلسلة فما
انا بحلقى ولا بسُتَيْهِىّ ولا اكون امام القوم فان الثانية انحس من الاولى * وانما انا
مستقبل لما استحسنت * آخذ بناصية ما استظرفت * رافض مكلف العادة *

It is also the case that snow, however much misery and trouble it may bring in reality to those who are familiar with it, often looks delightful to someone who has never seen it before. We have been told that a certain vagabond was once the guest of people who failed to honor and celebrate him[272] because he was inferior to them in terms of acquaintance and social eminence, their country being one in which snow never fell. When he left them and went to another, which he found to be a land of plenty and where he witnessed snow falling with his own eyes, he exclaimed and cheered at the sight and was as pleased as he could be, to the point that he claimed that it was a gift from God that the latter had made specific to that particular spot to distinguish it from all others, just as the Almighty had denied it to the first country in which he'd been a guest. 1.17.9

Of the same type are my words here,[273] for, despite all the digression and padding, the words that have been squeezed into figures of speech and the meanings that have been made knotty with allusions and *insinuations*, transformations and witty *formulations*, someone unused to such minglings may find it appealing; indeed his admiration may even drive him to seek to outdo and emulate it. Too late, though! The door has closed in the face of competitors. While I do not claim to be the first writer in the world to follow this path or thrust a pinch of it up the noses of those who pretend they are dozing, I do notice that all the authors in my bookcase are shackled to a single stylistic chain. I don't know whether they've changed their style now or not: more than five years have passed since I left them. Once you've become familiar with one link of the chain, you feel as though you know all the others, so that each one of them may truly be called a chain-man, given that each has followed in the footsteps of the rest and imitated them closely. This being established, know that I have exited the chain, for I am no chain-man and will not form the rump of the line; nor do I have any desire to be at its front, for the latter is an even more calamitous place to be than the former. I follow what I see to be good, seize what I find appealing by the forelock, reject the impositions of tradition. 1.17.10

الفصل الثامن عشر

في النحس

١،١٨،١ لقد ارحت سن القلم من كدم اسم الفارياق قليلا بعد ان تركته مع القسيس الربيط * وتلهّيت بالكلام على الثلج لما داخلنى من فرط الحدة عليهما معاً * اما على القسيس فلكونه خان صديقه الذى اواه الى منزله في حرمته * وكان ينبغى له ان يذهب الى مواجرة او يفعل كسائر القسيسين من اهل حرفته * اذ لو كان الله تعالى رزق ذلك التاجر ولدا على نيّته اى فتح له رحم امراته كما تقول التوراة لكان اربعة ارباع هذا الولد من القسيس والباقى وهو اسمه من التاجر * فيكون قد اقام نفسه مقام مَن يربُ النغول * مع ان اول ذكر فاتح رحم كما تقول التوراة مبارك ومعظم عند جميع الامم * ولهذا كان حق الوراثة عند الانكليز للبكر اى لفاتح الرحم * فكيف يحاول القسيس هنا جمع اللعنة والبركة على راس مخلوق واحد * اِنّ ذلك الّا محال * واما على الفارياق فلانه هو ٢،١٨،١

الذى كان السبب فى افشآ هذا السرّ بما ابداه من العناد والتصلّف فى حفظ ابياته التى لا اشك في انه ارتكب فيها المين والغلو والمبالغة المردودة لغير نفع * وهو مع ذلك يحسب انه يحسن صنعا * فاما مشابهة الولد اباه في الخَلق هل دلالة قطيعة على كونه ابنه فغير متفق عليها * فذهب بعض الى انها ليست علامة كافية * لان الام قد يحتمل في حالة كونها مسافحة ان تكون

Chapter 18

Bad Luck

The reason I gave the nib of my pen a little rest from the snapping teeth of the Fāriyāq's name, after leaving him with the self-denying priest, and distracted myself by talking about snow was that I was so angry at the two of them. Where the priest's concerned, I was angry that he'd betrayed his friend who had taken him in and had played fast and loose with his womenfolk; had the Almighty given that merchant a son whom he'd accepted in good conscience as his own—or, in other words, had He "opened his wife's womb," as it says in the Old Testament[274]—four quarters of the child would have been from the priest and the rest, which is his name, from the merchant, the latter thus putting himself in the position of a raiser of bastards, though the first male to open a womb is, as the Old Testament says, "blessed and magnified among the nations."[275] That is why, among the British, the right of inheritance goes to the eldest, or the "opener of the womb."[276] How could the priest have attempted, by doing so, to bring both a curse and a blessing down on the head of any of God's creatures? It's unthinkable. 1.18.1

As to the Fāriyāq, I was angry because he was the cause of the secret's being revealed[277] through the obstinacy and blustering that he demonstrated in hanging on to his verses, in which, I have no doubt, he was guilty of falsity, overstatement, and objectionable exaggeration to no purpose (despite which he thinks he's a great poet). As for the claim that the child's physical resemblance to its father constitutes definitive proof of his being his son, there is no consensus. Some believe it is an insufficient indication because it is possible that the mother, even while fornicating, might be thinking about her husband and picturing him to herself, in which case the fetus would take on the form of that image. Others say that the mother, 1.18.2

مفكرة فى زوجها ومتصورة له فياتى توزيغ الجنين بحسب هذا التصوّر * وذهب بعض الى ان الام وحدها لا فاعلية لها في التوزيغ فقد ياتى بعض الاولاد مشابها لعمّه او خاله او لآخر ممن لم تكن امّه قد راته قط * والان ينبغى لى ان استمر فى
١،١٨،٣
القصة * وان اعرضها على مسامع القارى من دون اجراض احدنا بغصّة * فاقول قد تقدم فى اول هذا الكتاب ان الفارياق وُلد والطالع نحس النحوس والعقرب شائلة بذنبها الى التيس * والسرطان واقف على قرن الثور * فاعلم هنا ان النحس على قسمين نحس ملازم ونحس مفارق * فالنحس الملازم ما لزم الانسان في يقظته ومنامه واكله وشربه وغدوه ورواحه وفى كل ما ياتيه * والنحس المفارق ما خالف ذلك اعنى ما لزم الانسان في حال دون حال * واعرف ما يكون لزومه فى الاحوال الخطيرة الشان كالزواج والسفر وتاليف كتاب ونحو ذلك * ثم ان ماهيات
١،١٨،٤
النحس الملازم مختلفة ايضا * فمنه ما يكون كالعقدة المحكاة * ومنه كالربقة ومنه كالمسمار * ومنه كالوتد ومنه كالمشبك * ومنه كالقفل بلا مفتاح ومنه كالغِرآ ومنه كالغِمجار * ومنه كالجِاذ ومنه كالشِراس * ومنه كالدبق والطِبق او كالرُومة او الثَرط واللِزاق * ومنه كالجلد ومنه كالدم السارى فى جميع اوصال الجسد ومفاصله * وجناجنه وسلائله * وسناسنه وشلاشله * وترائبه وتراقيه * وشراسيفه وبوانيه * وغضاريفه وحوانيه * ورَبَلاته ومذاخره * وعَضَلاته ونواشره * وعصبه وبوادره * واعصاله ومرادغه * وسافنه وناعوره * ووريده ووتينه * واسهريّه واخدعَيه * ومريّه وفليقه * وحلقومه وبخاعه * ونائطه ونخاعه * واوداجه وذِفراه * وثَفِنته وشظاه * ورواهشه وشراينه * ونسيسَيه واشلائه * وعموده واشوائه * فنحس الفارياق كان من هذا النوع * غير انه لا ينبغى ان يفهم هنا انه كان دمويا اى كثير الدم او محبّا لسفكه او ولّاجا فيه *

on her own, has no role in the shaping of the fetus; some children come out looking like their paternal or maternal uncles, or someone their mothers never ever set eyes on.

Now I must resume my tale, presenting it to the reader's *ears* without leading either of us to choke on his *tears*. Thus I declare: as stated earlier in this book, the Fāriyāq was born with the misfortune of having misfortune everywhere in the ascendant, the Scorpion raising its tail to strike at the Kid, or Billy Goat, and the Crab set on a collision course with the horn of the Ox. Here you must know that bad luck is of two kinds—inseparable bad luck and separable bad luck. Inseparable bad luck is the kind that dogs a person in his waking and sleeping, his eating and drinking, in his setting off of a morning and his coming home at night, and in everything that comes his way. Separable bad luck is the contrary, by which I mean that it is the kind that dogs a person under certain conditions and not others, the best-known such conditions being the critical ones, such as marriage, travel, writing a book, and the like. 1.18.3

The specificities of inseparable bad luck are various too. One kind is like a tightly tied knot, another like a noose, another like a nail, another like a peg, another like a clip, and another like a lock without a key; one is like fish glue, another like corn glue, another like flour paste, another like bookbinder's paste, another like birdlime or mistletoe slime, or like arrow-feather glue or shoe-maker's glue or chrysocolla; one is like the skin and another like the blood that courses through the body's every joint and member[278]—the breastbones and polyps, the vertebrae tips and osmotic membranes, the thoraces and collarbones, the rib cartilage and shoulder blades, the gristle and the four long ribs, the upper thighs and lower belly, the muscles and the sinews of the arm, the veins and the flesh between the shoulder and the neck, the intestines and fatty deposits, the vein that runs on the inner side of the spine and is joined to the aorta and the hemophilic vein, the jugular and aorta, the seminal ducts and the two hidden veins at the cupping-place on the neck, the esophagus and the cephalic vein, the gullet and the backbone nerve, the spinal vein that is cut to cure jaundice and the bone marrow, the jugular veins and the sweaty place behind the ear, the stifle joint and the small bone in the knee that is sometimes displaced, the inner-arm sinews and the arteries, the two veins that supply blood to the brain and the limbs, the spine and the extremities—and it was to this type that the Fāriyāq's bad 1.18.4

فانه كان منزها عن هذه الصفات كلها * وانما كان نحسه كالدم من جهة انه كان
ملازما له فى جميع احواله * فقد حكى وان يكن كاذبا فعليه كذبه انه بات ليلة وقد ١،١٨،٥
راى في المنام انه شرب مثلوجا ثم شرب عقبه سخينا فاصبح يشكو من وجع فى
اضراسه شديد ومن بحح فى حلقه * وكان يحلم انه يتهوّر من قنة جبل او يسقط
عن ظهر جمل فيغدو وظهره متقوّس * وكان اذا حلم انه اكل الكامخ مغسه فى
ليلته * او شرب أُجاجا او زعاقا قآ * او اشتمّ روائح كريهة غثت نفسه * وكان
اذا حدثه احد بانه راى فى حديقته رِبَحْلة راى هو فى المنام ليلته تلك انه في

وَيْل — واد فى جهنم او بئر او باب لها *
او فى المَوْبِق — واد فيها *
او فى الفَلَق — جهنم اوجبّ فيها *
او فى بُولَس — سجن فيها *
او فى سِجّين — واد فيها *
او فى اثَام — واد فيها *
او فى الحُطَمة — باب لها *
او فى غَيّ — واد فيها او نهر *
او فى الصَعُود — جبل فيها * وحوله
لُبَيْنَى — اسم بنت ابليس * ١،١٨،٦
او زَلَنْبُور — احد اولاد ابليس الخمسة *
او مِسْوَط — ولد لابليس يغرى على الغضب *
او السُرْحوب — شيطان اعمى يسكن البحر *
او خَنْزَب — شيطان *

luck belonged. It shouldn't be understood, however, that he was "bloody" in the sense of having much blood, or being fond of shedding or wallowing in it; he was innocent of all such characteristics. It's just that his bad luck was like blood in being inseparable from him under any circumstances.

He has said—and if he lied the responsibility is his—that one night he saw 1.18.5
in his dreams that he drank an iced drink and then, immediately after it, a hot drink and started complaining of a severe pain in his molars and of a hoarseness in his throat. On other occasions, he would dream he was plunging from a mountain top or falling off a camel's back, so that he ended up bent double. If he dreamed that he ate pickles, he would get a stomachache from them that same night, if he drank salty or brackish water, he would vomit, and if he smelled a bad smell, he would faint. And if anyone were to tell him that he'd seen a fair, full-bodied girl in his garden, that night in his dreams he would see himself

in Wayl,	"A valley in Hell, or a well or a gateway there"	
or in al-Mawbiq,	"A valley" there	
or in al-Falaq,	"Hell, or a pit therein"	
or in Būlas,	"A prison" there	
or in Sijjīn,	"A valley" there	
or in Athām,	"A valley" there	
or in al-Ḥuṭama,	"A gateway" there	
or in Ghayy,	"A valley" there, or "a river"	
or in al-Ṣaʿūd,	"A mountain" there with, ranged about it,	
Lubaynā	"Name of the daughter of Iblīs"	1.18.6
or Zalanbūr,	"One of the five sons of Iblīs"	
or Miswaṭ,	"A son of Iblīs who tempts men to anger"	
or al-Surḥūb,	"A blind devil that lives in the sea"	
or Khanzab,	"A devil"	

او السَرْفخ اسم شيطان *

او الجِمّ الشيطان او الشياطين *

او نُهُم شيطان *

او هَياه من اسمآ الشياطين *

او الحُباب اسم شيطان *

او الأزَبّ اسم شيطان *

او ازَبّ العقبة اسم شيطان * ١،١٨،٧

او الهرآ اسم شيطان موكّل بقبيح الاحلام *

او الوَلْهان شيطان يغرى بكثرة صبّ المآ فى الوضو *

او الخُبْث والخبائث ذكور الشيطاين واناثها *

او السَفِيف ابليس ويسمّى ايضا المبطل وكنيته ابو مُرّة وابو قِتْرة *

او عمرو اسم شيطان الفرزدق *

او القِلَّوْط من اولاد الجن والشياطين *

او الشَيْصبان والبَلأز والقاز والخابل والخنّاس والوَسواس والفَتّان والاَجْدع *

وكان اذا بصرمن كوّة بيته بكمكامة مكماكة خيّل له فى المنام أنه فى ١،١٨،٨

ارض خافية بها جنّ *

او فى البِراص منازل الجن *

او فى البَلُّوقة موضع بناحية البحرين فوق كاظمة يزعمون انه من مساكن الجن *

او فى البَقّار موضع برمل عالج كثير الجن *

او العازف ع سمّى لانه تعرف به الجن *

or al-Sarfaḥ,	"Name of a devil"
or al-Jimm,	"A devil, or a number of devils"
or Nuhm,	"A devil"
or Hayāh,	"A name used by devils"
or al-Ḥubāb,	"Name of a devil"
or al-Azabb,	"Name of a devil"
or Azabb al-ʿAqabah,	"Name of a devil" 1.18.7
or al-Hirāʾ,	"Name of a devil in charge of nightmares"
or al-Walhān,	"A devil who tempts men to use too much water when performing their ritual ablutions"
or al-Khubth and al-Khabāʾith,	"Male and female devils"
or al-Safīf,	"Iblīs, also called al-Mubṭil ('the Joker'[279]) and known by the patronymics Father of Bitterness and Father of Molten Brass"
or ʿAmr,	"The name of al-Farazdaq's devil"[280]
or al-Qillawṭ,	"One of the children of the jinn and the devils"

or al-Shayṣabān,[280] al-Balʾaz, al-Qāz, the Corrupter,[282] the Recoiler, the Whisperer, the Seducer, or Cut-nose.

Similarly, if he looked through the window of his house and saw a neat trim 1.18.8
little girl, it would seem to him in his dream that he was in

an *arḍ khāfiyah*	"a land of the jinn"[283]
or *birāṣ*,	"dwellings of the jinn"
or in al-Ballūqah,	"A place in the area of Bahrain, above Kāẓimah, that they claim is an abode of the jinn"
or al-Baqqār,	"A place in the Sands of ʿĀlij where there are many jinn"
or al-ʿĀzif,	[literally, "the Maker of Sounds"] "A place so named because the jinn make sounds there"

او فى الحَوْش بلاد الجن *

او فى وَبار وبار كقطام وقد يصرف ارض بين اليمن و رمال يبرين سميت بوبار بن اِرَم لما اهلك الله تعالى عادا و رَّث محلتهم الجن فلا ينزلها احد منا *

او فى عَبْقر ع كثير الجن *

او فى جَيْهم ع كثير الجن * ولديه

الشَّيْصَبان قبيلة من الجن * ١،١٨،٩

او بنو هنَّام قبيلة من الجن *

او بنو غَزْوان حىّ من الجن *

او دَهْرَش اسم ابى قبيلة من الجن *

او اَحْقَب اسم جنّى من الذين استمعوا القرآن *

او زِمزِمة قطعة من الجن *

او الشِقّ جنس من الجن *

او شِنِقْناق رئيس للجن *

او العِسْل قبيلة من الجن *

او العِسْر قبيلة من الجن وهو ايضا اسم ارض للجن *

او السِعْلاة والعَيْسَجور والشَّهام ساحرة الجن *

او السَعْسَلِق امّ السَّعالِى * ١،١٨،١٠

او العَضْرَفوط من دوابّ الجن *

او النَظْرة الطائف من الجن *

or in al-Ḥawsh,	"Lands of the jinn"
or in Wabār,	"Wabār: (of the pattern of *qaṭām*, with or without nunation[284])—a stretch of land between Yemen and the Sands of Yabrīn, called Wabār ibn Iram. [285] When the Almighty destroyed ʿĀd, He bequeathed their territory to the jinn, and thus no human may stay there"
or in ʿAbqar,	"A place full of jinn"
or in Jayham,	"A place full of jinn" or that he was facing
the Shayṣabān,	"A tribe of the jinn" 1.18.9
or the Banū Hannām,	"A tribe of the jinn"
or the Banū Ghazwān,	"A clan of the jinn"
or Dahrash,	"The name of the forefather of a tribe of the jinn"
or Aḥqab,	"The name of one of the jinn who gave ear to the Qurʾān"[286]
or Zimzimah,	"A sub-section of the jinn"
or the Shiqq,	"A kind of jinn"
or Shiniqnāq,	"A chief of the jinn"
or the ʿIsl,	"A tribe of the jinn"
or the ʿIsr,	"A tribe of the jinn and also the name of a territory belonging to the jinn"
or the Siʿlāh, or the ʿAysajūr, or the Shahām,	"Witches of the jinn"
or the Saʿsaliq,	"The mother of the Siʿlāh witches" 1.18.10
or a *ʿaḍrafūṭ*,	"A beast ridden by the jinn"
or the Naẓrah,	"Jinn that roam by night"

او الزَوبَعة رئيس للجن *

او الخافى والخافية الجن وكذا الخَبَل *

والخافيا

او التابع والتابعة الجنى والجنيّة يكونان مع الانسان يتبعانه حيث ذهب *

او العَكَنكَع والكعنكع الغول الذكر *

او الخيَدع الغول الخدّاعة *

او السِلتم والصَيدانة والخَيعل والخيَلع والخولع والختيعور والسَمَرمرة والسُمَّع والعَوَلق والعَلُوق والهَيرعة والهيعرة والملد والعَفَرناة (كلها من اسمآ الغول) *

او العِتريس الغول الذكر * ١،١٨،١١

او[1] التِمسَح المارد الخبيث *

او الدِرقِم اسم الدجال وهو ايضا المِسّيح كسكّين *

او الطُغمُوس المارد من الشيطان والخبيث من الغيلان *

او الزَبانية جمع زِبنية وهو متمرد الانس والجن ومثله العِكَبّ *

او الحَيزَبون وكانّ صاحبنا وَهِم فى هذه فانى لم اجدها فى القاموس فكيف يمكن رؤيتها فى منام * واسمها غير موجود فى قاموس الكلام * مع ان المص رحمه وزن عليها الحيزبور والختيعور والقيدحور والعيجلوف والعيطبول والهيجبوس والجيهبوق والزيزفون والجيثلوط والعيضفوط * ثم انه كان اذا سمع ١،١٨،١٢

خَنبة تكلم رجلا بمنطق رخيم سمع فى الليل عَزيفا وهَساهِس وتهويدا وزِيزيما[2] وهدهدا وزَهزَجا وزِى زِىّ * (كلها من اصوات الجن) (١) رَدَتْ الجارية رفعت رِجْلا

واذا راى جارية تَردى نصف النهار(١) جآه فى نصف ومشت على اخرى تلعب *

١ ١٨٥٥: أو. ٢ ١٨٥٥: زِيزما.

or the Zawbaʿah,	[literally, "the Whirlwind"] "A chief of the jinn"
or *al-khāfī* or *al-khāfiyah* or *al-khāfiyāʾ*,	[literally, "the Hidden Ones" (male, female, and collective)] "The jinn"; *al-khabal* means the same
or *al-tābiʿ* or *al-tābiʿah,*	[literally, "the Followers" (male or female)] "The male or female jinni, because they are among men and follow them wherever they go"
or the ʿAkankaʿ or the Kaʿankaʿ,	"Male ghouls"
or a *khaydaʿ*,	"A deceitful [female] ghoul"

or the Siltim, the Ṣaydānah, the Khayʿal, the Khaylaʿ, the Khawlaʿ, the Khaytūr, the Samarmarah, the Summaʿ, the ʿAwlaq, the ʿAlūq, the Hayraʿah, the Hayʿarah, the Mald, and the ʿAfarnāh, (all names of ghouls)

or a *ʿitrīs*,	"A male ghoul"	1.18.11
or a *timsaḥ*,	"An ignoble *mārid*"[287]	
or al-Dirqim,	The name of the Antichrist, also known as the Missīḥ (of the pattern of *sikkīn*)	
or a *ṭughmūs*,	"A rebellious devil or ignoble ghoul"	
or *zabāniyyah*,	Plural of *zibniyyah*. "Rebellious persons, whether humans or jinn"; synonym *ʿikabb*	
or a *ḥayzabūn*.	I think our friend must be wrong about this one:	

I can't find it in the *Qāmūs*,[288] and how can the Fāriyāq have seen it in a *vision* when it's nowhere to be found in that paragon of *precision*? On the other hand, the lexicographer,[289] God rest his soul, does use it as the pattern-word for *ḥayzabūr* (synonym of *ḥayzabūn*), *khaytaʿūr* ("fading mirage"[290]), *qaydaḥūr* ("person with an ugly face"), *ʿaylajūf* (the name of the ant mentioned in the Qurʾān),[291] *ʿayṭabūl* ("tall" (of a girl)), *hayjabūs* ("hasty, rough man"), *jayhabūq* ("rat feces"), *zayzafūn* ("fast" (of a she-camel)), *jaythalūṭ* (an insult invented by women, of unclear meaning), and *ʿayḍafūṭ* (synonym of *ʿaḍrafūṭ* (see above)).

and if he were to hear by day a sweet-toned coquettish girl talking in dulcet tones to a man, at night he'd hear the moaning and laughing of the jinn, their twitterings and whisperings, their cheepings and chitterings, their clamorings and their *ziy-ziy* (all of which are sounds made by the jinn); and if he saw a girl hopping(1) on one foot all day long, he'd be assailed in the middle of the night by a 1.18.12

(1) *radat al-jāriyah*: she raised a foot and moved using the other, in play.

١٣،١٨،١ الليل الكابوس والجاثوم والدُوَفان والنَيْدَل والبارُوك والدِئْثان والدَيْثانى * ورای
ليلة ما ان قد زفت اليه عروس فاتاه تيس وجعل ينطحه بقرنيه فاستيقظ فاذا
بقرن راسه مرضوض * ورای ليلة اخرى ان قد وجد على شاطى نهر دنانير
ودراهم فمدّ يده واخذ منها خمسة عشر درهما لا غير * فلما عبر الشط الثانى
رای شيخا بيده كرة يديرها * فكان كلما ادارها اخذ الفارياق فى ظهره وجع
شديد كوجع الدآ المعروف فى بلاد الشام بالوثّاب * فلما رمى الدراهم من يده
من شدة ما اصابه سكن عنه الوجع * ورای ليلة اخرى ان رجلا مغربيا
اتحفه بشى فتلقفه فى الحال مشرقى وذهب به * قال والى الان لم يرجع به مع
١٤،١٨،١ انتظارى له كل ليلة * وقس على ذلك سائر احلامه * ومما قاله فى الحلم نظما *

كانّ همومى وهى تحت مخدّتى   اذا بتّ تُغرى بى الهرآ لتُذْرئَه
تقول علىّ اليوم كان بُواله   وانّ عليك الليلَ ذا ان تخرّئه

وقال

أُسرّ اذا انقضى يومى لانى   ارجّى فيه احلاما تسرّ
فاحلم اننى اسعى واشقى   فليلى مثل يومى او اشرّ

وقال ايضا

ويارب حتى فى المنام تروعنى   باضغاث احلام تسوء وتزعج
فياليتنى اشقى نهارى وفى الكرى   أُسَرّ برويا من احبّ وابهج

bad dream—by the dream that lies prone upon the breast, by the incubus, by the succubus, by the dream that kneels on the chest, by the dream that pollutes, by the dream that humiliates, by the nightmare.

One night he saw a bride brought to him in procession, after which a billy goat came to him and started butting him with its horns. He awoke, and, lo and behold, the place on his head where horns would be was bruised. Another night he dreamed that he came across some gold and silver coins on the river bank, so he stretched out his hand and took fifteen silver coins, no more. When he crossed to the other side, he saw an old man who had a ball in his hand that he was twisting, and every time he gave it a twist, the Fāriyāq was taken by a severe pain in his back, like that of the illness known in the Syrian lands as "the jumper,"[292] and when the pain increased so much that he threw the coins from his hand, it went away. And another night he saw a man from the west bestow something on him, at which a man from the east immediately snatched it away and made off with it. "And," he declared, "he still hasn't brought it back, even though I've waited for him all night!" The rest of his dreams were of the same sort. 1.18.13

Among the verses that he composed on dreams are the following: 1.18.14

Meseems at night my cares, from underneath my pillow,
Draw al-Hirā'[293] to me, that him against me they may pit.
They say he spent the day upon me pissing
"So tonight you have to make him shit."

And

At day's end I'm happy
For I have hopes of dreams of pleasure.
But then I dream of strife and toil
And night and day are shrunk to equal measure.

And again

O Lord, you scare me even in my sleep
With dreams confused that torment and distress.
Would I might toil by day and then, when I'm asleep,
Enjoy the sight of my belov'd and there find rest.

١٥،١٨،١ وعنّ له يوما ان يمدح بعض ذوى السيادة والسعادة * فلما حظى بلثم اعتابه الشريفة وانشده القصيدة رجع القهقرى على عادة اهل بلاده من ان الصغير لا يُرِى الكبير قفاه * اشارة الى انه لا قذال الا قذال الكبير * ثم جآه الحاجب يقول ان الامير ادام الله دولته * وخلد صولته * وجعل الشمس والقمر نعلا لفرسه * وجعل يومه خيرا من امسه * وجعل ظله ممدودا على الارض ظليلا * وجعل طرف الكون بتراب نعله مكحولا * وجعل الثريا مقرا لرجليه * والعيوق شراكا لنعليه * وجعل الوجود باسمه مبتهجا وبابه لكل لائذ رتجا مرتجى * وجعل — فلم

١٦،١٨،١ يتمالك الفارياق ان بادره وقال دعنى من جَعَل ياجُعل * ماذا يقول الامير * قال يقول الامير المعظم * الخطير المكرم * ذو الالآ الغامرة * والنعم الوافرة * من اذا قال فعل * واذا سئل اعطى فاجزل * واذ تنخخ القى الرعب فى قلوب اعاديه * واذا سعل خفقت فَرَقا افئدة شانئيه * واذا مخط ارتجّ المكان لهيبته * واذا حبق تزلزل المجلس لحبقته * فقال الفارياق افّ لهذه الرائحة الخبيثة ياخبيث قل ما يقوله الامير * وارحنى من هذا التقعير * لقد برّزت على الشعرآ * بهذا الغلو والاطرآ * قال انه يقول لك انك قد احسنت فى ابيات القصيدة وابدعت ما شئت * لانك شبّهته بالقمر والبحر والاسد والسيف الماضى والطود الراسخ والسيل المنهمر مما هو خليق بالاتصاف به * الّا فى بيت واحد جعلته فيه قوادا * قال كيف ذلك جلّ الامير عن القيادة * قال نعم انك قلت انه يجود بالمال والنفائس ويولي الابكار * وقلت فى بيت آخر انه محمّد الذكر محمود المناقب وهو غير محمد ولا محمود * وبسبب هذا الخطا الفاحش حرمك من رؤيته * قال هذه عادة الشعرآ انهم لا يزالون يتلمّظون بذكر الخرائد والمحامد * وليس المقصود بذلك نسبة القيادة

One day it occurred to him to write a eulogy to one of those possessed of sovereign felicity. After he'd been permitted the privilege of kissing the latter's noble threshold and of reciting his ode and had retired backward in accordance with the custom of the people of that land, which dictates that a young man must not show the nape of his neck to an older (in acknowledgment of the fact that only older persons have backs to their heads), the chamberlain came to tell him that the emir, might God preserve his rule for ever and a *day* and immortalize his *sway*, make of the sun and moon *shoes* for his horse's *hooves*, make each day of his better than the one *before*, spread his shadow the earth as a protection *o'er*, anoint the eye of the universe with his slipper's *dust*, make the Pleiades his stepping-stone and Capella, through the eyelets of his boots, as laces, *thrust*, make all existence rejoice in his name and make his *portal* the desired gate of every *mortal*, make . . .—but here the Fāriyāq could no longer contain himself and interrupted by saying, "Enough 'makes,' you mayfly! What says the emir?" 1.18.15

The man replied, "The emir—the *magnified*, the important and highly *dignified*, he of the blessings *overflowing* and favors *ever-growing*, he who, when he speaks, passes forthwith into *action*, and who, when asked, is generous in *benefaction*; who, when he clears his throat strikes terror into the hearts of those who are his *foes*, and, when he coughs, makes those who hate him shiver to the tips of their *toes*; whose whole palace quivers at his majestic *pose* when he blows his *nose* and whose *fart* makes the whole council chamber *start*; whose . . . ." Said the Fāriyāq, "Pew to this vile smell, you villain! Tell me what the emir said and relieve me of these orotund *phrases*—you've outdone the poets with your lavish *praises*." He said, "He says you did a good job on your ode and achieved your ends very well when you likened him to the moon, the sea, a lion, a sharp sword, a firm-set mountain, and a watercourse in spate, all of which he is worthy of being compared to. Except that, in one verse, you called him a pimp." "How so?" said the Fāriyāq, "may the emir remain far above all pandering!" "It's true," said the other. "In one verse you said that he 'hands out money and gems with open hand, and befriends the virgin.' Also, in another you said that his name was 'worthy to be praised (*muḥammad*)' and that his virtues were 'praiseworthy (*maḥmūd*)' but he's no Muḥammad or Maḥmūd,[294] and because of this appalling mistake he has banished you from his sight." The Fāriyāq replied, "This is but the way of poets—they keep smacking their lips over 'unbored pearls'[295] 1.18.16

الى الممدوح * قال هذا غاية ما عندى فلا تطمع بعد فى المثول بحضرة اميرنا
المبجل * فمن ثم رجع الفارياق محروما من هذا المغنم الهنّى * وبلغ منه الغيظ ان ١،١٨،١٧
اضله عن الطريق المستقيم * فسار فى طريق آخر وما وصل الى منزله الا بعد اللتيّا
والتى * واخذ يفكر في نحس طالعه وشؤم قلمه * فظهر لهوسه ان القلم انحس
شى يتخذه الانسان سببا لمصالحه * وان اشفى الاسكاف انفع منه * وان تقديم
النون عليه فى قوله تعالى ن والقلم وما يسطرون ان هو الّا اشارة الى النحس * وان ما
قاله المنجم فى طالعه صحيح * فانه اوّل المراة التى زفّت اليه فى المنام بالعقرب * والجدى
بالتّيس الذى كان ينطحه * والسرطان بنفسه اذ رجع القهقرى من عند الامير فكاد
ان يعثر بحصير مجلسه السامى لولا ان تمسك ببعض اوتاده الشريفة * واوّل الثور
بالامير الممدوح * الا ان العبارة الاولى وهى قول المنجم نحس النحوس غير محصورة ١،١٨،١٨
فى حادث واحد * اذ هى تستغرق جميع الاحوال والحوادث كما سيرد بيانه * وذلك
ان الفارياق لما سمع من نجيّه الذى قايضه على الاعتراف ان المساومة فى قيل وقال
هى من البياعات الرابحة * والاسباب الناجحة * خلج فى صدره ان يجرب تنفيق
ما عنده من البضاعة المزجاة * الا انه لم يعرضها من اوّل وهلة على احد المشترين
من الجثالقة كما فعل صاحبه * بل اخذ فى تقليبها وتفليتها وتمشيطها وتنسيلها من
جهة واستشفافها من اخرى * فظهر له انها قديمة قد ركّت بحيث لا يكاد احد
ان يرغب فيها * واتفق وقتئذ ان قدم عنقاش يفدّد على شرآء السلع القديمة وعلى ١،١٨،١٩
اصلاحها او على مقايضتها او على صبغها * وادعى انه يقدر ان يعيدها الى لونها
الاول * وانه لا يعجزه شى من احوالها بحيث ان صاحب السلعة نفسه اذ رآها
بعد صبغها وتصليحها يتجب منها غاية العجب ولا يعود يعرفها * وانه اى العنقاش لما
بلغه فى بلاده فساد تلك السلع اقبل حفدا الى تلك البلاد وهو يحمل خرجا كبيرا فيه

and 'praiseworthy virtues,' but that doesn't mean that they're accusing the person praised of pimping." "That's all I have," said the other. "Don't even think of appearing in the presence of our venerable emir again."

Thence, then, the Fāriyāq returned, deprived of that happy source of profit, and his anger grew so fierce that it diverted him from the straight path, and he walked another road, reaching home only after many a mishap. He started thinking how ill-omened was the star under which he'd been born and how much bad luck his pen had brought him, and in his folly it seemed to him that the pen was the unluckiest thing any man could adopt as the instrument of his livelihood, that the cobbler's awl was more profitable, that the letter *nūn*, when preceding the words of the Almighty "*Nūn*. By the pen, and what they inscribe. . ." had been put there to indicate "bad luck,"[296] and that what the astrologer had said of his birth stars was correct. He interpreted the woman who was brought to him in a wedding procession in his dream as being the Scorpion, the billy goat that had butted him as the Kid, and himself, as he retreated from the emir's presence, as the Crab, for he would have tripped over the rugs of his sublime council chamber had he not grabbed onto its noble supporting poles. Likewise he interpreted the Ox as being the emir who was the object of his praise. 1.18.17

However, the earlier statement—namely, the astrologer's words concerning "the misfortune of having misfortune everywhere"—were not limited to one incident; rather, they encompassed every condition and event, as shall be explained. Thus, when the Fāriyāq heard from his confidant[297] with whom he'd exchanged confessions that trading in polemics was a profitable *affair*, with prospects *fair*, he was taken by the idea of trying his hand at making money out of the paltry supply he had of such goods. He did not, however, display them right away to some ecclesiastical bigwig in the hope that he might buy them, as his friend had done, but took, on the one hand, to turning them upside down and removing the *nits*, combing through them and picking them to *bits*, and, on the other, to holding them up to the light to check for defects, at which they appeared to him so old and worn that hardly anyone could be expected to want them. 1.18.18

Now, it so happened that, at this time, a roving peddler had arrived, crying that he would buy, mend, exchange, or dye old goods, claiming he could restore them to their original color, that nothing was impossible for him, and that the owner himself would be so amazed on seeing them after 1.18.19

من الاصباغ والادوات ما يرفأ كل خرق ويعيد كل لون نافض * فسار اليه الفارياق عجلا الى المقايضة وواطاه على ابدال ما عنده من السلعة القديمة باخرى جديدة راقت لعينه * فقد يقال لكل جديد بهجة * ثم قفل الى منزله مسرورا بصفقته *
١،١٨،٢٠ فلما علم اهله وجيرانه بذلك استشاطوا عليه غيظا وقالوا * لعمر رب الجنود ما جرت العادة فى بلادنا بتغيير البياعات ولا بمقايضتها ولا باصلاحها ولا بصبغها * ثم لم يلبث الخبر ان بلغ مطران الصقع وكان من الضواطرة الكبار * فكانما كان سكّينا سقط على حلقومه * او خردلا دخل فى خرطومه * فهاج وازبد * وابرق وارعد * وماج واضطرب * وضج وصخب * والّب وحزّب * وبربر وثرثر * واقبل وادبر * وزجر ونهر * ووثب وطفر * وفتل لحيته من الغيظ حتى صارت كالمقرعة * واغرى كل حنتوف مثله بان يهيج معه * ونادى ياخيل الله على الكفار * انهم صالوا النار * كيف تجرّا هذا الشقى المنحوس * المعتوه المهلوس * على ان يذهب مذهبا غير ما نهجه له جاثليقه * وسلكه فيه بطريقة * وكيف اقدم بوقاحته * وصفاقة وجهه وقباحته * على معاملة ذلك العنقاش اللئيم * ومبايعته ما ورثه من ابائه من الزمن القديم * اليس فى بلادنا صُلُب * وادهاق ويلب * هلموا به مُهانا * اجلدوه عريانا * اطرحوه نيرانا * القموه حيتانا * اطعموه دمانا * اقطعوا منه لسانا * اسقوه الزنانَى * علىّ به الآن الان * فابتدر بعض الحاضرين وقال انا آتيك بهذا الجُعشوش باسرع من رد طرفك اليك * ثم ولّى حفدا الى الفارياق فوجده مكبّا على قراة الدفتر الذى فيه اثمان السلعة * فتناوله
١،١٨،٢١ بالسيف فاصاب فروته * ثم سيق الفارياق الى الجزّار المشار اليه * فلما بصر به انتفخت اوداجه واتسع منخراه وتعقدت اسرّة جبينه واصفرت شفتاه * ورقص شارباه واحمرت حدقتاه * واحترقت اسنانه ودارت بينهما هذه المحاورة *

dyeing and mending that he wouldn't recognize them. He (the peddler, that is) also claimed that, when he'd heard back in his hometown of the dire state of the goods in these parts, he'd hot-footed it over, bringing with him a large saddlebag[298] full of dyes and containing the tools to darn any tear and restore any faded color. The Fāriyāq therefore hurried off to do some bartering and came to an arrangement by which he would exchange all his old goods for others that were new and pleasing to his eye, for, as they say, "All things new have appeal." Then he returned home, pleased with his bargain.

When, however, his family and neighbors found out, they erupted in rage against him, saying, "By the Lord of Hosts, it is not our custom in these lands to change, barter, mend, or dye goods" and soon thereafter the news reached the bishop of the district, one of the big-time fast-talking market traders.[299] You would have thought a knife had fallen on his windpipe or mustard got up his nostrils, for he fumed and frothed, thundered and lightninged, surged and thrashed, roared and bawled, conspired and plotted, jabbered and prattled, wheeled and dealed, remonstrated and reproached, and jumped up and down, braiding his beard, in his fury, into a whip, and trying to inveigle every other bilious beard-plucker like himself to rise up with him as he cried, "God's horsemen against the *infidel*![300] They shall *roast in Hell*![301] How dare this accursed rascal, this raving *lunatic*, choose a path other than that laid down for him by his masters *ecclesiastic*, that followed by his very own patriarch? How dare he, in his impertinence, brazenness, and *infamy*, have dealings with that miserable traveling peddler and barter away to him what's been passed down to him from his ancient *ancestry*? Are there in our land no *roods*, no stocks, no leathern *hoods*? Bring him to us in *disgrace*! Flog him in the nude! Throw him in the *fireplace*! Feed him to the *fishes*! Make him eat *ashes*! Cut out his tongue and make him drink camel *snot*! Bring him to me while the iron's *hot*!" At this, one of those present leaped forth and said, "I shall bring you the little squit 'before ever thy glance is returned to thee.'"[302] Then he hot-footed it over to the Fāriyāq, whom he found poring over the ledger in which were written the prices of the goods, and set upon him with his sword and injured his scalp, after which the Fāriyāq was handed over to the aforementioned butcher. 1.18.20

When the latter set eyes upon him, his jugulars swelled, his nostrils flared, his brow knotted, and his lips turned *blue*, his mustaches quivered, his eyes turned red, and from his teeth smoke *flew*, and they proceeded to engage in the following dialog: 1.18.21

قال الضوطار ويلك يامغبون * ما دعاك الى المساومة فى سلعتك *

الفارياق اذا كانت هى سلعتى كما اقررتَ فما الذى يمنعنى من ذلك *

الضوطار ضللت * هى سلعتك من حيث انك ورثتها من ابائك لا من حيث ان لك حق التصرف فيها *

الفارياق هذا خلاف العادة والحق فان ما يرثه الانسان يحقّ له التصرف فيه *

الضوطار كذبتَ * انك انما ورثتها لتحفظها لا لتضيعها ولا لتبادل بها *

الفارياق هى ميراثى افعل به ما اشآ *

الضوطار قُبحتَ * انى انا القيّم عليه الصائن له من الشوائب *

الفارياق ما بلغنا عن احد انه تولّى ميراث غيره الا اذا كان الوارث غير راشد *

الضوطار غويت * انك انت غير رشيد وانا وليّك ووصيّك وكفيلك ووكيلك وحسيبك *

الفارياق ما الدليل على انى لست من الراشدين ومن ذا الذى جعلك وصيّا ووليّا *

الضوطار زغتَ * انما الدليل على غوايتك وضلالك هو انك تبدلّت به متاعا غيره * واما كونى وصيّا فان جميع امثالى يشهدون لى به كما انى انا ايضا اشهد لهم بانهم اوليآ غيرك * ٢٢،١٨،١

الفارياق ليس تبديل شى بآخر دليلا على الضلال والزيغ اذا كان المبدل والمبدل منه من جنس واحد * ولا سيما انى رايت لون القديم يوشك ان ينصل وقد ركّت رقعته فتبدلته بما هو ازهى واقوى *

The Trader: Woe unto you, you sucker! What made you barter away your goods?

The Fāriyāq: If they're my goods, as you have just admitted, what's to stop me?

The Trader: Misguided man! They're your goods in the sense that you inherited them from your forefathers, not in the sense that they're yours to do with as you please.

The Fāriyāq: This is against custom and truth, for a man may do whatever he likes with his inheritance.

The Trader: Liar! You inherited them precisely so you could preserve them, not so you could squander them or exchange them for something else.

The Fāriyāq: It's my inheritance and I shall do with it as I wish.

The Trader: Accursed one! I am the warden of the inheritance and its preserver from all that might sully it.

The Fāriyāq: That's the first time we've heard of someone being put in charge of someone else's inheritance, unless the heir's incompetent.

The Trader: Dupe! You *are* incompetent and I am your guardian, your trustee, your sponsor, your agent, and the one who will hold you to account.

The Fāriyāq: What proof is there that I'm not competent, and who made you a trustee and a guardian?

The Trader: Deviant! The proof of your gullibility and error is precisely **1.18.22**
that you traded in your inheritance for other goods. As to my being a trustee, everyone else in my position attests to that fact, just as I attest that they are the trustees of others.

The Fāriyāq: Exchanging one thing for another isn't evidence of error and deviation if the thing exchanged and the thing it is exchanged for are of the same kind, especially since I'd observed that the color of the old had almost completely faded and that the material was worn through. That is why I exchanged it for something more attractive and stronger.

الضوطار كفرتَ * انه غشى على بصرك فما تستطيع ان تفرق بين الالوان *

الفارياق كيف ذلك ولى عينان ناظرتان ويدان لامستان*

الضوطار عميتَ * فان الحواس قد تغش ولا سيما حاسة البصر *

الفارياق اذا كانت حواسى قد غشت فكيف سلمت حواسك من الغش وانت بشر مثلى *

الضوطار حِنْتَ * انى وان كنت بشرا مثلك لكنى وكيل من طرف شيخ السوق * وقد افادنى مما اودع الله فيه من الاسرار العجيبة ان لا يطرا علىّ غبن ولا غش الّا وتبيّنته لانه هو منزه عن الغش *

فقال الفارياق وكان به فأفاة * واين شيخ الفسوق هذا ثم استدرك كلامه وقال ٢٣،١٨،١
انما اردت شيخ السوق * فلا تكن زيادة هذه الثمانين موجبة لحدّ الثمانين *

الضوطار لُعنت * هو بعيد عنا بيننا وبينه ابحار وجبال * غير ان انفاسه القديسة تسرى فينا *

الفارياق كيف به اذا مرض او جنّ او مسّه طائف من الجن او اصابه برسام * فكيف يمكن والحالة هذه تمييز المتاع الردى من الجيد *

الضوطار هلكتَ * ما هو ببَلُوٍ للعوارض لانه بوّاب رتاج عظيم وبيده مزلاجان عظيمان لاحكام الباب من قُبُل ومن دُبُر *

الفارياق ليس هذا بدليل فان كل انسان فى العالم يمكنه ان يصير بوّابا ذا مزلاجين *

الضوطار فسقت وفجرت * انه هو وحده مستبدّ بهذه الخطّة اذ قد فوضت اليه من المالك الآمر *

The Trader: Blasphemer! He blinded you so that you couldn't distinguish among the colors.

The Fāriyāq: How can that be, when I have two eyes to see with and two hands to touch with?

The Trader: Blind man! The senses can be deceived, especially sight.

The Fāriyāq: If my senses were deceived, how come you've been able to preserve yours from being deceived too when you're a human being just like me?

The Trader: May you perish! Though I was once a human being just like you, I am now an authorized agent of the Market Boss, who has let me in on the amazing powers that God has bestowed on him, which include my being able to see through any false claims or dishonesty that may come my way, because he himself could never cheat.

Said the Fāriyāq (who had a speech defect involving the letter *f*): And where is this "Boff of the Market Difgwace"[303] (then he corrected himself and said) "I mean 'the Marketplace'? Shouldn't the addition of these eighty require the eighty-lash penalty?"[304] **1.18.23**

The Trader: Curse you! He is far away and between us lie seas and mountains. But his holy spirit courses within us.

The Fāriyāq: What happens if he falls sick or goes mad, or is touched by some wandering jinni or afflicted with pleurisy? In such a state, how can he distinguish low-quality goods from high?

The Trader: May you perish! He is never afflicted by such attacks, for he is the keeper of a mighty gate, and he has in his hand two mighty keys to close the door tight, one from in front and one from behind.

The Fāriyāq: That's no proof, for any person in the world could become a doorkeeper with two keys.

The Trader: Depraved sinner! He alone has sole charge of this plot of land, for it was entrusted to him by its All-commanding Owner.

الفارياق متى كان ذلك *

الضوطار صُلبتَ * مذ الفى سنة تقريبا *

الفارياق اَوَ عاش هذا الشيخ الفى سنة *

الضوطار الحدثَّ * انما انتقلت اليه بالوراثة *

الفارياق ممّن ورثها اَمن ابيه وجده *

الضوطار نكلت * من انسان لا يُعدّ فى اهله *

الفارياق هذا امر عجيب كيف يرث الانسان شيا من رجل غريب فان ١،١٨،٢٤
الغريب اذا مات عن غير وارث انتقل ماله الى بيت المال فهو
اولى به من رجل على حدته *

الضوطار عُذّبت * هذا سرّ ليس لك ان تبحث فيه *

الفارياق ما الدليل على كونه سرّا *

الضوطار ا فحشت * هذا هو الدليل * وعند ذلك قام عجلا وا تى
بكتاب وا خذ يقلب فيه من اوله الى اخره حتى يجد فيه
مطلوبه اذ لم يكن كثير الدراسة له * الى ان وجد عبارة
مضمونها ان المالك كان احبّ مرة رجلا فوهبه هبات شتى
من جملتها كاس وطست وعصا فى راسها صورة ثعبان
وجبّة وتبّان ونعلان وباب له مزلاجان * وقال له قد
وهبتك هذه كلها فاستعملها واهنأ بها *

الفارياق لعمرى ليس فى هذه الهبة ما يدل على سرّ * هذا وقد مات كلّ
من الواهب والموهوب له وفُقد الموهوب كله * فكيف لم يبقَ الا
المزلاجان فقط وقد ضاع الباب وهما لا ينفعان من دونه شيا *

The Fāriyāq: When was that?

The Trader: May you be crucified! About two thousand years ago.

The Fāriyāq: You mean to tell me that this "boss" has been around for two thousand years?

The Trader: Atheist! It came to him by inheritance.

The Fāriyāq: From whom did he inherit it? From his father and grandfather?

The Trader: You should be punished as a warning to others! From a person not considered to be a member of his family.

The Fāriyāq: That's odd! How can a person inherit anything from a stranger? If a stranger dies without leaving an heir, his money goes to the public treasury, which has a better right to it than any individual. **1.18.24**

The Trader: May you be tortured! It's a sacrament that you have no right to discuss.

The Fāriyāq: And what proof is there that it's a sacrament?

The Trader: Now you've gone too far! Here's the proof (and he got up in a hurry, fetched a book, and started leafing through it from beginning to end, looking for what he wanted—for he hadn't studied it at any great length—until he found a passage that said, in summary, that the Owner had once loved a man, so he'd given him a number of gifts, among which were a cup, a basin, a stick with a carving of two snakes on the end, a robe, a pair of shorts, a pair of sandals, and a door with two keys, and had said to him, "All these things I give unto you. Use them and enjoy them.")

The Fāriyāq: I swear there's nothing in such a donation to prove it's a sacrament, not to mention that both the benefactor and the beneficiary have died and the whole gift has been lost. How can just the keys be left, when the door's gone and they're useless without it?

الضوطار فُتدت * لم يبقَ لنا فى غير المزلاجين من حاجة *

الفارياق بحق هذين المزلاجين عليك ياسيدى الّا ما أريتنى الكاس مرة فى العمر وحسبُ * ولك علىَّ بعد ذلك الإِمرة التامة *

١، ١٨، ٢٥ فلما ان ضغط الضوطار بين السلب والايجاب استنشاط وَغْرا وهمّ ان يلحق الفارياق بالباب والكاس لولا ان دعاه داعٍ الى اللوس * فقام ناشطا ووكل به بعض الاوغاد وكان وقتئذ يتضوّر جوعا فراى ان رؤية قعر القدر فى المطبخ اشهى اليه من النظر الى وجه الفارياق * فتغافل عنه فتملص الفارياق من هذه الورطة واقبل يهرول الى الخرجى وقال له * لقد خسرت تجارتى معك فان البضاعة كادت تمنينى بمبضع * فابتغى منك الاقالة * اَوْ لا فان يكن عندك فى الخرج راس يلائم جثتى حين تعدم هذا فارنى اياه ليسكن روعى * اذ لا يمكن لى ان اعيش بلا راس *

١، ١٨، ٢٦ فاما ان لم يكن فى الخرج غير اللسان فما لى به حاجة هذا متاعك فضمّه اليك * فقال له الخرجى ما هكذا حق التعامل * ينبغى ان تصبر على ما يلحقك من تبعة الصفقة كما هو داب جميع المتبايعين عندنا * وتلك من بعض خواص هذه التجارة * ولكن لا تخف فان من خواصها ايضا ان تقى الواقى لها وتحفظ المحافظ عليها * فيكون له بها غنًى عن الراس اذا نقف * وعن العينين اذا سُملتا * وعن اللسان اذا استلّ * وعن الساقين اذا غمزتا بالدَهَق * وعن اليدين اذا غلّتا بالكبل * وعن العنق اذا وُقصت * والكبد اذا فُرصت * قال ما ارى ما ترى فان الاسف لا يحيى مائتا * والندم لا يردّ فائتا * فان يكن عندك مخزن آمن فيه من العدوّ على السلعة فآونى اليه * والّا فهذا فراق بينى وبينك * فاطرق الخرجى ساعة ثم دخل به حجرة صغيرة واغلق الباب * واخذ يمتحن الفارياق كما سيرد بيانه فى الفصل الاتى *

The Trader: May you be shown up for the liar you are! The keys are all we need now.

The Fāriyāq: By the power of these two keys over you, My Lord, if you can show me just once in my lifetime the cup—that's all—you can have complete authority over me from that day on.

Faced by this resolute attitude, the trader burned with ire and was on the point of bringing the Fāriyāq the door and the cup when someone called him to table. Rising energetically, he appointed a few of his knaves to see to the Fāriyāq, for at that moment he was so convulsed with hunger that he believed the sight of the bottom of the pots in the kitchen would be more appetizing to him that that of the Fāriyāq's face, and he pretended to forget about him. The Fāriyāq thus escaped from that sticky situation and set off at a run to the Bag-man and told him, "I lost by my trade with you, for the goods almost landed me under the scalpel, so I want to revoke the deal—or if you will not, and you have in your bag a head that will fit my body when the latter's deprived of this one, show it to me now and calm my nerves, for I cannot live without a head. If all you have in the bag is the tongue, it is of no use to me. Here's your property. Take it." 1.18.25

Said the Bag-man, "This is no way to do business. You have to endure patiently the consequences of the deal, according to the way of all those where we come from who agree on terms, this being one of the distinguishing features of this trade. But do not fear: another of its features is that it protects those who protect it and preserves those who preserve it. He who engages in it will need no head if the top of his is lopped off, or eyes if his are put out, or tongue if his is pulled out, or legs if his are clamped in the stocks, or hands if his are shackled in irons, or neck if his is *snapped*, or liver if his is *popped*." The Fāriyāq replied, "I don't see things the way you do: being sorry doesn't revive the *dead*, regret doesn't bring back what's *fled*. If you have a storeroom in which I can keep my goods safe from the enemy, lodge me there. If not, this is the parting of the ways between us." The Bag-man hung his head for a while, then took him into a little room and closed the door, and he set about putting the Fāriyāq to the test, as will be explained in the following chapter. 1.18.26

الفصل التاسع عشر

فى الحس والحركة

١،١٩،١ قد جرت عادة الناس جميعاً بان يقولوا اذا احبوا شيا او اشتاقوا الى شى ان قلبى يحب هذا الشى * او يحسّ بمحبة هذا الشى * او يشتهى ذلك الشى * ولست ادرى علة هذا الاستعمال * فان القلب انما هو عضو فى الجسم من جملة الاعضآء فلا يمكن ان تكون حاسّيتها كلها مجموعة فيه * وبيانه انّ مَن احبّ مثلاً لوناً من الطعام بخصوصه فلينظر فى ادوات الاكل الباعثة على اشتهائه * ومن احبّ امراة فلينظر فى الاداة الباعثة على اشتهآئها * وما يميل اليه الطبع وهو غير محتاج الى اعمال اداة ظاهرة وذلك لحب الرئاسة والسعادة والدّين ينبغى ان يحمل على الراس * اذ هى امور معنويّة لا علاقة لها بتلك البضعة اى القلب * وكما ان الطحال الذى هو وزير الميمنة لا تعلق له بهذه الامور * فكذلك كان وزير الميسرة اى القلب * الا انه لما كانت حركة القلب اسرع من غيره لكونه اقرب الى الرئة التى هى حرز التنفّس * ظنّ الناس ان القلب اصل فى جميع اهوآء الانسان واشواقه * ومن عادتهم اجتناباً للبحث عن كثرة الاسباب والعلل والتيقّن للحقائق ان يقتصروا على سبب واحد من الاسباب المتعدّدة * وينسبوا اليه كل ما تسبّب عن غيره * كما تنسب الشعرآء مثلا دواعى النحس الى الدهر ودواعى البين والفراق

٢،١٩،١ الى الغراب * وبنآء على هذا الاعتقاد اى نسبة الاهوآء كلها الى القلب اراد

Chapter 19

Emotion and Motion[305]

It is the custom of people everywhere to say when they love or long for something, "My heart loves" that thing or it "feels drawn to" it or "desires" it. I don't know the underlying reason for this usage, for the heart is only one of the many organs of the body, and it's not possible that the sensory capacities of all the organs should be gathered together in just that one. The proof is that if someone loves a certain kind of food, for example, the cause is to be sought in the gustatory organs that give rise to his desire for it, and if someone loves a woman, the cause is to be sought in the organ that gives rise to his desire for her. Natural inclinations that do not call for the employment of any visible organ—such as love of leadership, good fortune, or religion—must be attributed to the head, these being abstractions that have nothing to do with that lump of flesh called the heart. By the same token, as the spleen, which is the Vizier of the Right-hand Side,[306] has nothing to do with these matters, so the heart, which is the Vizier of the Left-hand Side, can have none either. However, given that the motion of the heart is more rapid than that of other organs because of its greater proximity to the lungs, where breathing originates, people think that the heart must be a primary source for all a person's affections and desires. It is also their custom, to avoid having to search for numerous reasons and causes and of having to be certain of their facts, to reduce everything to one cause among the many. In the same way, poets, for example, attribute the proximate causes of bad luck to fate and of ill-fortune and separation to crows. 1.19.1

Based on this belief (namely, that all affections are attributable to the heart), the Bag-man wanted to test the Fāriyāq's in order to find out whether 1.19.2

الخرجى ان يمتحن قلب الفارياق ليعلم هل نبض فيه حبّ السلعة الجديدة نبضا قويا اَوْ لا * فجعل يقول له هل تحسّ فى قلبك بان السلعة الجديدة خير من الاولى * وهل يضطرب فرحاً وسروراً عندما تسمع بذكرها * وهل ينبسط ويتسع وينشرح عند خطور هذه ببالك * وينقبض ويضيق ويتضامّ عند ذكر تلك * وهل عند قرآتك دفتر الاثمان يُخيَّل لك اَن قد طُبع فيه اى فى قلبك كل حرف من حروف الدفتر * حتى لو اعوزك وجوده سدّت تلك الحروف مسدّه * وهل يضطرم ويتوقد مرة ويذوب ويضمحل اخرى * ثم يعود اقوى مما كان عليه كالسمندل المعروف * وهل تحسّ ايضا بان ناخسا ينخسه * وواخِزا يخزه * وعاصرا يعصره * وراهصا يرهصه * وممزقا يمزقه * وضاغطا يضغطه * فقال له الفارياق اما الاضطراب ٣،١٩،١
والخفقان فانه دائما على مثل هذه الحالة * وهو عُرضة لذلك فى حالتى الفرح والترح فان ادنى شى يوثر فيه * واما التوقّد والذَوَبان فلا ادرى * فقال المراد بالتوقد هنا وبالنخر والعصر الحميّة والتحمّس والتهوّس وتخيّل ما هو معدوم موجودا وما هو موهوم يقينا * ومَثَل ذلك مثل من يسافر فى فلاة لا مآء فيها فيبلغ منه الظمأ ان يتصوّر السراب مآءً وشعاع الشمس نِقرًا * ولا يزال يُمنّى نفسه بوجدان المآء حتى يقطع المفازة * فان شدة التخيّل والتهوّس تعين الانسان على تحمل المكاره والمشاقّ * فيكون رازحاً تحت ثقلها وهو يحسب انه من المتّكئين على الارائك * فيستوى بذلك عنده المجاز والحقيقة والمحسوس وغير المحسوس * حتى يحسب الصَفَر خِوانا والنعش عرشا والخازوق او الصليب منبرا * وربما كان ذا زوجة وعيال فيتّخذهم متخذ الماعون من الخزف فيغادرهم ويجرى فى البلدان القاصية لترويج السلعة * ويستغنى عن اهله واخوانه ورهطه بما لديه فى الخرج * فيحمله على كتفه مستبشرا مسرورا ويضرب فى مناكب الارض طولا وعرضا * فكل مَن مرَّ به من عباد

or not love for the new goods beat strongly within it. He started off by asking him, "Do you feel in your heart that the new goods are better than the old, and does it pound with joy and pleasure when you hear them mentioned? Does it feel happy, expansive, and care-free when the thought of them occurs to your mind and does it clench itself, shrink, and recoil at the mention of the other? When you read the price list, do you feel that every single letter in it has been imprinted on it (meaning, on your heart), so that, even if it weren't there, those same letters could take its place? Does it sometimes ignite and burn, and then at others go out, only to return more strongly, like the celebrated phoenix? Do you feel too that it's being prodded by a prodder, pricked by a pricker, squeezed by a squeezer, constricted by a constrictor, ripped by a ripper, and pressed by a presser?"

The Fāriyāq told him, "As for the pounding and the choking, my heart's **1.19.3**
always that way, being subject to such sensations in both joy and sadness, for the least thing affects it. As far as igniting and melting are concerned, though, I don't know what you mean." "What is meant by 'burning' here," replied the Bag-man, "and by 'prodding' and 'squeezing,' is ardor, enthusiasm, and obsessive interest, and imagining that what isn't there is present and what is a fantasy is real. An example would be someone walking in a waterless desert who becomes so thirsty that he thinks the mirage is water and the sun's rays, too, are pure, sweet water, and keeps on going in the hope of finding water until he's crossed the waste, because intense imagining and obsessive interest help a person put up with trials and tribulations, and, though he be sinking under their weight, he will imagine that he's reclining at ease on a couch. Thus the figurative and the real, the tangible and the intangible, all come to be on the same plane to him, to the point that he reckons hunger a dining table, the bier a throne, the impaling stake or cross a pulpit. He may have a wife and children and use them as though they were no more valuable than china plates and go running off through distant lands to promote his goods, giving up family, friends, and companions in favor of the contents of his saddlebag. This he carries on his shoulder, gladly and with high hopes, trudging high and low over the earth, offering to make any mortal who crosses his path his partner and co-financer. He goes on this way until his time is up, and nothing pleases him better than to die thus engaged. The bag! The bag! No other trade or work have we than it. The goods!

الله عرض عليه الشركة والمضاربة * ولا يزال دأبه كذلك حتى يقضى نحبه وطوبى
له ان مات على هذه الحالة * الخرجَ الخرجَ * ما لنا سواه من حرفة ولا شغل *
٤،١٩،١ السلعةَ السلعةَ * ليس لنا غيرها من جُعل * ثم طفق يبكى وينتحب * فلما افاق
بعد حين ساله الفارياق هل عندكم معاشر الخرجيّين سوق وشيخ للسوق * قال لا *
قال ومن يقوّم لكم المتاع قال كلّ منا يقوّم متاعه بنفسه ولا يحتاج الى آخر *
فتعجّب الفارياق وقال فى نفسه انّ فى هذا لعجبا * فانّ قوما من هولآء الصعافيق
لهم شيخ سوقٍ وما لهم خرج * وقوما لهم خرج وليس لهم شيخ * ولكن لعل
صاحبى هذا على الحق * اذ لو لم يكن كذلك لما تكلّف حمل الخرج من اقصى البلاد
وتجشّم اخطار السفر وغيره * ثم نخزه الخنّاس ان الخرجى ربّما لم يجد محترفا فى
بلاده فجآء بما عنده لينفقه فى بلاد اخرى * فان تاجرا لو استبضع من بلده مثلا
خزًا او كِرباسا الى بلد آخر لم يحكم له بانه قدم الى هذا البلد حبّا باهله * فقد جرت
العادة بان المتسبّبين يطوفون في كل الاقطار * ثم فكّر فى اَنّ اَناةَ الخرجى وما
هو عليه من الرزانة والصبر لا بدّ وان يكون قرينها الرشد والحزم * بخلاف النزق
والطيش فانه لا يكون الا قرين الغواية والضلال * فمن ثم حكم بان الخرجى كان على
٥،١٩،١ هُدًى وذلك لاناته وحلمه * وان المطران كان من الضالين لِحدّته وتترّعه * ثم قال
للخرجى قد وعيت ياسيدى كل ما اوعيتَه اذنى * وما ارى الحق الّا معك *
وانى مشايعك ومتابعك وحامل للخرج معك * ولكن اجرنى من هولآء الصعافيق
فانهم كالاسود الضارية لا تاخذهم فى خلق الله رافة ولا شفقة * وعندهم اَنَّ
اهلاك نفس غيرةً على الدين يكسبهم عند الله زُلْفَى * وقد تمسكوا بظاهر اقوال
من الانجيل فيما رأوه موافقا لغرضهم وزائدا فى جاههم وسلطانهم * فيقولون ان
المسيح بقوله ما جئت لالقى على الارض سِلْما لكن سيفا انما رخّص لهم فى اعمال

The goods! No other reward have we than they." At this point he broke down, weeping and sobbing.

When, after a while, he'd recovered his composure, the Fāriyāq asked him, "Do you Bag-men have a marketplace and a boss to take charge of it?" He said, "No." "Who, then," said the Fāriyāq, "checks the quality of the goods?" He replied, "Each of us does so himself and we don't need anyone else." The Fāriyāq was amazed and said to himself, "Now here's a wonder! We have a group of undercapitalized parasites who have a market boss but no saddlebags, and a similar group who have saddlebags but no boss. But perhaps my friend is in the right: if it were otherwise, he would not have undertaken to bring his bag from such distant lands or braved the dangers of the journey and all the rest." Now, however, the Recoiler poisoned his mind with the thought that perhaps the Bag-man hadn't found anywhere to set up shop in his own country, so he'd brought what he had in stock to get rid of here. If a merchant stocked up on, say, silk-wool, or cotton goods, and brought them to another country, he couldn't be regarded as doing so out of love for its inhabitants; it had, after all, become commonplace for those in search of work to roam the world. Next, though, it occurred to him that the Bag-man's perseverance and his equanimity and patience must inevitably be complemented by good sense and resolve, in contrast to rashness and flightiness, whose only complements are conceit and error, and he concluded that, in view of his said perseverance and mild manners, the Bag-man must be following the right path and that the metropolitan, with his vehemence and eagerness to do evil, must be among the misguided. 1.19.4

He said, therefore, to the Bag-man, "Sir, I have heeded everything with which you've filled my ears and believe the truth to lie with you alone. I am your partisan, your follower, and the co-carrier of your bag. Just protect me from these undercapitalized parasites, for they are like ravening lions that feel no mercy or pity for God's creatures. They think that destroying a soul out of zeal for religion will earn them a place close to Him. They hold tight to such exterior meanings of the words of the gospel as they believe are in keeping with their aims and will increase their standing and authority. They say, for instance, that Christ's words 'I came not to send peace, but a sword'[307] license them to apply the said instrument to people's necks to make them return to the true path. They have cast behind them the essence, substance, 1.19.5

هذه الاداة فى رقاب الناس ردًّا لهم الى طريقة الحق * وقد نبذوا ورآء ظهورهم خلاصة الدين وجوهره ونتيجته * وهى الالفة بين جميع الناس والمحبة والمساعدة وحسن اليقين بالله تعالى * وما صعبٌ على من زاغ وعمى عن الحق ان يستخرج من كل كتاب وَحيًا كان او غير وَحى ما يوافق غرضه وفساد عقيدته * فان باب التاويل واسع * ايجوزُ الان لامير الجبل اذا شاخ ولم يَعُد التدثّر بالثياب يدفّئه ان يتكوّى ببنت عذرآء جميلة اى يتدفّأ بها ويصطلى بحر جسدها كما فعل الملك داود * ام يجوز له اذا حارب الدروز وانتصر عليهم ان يقتل نسآهم المتزوجات واطفالهم ويستحيى ابكارهم لتفجر بهن فحول جنده * كما فعل موسى باهل مدين على ما ذكر فى الفصل الحادى والثلثين من سفر العدد * ام يجوز له ان يتزوج بالف امراة ما بين ملكة وسريّة كما فعل سليمن * ام يجوز لاحد من القسيسين ان ينكح زانية ويولدها النغول كما فعل النبى هوشع * ام يسوغ لاحد من الولاة ان يقتل من اعدائه كل رجل وكل امراة وكل طفل رضيع * كما فعل شاول بالعمالقة عن امر ربّ الجنود * حتى ان الرب غضب عليه لعدم قتله خيار الشآء والانعام ولابقائه على اجاج ملك العمالقة وندم على انه ملّكه على بنى اسرائيل فقام صمويل وقطّع الملك قطعا امام الرب فى جلجال * هذا وانى قد قرأت فى فهرست التوراة المطبوعة فى رومية فى حرف الهآء ما نصه * ينبغى لنا (اى لاهل كنيسة رومية) ان نهلك الهراطقة * اى المبتدعين او المشاحنين * واستشهدوا على ذلك بما كان يجرى بين اليهود واعدائهم من القتال والفتك والاغتيال على ما سبق ذكره * فان يكن دين النصارى يحلّل قتل الرجال والنسآء والاطفال والفجور بالابكار من النسآ ويبح التوثّب على عقار الغير من دون دعوة الى الدّين بل مجرد عتوّ وظلم كما كان يحلّله دين اليهود * فلاىّ سبب نَسَخَه اذًا وابطل احكامه * لكن دين النصارى

and consequence of religion, which are friendship among all men, affection, assistance, and a proper certitude as to the existence of God Almighty. Those who have gone astray and are blind to the truth find no difficulty in extracting from any book, divinely inspired or not, whatever may suit their purpose and corrupt creed, for the door of exegesis is a wide one. Should the Emir of the Mountain, once he's grown old and wrapping himself up in his clothes is no longer enough to keep him warm, be permitted to cozy up to a beautiful virgin girl, i.e., warm himself with her and heat himself with the warmth of her body, like King David? When he makes war on the Druze and God grants him victory over them, is he permitted to slay their married women and their children and leave their virgins alive for the stud bulls among his troops to debauch, the way that Moses did to the people of Midian, as stated in Numbers, chapter 33? Is he permitted to marry a thousand women, queens and concubines, as Solomon did? Is a priest permitted to have intercourse with an adulteress and beget bastards, as did the prophet Hosea? Or to tolerate one of his governors slaying every man, woman, and suckling child among his enemies, as Saul did at the Lord's command with the Amalekites, the Lord even being angry with him that he hadn't killed along with them the best of their sheep and oxen and had spared Agag, King of Amalek, and repenting that he had made Saul king over the Children of Israel, so that Samuel arose and hewed Agag in pieces before the Lord in Gilgal? Moreover, I have read in the index to the Old Testament printed in Rome, under the letter *h*, the following: 'We (i.e., the adherents of the Church of Rome) are obligated to destroy the heretics (i.e., innovators and schismatics)'; in justification, they cite the fighting, bloodshed, and assassination that occurred between the Jews and their enemies, as outlined above. Thus, if the religion of the Christians makes lawful the slaying of men, women, and children and the debauching of virgins, and allows the seizing of other people's property without first inviting the victims to join the true religion but out of mere ferocity and tyranny, as does the religion of the Jews, why did the first abrogate the second and declare its laws null and void? In fact, though, the Christian religion is built on high moral values and its aim from beginning to end is to maintain peace among men and urge them to what is righteous and good. Otherwise, we might as well go back to being Jews."

مبنىّ على مكارم الاخلاق * وغايته من اوله الى آخره ابقآء السِلْمِ بين الناس *
وحثّهم على الصلاح والخير * والّا فلنرجعْ يهودًا * فلما سمع الخرجىّ ذلك رأى ١،١٩،٦
ان ورآ هذا الكلام لباقعةً * فحرص على انقاذ الفارياق من ايدي العتاة * وارتاى
ان يبعثه الى جزيرة تسمى جزيرة الملوط استئمانًا فيها * فركب الفارياق فى سفينة
صغيرة سائرة الى الاسكندرية * فلما ان سارت به غير بعيد هاج البحر واضطرب
بالسفينة فلزم صاحبنا فراشه من الدوار * وطفق يشكو من الم البحر وينوح قائلا *

نواح الفارياق وشكواه

ويلى من السَفَر ومّما اشتق منه ماكان اغنانى عن مقاساة هذا الضر الاليم * ١،١٩،٧
ماكان اغنانى عن هذه المساومة التى سامتنى هذا الكرب العظيم * ماذا وسوس
الىّ حتى دخلت بين الضواطرة ولا عائدة لى من هذا الفضول الذميم * لقد ولدت
فى الدنيا وعشت زمانا ولم يخطر ببالى ما اختلف فيه عَبام وبعيم * فلاى شى
دخلت فى هذه المضايق وتورّطت فى هذا الشرّ العقيم * هل كان يعنينى ما تهاتر
عليه اهل المشرقين من فساد رايهم وخلقهم اللئيم * لهفى على القلم وان يكن فى شِقه
شَقّ وحول مُجاجه الوَنِيم * لهفى على الحمار الذى كان يرقع ويرفس من لى بذلك
البهيم * لعله الان احسن حالا منى ولعله فى نعيم مقيم * وانا اليوم بما فرّطت
مُليم * مَن لى بالخان والاخوان فيهم كل بزيع نديم * زمانَ لا شغل الا معاقرة المدام
والتطريب والترنيم * ليتنى قلت ما قال الناس وعبدت معهم البعيم * (استغفر
الله قد كفر صاحبنا) ليس كل وقت وقت جدال ومناقشة خصيم * لقد نصحنى
المطران بقوله ان الحواسّ قد تغش فى الضئيل والجسيم * والغبى والحكيم * والجاهل
والعليم * انه يعرف الحق ويقول غيره خوفَ كل عتلّ زنيم * اذ الجاهلون لا يحبهم

When the Bag-man heard this, he decided that behind the words was a sly dog, so he exerted himself to save the Fāriyāq from the hands of the arrogant,[308] thinking it best to send him to an island known as the Island of Scoundrels,[309] believing it would make a safe haven for him. The Faryāq thus embarked on a small ship going to Alexandria, but before they had gone far, the sea rose and threw the ship about, and our friend became so dizzy he had to stick to his bunk, where he set to complaining of the dolors of the sea and to lamenting, as follows: 1.19.6

The Faryāq's Lament and Plaint

"Alas for my traveling and alack for my *travail*! Why do I endure this painful distress to *no avail*? What good this bargain when this mighty affliction is all it *earns*? What tempted me to take on the traders when such low meddling could bring me no *returns*? I was born into this world and lived there many a year *before*, without giving a thought to the squabbles of every dolt and *boor*. Why did I enter these *straits* and get embroiled in these sterile *debates*? Why should the shouting matches engaged in by people west and *east*, with their corrupt thinking and low characters, concern me in the *least*? Ah how I miss the pen, however hard over its nib-notch I've *toiled* and even if the page onto which it spits its ink with fly shit's *soiled*! Ah how I miss the donkey that brayed and kicked—who will bring me back that *beast*? He may be better off than me these days—he may be living a life of *ease*, while I, today, am cut off from all I once held *dear*. Who will bring me back the inn and brethren—each one a gracious and companionable *peer*? All I had to do then was sing, warble, and *quaff*—would that I'd gone along with all the rest and worshipped the *golden calf*!"[310] (I seek refuge with God—our friend has blasphemed!). "Not every second has to be given over to wrangling and trying to grab your opponent by the *collar*. The metropolitan gave me sound advice when he said the senses deceive mighty and meek, stupid and wise, ignoramus and *scholar*. He knows the truth but says something different, fearing all who are 'ignoble and, beside that, basely *born*,'[311] for nothing pleases the ignorant more than to distract and *suborn*. Did he not tell me, 'You cannot 1.19.7

الا التضليل والتهييم * الم يقل لى انك لا تقدر على تجديد القديم * وعلى تقويم ما لا يستقيم * نعم ان الحواس تغش وسيّان فى ذلك السفيه والحليم * والكريم واللئيم * ثم وقف قليلا حتى يورد امثلة على هذا واذا به يقول * ان القبيحة ١،١٩،٨
الشوهآء اذا نظرت وجهها فى مرآة تقول ان كنت شوهآ عند بعض فانى حسنآ عند آخرين * ولذلك قال صاحب القاموس الشوهآ العابسة والجميلة ضدّ * وان القُناف اذا نظر جلمود انفه قال يحتمل ان بعض الحسان يرغبن فيه وما يرين به اَمْتا ولا عَوجا * وان سادتنا القباح من الملوك والملكات وذوى السعادة والجَدّ لا يصورهم المصّورون الّا حسانا * وهم لا ينظرون انفسهم فى العِناس الا كما صوّرهم المصورون * وانّا لنرى الشمس طالعة ولمّا تكن قد طلعت كما يقول الرياضيون * ونرى العصا فى المآ معوّجة وهى غير ذات عوج * وان السراب يرى الشخص اثنين * وان بعض الالوان يبدو بلونين * وان السحرة يخيّلون للناظرين انهم يمشون على المآ ويدخلون فى النار ولا يحترقون * ومَن يكُ فى سفينة ماخرة قابلة ديار وعقار فانه يرى ما يقابله فى الارض متحركا ماشيا وهو ساكن ثابت * ومن يعقد فى شباك مناوح لشباك آخر مساوٍ له فى الارتفاع فانه ينظره اعلى من شباكه * ولعل صاحبى الخرجى كان بكآوه لداعٍ غير داعى السلعة * فانه يبلغنى عن اللاعبين واللاعبات فى الملاهى انهم يبكون ويضحكون ايان شاوا فلعل البكآ عندهم من الصنائع التى يتعلمونها على صِغَر * ماذا يفيدنى الخرج الان * اادعوه ويتركنى[1] * ااحبه ويبغضنى * ااحمله وينبذنى * فلما ابتدا هذه السفاهة التى ١،١٩،٩
تعدّ عند الخرجيّين كفرا * وعند السوقيين تسبيحا * وعند المتوسطين بينهم سفاهة ناشئة عن الجزع * اذ الناس لم يتفقوا الى الان الّا على الخلاف * مادت به

---

١ ١٨٥٥: يتزكّى.

renew the old, or straighten what is *bent*?' True, the senses deceive and alike in this are the murderer and the man of mercy, the vile and the *benevolent*."

After pausing for a moment to marshal examples of the preceding, he resumed, "When an ugly, misshapen (*shawhā'*) woman looks at her face in the mirror, she says, 'I may be ugly and misshapen to some but to others I am handsome,' which is why the author of the *Qāmūs* says, '*Shawhā'* means both "a woman who frowns" and "a beautiful woman"; a word with two opposite meanings.' When a man with a big nose looks at that crag on his face, he says, 'It may well be that some good-looking women will desire it and see in it no crookedness or curve.' Painters portray our ugly overlords, kings, queens, and any others on whom fortune has smiled as though they were comely and they, in their years of spinster- and bachelorhood, see themselves exactly as the painters have portrayed them. We see the sun as though it had risen, when according to the scientists it hasn't yet done so, and we see a stick in water as though it were crooked, though 'there is no therein no crookedness.'[312] A mirage shows a person as though double and certain colors appear in two different forms. Magicians make observers think they are walking on water or going through fire without being burned. To a person in a ship plowing along opposite houses and property, the part of the land closest to him appears to be moving and mobile, when it is unmoving and fixed. A person who sits at a window opposite another at the same level sees the latter as though it were higher than his own. Maybe, then, the Bag-man's tears were not for his goods but for some other cause, for I hear that the players in theaters weep and laugh at will. Maybe weeping is one of those arts that the Bag-men are instructed in when young. What benefit to me is the saddlebag now? I call on it, and it abandons me? I love it, and it hates me? I pick it up, and it spurns me?" 1.19.8

When he started in on this foolishness—which the Bag-men regard as blasphemy, the Market-men as glorification of the Lord, and those in between as generated by fear (for to this day people can agree only to disagree)—the ship gave him a violent shove, such as the Bag-men would consider to be the Lord's revenge and the Market-men entirely incidental, and he began yelling, "Forgive me, Market Boss! By your beard, which is at the barber's, save me! Bag! Goods! Price list! Traders! Undercapitalized parasites! You who weave the goods and you who dye them, you who warp and you who weft them, you who hem and you who embroider them, you who 1.19.9

السفينة ميدة شديدة يحسبها الخرجيون انتقاما من الرب * والسوقيون عارضا من العوارض *فجعل يصرخ ويقول الا ياشيخ السوق عفواً بحق لحيتك التى عند الحلاقين الا ما اجرتنى * ياخرج * ياسلعة * يادفتر * ياضواطرة * ياصعافقة * ياتسّاجى السلعة * ياصبّاغيها * يامسدّيها يامُلْحميها يامنيّريها يامطرزيها ياموشيها يارقّاميها يارفّائيها ياشصّاريها ياخياطيها ياكفافيها ياشرّاجيها ياتشاريها ياطوآئيها ياقسّاميها(١) يالفافيها ياملفقيها * تداركونى بحقكم قد هلكت * فما كاديتم هذا الدعآء الّا ومالت به السفينة ميلة تدحرج بها راسه الصغير كالبطيخة *فجعل يصرخ ويستغيث ويقول لقد عدّيت عن التقديد * هذا اثره ظهر من اول الطريق فكيف يكون فى آخره * ثم غشى عليه وصار يهذى ويقول الخُرّ الخُرّ * فسمعه احد الركّاب يكرر ذلك فظن انه يشكو من احد الاخثين فى فراشه * فلما لم يجد شيا قال هو يهذى من الاَلَم وتركه *
١٠،١٩،١ ثم قدّر الله ان سكن البحر وصفا الجو وظهرت بعد ساعات ارض الاسكندرية * فجآ ذلك الرجل وبشّر الفارياق برؤية الارض * فقام متجلدا وغسل وجهه وبدل ثيابه * فلما خرجوا من السفينة سبقهم الفارياق وما كاد يطا الارض حتى تناول منها حصاة والتقمها وقال هذه اُمّى * واليها اَمّى * فيها ولدت وفيها اموت * ثم انه توجه الى خرجى كان فى المدينة وادّى اليه كتاب توصية من الخرجى الآخر * ولبث عنده ينتظر سفينة تسافر الى تلك الجزيرة * فلنهنئه بوصوله سالما آمنا * ولنقدم عرض حال للسدّة الاميرية * والحضرة الملكية * حضرة بطرك الطائفة المارونية كائنا ماكان * ثم نعرج قليلا على السوقيين والخرجيين ونذكر الفرق بينهم *

(١) القَسامىّ مَن يطوى الثياب اول طيّها حتى تتكسر على طيّه *

ornament and you who stripe them, you who darn and you who stitch them, you who sew and you who edge them, you who baste and you who unroll them, you who fold and you who crease them,(1) you who wrap and you who sew them edge to edge, catch me, by your lives, or I am done for!" This cry had barely left his lips before the ship gave a list to one side that sent his little head rolling like a watermelon, so he started yelling and calling for help, saying, "I'll never cry goods for sale again! If this is what's in store for us at the start of the road, where will it all lead?" Then he fainted and started raving, saying, "Sh . . . ! Sh . . . !" which made a passenger who overheard him repeating it again and again think he must be complaining that there was one of "the two impure things" in his bed.[313] Finding nothing, though, he said to himself, "He must be raving with pain" and left him.

(1) The "creaser" (*al-qasāmī*) is "the person who gives clothes their first folding, so that they take their creases according to the way he makes them."

Then God decreed that the sea grow calm and the weather turn fair, and **1.19.10** after some hours the Alexandrine shore appeared, and the same man came and gave him the good news that land was in sight, so he arose stoically, washed his face, and changed his clothes. When they left the ship, the Fāriyāq was ahead of them all, and no sooner had he set foot on the ground than he picked up some pebbles from its surface and swallowed them, declaring, "This is my mother and to it I return. On it I was born and on it I shall die." Then he made his way to a Bag-man who was in the city and presented him with his letter of recommendation from the other Bag-man, and he stayed with him while waiting for a ship leaving for the island. Let us then congratulate him for arriving safe and sound, and let us present a memorandum to the Princely See and Royal Presence, His Excellency the Patriarch of the Maronite Sect, whoever he may be, after which we shall turn our attention for a short while to the Market-men and the Bag-men and set out the differences between them.

عرض كاتب الحروف

١،١٩،١١ قد تفلّت الفارياق من ناديكم * وانملص من بين اياديكم * وعَنْجَر فى وجوهكم جميعا
واصبح لا يخاف لكم وعيدا * وبقى الان ان اذكركم ما اشططتم به من الظلم والطغيان
والجور والعدوان على اخى المرحوم اسعد * اذ اودعتموه السجن فى داركم الوزيرية
بقنوبين نحوست سنين * وبعد ان اذقتموه جميع ضروب الذلّ والهوان والبوس
والضنك فى صومعة صغيرة لزمها فلم يكن يخرج منها الى موضع يبصر فيه النور او
يستنشق الهوآ اللذين يمنّ بهما الخالق على الابرار والفجّار من عباده قضى نحبه وما
كان سجنكم له الا لمخالفته لكم فى اشيآ لا تقتضى عذابا ولا عتابا * وماكان لكم عليه
من سلطان دينى ولا مَدَنىّ * اما الدّين فان المسيح ورسله لم يامروا بسجن من كان
يخالف كلامهم وانما كانوا يعتزلونهم فقط * ولوكان دين النصارى نشا على هذه
القساوة الوحشية التى اتصفتم بها الان انتم رعاة التائهين وهداة الضالّين لما آمن
به احد * اذ لا احد من الناس يَصْبُؤُ الا اذا كان يرى الدين الذى خرج اليه خيرا
من الذى خرج منه * وكل انسان فى الدنيا يعلم ان السجن والتجويع والاذلال والتوعّد
والتأويق والتشنيع ليس من الخير فى شى * وناهيك ان المسيح ورسله اقرّوا ذوى
السيادة على سيادتهم وإِمْرتهم * ولم يكن دابهم الّا الحضّ على مكارم الاخلاق
والامر بالبِرّ والدعة والسِلم والاناة والحلم * فانها هى المراد من كل دين عُرف بين
١،١٩،١٢ الناس * واما المدنى فلان اخى اسعد لم ياتِ منكرا ولا ارتكب خيانة فى حق جاره
او اميره او فى حقّ الدولة * ولو فعل ذلك لوجب محاكمته لدى حاكم شرعىّ * فاساَة
البطرك اليه انما هى اساَة الى ذات مولانا السلطان * لأنّا جميعا عبيد له مستامنون
فى امانه وحكمه * وكلنا فى الحقوق سوآ * اذ البطرك ليس له حق فى ان يخطف من
بيتى درهما واحدا لو شآه فانّى له ان يخطف الارواح * وهَبْ ان اخى جادل

A Memorandum from the Writer of These Characters

The Fāriyāq now has escaped your *lands* and slipped through your *hands*. 1.19.11
He's blown a raspberry in all your *faces*, and at your threats his pulse no longer *races*. All that remains is for me to remind you of the injustice, tyranny, oppression, and aggression that you carried to such great lengths against my brother, the late Asʿad,[314] to wit, that you held him in your prison at your official abode at Qannūbīn[315] for around six years and that, after you had forced him to taste every form of humiliation, degradation, misery, and distress in the small cell that was his sole abode—for he never left it for a place where he could see the light or breathe the air that the Creator has bestowed on the innocent and guilty alike among his creatures,—he gave up the ghost. Your only reason for imprisoning him was that he was at odds with you over matters that call for neither punishment nor reproach. You had no authority over him, either religious or civil. As for the religious aspect, Christ and his apostles never ordered the imprisonment of those who disagreed with what they had to say; they merely held themselves aloof from them. If the Christian religion had adopted from its beginnings the same vicious cruelty that characterizes you now—you, the shepherds of the lost and guides of the erring—no one would have believed in it, for no one converts unless he believes that the religion he is adopting is better than the one he is abandoning. Everyone in the world knows that there is nothing good to be said for imprisoning, starving, humiliating, threatening, discomforting, and reviling people, not to mention that Christ and his apostles acknowledged the authority and government of the sovereign and never themselves did more than urge on people the noble virtues and command them to piety, modesty, peace, endurance of suffering, and mildness of behavior, which are the goals of every religion known to man.

And as for the civil aspect, given that my brother Asʿad did nothing repre- 1.19.12
hensible and committed no crime against his neighbor or his emir, or against the state—which, if he had done so, would have required that he be tried before the legal authorities—the patriarch's maltreatment of him is no less than maltreatment of the person of Our Lord the Sultan, whose slaves we all are and to whose safekeeping and rule we all appeal. All of us are equal in

فى الدين وناظر وقال انكم على ضلال فليس لكم ان تميتوه بسبب هذا * وانما كان يجب عليكم ان تنقضوا ادلّته وتدحضوا حجته بالكلام او الكتابة اذا انزلتموه منزلة عالم تخشون تبعته * والا فكان الاولى لكم ان تنفوه من البلاد كما كان هو يطلب ذلك * بل اصررتم على عتوكم فى تنكيله وزعمتم ان فراره من داركم مرة لنجاة نفسه
كان زيادة فى جنايته وجريرته فزدتم تجبرا عليه وظلما * وكانّى بكم معاشر السفهآ ١،١٩،١٣
تقولون ان اهلاك نفس واحدة لسلامة نفوس كثيرة محمدة يُندَب اليها * ولكن لو كان لكم بصيرة ورشد لعلمتم ان الاضطهاد والاجبار على شى لا يزيد المضطهد وشيعته الّا كلفاً بما اضطهد عليه * ولاسيما اذا علم من نفسه انه على الحق وان خصمه القاهر له على ضلال * او انه متحلّ بالعلم والفضائل وقرينه عُطُل عنها * فقد فاتكم على هذا العلم الدينى والسياسىّ * وعرّضتم عرضكم للقذف والتسويد * وذكركم للمقت والتفنيد * ما دامت السمآ سمآ والارض ارضا * وان اخى رحمه الله وان يكن قد مات فذكره لن يموت * وكلما ذكره ذاكر من اهل الرشد والبصيرة ذكر معه ايضا سوفعلكم وافحاشكم وغلوكم وجهلكم وشناعتكم * وقد لعمرى اخرج عنكم بموته من شيعتكم هذه المتوحّمة على سفك الدم اكثر مما لو بقى حيّا * وحسبك
بالخواجا ميخائيل مشاقه الاكرم وبغيره من ذوى الفضل والبراعة مثالا * لم تاخذكم ١،١٩،١٤
ياغلاظ الاعناق رافة فى شبابه وجماله * الم تتاثر قلوبكم التارزة لصفرة وجهه حين حجبتموه عن النور والهوآء * وحين ذوت غضاضة جسمه وبضاضته * وحين لم يبق ترارته غير الجلد والعظم وبخلتم عليه ايضا ان تطلقوه بهما * الم تشفقوا عليه اذ رايتم انامله قد ضنيت لعوز ماكان يتمتع به حُمُر ديركم * ولقد طالما والله اخذت القلم فخطّت ما يعجب به الملوك * ولقد طالما والله صعد المنبر فخطب فيكم ارتجالا والعَرَق يتصبّب من جبينه ذاك الصليت * ولشدّ ما ابكى سامعيه تذكيرا وتزهيدا *

rights, for the patriarch has no right to take a single silver coin from my house by force; how much less then is his right to take a life by force! Even if we concede that my brother debated and argued over religion and said that you were misguided, it was not yours to kill him for that reason. If you acknowledged his status as a scholar and feared the consequences of his activities, you ought to have pulled apart his evidence and refuted his arguments orally or in writing; if not, you should have banished him from the country, as he asked you to do. Instead, though, you persisted in your ferocious punishment in order to make an example of him and claimed that the fact that he once escaped from your abode in an attempt to save himself exacerbated his crime and increased his guilt, meaning that your own tyranny and injustice toward him should also be increased.

Do I hear you, you confederacy of cretins, claiming that to destroy one 1.19.13
soul for the salvation of many is a praiseworthy act that should be encouraged? If you had any insight or good sense you would know that persecution and compulsion only increase the persecuted in his love of that for which he is persecuted, especially if he is convinced in his heart that he is right and his tormentor wrong, or that he is blessed with knowledge and virtue while the other is innocent of them. The fact is, you are without either religious or political understanding and have exposed your honor to defamation and blackening and your reputation to revulsion and condemnation for as long as sky is sky and earth earth, and that my brother's reputation, God have mercy upon him, though he be dead, will never die. Whenever anyone of good sense and insight mentions him, he will mention along with him your misdeeds, your atrocities, your excesses, your ignorance, and your ugliness. I swear, he drove more of your blood-thirsty community out of their allegiance to you by his death than he would have done if he had remained alive—suffice it to mention the Most Honorable Khawājā Mikhā'īl Mishāqah[316] and other persons of wealth and capability.

Did you feel no compassion, you bull-necked thugs, for his youth and 1.19.14
beauty? Were your hard hearts not affected by the pallor of his face when you kept him from the light and air, when his firm and tender body withered and nothing was left of his well-turned physique but skin and bones (and even then you were too stingy to release him with just those)? Did you take

وطالما الّف وعرّب لكم كتبا ركيكة وعلّم حمقى رهبانكم واخرجهم من ظلمات الجهل * الم يخزِ وجوهكم الصفيقة ما كان يترقرق فى وجهه من مآء الحيآ فكان اشدّ خفرا من مخدَّرة * وانّه كان عزيزا فى اهله * مكرما عند الامرآء محبَّبا الى الخاصة والعامة * نزيه النفس * كريم الخلق * فصيح اللهجة * انيس المحضر * اَمِثْله يحبس ست سنين ويذل وينكل ويموت والله يعلم باى شى مات * ما بال الكنائس ١٥،١٩،١
الفرنساوية والنمساوية والانكليزية والمسكوبية والرومية الارثوذكسية والرومية الملكية والقبطية واليعقوبية والنسطورية والدرزية والمتوالية والانصارية واليهودية لا تفعل هذه الفظاعة والشناعة التى تفعلها الكنيسة الماورنية * ام هى وحدها على الحق والناس اجمعون على الباطل * الستم تزعمون ان ملك فرنسا هو مجير الدين وناصره * والناسُ من اهل مملكته الكاتوليكيين ما زالوا يطبعون كتبا يندددون فيها بعيوب رؤسآء كنيستهم وقبائحهم وسفاهتهم وفحشهم وشراهتهم والحادهم * بل ان كثيرا منهم قد الّفوا تواريخ خاصة بما كان عليه الباباوات من الفسق والفجور وسوء التصرف * وبكفرهم بخلود النفس والوحى وبالهيّة المسيح * فمنهم من قال ١٦،١٩،١
ان البابا ارماديوس الثامن ويعرف بدوق صَفوَى رقى الى درجة بابا وهو عامى * ومنهم من قال ان مجمع باسيل انما كان انعقاده لخلع البابا يوجين وانهم حكموا عليه بالعصيان والارتشآ والشقاق والبِدَع ونكث اليمين * ومنهم من قال ان البابا نيقولاس الاول كان قد حرم كونتيار مطران كولون لمخالفته له فى المجمع الذى عقد فى مَتْز سنة ٨٦٤ * فكتب المطران المذكور رسائل الى جميع كنائسه يقول فيها * ان المولى نيقولاس الذى اتخذ له لقب بابا ويحسب نفسه انه بابا وسلطان معا وان يكن قد حرمنا فقد علونا على سفاهته * ومنهم من قال ان امبروسيوس حاكم ميلان حصل على درجة مطران مع انه كان غير صحيح الاعتقاد بدين النصارى *

no pity on him when you saw that his fingertips had been worn away for want of those very things to which the asses in your monastery had unfettered access? How many a time, by God, did they take up the pen only to use it to write out what kings wished to hear and how many a time, by God, did he ascend the pulpit and preach to you extemporaneously, the sweat pouring from that shining brow, and how hard did his listeners weep as they remembered their sins and determined to renounce them! How many a time did he write and translate insipid books for you and instruct your stupid monks and bring them out from the shadows of their ignorance! Did not the modest decency that shone from his face put your own impudent countenances to shame—he who was more bashful than the most demure of women? Or his dearness to his family, the honor paid him by emirs, the love shown him by lords and commoners? His unblemished purity and honorable morals? The elegance of his language, the good cheer he brought to those he was with? Is one such as him to be imprisoned for six years, humiliated, punished, and to die (and God alone knows of what he died)?

How do you explain that neither the French churches nor the Austrian 1.19.15
nor the English nor the Muscovite nor the Greek Orthodox nor the Greek Catholic nor the Coptic nor the Jacobite nor the Nestorian nor the Druze nor the Mutawālīs[317] nor the Anṣārīs[318] nor the Jews perform such abominable and vile acts as are performed by the Maronite church? Or is it alone possessed of the truth, while all others are in error? Do you not claim that the King of France is the protector and defender of religion? Yet at the same time, the Catholic citizens of his kingdom continue to print books condemning the vices, shameful deeds, stupidity, obscenity, lustfulness, and atheism of the leaders of their church. Some of them, indeed, have written histories devoted to the immorality, depravity, and bad conduct of the popes, as of their denial of the truth of the immortality of the soul, of divine inspiration, and of the divinity of Christ.[319]

One has said that Pope Amadeus VIII, known as the Duke of Savoy,[320] 1.19.16
was elevated to the papacy when he was a layman. Another that the Council of Basel was convened specifically to depose Pope Eugene[321] and found him guilty of sedition, bribery, sowing discord, and betraying his vows. Another that Pope Nicolas I excommunicated Bishop Günther of Cologne because of

ومنهم من قال ان البابا يوحنا الثامن ارسل نوابا من طرفه الى القسطنطينية * فعقدوا ثمّ مجمعا اجتمع فيه اربعمائة اسقف وكلهم حكموا ببرآة فوتيوس وانه جدير برتبة مطران * ومنهم من قال ان البابا اسطفانوس السادس امر بان تنبش جثة فرموسيوس اسقف بورطو من القبر لانه كان قد اثار شَغْبا على سلفه البابا يوحنا الثامن * ثم حكم عليه حالة كونه ميتا بقطع راسه وثلث من اصابعه والقيت جثته في طيبر * وان البابا سرجيوس كان قد استوزر ثاودورة ام ١٧،١٩،١
ماروزيا التى تزوّجت بمركيز طوسكانى * وانه اى البابا اولد ماروزيا هذه ولدا ربّاه عنده داخل قصره من دون محاشاة احد من اهل رومية * ثم تزوجت ماروزيا بعد ذلك بهوك ملك ارلس وعملت على قتل البابا يوحنا العاشر لانه كان يهوى اختها * فخنقته بين فراشين واستبدّت بالامر * ثم احتالت ان ولّت ليو هذه الرتبة ثم قتلته فى السجن بعد اشهر * ثم ولّت من بعده رجلا خامل الذكر فولى بعض سنين ثم عزلته ونصبت يوحنا الحادى عشر وهو ابنها من سرجيوس الثالث وكان قد اتى عليه اربع وعشرون سنة لا غير * وشرطت عليه ان لا يباشر من الاحكام الا ما كان مختصا برتبة البابوية * وانها سمّت زوجها ثم تزوجت بسلفها ملك لومباردى وفوضت اليه الحكم * فقام احد ولدها من زوجها الاول وشغب عليها اهل رومية وحبسها وابنها البابا فى صانت انجلو * وانه وَلِى بعده اسطفانوس الثامن * غير انه لما كان بغيضا عند الرومانيين لكونه من جرمانية شوّهوا وجهه فلم يقدر بعدها على الظهور بين الناس * ثم انتُخب ابن ولد ماروزيا المسمى اكطافيانوس وله من العمر ثمانى عشرة سنة وسّمى من بعد ذلك يوحنا الثانى عشر * وكان خليعا ماجنا فحّاشا مستهترا منهمكا فى اللذات وهوى النفس مولعا بركوب الخيل والفروسية * وانما لم يخلّ ذلك بامور الكنيسة لان اكثر الدول

a disagreement with him at the council that was convened in Metz in 864 and that the aforementioned bishop sent letters to all his churches in which he said, "Although Vicar Nicholas, who has taken the title of pope and considers himself to be simultaneously pope and secular leader, has excommunicated us, we have dismissed his folly."[322] And another that Ambrose, governor of Milan, obtained the rank of bishop, even though his belief in the Christian religion was unsound.[323] Another has said that Pope John VIII sent delegates to Constantinople, where they convened a synod at which four hundred bishops met and that all of them found Photius innocent and declared him to be worthy of the rank of bishop.[324] Another that Pope Stephen VI ordered that the body of Formosus, Bishop of Porto, be exhumed from its grave because he had incited strife against his predecessor John VIII, and then sentenced him, dead as he was, to have his head and three of his fingers cut off, after which his body was thrown into the Tiber.[325]

And that Pope Sergius[326] appointed Theodora, the mother of Marozia,[327] **1.19.17**
who was married to the Count of Tuscany, a senator[328] and that he, that is, the pope, fathered a boy[329] on the said Marozia and had him raised inside his palace far from the eyes of the people of Rome, after which Marozia married Hugh, king of Arles,[330] and intrigued to have Pope John X[331] killed because he was in love with her sister, smothering him between two pieces of bedding and assuming absolute power. Next, she schemed to appoint Leo[332] to the same position, and then, a few months later, murdered him in prison; after him, she appointed another man whose name has now fallen into oblivion[333] and he ruled for a few years, after which she deposed him, placing John XI—her son by Sergius III—on the throne when he was only twenty-four years old, imposing on him the condition that he should implement no decision that did not directly derive from his rank as pope. She also poisoned her husband[334] and married her brother-in-law the king of Lombardy,[335] to whom she delegated the rule of the Papal States. One of her sons by her first husband[336] rose up and incited the people of Rome against her, imprisoning her and her son, the pope, in Sant'Angelo. After him, Stephen VIII[337] held office but he was hated by the Romans because he was from Germany, and they so disfigured his face that he could not show himself among the people.[338] Then Marozia's grandson Octavianus was elected pope at the age

والكنائس كان على هذه الحال * وان اوثو الامبراطور لما علم ان هذا البابا قد اضمر ١٨،١٩،١
العصيان وكان اهل ايطاليا قد استدعوا حضوره لاصلاح ما اختلّ من احوالهم توجّه من باڤيا الى رومية * وبعد ان استتبّ له الامر فى المدينة عقد مجمعا حضر فيه البابا بنفسه وكثير من امرآء جرمانية و رومية واربعون اسقفا وسبعة عشر كردينالا وذلك فى كنيسة مار بطرس * وشكى البابا بحضرتهم اجمعين انه فسق بعدّة نسآء وخصوصا ايتَنّت التى ماتت وهى نُفَسآ * وانّه قلّد مطرانيّة طودى لغلام كان سنّه عشر سنين لا غير * وانه كان يبيع الرتب والدرجات الكنائسية بيعا وسمل عينى اشبينه فى المعمودية سملا * وجَبّ اى خصى احد الكرادلة او الكردينالات جبّا * ثم قتله * وانه لم يكن يومن بالمسيح وغير ذلك مما اوجب على الامبراطور خلعه ونصب ليو الثامن فى مكانه * الا انه لم يكد الامبراطور يخرج من رومية حتى هاج البابا عليه اهل المدينة * وعقد مجمعا خلع فيه ليو الثامن وامر بقطع يد الكردينال الذى كتب الشكوى عليه * وقطع ايضا لسان الكاتب الذى كان يقيّد الحوادث وأنفه واثنتين من اصابعه * ثم قُتل البابا يوحنا الثانى عشر وهو معانق
لامراة * وكان القاتل له على ما قيل زوجها * ثم ان القنصل كريسنتيوس ابن البابا ١٩،١٩،١
يوحنا العاشر من ماروزيا جيّش اهل رومية على اوثو الثانى وسجن بندكتوس وكان من حزب الامبراطور فمات فى السجن * فلما بلغ ذلك مسامع اوثو ولّى يوحنا الرابع عشر * فقام عليه بونيفاس السابع الذى كان ولى الرئاسة من قِبَل القنصل وقتله * وبقى القنصل مستقلا بتدبير الامور ومباشرة الاحكام الى ان قام غرغوريوس ابن اخت الامبراطور وخلعه[1] اوثو الثالث * ثم احتال عليه الامبراطور وضرب عنقه وامر بان تعلق جثته من القدمين * وسُملت عينا البابا يوحنا الخامس عشر الذى انتخبه الرومانيون وقُطع انفه ثم رُمى به من ذروة قلعة صانت انجلو *

١ ١٨٥٥: خلع.

of eighteen, being known thereafter as John XII.[339] He was licentious, indecent, depraved, a scoffer at religion, entirely given over to the satisfaction of sensual pleasures and his appetites, infatuated with horse-riding and chivalry—a situation that failed to disturb the church only because most other churches and nations were in the same state.

When Otto, the emperor,[340] learned that this pope was secretly in revolt **1.19.18** against him, and the people of Italy called on him to come and set their affairs to rights, he made his way from Pavia to Rome and, after settling the affairs of the city, convened a synod that the pope himself attended along with many princes of Germany and Rome, forty bishops, and seventeen cardinals, in the church of Saint Paul. There, in the presence of all, the emperor made a complaint against the pope that the latter had fornicated with a number of women, and specifically with Étiennette, who died in childbirth, that he had ordained as bishop of Todi a boy who was only fourteen years old, that he used to sell church titles and offices for money, that he had put out the eyes of his godson at his baptism, that he had "snipped" (i.e., castrated) a cardinal and then murdered him, and that he did not believe in Christ, along with other charges, the emperor thus being obliged to depose him and install Leo VIII[341] in his place. Barely, however, had the emperor left Rome before the pope (John XII) whipped up the people of the city, convened a synod at which Leo VIII was deposed, and ordered the amputation of the hand of the cardinal who had recorded the complaint against him. He also had the tongue of the clerk who had recorded these events cut off, as well as his nose and two of his fingers. John XII was later murdered while embracing a woman—the murderer being, according to some, the woman's husband.

Next, Consul Crescentius,[342] son of Pope John X by Marozia, mobilized **1.19.19** the people of Rome against Otto II and imprisoned Benedict,[343] who was of the emperor's party, and he died in prison. When this reached Otto's ears he appointed John XIV,[344] but Boniface VII,[345] who had been appointed to the top position by the consul, rose up against him and killed him, leaving the consul a free hand in the running of affairs and execution of decisions until Gregory,[346] the emperor's sister's son, was installed and Otto III[347] deposed Crescentius; the emperor then played a trick on him, cut off his head, and

ثم عُرضت الرئاسة البابا وية على البيع فاشتراها كلٌّ من بندكتوس الثامن ويوحنا التاسع عشر واحدا بعد واحد * وكانا اخوى مركيز طوسكانى * ثم اشتُريت لولد سنّه عشر سنين وهو بندكتوس التاسع * ثم انتخب باباوان اخران وكان احدهما يكفّر الاخر ويحرمه * ثم اصطلحا على ان يتقاسما دخل الكنيسة فيما بينهما وان يعيش كل منهما مع سرّيته * ومنهم من قال ان كنيسة رومية اصدرت مرة ٢٠،١٩،١
منشورا حكمت فيه على بعض ملوك فرنسا بان يطلّق امراته ويباشر دواعى التوبة سبع سنين * وانه لما شهر المنشور فى المملكة سقطت حرمة الملك من عيون الناس فتجنّبته الخاصة والعامة حتى لم يبق عنده غير خادمَيْن * ومنهم من قال ان البابا غريغوريوس السابع عقد مجمعا فى رومية على آنرى الرابع سلطان جرمانية وقال فيه * قد خلعت آنرى عن ولاية النمسا وايطاليا وأَعْفيت جميع النصارى من الطاعة له ونقضت عهدهم له * ولست آذن لاحد فى ان يخدمه باعتبار انه ملك ذو سلطان * وان آنرى لما ضاق بذلك ذَرعا اضطر الى الذهاب الى رومية * فلما قدم على البابا وجده خاليا بالكُنْتس ماتيلدة فى كانوزا(١) فوقف السلطان يستاذن فى الدخول لدى الباب ولم يكن معه احد يخفره * فلما دخل المقام الاول اعترضه بعض حشم البابا ونزعوا عنه حلّته الملكيّة والبسوه ثوبا من الشعر * ووقف ايضا ينتظر الاذن فى صحن القصر حافيا وكان ذلك فى قلب الشتآء * ثم اُلزم ان يصوم ثلثة ايام قبل تقبيل قدم البابا * فلما انقضت الايام الثلثة دُخل به الى مجلس البابا فوعده بالعفو بشرط ان ينتظر ما يحكم به عليه فى مجلس اغوسبرغ * الى ان قال ثم مات البابا المذكور وخلفه رئيس ديرسُمّى اوربانوس الثانى * وكان مثل سلفه فى العتوّ والتجبّر * فمن ثم جعل يحرّض ابنَى آنرى على قتال ابيهما * وهذه ثانى مرة هاج البابا فيها الابنآء

(١) الكنتس مونث الكُنت من القاب الشرف عند الافرنج

ordered that his body be hung up by the feet.[348] Pope John XV, who had been elected by the Romans, had both eyes put out and his nose cut off,[349] and was then thrown from the top of the castle of Sant'Angelo. After this, the papacy was put up for sale, to be bought successively by Benedict VIII[350] and John XIX,[351] who were brothers to the Count of Tuscany. Then it was bought for a boy aged ten, Benedict IX.[352] Then two further popes were elected, each of whom excommunicated the other,[353] only to reconcile later on the basis that they divide the wealth of the church between them, each living with his concubine.[354]

Others have stated that the Church of Rome once issued an edict **1.19.20** by which it ruled that one of the kings of France should divorce his wife and perform acts of penance for seven years[355] and that, when the edict was published in the kingdom, the king lost his sanctity in the eyes of the people, who, lords and commoners alike, ostracized him to the point that he was left eventually with no one but two servants. Some say that Pope Gregory VII[356] convened a synod against Henry IV,[357] king of Germany, in Rome, where he declared, "I hereby depose Henry as ruler of Austria and Italy and absolve all Christians from obedience to him, and I will permit no one to serve him as a sovereign king." When Henry IV could stand it no longer, he was forced to go to Rome. When he went to the pope, he found him alone with Countess(1) Matilda[358] at Canossa,[359] and the emperor stood at the gate, with no guard of his own, asking for permission to enter. When he entered the first courtyard, his way was barred by some of the pope's servants, who stripped him of his royal mantle and dressed him in a hair shirt, and again he stood and waited for permission, barefoot in the castle courtyard, in the middle of winter. Then he was told he had to fast for three days before he could kiss the pope's foot. When the three days were over, he was brought into the pope's council chamber, where the pope promised to pardon him provided he should wait to see what sentence the Diet of Augsburg might pass on him. The writer goes on to say that the aforementioned pope died and was succeeded by the abbot of a monastery, under the name Urbanus II,[360] who was as arrogant and tyrannical as his predecessors and, as such, set about inciting the two sons of Henry IV[361] to fight

(1) "Countess" is the feminine of "Count," a title of nobility among the Franks.

على آبائهم * فقاما عليه واودعاه السجن ثم فرّ منه ومات فى لياج مسكينا ذليلا *
ومنهم من قال ان آنرى السادس ولد فريدريك الثانى سار الى رومية ليتوجّه البابا
سيلستانوس * ولما كان الامبراطور متطاطئا لتقبيل قدمه وعلى راسه تاج الملك
رفع البابا رجله ورفس بها التاج عن راسه فوقع على الارض وكان سنّ البابا وقتئذ
ستا وثمانين سنة * ومنهم من قال ان بعض الباباوات واظنه اينوصنت الثالث ٢١،١٩،١
حرم الملك لويس واباه * غير ان مطارين فرنسا نسخوا حكمه وامروا بالغائه * وان
البابا اينوصنت الرابع عقد المجمع الثالث عشر على الامبراطور فريدريك الثانى وذلك
فى سنة ١٢٤٥ وحكم عليه فيه بكفره وبانه كان يتسرّى بجوارى مسلمات * فناضل
عن الامبراطور خطباوه وحزبه وردّوا على البابا انه افتضّ بنتا وارتشى غير مرة *
ومنهم من قال ان البابا المذكور اغرى طبيب الامبراطور المشار اليه بان يدسّ له
السمّ فى طعامه * وان البابا لوقيوس الثانى وَلِىَ مرة حصار رومية بنفسه ومات
من رمية حجر على راسه * وان البابا اكليمنضوس الخامس عشر كان يجول فى قُنَّى
وليون لجمع المال ومعه عشيقته * وان راهبا من الدومينيقيين سمّ الامبراطور آنرى
عن امر البابا وذلك فى القربان * وانه فى سنة ١٢٠٠ تزاحم باباوان على الرئاسة وجمع
كل منهما حزبه للقتال وعلى راية كلٍ صورة المفاتيح * وان احدهما تصرف فى آنية
كنيسة مار بطرس وانفقها فى اهبة الحرب * وان البابا اوربانوس كان يعذب كل
من خالفه من الكرادلة او الكردينالات * وفى ذلك الوقت انكرت دولة فرنسا رئاسة
البابا واستبدّت اساقفتها بامور رعيتهم * ومنهم من قال ان البابا يوحنا الثالث
والعشرين شُكى بانه سمّ سلفه وباع الوظائف الكنائسية وقتل عدة ابرئآ * وانه كان
كافرا ولوطيّا معا * فمن ثم خُلع بحضرة الامبراطور * الى غير ذلك مما يضيق عنه
هذا الكتاب فانى لم اضعه فى الدين وانما اوردت ما مرّ بك على سبيل الاستطراد *

their father, which was the second time the pope had set the sons against their father. They rose up against him and put him in prison but he escaped and died at Liège, pitiful and humiliated. Some say that Henry VI,[362] son of Frederick II, went to Rome to have himself crowned by Pope Celestine[363] and that when the emperor, crown on head, bent over to kiss the pope's foot, the pope lifted his leg and kicked off the crown, which fell on the ground; the pope was eighty-six at the time.

Someone else says that one of the popes, Innocent III[364] I think, excom- **1.19.21**
municated King Louis and his father but that the French bishops abrogated the sentence and ordered him to cancel it, and that Pope Innocent IV[365] convened the thirteenth synod against the emperor Frederick II[366] in 1245 and there found him guilty of unbelief and of taking Muslim girls as concubines. The emperor's preachers and the members of his party stood up for him and responded by accusing the pope of having deflowered a virgin and of taking bribes on more than one occasion. Another has said that the aforementioned pope seduced the aforementioned emperor's physician into slipping poison into his food, and that Pope Lucius II[367] on one occasion took command in person of besieging Rome and died as the result of a stone striking him in the head; that Pope Clement XV[368] used to roam about in Vienne[369] and Lyons collecting money with his mistress, that a Dominican monk poisoned Emperor Henry on the orders of the pope (and at communion too!), that in 1200 two popes jostled for the throne, each gathering his party in readiness for a fight, on the banner of each the image of the keys, that one of these seized the liturgical vessels of the church of Saint Peter and sold them in preparation for the war, and that Pope Urban[370] used to torture any cardinal who disagreed with him. At this time also, the French state refused to acknowledge the pope and its bishops ruled tyrannically over the people. Some say that Pope John XXIII[371] was accused of poisoning his predecessor, selling church offices, murdering a number of innocents, and being both an unbeliever and a sodomite, as a result of which he was deposed by the emperor.[372] And so it continues, beyond the scope of this book, for it has not been my intention to belittle religion; I simply provide the foregoing by way of a digression.

فان كان ما قاله هولآ المولفون من الفرنساويين حقاً كان ابرّ من هولا الائمّة واتقى * ٢٢،١٩،١
اذ لم يُشَكَّ قط بانه لاط او زنى اوسمّ احدا او هاج الابنآ على ابائهم ليقتلوهم *
او انه اختلس انية الكنائس او طغا وتجبّر على سلطانه او ارتشى * وانما هى
مماحكات جرت بينه وبين بطركه على اشيآ غير مقيسة ولا معدودة ولا موزونة
ولا مكيلة * فانت تقول مثلاً ان دركات قنوبين المودّية الى سجّين ثلث * وهو قال
ثلثمائة * وانا اقول ثلثة الاف * فما مدخل السجن هنا والعذاب * وان كان ما قالوه
كذبا وافترآء كان ذلك ادعى الى تنكيلهم والاقتصاص منهم * لافترائهم على
احبار الله وخلفائه فواحش لن يستطيع عبّاد الفتيش ان ياتوا بافظع منها * مع انّا لم
نرَ احدا منهم عُذّب او نُفى او استفزّ من داره او اُنف من محضره * بل قد طُبعت
كتبهم المرة بعد المرة * وسعرها فى الاسواق كسعر كتب العلم * ولعل قائلا يقول ان ٢٣،١٩،١
عَرضك هذا موجّه الى البطرك المتولّى الان وهو من اهل الفضل والمكارم وليس
هو الذى سجن اخاك وقتله وانما سلفه * قلت عندى علم ذلك * غير انه ما دام هو
يعتقد بان ما فعله سلفه كان صوابا فهو شريك له ولا يلبث ان يعامل من يقتدى
باخى معاملة سلفه * وكذلك يعم اللوم جميع المطارنة والاساقفة والقسيسين
والرهبان ان كانوا يصوّبون ما فعله البطرك المتوفى * وكنت اودّ لو اختم هذا
العرض بعتاب اوجهه الى حضرة المطران بولس مسعد ابن خالى وخال اخى وكاتب
اسرار البطرك * ولكنى خشيت الان من الاطالة * وفيما قلت ما يغنى اللبيب *

However, if what these French authors say is true, then my brother was far more pious and godly than these leaders of the church, for no one ever accused him of practicing sodomy or adultery or poisoning anyone or inciting sons to kill their fathers, or of making off with the church plate or behaving unjustly or rebelling against his sovereign or taking bribes. The whole matter comes down to no more than arguments between him and a patriarch over things that have no fixed measure or number or weight or volume. *You* might say that the steps from Qannūbīn to Sijjīn[373] are three in number; *he* might say three hundred; *I* might say three thousand—what role do prison and torment have to play in such matters? If, on the other hand, what these writers say is lies and slanders, that would call for them to be punished and for retribution to be exacted upon them for slandering God's priests and successors with libels so vile no fetish-worshipper could come up with anything more appalling. In fact, however, we are not aware of any of them having been tortured or banished or scared out of their houses or summarily removed from their abodes—quite the opposite, as their books have been printed time and time again and are priced in the market as scholarly works. 1.19.22

Someone may say, "This memorandum of yours is addressed to the present patriarch, who is a man of virtuous and noble qualities and not the one who imprisoned and killed your brother, who was his predecessor." I reply, "I am aware of that, but so long as he believes that what his predecessor did was right he is his partner and sooner or later will mete out the same treatment to those who have followed in my brother's footsteps. By the same token, all metropolitans, bishops, priests, and monks are equally blameworthy if they condone what the deceased patriarch did. I would have preferred to conclude this memorandum with a word of censure addressed to His Excellency Metropolitan Būlus Mus'ad, our maternal uncle and confidential secretary to the patriarch. But I see that I'm in danger of going on too long, and what I've said above should be enough for the wise." 1.19.23

الفصل العشرون

في الفرق بين السوقيين والخرجيين

١،٢٠،١ اعلم ان للسوقيين شهرة عظيمة فى جميع الاقطار * وذلك انهم احتكروا السلعة منذ القديم فى مخازن لهم * وقالوا كل من لم يشترِ من مخازننا انزلنا به القصاص * ثم انهم اخفوا دفتر اسعار البياعات عن المشترين وغالوا بثمن الاصناف واشطّوا * فكانوا يتقاضون من المشترى اضعاف القيمة * ثم اتخذوا لهم معامل ومخازن فى جميع الامصار وجعلوها مظلمة خالية عن الكُوَى ومنافذ النور * فكانوا يبيعون منها من غير ان يُبدوا حقيقة لون السلعة ورقعتها * وكانوا يجعلون ما يبيعونه من اصنافها ملفوفا مظروفا فياخذه الشارى وينطلق به ولا يرى منه شيا * وكان عندهم من النسّاجين والخياطين والرفّائين والصبّاغين ما يفوق العدد * فكان هولآ

٢،٢٠،١ يصنعون لهم كل ما يامرونهم به * واتفق فى بعض السنين ان وقع مُوات ذريع فى الماشية وامحلت البلاد فقلّ الصوف والحرير عندهم وكادت الانوال والمعامل تتعطل * فارتاى رجل منهم من اهل الحصافة والحذق ان يستعمل الشعر وبعض اصناف الحشيش بدل ما اعوزهم من الحرير وغيره * وجآ عمله هذا متقنا محكما حتى اشتبه على اكثر الناس * ثم ان نفرًا من المعسرين الذين حملهم الضنك فى المعيشة على توسيع دائرة الفكر والنظر فى الامور والتمييز لها * (فان جل العلمآ والمستنبطين من الصعاليك) ذهبوا يوما الى بعض المخازن لشراء ما لزم لهم وجآوا بما اشتروه

Chapter 20

The Difference between Market-men and Bag-men

You must know that the Market-men are famous everywhere, for they have, since ancient times, held a monopoly over the goods, which they keep in warehouses of theirs, declaring, "We shall exact revenge on anyone who does not buy from our warehouses." They have also hidden the price list from the buyers and jacked up the prices of the various items to an exorbitant degree, demanding from the buyer several times the original price. More recently they opened workshops and warehouses in all the cities, and they have kept these dark, with no apertures or openings for the light, and they sell from them without showing the true colors of the goods or the kind of cloth. They keep the items they sell wrapped and packaged, and the buyer takes them and goes off without having set eyes on them. They have innumerable weavers, tailors, darners, and dyers, and these make them whatever they ask for. 1.20.1

One year it happened that a devastating die-off of cattle occurred, and the land was laid waste. Their stocks of wool and silk were thus reduced, and the looms and workshops were close to falling idle. One among them, a man of sound judgment and perspicuity, decided to use hair and certain kinds of plant in place of the silk and other stuffs that they could not find, and the work that he did with such materials was so well and cleverly made that most people were taken in. Then a company of those hard-pressed types who have been driven by their poverty-stricken situations to broaden the scope of their thinking and to look into and compare and contrast things—for the majority of scholars and original thinkers are vagabonds—went to one of the warehouses to buy what they needed and took what they'd bought to their homes, wrapped and untouched, as usual. 1.20.2

٣،٢٠،١ الى منازلهم ملفوفا مصونا على العادة * وكان احدهم يهوى امراة يريد ان يتزوج بها وقد اشترى لها منديلا * فلما اهداها اياه بحضرتهم وكانت ذات استشراف واستطلاع واستكشاف للمستور كما هو شان سائر النسآ * اخذت المنديل وقبل ان تشكره على معروفه ادنته من نور السراج اذ كانت زيارتها له فى الليل * فرات فيه خللا كبيرا مع ان النور كان طفيفا يوشك ان ينطفى * واذا بها صرخت تقول * بئس من باعك هذا انه قد غبنك * ان فيه خللا مثل الذى قد فتنك * فلما سمعوا ذلك تنبهوا فاخذ بعضهم ينسّل حاجته * وصار الاخر يقيس ثوبه على قامته وهلمّ جرّا * فظهر لهم ان البضاعة ليست على وفق مرادهم * لان من ذهب ليشترى حاجة بلون احمر وجدها سودآ * ومن اراد ثوبا طويلا وجده

٤،٢٠،١ قصيرا * ومن اراد حريرا وجده كرباسا * فرجعوا بها فى الغد الى الباعة وقالوا لهم قد بعتمونا ما لم نرده * واوردوا لهم عللا واسبابا للاقالة * فقال صاحب المنديل لقد كدتم تسوّدون وجهى عند محبوبتى البيضآ * وكادت تغاضبنى لما اتحفتها من سقط المتاع لولا انها طمعت فيما يكون خيرا منه * فقالت لهم الباعة انما بعناكم ما طلبتم ولكن على ابصاركم غشاوة فلستم تبصرون اللون ولا الرقعة ولا تعرفون المقادير ولا المقاييس * فقال مَن اشترى الثوب كيف يمكن ان يجهل الانسان قامته ويعرفها آخر غيره * وقال صاحب اللون الاسود انما اردت اللون الاحمر وها ان ثوبك اسود و رفيقاى هذان يشهدان لى وما هو واضح لكل ذى عينين * فقال له البائع انت اعمى لا تميز الالوان ثم ذهب لياتيه بلُماك ليكحله به فابىَ ذاك وقال لا بل انت عَمِه اعمى * وقال من اشترى الكرباس بدل الحرير هب ان البصر يُغَشّ افينخى اللمس على الاعمى * فلجّ بينهم الجدال والعناد وملاوا المكان صخبا وضجيجا *

٥،٢٠،١ وفيما هم على ذلك اذا برجل اقبل يسعى وهو يلهث بُهَرا وقد اندلع لسانه ووضع يديه

Now one of them was in love with and wanted to marry a woman, and he'd bought her a handkerchief. When he presented it to her in the presence of the others—it being noted that she was, like all women, skilled at examination and inspection and the uncovering of what is hidden—she took the handkerchief and, before thanking him for his kindness, brought it close to the light of the lamp (for she was visiting him at night), only to find in it a large hole, even though the light was weak and on the point of going out. Before them all, she cried, "Woe to him who sold you this! He cheated you. It's got a hole in it as big as the one that holds you in thrall!" When they heard this, they were put on their guard, some picking apart what they'd bought, others measuring their clothes against their bodies, and so on, until it became plain to them that the wares were not what they'd asked for. He who had gone to buy something red found it was black, he who had wanted a long robe found it was short, and he who had wanted silk found it was cotton. 1.20.3

The next day, they returned to the salesmen and told them, "You sold us things we didn't ask for" and gave them reasons and justifications for returning the goods. Said the owner of the handkerchief, "You almost blackened my face in front of my white-skinned beloved, and she would have quarreled with me over the low quality of what I gave her, had she not been anxious to get something better." The salesmen, however, told them, "We sold you what you requested but 'over your eyes there is a covering'[374] that stops you from seeing the colors or kinds of cloth and from recognizing either quantities or measurements." "How," asked the one who had bought a robe, "can a person be ignorant of his height and another know it?" And the man who had the black but had wanted red said, "Look! The robe you sold me is black, and these two companions of mine will bear witness to what I say. See! It's clear to anyone with eyes." "You are blind and cannot distinguish colors," said the salesman. Then he went to fetch some eye-wash with which to treat the man's eyes, but the other refused, saying, "On the contrary, it's you who are blind, and stupid, too." The one who'd bought cotton instead of silk now said, "Suppose the eyes can deceive. Can touch also mislead the blind man?" Thus debate and intransigence did battle between them, and they filled the place with shouting and uproar. 1.20.4

While they were so engaged, a man came up at a run, panting and gasping. His tongue was hanging out, and he was holding his midriff with his hands. He had barely entered the store before he fell to the ground and could move 1.20.5

على كشحيه * فما كاد يدخل الحانوت حتى سقط لا يستطيع حراكا وغدا يئن ويقول آه امراتي اه امراتى * ثم غشى عليه ساعة * فلما افاق ادار نظره يمنة ويسرة فراى غريمه * فلم يتمالك ان وثب من مجثمه وقال * ياأهل الفساد * ومروّجى الكساد * ومسبّبى الفتن بين المرء وزوجته * ومفرقى الاب عن ابنه وابنته * وغابنى الاغرار من الشارين * ومبرقعى وجوه المبصرين * كيف حلّ لكم من الله ان تغشونى وتبيعونى ما لا حاجة لى به * انى اتيتكم بالامس اطلب منكم ان تبيعونى لحمًا لاتخذ منه مرقا لزوجتى لانها عليلة مذ ايام * فبعتمونى كِسَر خبز وقلتم لى انه لحم غريض * فلما اوقدت النار لاطبخه اذا به خبز * فباتت امراتى من غير ان تذوق شيا وقد اصبحت لا حراك بها الّا بلسانها * فهى لا تزال تلعن تلك الساعة التى راتنى فيها قبل الزواج * وتسب القسيس الذى كان السبب فيه * وقد حلفت انها اذا برئت من مرضها لَتامرنّ النسآ جميعا بان يكنّ مع ازواجهن ضُجُعا مفسّلات مناشيص(١) وكانه لما قال ذلك فار دَمُه فى دماغه فوثب من مكانه وكاد ان يبطش بالبائع * لولا ان تداركه بعض الصنّاع فى الحانوت * فلما تملّص البائع من يديه صعد منبرا وقال * اسمعوا ايها الخصمآ * ولا تعجلوا الى اللَوْم فانه من داب اللؤما * ان عيونكم قد غشى عليها فهى تبصر الاحمر اسود * وذوقكم قد فسد فعندكم ان اللحم خبز مُفْتأد * وعقلكم قد ركّ وحرض فانتم تحسبون الحرير قطنا * والجوهر عهنا * فما ينصفنا الّا قيّم السوق * فهلمّوا[1] اليه والّا فانتم من اهل الكفر والفسوق * فلما سمعوا مقالته وعلموا ان محاكمته لهم عند شيخ السوق شطط لكونه اضعف ٦،٢٠،١

(١) الضجع جمع ضَجوع وهى المراة المخالفة لزوجها * قلت وهو غريب فان اشتقاقه من ضجع فكان يقتضى ان يكون معناه الطاعة * والمفسّلة المراة التى اذا اريد غشيانها قالت انا حائض لترده والمناشيص جمع مِنْشاص للتى تمنع زوجها فى فراشها *

[1] ١٨٥٥: فهلّموا.

no more, and he started moaning and saying, "Ah my wife! Ah my wife!" Then he passed out for a time. When he revived, he cast looks right and left, caught sight of his foe, and could not restrain himself from leaping up from where he lay and saying, "You wicked people! You pushers of goods that have exhausted their *life*! You stirrers-up of conflict twixt a man and his *wife*! You drivers of wedges between father, son, and *daughter*! You veilers of the eyes of those who can see and cheaters of gullible buyers without *quarter*! How can you think that it is allowable in God's sight to cheat me and sell me something of which I have no need? Yesterday I came to you and asked you to sell me meat so that I could make broth for my wife who has been sick for some days, and you sold me crusts of bread and told me they were tender flesh. When I lit the fire to cook them, I found they were bread, and my wife went the whole night without tasting food and when morning came nothing of her moved, except her tongue, which never ceased cursing the wretched hour in which she set eyes on me before we married and abusing the priest who was the cause of our doing so, and she swears that, if she recovers from this sickness, she will give orders to all women to be to their husbands contrarians, excuse-makers, and bed-deniers."(1) As he said this, the blood in his brains apparently boiled, and he leaped up from where he lay and would have beaten the salesman had not some of the workers in the store grabbed hold of him.

(1) "contrarians, excuse-makers, and bed-deniers": *ḍuju'* is the plural of *ḍajū'*, meaning "a woman who is at odds with her husband" (I hold the form to be strange, for it derives from *ḍaja'a* ("to lie down") so it ought to imply obedience); *mufassilah* means "a woman who tells her husband when he wants to sleep with her, to keep him away, 'I am having my period'"; and *manāshīṣ* is the plural of *minshāṣ*, meaning "a woman who keeps her husband from her bed."

When the salesman had wriggled from his grasp, he mounted a pulpit and declared, "Listen, all you adversaries, and do not rush to criticize. Typically, as critics, your eyes have become so clouded you see black as *red*, your taste buds so corrupted you think meat toasted *bread*, your minds so enfeebled and *jaded* you believe jewels to be colored pompoms that have *faded*. Only the Market Boss can judge fairly between us, so off with us to *him*, otherwise you must be counted people of unbelief and *sin*!" When the others heard the man's words and realized that for him to have them tried before the Shaykh of the Market would be fast practice because the latter, by reason of his extreme old age, was weaker both in sight and judgment than they, they erupted in anger and started overturning the goods, jumbling them, and scattering 1.20.6

منهم بصرا وبصيرة لهرمه * التهبوا غيظا فجعلوا يركسون الامتعه ويشوّشونها
ويبعثرونها ويمزقون كل ما قدروا عليه * ويطأون ما امكن لهم وطؤه * ويكسرون
كل ما اصابوا من معدّ وصندوق وكؤس واكواب وخرجوا وهم سامدون * ثم
٧،٢٠،١ تواطاوا على ان يعقدوا مجلسا تلك الليلة ليتدبروا فى امورهم * فلما كان المسآ
اجتمعوا وقالوا قد اتضح لنا ان هولآء الباعة ظالمون غابنون * وان حواسنا لم ترَ
الشى الا على ما هو عليه * فشكرا لله ولصاحبة المنديل التى هدتنا الى هذا *
فتعالوا نستقلّ بامورنا ونعمل لنا مخازن ومعامل كما عملوا هم * ثم اتخذوا لهم شيعة
واخدانا * واصحابا واعوانا * واسقطوا عنهم من السعر ما امال اليهم كثيرا
من الناس * وقالوا لهم ان عهدنا اليكم ان نبيعكم البضاعة بمراى اعينكم ولمس
ايديكم وذوق السنتكم * ومن لم يرضَ شيا اشتراه فانّا نبدّله له بما هو خير منه *
ثم بحثوا عن الدفتر ونشروه فى جميع البلاد واستعملوا لذلك وسائل مختلفة * وقالوا
للناس هاوكم الدفتر الانور * والدستور الاكبر * فلا تشتروا منا حاجة الا على
مقتضى تسعيره * ولا تذهبوا الى شيخ السوق فانه هالك فى غروره * فرضى
الناس بما اشترطه هولآ على انفسهم * وانفصلوا عن الشيخ المذكور وعن حزبه *
وغدا كلّ من الحزبين يكذّب حريفه ويسوئ عليه ويخطّئه ويسفّهه ويحمّره ويفنّده
ويخرّفه ويلعنه ويكفّره ويوثّمه ويفسّقه * وسبحان من يداول الايام * بين الانام *

انتهى الكتاب الاول

them, ripping to pieces everything they could lay hands on, stamping on everything they could stamp on, and smashing every implement, box, glass, and cup they could reach. Then they left, heads held high. Next, they agreed among themselves to convene a council that night to arrange matters.

When it was evening, they met and said, "It's become clear to us that these salesmen are oppressors and cheats and that our senses perceived everything the way it really is. Thanks then to God and to the Lady of the Handkerchief, who guided us to this. Come, let us be independent in our *affairs* and set up our own warehouses and workshops as they did *theirs*," and they found themselves partisans and confidants, friends and assistants, and brought prices down so much that many became well disposed toward them. To these they said, "Our covenant with you is that we will sell you the goods in such a way that your eyes can see them, your hands touch them, and your tongues taste them, and if anyone's unhappy with what he's bought, we'll exchange it for something better." Then they looked for the price list and published it in all the lands, using a variety of means to that end, and they said to the people, "Behold the clearest of *ledgers*, the most extensive of *registers*. Buy from us nothing that isn't according to the price *sheet*. Don't go to the Market Boss; he is beyond redemption in his *conceit*." The people, pleased with the conditions these men had set themselves, split off from the aforementioned Market Boss and his party, and each of the two parties took to accusing their opposite numbers of lying, and calumny, calling them stupid, excoriating them, rebutting their claims, accusing them of feeble-mindedness, cursing them out, calling them unbelievers, and charging them with sin and *fornication*—glory be to Him who makes each of man's days succeed the one that went before, in never-ending *fluctuation*. 1.20.7

END OF BOOK ONE

Notes

1 Buṭrus Yūsuf Ḥawwā: one of a group of Lebanese merchants living in London, on whom al-Shidyāq depended for financial and moral support during his third sojourn there, between June 1853 and the summer of 1857, during which period he was also visiting Paris to oversee the printing of *Al-Sāq*; Ḥawwā provided al-Shidyāq with employment as a commercial agent in his offices.

2 "that house" (*hādhā l-bayt*): i.e., either the Ḥawwā family or the trading house it owned.

3 "the oddities of the language, including its rare words" (*gharā'ibi l-lughah wa-nawādirihā*): works on oddities and rarities of the "classical" or literary Arabic language form a well-established genre of Arabic letters, originally intended to clarify the use of unusual words in the Qur'ān and hadith.

4 "morphologically parallel expressions" (*ʿibārāt muraṣṣaʿah*, from *tarṣīʿ*, literally, "studding with gems"): a device used in rhymed prose (*sajʿ*), e.g., *ḥattā ʿāda taʿrīḍuka taṣrīḥan wa-ṣāra tamrīḍuka taṣḥīḥan* ("until your obscurity reverted to plain statement and your deficient rendering became sound").

5 "substitution and swapping" (*al-qalb wa-l-ibdāl*): on the evidence of his work devoted to the topic, *Sirr al-layāl fī l-qalb wa-l-ibdāl*, the author includes, under *qalb*, not only palindromes (the conventional definition of the term; see Julie Scott Meisami and Paul Starkey, *Encyclopedia of Arabic Literature*, 2 vols. (London and New York: Routledge, 1998), 2:660) but also the substitution of one letter in a word by another without change of meaning (see, e.g., *Sirr* 46, *bāḥah* and *sāḥah* ("open space, plaza")); by "swapping" the author means variation of the dots used to distinguish certain consonants over an identical or nearly identical ductus to produce different, related, words.

6 Unless otherwise noted, definitions added by the translator have been taken, here and throughout the translation, from Muḥammad ibn Yaʿqūb al-Fīrūzābādhī (= Fīrūzābādī), *al-Qāmūs al-muḥīṭ*, 2nd ed., 4 vols. (Cairo: al-Maṭbaʿah al-Ḥusayniyyah, 1344/1925–26) (see Glossary), from which only one of what are frequently several possibilities has been chosen.

7 *Muntahā l-ʿajab fī khaṣāʾiṣ lughat al-ʿArab*: this work is also mentioned by the author in his *Sirr al-layāl fī l-qalb wa-l-ibdāl* (Mattityahu Peled, "Enumerative Style in *Al-Sāq ʿalā al-sāq*," *Journal of Arabic Literature*, vol. 22, no. 2 (1991), 132); it was multi-volumed and

may have been lost in a fire (Mohammed Bakir Alwan, *Aḥmad Fāris ash-Shidyāq and the West* (Ph.D. diss., Indiana University, 1970), app. B).

8 i.e. "space for the avoidance of falsity."

9 The author's implicit claim appears to be that the uncommon "second" or "augmented" form of the quadriliteral verb is associated with intensity.

10 Jalāl al-Dīn al-Suyūṭī (d. 911/1505): a prolific polymath, much of whose 500-work oeuvre compiles material taken from earlier scholars.

11 *Al-Muzhir fī l-lughah*: the full title of the work is *Al-Muzhir fī ʿulūm al-lughah wa-anwāʿihā* (*The Luminous [Work] on the Linguistic Sciences and Their Branches*).

12 Aḥmad ibn Fāris (d. 395/1004), known as al-Lughawī ("The Linguist"), wrote on most areas of lexicography and grammar. It may be that the author's choice of the name "Aḥmad" on his conversion to Islam was an act of homage to this scholar.

13 i.e., the author does not regard such a straightforward figurative usage as a distinguishing characteristic of Arabic.

14 By "the Fāriyāqiyyah" the author has been generally assumed to mean the Fāriyāq's wife, but Rastegar makes the point that, "while the noun is feminine, it is not simply a feminization of his name (which would be Fāriyāqah). Fāriyāqiyyah should more correctly be translated as 'Fāriyāq-ness,' although as a grammatical formulation, it is feminine. Within the text, it is not always clear that it refers to his wife (although at times it clearly does)" (Kamran Rastegar, *Literary Modernity between the Middle East and Europe: Textual Transactions in Nineteenth-century Arabic, English, and Persian Literatures*, 105–6). The Fāriyāqiyyah does not appear again until Volume Three.

15 Rāfāʾīl Kaḥlā of Damascus: a litterateur and collaborator of al-Shidyāq's in Paris, who paid for the printing of *Al-Sāq*.

16 "the table enumerating synonyms": i.e., the Enumeration of Synonymous and Lexically Associated Words in This Book (in fact, a list of the lists of synonyms, etc.) that occurs near the end of Volume Four and to which the author added further items.

17 See 2.3.3.

18 "had not been mentioned" (*lam takun shayʾan madhkūran*): cf. Q Insān 76:1.

19 "dots that shine": perhaps refers to the manuscript writers' tradition of embellishing dots and other diacritical points with colored ink or even gold leaf.

20 "with pulicaria * Plants . . . ." (*bi-l- * rabalāti . . . .*): *Pulicaria undulata* (*rabal*) is a plant with medicinal properties that grows in the region; however, *rabalāt* may also mean "the fleshy thighs of women," in which case it would prefigure "From them will come to you the scent of statuesque slave girls" three lines further on.

21 "statuesque slave girls . . . plump slave girls" etc.: this list of desirable women is not simply a high-flown metaphor for the joys that the book holds, since the same (mostly rare) words used occur also in the main text.

22 "And be not lazy in pursuing and realizing *cunsummation*" (*wa-lā tatarakhkhā ʾan tudrika l-khurnūfā*): the 1855 edition reads *ḥurnūfā,* a word not attested in the dictionaries; we have preferred to read *khurnūfā* (=*khurnūfah*) ("vagina"), supposing its usage here to be figurative, i.e., "the desired goal"; it then parallels the phrase used thirty-four lines later *fa-tukhṭiʾa l-khur . . . fah* (the ellipsis is the author's) ("and so miss . . . summation").

23 Shiẓāẓ: a thief of proverbial skill.

24 "I guarantee . . . hunger" etc.: i.e., the book will distract you from all pleasures and keep you awake at night, but everyone will realize that the book is the cause.

25 ". . . summation" (*al-khur . . . fah*): see n. 22 above.

26 "cutting character" (*ḥarf bātir*): or, punningly, "cutting edge."

27 "will pull back from you blinded" (*yakuffu ʿanka kafīfā*): or, punningly, "will pull back from you entirely."

28 "Isn't 'of a certain stamp' the same in meaning as * 'Of a certain type,' with the addition of the thwack of a stick?" (*a-wa-laysa inna l-ḍarba mithlu l-ṣanfi fī l-maʿnā wa-qarʿu ʿaṣan ilay-hi uḍīfā*): *ḍarb* has "blow, stroke" as its basic meaning but also a subsidiary meaning of "type, kind" (synonym *ṣanf*); hence, things that are of a certain *ḍarb* may be conceived of (jokingly) as delivering a certain percussive force. The overall sense of these two couplets seems to be "Do not be offended if the contents of the book, and (perhaps especially) the various lists that I have compiled, is somewhat rebarbative."

29 "It does not strike the noses of mortals": i.e., its injurious consequences harm none but me.

30 "Raising a Storm" (*Fī ithārat riyāḥ*): compare the earlier description of the book as falling "like the wind in the valley when / Stirred up" (0.4.9); the first chapter of each of the four books of which the work is composed bears a title that, like this one, has little to do with the events recounted in that chapter but denotes the initiation of some energetic activity. For further discussion of chapter titles, see the Translator's Afterword (Volume Four).

31 "How many a pot calls the kettle black!" (*wa-muḥtaris min mithlihi wa-hwa ḥāris*): "From many a one such as he does he guard himself though he is himself a guardian," a proverb "alluding to him who finds fault with a bad man when he is himself worse than he" (Edward Lane, *An Arabic-English Lexicon,* 8 vols., London: Williams and Norgate, 1863 (offset ed. Beirut: Librairie du Liban, 1968), s.v. *muḥtaris*).

32 "You've made a bad business worse!" (*ʿāda l-ḥays yuḥās*): "The sloppy date mixture has been made sloppier," said when someone is called upon to make good something done

badly by another and makes it worse (Aḥmad ibn Muḥammad al-Maydānī, *Majmaʿ al-amthāl*, 2 vols. (Cairo: al-Maṭbaʿah al-Khayriyyah, 1310/1892–93), 1:316).

33 "Make the most of what you're given!" (*khudh min Jidhʿ mā aʿṭāk*): "Take from Jidhʿ whatever he may give you." The pre-Islamic Ghassanid Arabs had been obliged to pay a certain king protection money; when the king died and his son came to collect his money from a Ghassanid named Jidhʿ, the latter beat him with his sword and pronounced the words in question, after which the Ghassanids stopped paying the tax (al-Maydānī, *Majmaʿ*, 1:156).

34 "So what are you going to do about it?!" (*shaḥmatī fī qalʿī*): "My fat is in my shepherd's bag." The wolf, asked what he would do if he came upon sheep guarded by a shepherd boy, replied that he would fear the boy's arrows that were in his shepherd's bag, but when asked, "What if the shepherd were a girl?" replied as given, meaning "I should do with them as I liked" (al-Maydānī, *Majmaʿ*, 1:246).

35 To confound his putative critic, the author produces four impeccably classical proverbs, each of which consists of the words *ʿalā ẓalʿak* "regarding thy limping" preceded by an imperative verb: *irbaʿ ʿalā ẓalʿak* ("Restrain thyself because of thy limping," i.e., "Do not overreach yourself"), *irqa ʿalā ẓalʿak* ("Ascend thou the mountain with knowledge as to thy limping," i.e., "Do not make idle threats"), *irqaʾ ʿalā ẓalʿak* (apparently meaning "Be gentle with thyself, and impose not upon thyself more than thou art able to perform . . . or abstain thou, for I know thine evil qualities or actions . . . or . . . rectify thou, or rightly dispose, first thy case, or thine affair"), and *qi ʿalā ẓalʿak* ("Be cautious as to thy limping," i.e., "If you live in a glass house, don't throw stones") (see Lane, *Lexicon*, s.v. *ẓalaʿa*).

36 "Another of Khurāfah's tales, Umm ʿAmr!" (*Ḥadīthu Khurāfah yā Umma ʿAmr*): Khurāfah was a man of the tribe of ʿUdhrah who claimed to have been carried off by the jinn but whose tales of which were, on his return, dismissed as lies; thus *khurāfāt* has come to mean in modern usage "superstitions, fables, fairy stories." Umm ʿAmr ("Mother of ʿAmr") is an epithet of the hyena; her frequent apostrophization in proverbs and anecdotes appears to be related to the conventional view of the hyena as "the stupidest of beasts" (see al-Maydānī, *Majmaʿ*, 1:160); thus the sense is something like "It's all a pack of lies, you imbecile!"

37 *abīlīn*, pl. of *abīl*, "one who beats the *nāqūs*," a plank beaten with rods to summon Christians to prayer.

38 "the Great Catholicos" (*al-jāthilīq al-akbar*): the leader of Eastern Orthodox Christians living under Muslim rule.

39 "the Supreme Pontiff" (*al-ʿasaṭūs al-aʿẓam*): the Pope of Rome.

40 "Ascribing partners to God" (*al-shirk*): i.e., polytheism.

41 "pronounce letters like Qur'ān readers" (*tuqalqilūn*): *qalqalah* is "a quality unique to recitation [consisting of] the insertion of [ə] (schwa) after syllable-final [q], [d], [ṭ], [b], and [j]" (Kristina Nelson, *The Art of Reciting the Qur'an* (Cairo: American University in Cairo Press, 2001), 22). Such a pronunciation would sound bizarre in non-Qur'anic contexts.

42 "falter" (*taḥṣarūn*): the repetition is the author's.

43 "tightened" (*mufarram*): cf. the *Qāmūs*, "*al-farm* . . . is a medicament with which a woman becomes narrower" and Lane, *Lexicon*, "*farama* . . . to constrict the vulva with raisin stones."

44 "in two different forms" (*al-ʿakhtham wa-l-khathīm*): while the second word reads in the text *wa-l-khashīm*, this word, which is not found in the lexica, must be a misprint for *wa-l-khathīm*, which the *Qāmūs* gives as a synonym of the former.

45 "the just plain large one" (*al-ʿumāriṭī*): defined in the *Qāmūs* as *farj al-mar'ah al-ʿaẓīm* ("a woman's large vagina").

46 "the buttocks but with a slightly different spelling" (*al-būṣ*): the author has already used *al-bawṣ* above; the *Qāmūs* gives both spellings.

47 *al-ḥāriqah*: literally "the woman who rubs, or burns." The *Qāmūs* gives other possibly appropriate meanings, such as "the woman who is so overcome by lust that she grinds her teeth one upon another out of fear lest that lust take her to the point of neighing and snorting."

48 "the woman whose vagina is wide open and the woman whose vagina is open wide" (*al-khijām wa-l-khajūm*): according to the *Qāmūs*, the two forms are synonymous.

49 "the woman with the tiny vagina a man can't get at (again, but a different word)" (*al-marfūghah*): cf. twenty-one items earlier (*al-marṣūfah*).

50 *al-maṣūṣ*: also (the *Qāmūs*), the "vagina that dries the liquid from the surface of the penis."

51 *al-bayẓ*: also (the *Qāmūs*) "the water of the woman or man."

52 "the clitoris said with a funny accent" (*al-ʿuntul*): "the clitoris (*baẓr*); a dialectal variant of *ʿunbul*" (*Qāmūs*).

53 "a man's practicing coitus with one woman and then another before ejaculating and a man's practicing coition with one woman and then another before ejaculating" (*al-fahr wa-l-ifhār*): the *Qāmūs* states that these two verbal forms from the same root are synonymous.

54 "a little-used word for plain copulation" (*al-nashnashah*): defined in the *Qāmūs* simply as *nikāḥ* ("copulation").

55 “a noun meaning copulation from which no verb is formed” (*al-ʿaṣd*): the definition in the *Qāmūs* runs *al-nikāḥ lā fiʿla lahu.*

56 “dashing water on one’s vagina”: the next word in the text—*al-ʿaṣd*—has occurred eight items earlier (see n. 56); here the author may have intended *al-ʿazd*, which is synonymous with the former (though it has a verbal form).

57 “the flesh of the inner part of the vulva” (*al-kayn*): this is followed in the text by *al-ṭuʾṭuʾah*, for which no meaning has been found.

58 “the vulva said four other ways”: the author supplies four more items (*bizbāz*, *fāʿūsa*, *khurnūf*, *mashraḥ*) that the *Qāmūs* defines simply with the words *farj* and *ḥir* (“vagina” and “vulva”).

59 “the flabby vagina”: in the text *al-ghuḍāriṭī*, which is not to be found in the *Qāmūs* (or other dictionaries) and is probably a misprint for *al-ʿuḍāriṭī*, in which case it is a repeat from above; this possibility seems stronger, given that the following word is also a repeat (see the following note).

60 “the vagina that dries the liquid from the surface of the penis” (*al-maṣūṣ*): a repeat from above where, however, the second sense given in the *Qāmūs* seems more appropriate.

61 “another name for the vagina” (*al-ṭanbarīz*): defined in the *Qāmūs* simply as *farj al-marʾah* (“a woman’s vagina”).

62 “the bizarrely spelled” (*al-khafashanfal*): the word, defined simply as “a woman’s vagina,” is of a particularly unusual form and without related words that might throw further light on its meaning.

63 “the ‘nock’” (*al-fūq*): after the notch in the end of the arrow that fits the bowstring.

64 “and the vagina again in another exotic spelling” (*al-qaḥfalīz*): as *al-khafashanfal*, see preceding note.

65 “instruments of erection” (*adawāt al-naṣb*): *adawāt* is a grammatical term (literally, “instruments”) applied to particles (prepositions, adverbs, conjunctions, and interjections) that govern other words; *adawāt al-naṣb* (e.g., *an*, *lan*, *idhan*, *kay*) require that words they govern end in a *naṣb*; however, *naṣb*, in its non-grammatical sense, means “lifting up, erecting,” and the author puns on this.

66 “the thrower, the catapult,” etc.: many of the items in this and the next list appear to be epithets.

67 *khabanfatha*: defined simply as “a name for the anus” (*Qāmūs*).

68 “the fontanel” (*al-rammāʿah*): so called “because of its elasticity” (Jamāl al-Dīn Muḥammad ibn Mukarram al-Ifrīqī Ibn Manẓūr, *Lisān al-ʿArab*, http://www.baheth.info/).

69 "the dry and sweaty smelling" (*al-ṣumārā*): cf. *al-ṣamīr* "the man whose flesh is dry on his bones and who gives off a smell of sweat" (*Qāmūs*).

70 "the draining vent" (*al-ʿazlā* or *al-ʿazlāʾ*): literally, the mouth at the bottom of a water-skin used to drain off the last remains of the water.

71 "the black one" (*al-saḥmāʾ*): in the text this is followed by *al-funquṣah*, for which no meaning has been found.

72 "the bunghole and the butthole" (*al-burʿuth wa-l-buʿthuṭ*): two further words meaning "anus," with no further senses and with no other members to their respective roots.

73 *adawāt al-jazm*: particles (see n. 66) that govern words ending with a closed syllable (*jazm*), e.g., negational *lā*, *lam*; in its non-grammatical sense, *jazm* means "cutting off or amputation," whence the expression in the *Qāmūs*, *jazama bi-salḥihi* "he voided part of his excrement, part thereof remaining" or simply "he cast forth his excrement" (Lane, *Lexicon*).

74 "another word for the penis": *al-suḥādil* defined simply as *dhakar* ("penis").

75 "the strong, crafty wolf" (*al-ḍabīz*): such is its definition in the dictionaries, with no indication that it may be used figuratively.

76 "the thimble" (*al-qusṭubīnah*): this and the next item refer presumably to the glans penis.

77 "the prick" (*al-qahbalīs*): a word not found in the dictionaries, though the related *qahbalis* occurs, defined in the *Qāmūs* as *zubb* ("penis," a vulgarism).

78 the *qaṣṭabīr*: an orphan word, the only one in its root and cited in only one dictionary (*Qāmūs*), where it is defined simply as "penis" (*dhakar*).

79 "the tassels" (*al-jazājiz*): assuming that their use in the sense of "penises" derives from the underlying meaning of "tassels of colored wools with which the [women's] camel-litter is decorated" (*Lisān*); singular *jizjizah*.

80 *adawāt al-jarr*: particles that govern words ending in *i*, i.e., prepositions that govern the genitive case; in its non-grammatical sense, *jarr* means "drawing toward, attracting," prepositions being so called because the governed word is "attracted to," or governed by, them.

81 "to shtup" (*ʿazaṭa*): described in the *Lisān* as "seemingly a metathesis of" (*ka'annu maqlūbun min*) *ṭaʿaza* (the next to preceding item in this list).

82 "another word of similar form but dubious status" (*ʿazlaba*): the author of the *Lisān* writes, "I cannot confirm it" (*lā aḥuqquhu*).

83 "to bridge" (*qanṭara*): assuming the use of this denominal verb in the phrase *qanṭara l-jāriyah* ("he had intercourse with the slave girl") derives, perhaps via a visual image, from the base sense of the noun *qanṭarah* ("bridge").

84 “to fuck hard” (*qasbara*): assuming the verb derives from the nouns *qisbār* or *qusburī* meaning “a hard penis.”

85 “to fill her up” (*qamṭara*): cf. (*Lisān*) “to fill a water skin” and “to tie off a water skin with its thong.”

86 “to kick her” (*laṭaza*): if we assume that this sense derives from that of “to kick (its calf), of a she-camel.”

87 “and a variant of the same” (*lamadha*): the latter is a dialectal form of the preceding, i.e., *lamaja* (*Lisān*).

88 i.e., beginning with the first letter of the Arabic alphabet and ending with the last.

89 Meaning here the Arabs of the Arabian Peninsula in the days before, during, and shortly after the appearance of Islam, that is, the speakers of the pure Arabic language before its corruption by contact with other peoples and its decadence as the result of the passage of time.

90 The *Qāmūs* equates the two words at the point in its entry from which the author takes this definition; elsewhere, however, he defines *khajawjāh* as “a wind that blows constantly,” thus supporting the author’s argument.

91 “his ‘ocean’” (*qāmūsuhu*): see Glossary.

92 “the *zaqqūm* tree”: a tree that grows in Hell and whose fruit are exceedingly bitter (Q Wāqiʿah 56:52).

93 “she is to be excused because she was unaware that I, in fact, was only feigning sleep”: the argument seems to be circular, i.e., she is to be excused for not visiting him while asleep because, in fact, he was not asleep.

94 “paronomasia”: (*tajnīs* (or *jinās*), literally “making similar”): perhaps the most used rhetorical figure, it consists of deploying in proximity two words that are identical, or almost so, in the ductus but differ in vowelling and diacritics (e.g., حسن “handsome” and خشن “coarse” or أفعاله “his deeds” and أمواله “his money”)

95 i.e., Buṭrus Yūsuf Ḥawwā, to whom the book is dedicated.

96 Saʿd al-Dīn Masʿūd ibn ʿUmar al-Taftazānī (d. between 791/1389 and 797/1395) was the author of commentaries (*Al-Muṭawwal*, *Al-Mukhtaṣar*) on al-Khaṭīb al-Qazwīnī’s *Talkhīṣ al-miftāḥ* (*The Summary of the Key*) that were accepted for centuries as “the primary authoritative texts for the advanced study of rhetoric” (Meisami and Starkey, *Encyclopedia*, 2:751).

97 Abū Yaʿqūb Yūsuf ibn Abī Bakr al-Sakkākī (d. 626/1229) is best known for his *Miftāḥ al-ʿulūm* (*The Key to the Sciences*). His definitions and formulations “became standard in the science of Arab rhetoric” (Meisami and Starkey, *Encyclopedia*, 2:679).

98 Abū l-Qāsim al-Ḥasan ibn Bishr al-Āmidī (d. 370/980), whose *Al-Muwāzanah bayna Abī Tammām wa-l-Buḥturī*, which compares the poetry of Abū Tammām and al-Buḥturī, is "one of the most important monuments of Arabic literary criticism" (Meisami and Starkey, *Encyclopedia*, 1:85).

99 Abū l-Ḥasan ʿAlī ibn Aḥmad al-Wāḥidī (d. 468/1076), commentator and literary critic.

100 Abū l-Qāsim Maḥmūd ibn ʿUmar al-Zamakhsharī (467–538/1075–1144), best known for his commentary on the Qurʾān, also wrote in the fields of rhetoric, grammar, lexicography, and proverbs (Meisami and Starkey, *Encyclopedia* 2:820); the author may have had particularly in mind his *Maqāmāt*, which are written in "carefully crafted *sajʿ*" (Devin Stewart, "Maqāma," in *Arabic Literature in the Post-classical Period*, edited by Roger Allen and D. S. Richards, vol. 6 of *The Cambridge History of Arabic Literature* (Cambridge: Cambridge University Press, 2008), 155).

101 Abū Ḥātim Muḥammad ibn Hibbān al-Bustī (270–354/884–965), also known as Ibn Hibbān, was best known as a traditionist, but one of his few surviving works is a literary anthology, *Rawḍat al-ʿuqalāʾ wa-nuzhat al-fuḍalāʾ* (*The Meadow of the Sagacious and Promenade of the Virtuous*) (Meisami and Starkey, *Encyclopedia*, 2:334).

102 Abū l-ʿAbbās ʿAbdallāh ibn al-Muʿtazz (247–96/861–908) was a poet and critic who wrote *Kitāb al-badīʿ* (*The Book of Rhetorical Figures*), the first treatise covering this area of Arabic poetics (Meisami and Starkey, *Encyclopedia*, 1:354).

103 Kamāl al-Dīn Abū l-Ḥasan ʿAlī ibn Muḥammad ibn al-Nabīh (ca. 560–619/1164–1222), a poet, probably included in the list because of his love of morphological parallelism (see, e.g., lines 14 to 18 of the poem starting *afdīhi in ḥafiẓa l-hawā aw ḍayyaʿā* (http://www.adab.com/modules.php?name=Sh3er&doWhat=shqas&qid=55259, accessed March 15, 2012)).

104 The author probably means Jamāl al-Dīn Muḥammad ibn Shams al-Dīn ibn Nubātah (known as al-Miṣrī, "the Egyptian") (686–768/1287–1366), a poet known for his love of punning (*tawriyah*) and a writer on literature and stylistics to whom he refers later (Volume Four, 4.17.5). However, the latter's ancestor, Abū Yaḥyā ʿAbd al-Raḥīm ibn Muḥammad ibn Nubātah (known as al-Khaṭīb, "the preacher") (d. 374/984–85), whose sermons in rhymed prose were regarded as models of stylistics, may be intended.

105 *ghāniyah* ("beautiful woman"): the *Qāmūs* states that the *ghāniyah* may be so called because she is "the woman whose beauty is such that she may dispense with adornment" (*al-ghaniyyatu bi-ḥusnihā ʿan al-zīnah*).

106 "the Fāriyāq": the name of the author's alter ego, formed by combining the first part of his first name and the last part of the last, thus Fāri(s al-Shid)yāq.

107 "monopods ... monopodettes" (*nisnās ... nasānis*): according to the dictionaries (which have some difficulty in distinguishing between the two), the *nisnās* is, among other things, "an animal numbered among the monsters, that is hunted and eaten, has the form of a person with one eye, a leg, and a hand, and speaks like a person" (*Lisān*) whereas the *nasānis* may be either the same as, or the plural, or the feminine, of the former.

108 *al-ḥinn*: a species of jinn or their dogs, or half-men half-jinn (see Volume Two, 2.4.44).

109 Kufah and Basra: cities in Iraq from which emerged the two main contending schools of Arabic grammar. The author is unlikely to have meant this to be taken literally.

110 The Arabic letters *ḥ-m-q* used in the text spell out the word *ḥumq*, meaning "stupidity."

111 i.e., in Lebanon.

112 By the Arabic language the author means literary or formal Arabic; Syriac is the liturgical language of the Maronite church.

113 "his Frankish brethren" (*ikhwānihi l-ifranj*): i.e., the Roman Catholics of Europe.

114 "turning triliteral verbs into quadriliterals and vice versa": in another work the author provides the example of allowing the use of *rafrafa* instead of *raffa* in the sentence *raffa l-ṭā'ir janāḥayhi* ("the bird flapped its wings") (Aḥmad Fāris al-Shidyāq, *Kitāb al-jāsūs ʿalā l-qāmūs* (Constantinople: Maṭbaʿat al-Jawāʾib, 1299/1860–1), 13).

115 For example, by saying *wathiqa fī-hi* ("he trusted him") instead of *wathiqa bi-hi* or *ista'dhana bi-hi* ("he asked permission to do something") instead of *ista'dhana fī-hi*.

116 "*Durrat al-thīn ...*": the author mimics the extravagant rhymed book titles typical of his day.

117 "the country's ruler": Emir Bashīr II al-Shihābī (1767–1850), ruler of Mount Lebanon, with interruptions, from the 1780s until 1840.

118 "Abtholutely not" (*tuʿ tuʿ*): though the lexica do not appear to recognize this item as an interjection, the verb *taʿtaʿa* is defined as *fa'fā'* ("lisping") or *ratratah* ("tripping over the letter t"), among other meanings.

119 The interjection *way way* should perhaps be understood here as a reference to the words of the Qur'ān (Q Qaṣaṣ 28:82) *wayka'anna llāha yabsuṭuka l-rizq* ("Alas we had forgotten that it is God Who increases the provision [of those of his servants whom He will]") (Maududi), where *way* is considered by Sībawayh to be a separable particle meaning *waylaka* ("Alas for you!") (see *Qāmūs* s.v. *way*).

120 "the ten head wounds" (*al-shajjāṭ al-ʿashar*): the significance of the categorization lies in the various penalties owed the victim under the rule of *qiṣāṣ* ("retribution"), the first five requiring no *qiṣāṣ*, the second from five camels to a third of the monetary penalty for murder. Al-Shidyāq in fact increases the number to eleven by adding one category (the

first) in an attempt to correct an error in the original, which appears to be the *Lisān* (the *Qāmūs* contains no similar passage).

121 "The Great Christian Master Physician" (*al-sāʿūr al-akbar*): meaning, perhaps, al-Ḥunayn ibn Isḥāq (194–260/809–73), the translator of Galen.

122 "If it be said (*fa-in qīla*) . . . I reply": the author deploys a technique known as *fanqalah* (derived from the preceding Arabic words), common in Arabic exegetics and literary criticism, by which the author poses, and then responds to and dismisses, an objection to an argument he has put forward.

123 *ṭanāṭīr*: cone-shaped woman's headdresses, singular *ṭanṭūr*; "The height and composition of the tantour were proportional to the wealth of its owner, with the most splendid tantours made of gold and reaching as high as thirty inches. Some were encrusted with gems and pearls. The tantour was a customary gift presented to the bride by her husband on their wedding day" (http://en.wikipedia.org/wiki/Tantour, accessed April 20, 2012, with illustration; see also R. P. A. Dozy, *Dictionnaire détaillé des noms des vêtements chez les Arabes* (Amsterdam: Jean Müller, 1843; offset, Beirut: Librairie du Liban, n.d.).)

124 *qarn*: cf. Latin *cornu*, French *corne*, etc.

125 *ṣābūn*: cf. Latin *sāpon-*, English "soap," French *savon*.

126 *qiṭṭ*: cf. Latin *cattus*, English "cat," French *chat*.

127 *mazj*: not in fact cognate with English "mix" or French *mélange*, etc.

128 Cf. "the horns of the righteous shall be exalted" (Ps. 75:10) and "in my name shall his horn be exalted" (Ps. 89:24), etc.

129 "the word . . . is not derived from any verb" etc.: typically, Arab scholars of the classical period regarded nouns as derived from verbs; in this case, however, there is no verb with a meaning related to the noun *qarn* in either its literal or figurative senses.

130 Jirmānūs (Germanus) Farḥāt (1670–1732) was a Maronite cleric, grammarian, lexicographer, poet, and educator from Aleppo; his *Bāb al-iʿrāb ʿan lughat al-Aʿrāb* is an updating of the *Qāmūs*. Jirmānūs's efforts, portrayed as part of a "revival" of literary Arabic are sometimes better understood in the context of the transition from Syriac, the original spoken and literary language of many Levantine Christians. On Farḥāt's life and works, see Kristen Brustad, "Jirmānūs Jibrīl Farḥāt," in *Essays in Arabic Literary Biography 1350–1850*, edited by Joseph Lowry and Devin J. Stewart (Wiesbaden: Harrassowitz Verlag, 2009), 242–51.

131 *Abū l-ʿIbar*, etc.: one of the most famous buffoons and comic poets of his age, whose real name was Abū l-ʿAbbās Muḥammad ibn Aḥmad al-Hāshimī (ca. 175–250/791–864). Having changed his *kunyah* ("patronymic") from Abū l-ʿAbbās to Abū l-ʿIbar ("Father of Warnings" or "of Tears"), he thereafter added a letter with each succeeding year, ending

with the nonsensical appellation given above. His works include a comic sermon on marriage. See further Meisami and Starkey, *Encyclopedia,* 1:37.

132 "from the drain" (*mina l-balūʿah*): the sense is not obvious but perhaps recalls some anecdote concerning Abū l-ʿIbar.

133 The humor of many of the following anecdotes seems to lie in the unexpected and, especially, ridiculous nature of the protagonist's actions and reactions and the crossed purposes at which he always seems to be with his interlocutors.

134 The joke being perhaps that the response fails to answer the question either way.

135 The formulation of the question seems to imply a fuller version, such as "If he grew large, I'd ask him 'Why . . .' etc." This would be ridiculous, since the man cannot control how he grows and hence cannot be blamed for it.

136 The humor may lie in the phrase "to see her" (*li-anẓurahā*), which might be taken to mean "to cast the evil eye on her."

137 "May God be protected from every eye!" (*tabāraka llāhu min kulli ʿayn*): the man confuses the verbs *bāraka* and *tabāraka*.

138 Buhlūl, ʿUlayyān: moralizing "wise fools" of the early Abbasid period (see Naysābūrī, *ʿUqalāʾ*).

139 Ṭuways: Abū ʿAbd al-Munʿim ʿĪsā ibn ʿAbdallāh (10–92/632–711), nicknamed Ṭuways ("Little Peacock"), a celebrated singer and *mukhannath* ("effeminate") of Medina during the early days of Islam, known for his comical sayings.

140 Muzabbid: Muzabbid al-Madanī, a much-cited early Medinan comic.

141 The Fāriyāq: the author seems to have forgotten that the Fāriyāq is already speaking.

142 Waist-bands (*himyān*): i.e., sashes, in which money was carried.

143 "The Fāriyāq's father was one of those who sought to depose the emir" etc.: Yūsuf, Fāris's father, though employed by Emir Bashīr II al-Shihābī, became involved in a 1819 Druze revolt against him, led by his relatives Emir Ḥasan ʿAlī and Emir Sulaymān Sayyid Aḥmad and caused by his ever more oppressive tax levies. With the failure of the uprising, Yūsuf fled along with these to Damascus, where he died in 1821 (on the political situation in Mount Lebanon in the early nineteenth century and the Shidyāq family's role in it, see Ussama Makdisi, *The Artillery of Heaven: American Missionaries and the Failed Conversion of the Middle East* (Ithaca: Cornell University Press, 2008)), 72–76, al-Maṭwī, *Aḥmad,* 47–48, and Paul Starkey *Fact and Fiction in al-Sāq ʿalā l-Sāq,* in Robin Ostle, Ed de Moor, and Stephan Wild (eds.), *Writing the Self: Autobiographical Writing in Modern Arabic Literature* (London: Saqi Books, 1998), 36).

144 "a tambour" (*ṭunbūr*): a long-necked fretted lute. According to Starkey, the author uses "the *ṭanbūr* as a symbol of art, of freedom, almost of life itself" (Starkey, *Fact and Fiction*, 36).

145 "their Frankish shaykhs": i.e., the clergy of the Roman Catholic church, with which the Maronite church is in communion.

146 "schlup-flup" (*khāqibāqi*): "the sound of the vagina during intercourse" (*Qāmūs*).

147 "A Priest and a Pursie, Dragging Pockets and Dry Grazing" (*Fī qissīs wa-kīs wa-taḥlīs wa-talḥīs*): the priest is mentioned at 1.5.8, the pursie at 1.5.10; *taḥlīs* does not occur in the dictionaries but may be based on *maḥlūs* (a word already used, see 1.1.6) which, according to the *Qāmūs*, means "scantly fleshed" (of the vagina), in which case it would relate to the figurative use of "pursie" (see n. 10 below) in such sentences as "When my pursie grew light while within your Happy Purlieu, which is to say, when it grew to be a drag . . ." and/or on *iḥlās* meaning "bankruptcy"; *talḥīs* is likewise absent from the dictionaries but may be based on *laḥisat al-māshiyatu l-arḍ* ("the herds grazed the land to the roots"), in which case it would refer to the Fāriyāq's general state of penury.

148 "whose name rhymes with Ba'īr Bay'ar": i.e., Amīr [= Emir] Ḥaydar [ibn Aḥmad al-Shihābī] (1763–1835), cousin of Emir Bashīr II, ruler of Mount Lebanon (see 1.1.20, n. 117). The book referred to in the following lines as "ledgers" is Ḥaydar ibn Aḥmad's *Al-Ghurar al-ḥisān fī ta'rīkh ḥawādith al-zamān*, a history of Lebanon from the earliest times to the Egyptian invasion of 1831.

149 Alphonse de Lamartine (1790–1869), writer, poet, and politician; for these quotations, see Alphonse de Lamartine, *Oeuvres de A. Lamartine: Méditations Poétiques* (Paris: Charles Gosselin, 1838), 21, 23–24, and 25. The author's translations of Lamartine and Chateaubriand that follow are discussed by Alwan, who characterizes them as "smooth, readable, and reasonably accurate" (Alwan, *Aḥmad*, chap. 3).

150 'Antar ibn Shaddād: a pre-Islamic poet whose life gave rise at a later date to a popular epic of chivalry.

151 The name of the deity is used to express deep feeling incited by music or poetry.

152 *Poetry's Destiny*, etc.: Lamartine's essay is entitled *Des destinées de la poésie* and contains the words "je vois . . . des générations rajeunies . . . qui reconstruiront . . . cette oeuvre infinie que Dieu a donné à faire et à refaire sans cesse à l'homme, sa propre destinée. Dans cette oeuvre la poésie a sa place." (Lamartine, *Oeuvres* 56).

153 François-René de Chateaubriand (1768–1848): writer, politician, diplomat, and historian, considered the founder of Romanticism in French literature, who lived in America from 1791 to 1792. The originals of the two passages quoted below are to be found at

Chateaubriand, *Oeuvres complètes de Chateaubriand,* vol. 6, *Voyages en Amérique, en Italie, au Mont Blanc: Mélanges littéraires* (Paris: Garnier, [1861]), 54 and 62.

154 When Bilqīs, Queen of Sheba, visited Sulaymān from her kingdom in Yemen, he had a splendid pavilion built for her reception (Q Naml 27:44).

155 The verses are by Hammām ibn al-Salūlī (d. 100/718).

156 "a Magian": a Zoroastrian, and thus supposedly a worshipper of fire.

157 "pursies, and other things that have similar-sounding names" (*li-l-akyās wa-li-mā jā'a 'alā waznihā wa-rawiyyihā*): literally, "purses, and things that have the same syllabic structure and rhyme-letter"; the author probably intends the Arabic reader to think of *aksās* ("cunts"), just as the translator hopes the English reader will think of "pussies."

158 Mount Raḍwā: a mountain in Medina.

159 "Words... Matter... Form": the terminology is Aristotelian and was adopted by Muslim philosophers writing on physics, psychology, and metaphysics, with "Matter" meaning the substratum from which any entity is formed (thus, the soul is the matter from which the body is formed, wood the matter from which the chair is formed). The application of this analogy to the relationship between speech and meaning may be original to the author, whose intention seems to be to give a twist to the widely accepted notion that man is superior to other beings by virtue of having the capacity to speak, his point being that, if you have little to say, any such superiority is moot.

160 Abū Dulāmah: buffoon poet to the first three Abbasid caliphs (d. 161/777–78).

161 "al-Ku'aykāt... al-Rukākāt": comic names, meaning "Cookies" and "Simpletons" (or "Cuckolds") and perhaps joking allusions to the village of al-Shuwayfāt (Choueifat)—which is next door to al-Ḥadath, where the author lived in his youth and which has long been a transit point for trade among Beirut, the south, and Mount Lebanon—and another location as yet unidentified.

162 "capital (and assets)" (*ra's al-māl wa-dhanabuhu*): literally, "the head of the money (*ra's al-māl*) and its tail," the author playing with the literal meaning of the Arabic expression meaning "(financial) capital."

163 "faces radiant" (*wa-l-wujūhu nāḍirah*): cf. Q Qiyāmah 75:22 *wujūhun yawma'idhin nāḍirah* "Some faces will be radiant on that Day."

164 "those lands" (*tilka l-bilād*): i.e., Lebanon, or Mount Lebanon.

165 "every judge" (*kullu qāḍin*): or "each party to the transaction."

166 "her c . . ." (*mabā . . .*): the missing Arabic word is *mabālahā.*

167 Di'bil: Di'bil ibn 'Alī al-Khuzā'ī (148–246/765–860), a poet of invective (*hijā'*) and philologist who lived in Kufa.

168 "'O feeder of the orphans' . . . etc." (*a-muṭʿimata l-aytāmi ilā ākhirihi*): a reference to the widely cited but unattributed verse *a-muṭʿimata l-aytāmi min kaddi farjihā * a-lā lā taznī wa-lā tataṣaddaqī* ("O you who feed the orphans from the labor of your vagina, * I say to you, [better that] you neither fornicate nor give alms!"), i.e., it is better to do nothing than to seek to do good through illicit means.

169 "Unseemly Conversations and Crooked Contestations" (*Muḥāwarāt khāniyah wa-munāqashāt ḥāniyah*): alternatively, *Muḥāwarāt khāniyyah wa-munāqashāt ḥāniyyah* ("Inn-style Conversations and Tavern-style Discussions").

170 "which is why it's called *qahwah*": the author links *qahwah* ("wine") to the verb *aqhā ('an al-ṭaʿām)*, "to be put off (one's food)," though the roots are different.

171 Daʿd, Laylā: women's names.

172 "the ankleted honies": i.e., the women of his household.

173 "Each day some new matter he uncovers" (*fa-huwa kulla yawmin fī shān*): Q Raḥmān 55:29.

174 "the two best things" (*al-aṭyabayn*): i.e., eating and coitus.

175 Al-Qāsim ibn ʿAlī al-Ḥarīrī (446–516/1052–1122), Iraqi prose writer, poet, and official, wrote fifty immensely popular *maqāmāt*, which he compiled into a work of the same name.

176 "the *Nawābigh*": *Al-Kalim al-nawābigh*, a brief homily written in a mannered, ornamental style.

177 "his grandfather" (*jaddihi*): i.e., his mother's father, Yūsuf Ziyādah Musʿad, of ʿAshqūt (al-Maṭwī, *Aḥmad* 1:49), his father's father, Manṣūr, having died in 1793.

178 "*she . . . degree . . . awry . . . eye*": despite his protestations, the author slips into rhymed prose at this moment of heightened emotion, possibly without noticing, and continues to do so at similar moments throughout the chapter.

179 "she had an eye that was 'dried up'" (*dhābilatuhu*): meaning, presumably, that her eye had lost its moistness by having taken on that "sleepiness" that is said to characterize "bedroom" eyes.

180 "the whole entry . . . too noble to speak of": the entry for the root *ḥ-sh-f* includes words meaning "it (a camel's udder) became contracted and withered" and "dry bread" and "the worst quality of dates," as well as *ḥashafah*, "the head of the penis."

181 "Such a contrast . . .": *ṭibāq* ("antithesis"), consisting of the "inclusion of two contraries in one line or sentence" (Meisami and Starkey, *Encyclopedia*, 2:659), is a rhetorical staple of traditional Arabic poetics.

182 "or I do on their authority": by implying that he wrote the lines himself, the author may be seeking to undermine the sometimes spurious authority lent to ideas stated in prose

by topping them off with a couple of lines of verse, a standard technique used by writers of earlier generations.

183 Both are labial consonants.

184 "for a boy I teach": the author refers to the practice of addressing the beloved as though she were a male (*tadhkīr*), a feature of Arabic poetry and song from the earliest times until today.

185 The author deploys two contradictory arguments: that *tadhkīr* is used because some "men who can see no good in women" prefer to do so, and that it reflects an underlying grammatically masculine referent, namely the word *shakhṣ*; thus, according to the second argument, when the poet refers to "he" or "him," he really means "that person" and is thinking of a female. The French and Italian equivalents of *shakhṣ* that the author has in mind are, presumably, *personne* and *persona*.

186 "Ibn Mālik's *Sharḥ al-Mashāriq*": the author's name as given by al-Shidyāq is apparently a mistake for (ʿAbd al-Laṭīf ibn Firishtah ʿIzz al-Dīn ibn Amīn al-Dīn) Ibn Malak (d. after 824/1421), whose *Mabāriq al-azhār (fī) sharḥ Mashāriq al-anwār*, a hadith collection with extended commentary, was regarded as a classic and reprinted several times in the nineteenth century (*Encyclopaedia of Islam*, edited by P. J. Bearman, Th. Bianquis, C. E. Bosworth, E. van Donzel, and W. P. Heinrichs et al., 2nd ed., 12 vols. (Leiden: E. J. Brill, 1960–2005), 2:923–24); it has, however, proven impossible to confirm the reference in the absence of any mention of the hadith from the commentary on which this passage is presumably taken.

187 "Hind . . . Zaynab": generic female names.

188 "the 'novel' style": poetry in the style called *badīʿ*, i.e., that relying largely on rhetorical and technical artifices.

189 "That Which Is Long and Broad" (*Fī l-ṭawīl al-ʿarīḍ*): perhaps an allusion to the long, broad path facing the grammarian.

190 "Zayd struck ʿAmr" (*ḍaraba Zaydun ʿAmran*): Zayd and ʿAmr are generic names used in sentences constructed to demonstrate grammatical rules.

191 "the daughter of Abū l-Aswad al-Duʾalī" etc.: al-Duʾalī (d. 69/688) is known as "the father of Arabic grammar"; the story goes that his daughter said to him *mā ajmalu l-samāʾ* ("What is the most beautiful thing in the sky?") when she intended *mā ajmala l-samāʾ* ("How beautiful the sky is!"), and he corrected her, thus starting the process of the recording and codification of "chaste speech."

192 "the ship sails, or the mare runs": these are two-step metaphors because the ship is propelled by the wind, which in turn blows at God's behest, while the mare runs because she is made to do so by her rider, who is himself a creature propelled by God.

193 "aeolian" (*ʿiqyawniyyah*): for a definition of the noun *ʿiqyawn* from which this adjective derives, see Volume Two (2.14.43).

194 From this point, the nomenclature leaves the realm of reality and devolves into a series of fanciful and bizarre-sounding terms based largely on onomatopoeia (*farqaʿiyyah, qarqaʿiyyah,* etc.) or, toward the end of the list, hapax legomena known only from a single line of ancient verse (*jaḥlanjaʿiyyah, ʿuṭrūsiyyah*) or having only a precarious foothold in the language (such as *shunṭafiyyah,* of which the *Qāmūs* says, "a colloquialism, mentioned by Ibn Durayd, who does not explain it").

195 "tongue-smacking" (*ṭaʿṭaʿiyyah*): according to the *Qāmūs, ṭaʿṭaʿah* is a sound one makes by "sticking the tongue against the hard palate and then masticating [? *yanṭiʿ*] because of the good taste of something he is eating, so that a sound may be heard from between the palate and the tongue."

196 "panthero-dyspneaceous" (*khuʿkhuʿiyyah*): the word *khuʿkhuʿ* refers to a certain plant and thus does not lend itself to an onomatopeic interpretation; it may, however, be related to the verb *khaʿʿa* "to make a sound from the back of its throat when it has run out of breath running after its enemy (of a leopard)."

197 "the skrowlaceous" (*ʿuhʿukhiyyah*): of this word the *Lisān* says, "Al-Azharī said, 'We heard Khalīl ibn Aḥmad say, "We heard a hideous word, not to be permitted by the rules of word formation: a Bedouin was asked about his she-camel, and he said, 'I left her grazing *ʿuhʿukh*.' I asked reliable scholars, and they denied that this word could belong to the language of the Arabs."'" The *Qāmūs* says that the word, meaning a certain medicinal plant, is a deformation of *khuʿkhuʿ* (see n. 195 above) and, as such, does not offer an obvious onomatoeic association.

198 "skraaaghhalaceous" (*ʿuhkhaghiyyah*): the word is not found in the dictionaries.

199 "the transtextual and the intertextual" (*kashaʿthajiyyah wa-kashaʿẓajiyyah*): the *Qāmūs* says of these words only that they are "recently coined" (*muwalladān*), without definition.

200 "a book's prologue" (*khuṭbat al-kitāb*): the invocation with which pre-nineteenth-century Arabic books usually begin, which weaves a statement of the work's concerns into an encomium of the Prophet Muḥammad, his Companions, etc.

201 "opposition" (*ṭibāq*): al-Ḥillī describes *ṭibāq* as consisting of "using two words of opposite meaning, so that it is as though the poet were opposing (*ṭābaqa*) the one to its opposite" (al-Ḥillī, *Sharḥ* 72).

202 Al-Farrāʾ: Abū Zakariyyāʾ Yaḥyā ibn Ziyād al-Farrāʾ (144–207/761–822), a grammarian of the Kufan school, most famous for his grammatical commentary on the Qurʾān, entitled *Maʿānī al-Qurʾān*.

203 *ḥattā*: a particle (meaning approximately "until") whose usage is complex.

204 "**nna*": a particle (approximately "that") whose initial vowel varies according to environment.

205 "connective *fā'*" etc.: on the copula *fa-* (consisting of the letter *fā'* plus *a*) and its multiple uses and significations, see e.g., W. A. Wright, *Grammar of the Arabic Language*, 3rd ed., rev. W. Robertson Smith and M. J. de Goeje (Cambridge: Cambridge University Press, 1951), whose index cites ten distinct usages.

206 al-Yazīdī: Abū Muḥammad Yaḥyā ibn al-Mubārak al-Yazīdī (d. 202/817 or 818) was the author of several works on grammar and lexicography; these have not survived, although anecdotes about him abound in anthologies (Meisami and Starkey, *Encyclopedia* 2:812).

207 "connective *wāw*" etc.: on the copula *wa-* (consisting of the letter *wāw* plus *a*) and its multiple uses and significations, see e.g., Wright, *Grammar*, whose index cites five distinct usages.

208 "the right-related . . . uses of *lām*": on the particles *li-* and *la-* (consisting of the letter *lām* plus *i* or *a*), see e.g., Wright, *Grammar*, whose index cites seven distinct usages.

209 al-Aṣmaʿī: Abū Saʿīd ʿAbd al-Malik ibn Qurayb al-Bāhilī al-Aṣmaʿī (122–213/740–828) was one of the most influential early lexicographers and philologists. Sixty of his works are extant, although it is not clear if any dealt with the orthographic issue raised here.

210 "*aw . . . am*": two particles that may be translated "or."

211 "[the words] *qā'il* or *bā'iʿ*": because the proscribed orthography—*qāyil* and *bāyiʿ*—might be taken to represent a colloquialized pronunciation.

212 "when pronounced without vowels at the end" (*sākinan*): the author implies that most writers do not know enough grammar to use correct desinential inflections and their "concoctions" are therefore less offensive to the ear when read without them, in keeping with the adage *sakkin taslam* ("read without endings and be safe").

213 "the 'doer' and the 'done'": in Arabic grammatical terminology, the subject of a verb is referred to as the *fāʿil* ("doer"), the object as the *mafʿūl* ("done"). In the following, the author plays, as many have done before, on these and other, non-grammatical, meanings of the same words, e.g., "doer" in the sense of "manual worker" and "fucker," and "done" in the sense of "fucked."

214 "'raised' . . . 'laid'": the vowel *u*, called "raising" (*rafʿ*), is the marker of the subject, while *a*, called "laying" (*naṣb*), is, among other things, that of the object.

215 "the doer of the . . ." (*fāʿil al- . . .*): perhaps meaning, in grammatical terms, "the subject of the verb" (*fāʿil al-fiʿl*), which in non-grammatical language would mean "the doer of the (dirty) deed."

216 "who are steadfast" (*min al-qurrā' al-ṣābirīn*): evocative of a number of passages in the Qur'ān, e.g., *sa-tajidunī in shā'a llāhu min al-ṣābirīn* ("and, God willing, you will find me steadfast") (Q Ṣāffāt 37:102).

217 "switching persons" (*al-iltifāt*): a rhetorical figure consisting of an "abrupt change of grammatical person from second to third and from third to second," as in the words of the poet Jarīr "When were the tents at Dhū Ṭulūḥ? O tents, may you be watered by ample rain!" (Meisami and Starkey, *Encyclopedia* 2:657).

218 *māghūṣ*: a nonce-word apparently used to mean "bore, pest."

219 "Faid al-Hāwif ibn Hifām in lifping tones" (*ḥaddasa l-Hāris ibn al-Hithām*): the author substitutes the letter *s* for *th*, *h* for *ḥ*, and *th* for *sh*; without these substitutions, the sentence would read *ḥaddatha l-Ḥārith ibn Hishām*. The name evokes those of the narrators of the best known *maqāmāt* series, by al-Hamadhānī, whose narrator is called ʿĪsā ibn Hishām, and those by al-Ḥarīrī, who names his narrator al-Ḥārith ibn Hammām. At the same time, the name in its "lisped" form may be translated as "Masher, son of Pulverizer."

220 *The Balancing of the Two States and Comparing of the Two Straits* (*Kitāb Muwāzanat al-ḥālatayn wa-murāzanat al-ālatayn*): the title may be intended to evoke the *Kitāb al-Muwāzanah bayna Abī Tammām wa-l-Buḥturī* of al-Āmidī (see 1.1.11 above), although the latter compares not good and evil but the literary accomplishments of two poets and does not employ the "facing tables using a columnar system" referred to below.

221 Abū Rushd "Brains" ibn Ḥazm (Abū Rushd Nuhyah ibn Ḥazm): the name evokes two of the best known writers of the Maghreb—Ibn Rushd, known in the West as Averroës (520–95/1126–98), and Ibn Ḥazm (384–456/994–1064)—although the significance of the choice of these writers is not obvious. *Nuhyah*, literally "mind," is not part of the name of either writer.

222 "by even a jot" (*naqīran*): an echo of Q Nisā' 4:53 and 124.

223 "those who hold to the humoral theory" (*al-ṭabā'iʿiyyīn*): i.e., those who hold to Galen's theory that one's physical state is determined by the balance therein of the humors (*al-ṭabā'iʿ*—phlegm, blood, yellow bile, and black bile).

224 "by insisting on the impossible and making from the non-existent something necessarily existent" (*bi-farḍ al-mustaḥīl wa-jaʿl al-maʿdūm ka-l-mawjūd al-wājib*): the terms "(im) possible" and "necessary" pertain to Aristotelian logic (see also above 1.6.4, n. 158) and were introduced into Islamic philosophy by al-Fārābī (ca. 259–339/872–950). Al- Fārābī postulated that it is inconceivable to posit the impossible (e.g., a square circle), while the author's jurisprudent insists that to do so constitutes the very essence of his trade.

225 "I added him then to the three, making him number four" (*fa-ṣayyartuhu rābiʿa l-thalāthah*): an echo of Q Kahf 18:22 *sa-yaqūlūna thalāthatun rābiʿuhum kalbuhum*

"Some will say, 'They were three, the fourth was their dog'" (in reference to "the people of the cave").

226 "mindful men" (*dhī ḥijrin*): an echo of Q Fajr 89:5.

227 "A Sacrament" (*Sirr*): the allusion may be either to the sacrament of confession (1.14.4) or to the secret (also *sirr*) referred to at the end of the chapter (1.14.9).

228 "its number": i.e., the number thirteen.

229 "seized by their forelocks" (*yu'khadhu bi-l-nawāṣī*): Q Aḥzāb 33:37.

230 "the 'buttocks' of 'Halt and weep'" (*aʿjāz qifā nabki*): *qifā nabki* ("Halt and weep") are the opening words of the celebrated "suspended ode" (*muʿallaqah*) of the pre-Islamic poet Imru' al-Qays; the word "buttocks" occurs later, when the poet says "I said to the night, when it stretched its lazy loins followed by its fat buttocks, and heaved off its fat breast, 'Well now, you tedious night, won't you clear yourself off, and let dawn shine?'" (Arthur J. Arberry, *The Seven Odes: The First Chapter in Arabic Literature* (London: George Allen and Unwin, 1957), 64). The author links, bathetically, the misfortunes of the speaker with those of one of Arabic literature's most heroic figures.

231 *karshūnī*: Arabic written in Syriac script.

232 "soul (*nafs*) . . . breath (*nafas*) . . . breathes (*yatanaffas*)": the author plays with the fact that the words for "breath" and "soul" are spelled the same when vowels are not indicated, with a resulting potential for confusion; the reference to orifices and "a certain school" may be no more than a joke to the effect that some people count farting, belching, hiccupping, etc. as "points of exit and entry" for the breath.

233 "open his wife's womb": see, e.g., Gen. 30:22: "And God remembered Rachel, and God hearkened to her, and opened her womb."

234 "long converse and closeness in bed" (*qurb al-wisād wa-ṭūl al-siwād*—literally, "closeness of pillow and length of converse"): Bint al-Khuss (a semi-legendary figure dating to perhaps the third century before Islam and famed for her ready wit) was asked, "Wherefore didst thou commit fornication?," and this phrase was her response (Lane, *Lexicon*, s.v. *sāwada*; al-Maydānī, *Majmaʿ*, 2:37).

235 "the two cs": in the Arabic, "the two ks" (*al-kāfayn*). Since there appears to be no conventionally recognized "two ks," the meaning is open to speculation. In the opinion of the translator, the phrase is probably code for *al-kuss wa-l-kutshīnah* ("cunt and cards"), the topics of this chapter.

236 The following catalog lists activities, such as gambling, dishonest dealing, speculation, and usury that are forbidden in Islam.

237 "such people": meaning presumably, and presumably ironically, ships' captains.

238 *irtisām . . .* : the following list of 104 words is, in effect, redundant, because all but fifteen of them are repeated, with definitions, in a table at the end of the chapter (1.16.9); on the author's evolving approach to the formatting of such lists, see the Translator's Afterword in Volume Four. Words that are not repeated in the table, and that thus remain unglossed, are *tashā'um, taṭayyur, tafā'ul, taḥattum, tayammun, tasa''ud, tamassuḥ, kahānah, intijā', ṭalāsim, 'azā'im, ruqā, tamā'im, 'ūdhah,* and *siḥr*; these items are glossed here, in the endnotes. Presumably the author did not regard them as rare enough to need definition.

239 *tashā'um*: "to draw an evil omen."

240 *taṭayyur*: "to draw auguries."

241 *tafā'ul*: "to draw a good omen."

242 *taḥattum*: "to believe in the inevitability of a thing."

243 *tayammun*: "to draw a good omen."

244 *tasa''ud*: "to draw a good omen."

245 *tamassuḥ*: "to seek blessing from holy men by drawing the hands over them" (*Lisān*: "blessing is sought from so-and-so by drawing of the hands [over the object of veneration] (*yutammasaḥu bi-hi*) because of his merit and [the devotedness of] his worship, as if one were drawn closer to God by proximity to him").

246 *'āṭis*: defined in the list of definitions at the end of the chapter under *al-'āṭūs*, following the *Qāmūs*.

247 "or *qa'īd*, or *dākis*": defined in the list of definitions at the end of the chapter under the entry for *kādis*, following the *Qāmūs*.

248 *kahānah*: "soothsaying, divination."

249 *intijā'*: the author does not include this in his list of definitions below, nor does it appear in a relevant sense in the dictionaries, but *al-intijā'* is described by some of these as synonymous with *al-tanājī*, or "talking to one another in secret," and there may be a reference here to Q Mujādilah 58:9: "O believers, when you conspire (*idhā tanājaytum*), conspire not together in sin and enmity and in disobedience to the Messenger, but conspire together in peace and God-fearing" (58:9; Arthur J. Arberry, *The Koran Interpreted* (Oxford: Oxford University Press, 1982), 570); see also *tanajjā* above and in the list of definitions.

250 *ṭalāsim*: "talismans."

251 *'azā'im*: "spells."

252 *ruqā*: "incantations, charms."

253 *tamā'im*: "amulets."

254 *'ūdhah*: "spell."

255 *siḥr*: "magic."

256 *ṣadā*: in the list of definitions at the end of the chapter, this word is defined under the entry for *al-kādis*, following the *Qāmūs*.

257 "those lands" (*tilka l-bilād*): presumably, the lands to which he was bound before the ship turned back.

258 "the *mankūs*": "three lines following one another immediately, then one on its own" (*Lisān*).

259 The wording seems to be the author's, not that of a dictionary, and he interprets *ḥazā* as being of the root *ḥ-z-w* rather than *ḥ-z-y*, an alternative given by the *Lisān* but not the *Qāmūs*; *al-taḥazzī* is the noun formed from the reflexive variant of the verb.

260 "a tree": presumably of the kind also called *ratīmah*.

261 "or etc.": indicating that the entry in the *Qāmūs* continues with other less relevant definitions.

262 "pronounced like *kataba*" (*ka-kataba*): a word having the same pattern of consonants and vowels as that of the subject of the definition is used to disambiguate its spelling, a necessary procedure given that short vowels and other morphological features are not always indicated in writing and, if indicated, are vulnerable to error; the meaning of the word used (*kataba* "to write") is irrelevant.

263 "the minor magician who claims powers of divination and knocks small stones together" (*al-ḥāzī al-mutakahhin al-ṭāriq bi-l-ḥaṣā*): the *Qāmūs* quotes an authority to the effect that the *ḥāzī* "has less knowledge than the *ṭāriq* ('one who bangs small stones together'), and the *ṭāriq* can scarcely be said to divine; the *ḥāzī* speaks on the basis of supposition and fear."

264 *al-naffāthāt fī l-ʿuqad*: the phrase is taken from Q Falaq 113:4 and means literally "the women who blow on knots."

265 "too well known to require definition" (*m*): here, as frequently elsewhere, the *Qāmūs* uses the abbreviation *m*, standing for *maʿrūf* ("well known").

266 "a separate book": unidentified, but not, as one might expect, his *Al-Jāsūs ʿalā l-Qāmūs* (the verb *iḥtawā* is dealt with there but in terms of transitivity versus intransitivity, not root-assignment or semantics).

267 Q Insān 76:10.

268 "the moon and money-wagering" (*al-qamar wa-l-qimār*): perhaps because exposure to moonlight was considered by the ancient Arabs to be hazardous, as, of course, is wagering.

269 "cold talk" (*al-kalām al-bārid*): idiomatically, "rudeness."

270 "an instrument containing drink, or . . . one containing meat" (*adātun fī-hā sharāb . . . ukhrā fī-hā laḥm*): i.e., a bar or a restaurant, amenities that the author puts on the same level as bed-warmers and hot-water bottles by referring to each as an *adāh* ("instrument, device").

271 "their precipitation is bottom up, or in other words from the heads of people who are themselves ruled to the heads of those who rule" (*lafẓuhā min siflin ilā ʿilwin ay min ruʾūs nāsin masūdīn ilā ruʾūsi nāsin sāʾidīn*): apparently meaning that judges, being themselves subjects of the ruler, cannot impose the law upon him.

272 "a certain vagabond was once the guest of people who failed to honor and celebrate him": perhaps a reference to the author's treatment in Malta, or Egypt, versus that which he received in England or France.

273 "here": i.e., in this book.

274 "Old Testament": see 1.16.2, n. 232.

275 The reference is unidentified.

276 "opener of the womb": the referent has changed, being now the first-born child and not God; for the two different usages, see, e.g., Gen. 29:31 and Exod. 13:2.

277 "the secret's being revealed" etc.: cf. 1.14.9 above.

278 The following list reflects the medical science not of the mid-nineteenth century but mainly of the pre-Islamic and early Islamic periods, whose language provides the corpus for the *Qāmūs*. It thus includes terms not recognized by modern science, some of which are based on medieval understandings of camel and horse, rather than human, anatomy.

279 "the Joker": or "the Liar."

280 "The name of al-Farazdaq's devil": pre-Islamic and early Islamic Arabs believed that major poets had their verses dictated to them by personal devils; Hammām ibn Ghālib al-Farazdaq (ca. 20–110/640–728) identified his demon as bearing the name ʿAmr.

281 "al-Shayṣabān": a name of the Devil (as the two following items), but also the name of a forefather of a certain tribe of the jinn and as such repeated below.

282 "The Corrupter . . . the Beguiler": unlike the preceding, the majority of which are proper names, the following five items are common epithets of Satan.

283 *arḍ khāfiyah*: on *khāfiyah* in the sense of "jinn (collectively)," see further down this list.

284 "with or without nunation" (*wa-qad yuṣraf*): certain indefinite nouns are inflected with terminations ending in the letter *nūn* (n), a feature known as nunation, others with terminations not ending in *nūn*, and a few according to either regime; thus Wabār when fully inflected may be pronounced (in the nominative) either Wabārun or Wabāru.

285 "Wabār ibn Iram": Iram was one of the five sons of Sām, son of Nūḥ; among his descendants was Wabār, forefather of the tribe of ʿĀd, which God destroyed for practicing false belief in the sanctuary of the Kaaba.

286 "The name of one of the jinn who gave ear to the Qurʾān": a reference to "Remember how We sent to you a band of the jinn who wished to hear the Qurʾān and as they listened they said to one another, 'Be silent and listen' . . . ." (Q Aḥqāf 46:29); the jinn heard Muḥammad reciting during his retreat from al-Ṭāʾif and became believers.

287 "*mārid*": a sub-species of jinn, literally "the rebellious."

288 "I can't find it in the *Qāmūs*": it does in fact appear there, although without a definition, being glossed simply as synonymous with *ʿaḍrafūṭ* (see below); other dictionaries (e.g., the *Lisān*) define it as meaning "old woman." As the author points out, the word also occurs in the *Qāmūs* as the word used to disambiguate the pronunciation of most of these (in Arabic terms) bizarre-sounding words.

289 "the lexicographer" (*al-m.ṣ.*): an abbreviation for *al-muṣannif.*

290 "fading mirage": and twelve other definitions (in the *Qāmūs*), including "ghoul" and "devil."

291 "the ant mentioned in the Qurʾān": ". . . and when they came to the Valley of the Ants, one ant said, 'Ants! Go into your dwellings lest [Sulaymān] and his hosts inadvertently crush you'" (Q Naml 27:18).

292 "the jumper" (*al-waththāb*): neck-muscle spasm.

293 al-Hirāʾ: "a devil charged with [causing] bad dreams" (*Qāmūs*).

294 "Muḥammad or Maḥmūd": names specific to Muslims, while the emir was a Christian.

295 "unbored pearls": virgins, in conventional poetic imagery.

296 "the letter *nūn*": twenty-nine of the *sūra*s ("chapters") of the Qurʾān commence with one or more letters of the alphabet of unknown significance. The Fāriyāq takes the *nūn* preceding the verse quoted here (Q Qalam 68:1) to stand for *naḥs* ("bad luck").

297 "his confidant . . . polemics . . . ecclesiastical bigwig": the "confidant" (*najī*) was his elder brother Asʿad, whom the author visited, with other members of his family, following his adoption of Protestantism and who talked to him at length about his beliefs (al-Maṭwī, *Aḥmad,* 1:69); by "polemics" (*qīla wa-qāla*) the author means "religious controversy and debate"; the "ecclesiastical bigwig" (*aḥad . . . min al-jathāliqah*) must be the Maronite patriarch, to whom Asʿad frankly declared his beliefs in the hope of securing internal reform.

298 "saddlebag" (*khurj*): this introduces the theme of "the Bag-men" (*al-khurjiyyūn*), the author's term for Protestant missionaries (see Glossary).

299 "one of the big-time fast-talking market traders" (*mina l-ḍawāṭirati l-kibār*): see Glossary.

300 "God's horsemen against the infidel!" (*yā khayla llāh ʿalā l-kuffār*): the first half of the cry used to assemble the first Muslims before battle and subsequently used as a pious invocation to action on behalf of Muslims in danger.

301 "They shall roast in Hell!" (*innahum ṣālū l-nār*): Q Ṣād 38:59.

302 "I shall bring you the little squit 'before ever thy glance is returned to thee'" (*anā ātīka* etc.): the wording evokes the Qur'ān (Q Naml 27:40), when a member of Sulaymān's council volunteers to bring him the Queen of Sheba's throne.

303 "who had a speech defect involving the letter *f*" (*wa-kāna bi-hi faʾfaʾah*): the defect called *faʾfaʾah* is defined as "repeating and over-using the letter *fāʾ* in speech" and causes the Fāriyāq to say *shaykh al-fusūq* (literally "the Boss of Disgrace") for *shaykh al-sūq* ("the Boss of the Marketplace").

304 "Shouldn't the addition of these eighty require the eighty-lash penalty?" (*fa-lā takun ziyādatu hādhihi l-thamānīna mūjibun li-ḥaddi l-thamānīn*): the addition of *fāʾ* to *sūq* (see preceding endnote) produces *fusūq*; the numerical value of the letter *fāʾ* in the counting system known as *ḥisāb al-jummal* is eighty; and the penalty specified in the Qur'an for the *fāsiq* ("committer of *fusūq*" or depravity) is eighty lashes (cf. Q Nūr 24:4).

305 "Emotion and Motion" (*Fī l-ḥiss wa-l-ḥarakah*): both emotion and motion (of the heart) are mentioned in the opening passage.

306 "the Vizier of the Right-hand Side ... the Vizier of the Left-hand Side" (*wazīr al-maymanah ... wazīr al-maysarah*): terms derived from popular conceptions of the organization of the courts of the caliphs, but meaning here, presumably, the primary organs on the right- and left-hand sides of the body, respectively.

307 "I came not to send peace, but a sword": Matt. 10:34.

308 "he exerted himself to save the Fāriyāq from the hands of the arrogant": following his brother Asʿad's arrest by the Maronite patriarch in March 1826 (see below), the author himself sought refuge with the Protestant missionaries with whom Asʿad had consorted, and these hid him in Beirut before sending him abroad in December of the same year.

309 "the Island of Scoundrels" (*Jazīrat al-Mulūṭ*): i.e., Malta, normally *Māliṭah*.

310 "the golden calf" (*al-baʿīm*, literally, "the idol"): presumably a reference to the "idolatry" implied by the presence of statues of the Virgin Mary and saints in Maronite churches.

311 "ignoble and, beside that, basely born" (*ʿuṭullin wa-baʿda dhālika zanīm*): Q Qalam 68:13.

312 "there is therein no crookedness" (*ghayru dhāti ʿiwajin*): an echo of Q Zumar 39:28 ("[an Arabic Koran,] wherein there is no crookedness" (Arberry, *Koran,* 473).

313 "Sh . . . ! Sh . . . !" (*al-khur! al-khur!*): the passenger thinks the Fāriyāq is trying to say "The shit! The shit!" (*al-khur'! al-khur'!*), when, in fact, he is trying to say, in his delirium, "The saddlebag! The saddlebag" (*al-khurj! al-khurj!*).

314 As'ad: As'ad al-Shidyāq (1798–1830), the third eldest brother in the family (the author being the fifth and youngest), became convinced of the truth of Protestantism after associating with American evangelical missionaries in Beirut and was detained on charges of heresy by Maronite patriarch Yūsuf Ḥubaysh at his palace at Qannūbīn, where he died after some six years of maltreatment. For a detailed account of the events leading to and surrounding As'ad's death and their significance, see Makdisi, *Artillery*, and Alwan, *Aḥmad,* chap. 1.

315 Qannūbīn: a valley in northern Lebanon, site of numerous Christian monasteries, including a former seat of the Maronite patriarch.

316 Mikhā'īl Mishāqah (1800–1888 or 1889): first historian of later Ottoman Lebanon, who converted from Greek Catholicism to Protestantism in 1848.

317 "the Mutawālīs": the Twelver Shiites of Lebanon.

318 "the Anṣārīs": a Shiite sect with distinctive teachings and cosmology, with followers in Lebanon, Syria, and elsewhere in the region.

319 "Some of them . . . have written histories": the material that follows, even though attributed below by the author to several writers, appears to be taken mostly—and in some cases word for word—from Voltaire's *Essai sur les moeurs et l'esprit des nations*, chaps. 35–37 (see, e.g., http://fr.wikisource.org/wiki/Essai_sur_les_mœurs, accessed 6 March 2013).

320 "Pope Amadeus VIII": the name and number refer, in fact, not to a pope but to Duke Amadeus VIII of Savoy (1383–1451), who did, however, become antipope, assuming the papal name of Felix V, when elected by the dissident rump of the Council of Basel. The spelling Armadiyūs in the Arabic is an error.

321 "the Council of Basel was convened to depose Pope Eugene": the Council of Basel was convened in 1431 to limit the powers of the papacy. Pope Eugene IV (r. 1431–47) sought to disband the council, a rump of which remained at Basel and elected the antipope Felix V.

322 Nicholas I (r. 858–67) excommunicated the Bishop of Cologne over the latter's support for Emperor Lothar II's petition for an annulment of his marriage that would allow him to marry his mistress.

323 "Ambrose, governor of Milan": Aurelius Ambrosius (Saint Ambrose) (ca. 340–97) became Bishop of Milan after originally being governor of Emilia and Liguria, with headquarters at Milan. The author's reference to his "unsoundness" of belief may derive

from the fact that Ambrose was neither baptized not formally trained in theology when elected bishop by popular acclaim, but his later contributions to theology resulted in his being numbered among the four Latin Fathers of the Church.

324 "Pope John VIII... Photius": Pope John VIII (r. 872–82) recognized the reinstatement of Photius as the legitimate patriarch of Constantinople after he had been condemned by Adrian VII. Photius (ca. 810–93) gained, lost, and regained the patriarchate of Constantinople against a background of the struggle between rival candidates for the Byzantine throne, a struggle in which the Western church attempted to intervene. The Western church eventually anathematized Photius, while the Eastern canonized him.

325 "Pope Stephen VII... Formosus": under pressure from a leading Roman family supportive of Pope John VIII and opposed by Formosus, then Bishop of Porto, Stephen VI (r. 896–97) had the remains of Formosus (pope, r. 891–96, and Stephen's last predecessor but one) exhumed, put him on trial, and sentenced him to the punishments described.

326 i.e., Pope Sergius III (r. 904–11).

327 Marozia (ca. 890–936): a Roman noblewoman who, with her mother Theodora, was actively involved in the affairs of the papacy, as described in what follows. The accession to the papacy of her bastard son, grandson, two great grandsons, and a nephew has led hostile commentators to refer to the period of her ascendancy as a "pornocracy" (rule by prostitutes).

328 According to most accounts, it was Pope John X rather than Sergius III who awarded Marozia, rather than her mother Theodora, the unprecedented title of senatrix ("senatoress") of Rome.

329 Later, Pope John XI (r. 931–35).

330 "Hugh, King of Arles": i.e., Hugh of Arles (before 885–948), who was elected King of Italy.

331 Pope John X (914–28) was a protégé of Theodora and perished as a result of the intrigues of her daughter Marozia.

332 i.e., Leo VI (reigned for seven months in 928).

333 i.e., Stephen VII (r. 928 (?) to 931), hand-picked by Marozia as a stopgap until her son could assume the papacy as John XI.

334 "her husband": Alberic I, Duke of Spoleto; it is not usually reported that she poisoned him.

335 i.e., the aforementioned Hugh of Arles, King of Italy.

336 i.e., Alberic II (912–54), who had his mother imprisoned until her death.

337 Stephen VIII: reigned 939–42.

338 "disfigured his face": perhaps a reference to the claim that Stephen VIII was the first pope to shave and that he ordered the men of Rome to do likewise.

339 John XII reigned from 955–64, dying at the age of twenty-seven.

340 i.e., Otto I (912–73), who in 962 made a pact with Pope John XII that made the Western Roman Empire guarantor of the independence of the Papal States. Soon, however, the pope, fearful of the power thus bestowed, began to intrigue with the Magyars and the Byzantines against the Western Empire. Otto returned to Rome in 963, convened a synod of bishops, and deposed the pope.

341 Leo VIII was an antipope from 963 to 964, when he was illegally elected by the 963 synod that illegally deposed John XII, and a true pope from 964 to 965, having been legally re-elected following the death of John XII.

342 Crescentius: i.e., Crescentius II (d. 992), son of Crescentius I and not, as the author states, of John X and Marozia, was a leader of the Roman aristocracy who made himself de facto ruler of Rome, was deposed by Otto III, rose again in rebellion, appointed an antipope (John XVI), and was eventually defeated and executed.

343 Benedict: Pope Benedict VII (d. 983); other sources do not confirm that he died in prison; the author appears to have confused him with John XIV (see below).

344 John XIV: pope from 983–84, who was imprisoned by the antipope Boniface VII in Sant'Angelo, where he died.

345 Boniface VII: ruled as antipope (974, 984–85) under the patronage of Crescentius and the Roman aristocracy.

346 Gregory: i.e., Pope Gregory V (ca. 972–99), cousin and chaplain of Otto III; although he consistently supported the emperor, his death was not without suspicion of foul play.

347 Otto III (980–1002): son of Otto II, in 996 he came to Rome to aid Pope John XV (985–96) (see below) against Crescentius, whom he eventually killed.

348 "played a trick on him": Otto III promised Crescentius the right to live in retirement in Rome but reneged and had him murdered and hung from the walls of Sant'Angelo.

349 Pope John XV (r. 985–86) succeeded Pope Boniface VII; according to other accounts he died of fever, while it was the antipope John XVI, appointed by Crescentius, who, on the latter's defeat, had his eyes put out and nose cut off before banishing him to a monastery.

350 Benedict VIII: reigned 1012 to 1024.

351 John XIX: succeeded his brother Benedict VIII and reigned from 1024 to 1032.

352 Benedict IX: said by most sources to have been between eighteen and twenty years of age when he succeeded his uncle, John XIX, he is the only pope to have reigned three times (1032–44, 1045, 1047–48) and to have sold the papacy (to Gregory VI in 1045), although he later attempted to reclaim it.

353 Meaning presumably Sylvester III and the restored Benedict IX.

354 "with his concubine" (*maʿa surriyyatihi*): thus the Arabic, although one wonders if *maʿa sariyyatihi* ("with his detachment of soldiers") is not what is meant.

355 "one of the kings of France": i.e., Robert II (972–1032), who was excommunicated by Pope Gregory V when he insisted on marrying his cousin, a marriage denied by the pope on grounds of consanguinity.

356 Gregory VII: reigned from 1073 to 1085. His attempts to strengthen papal hegemony against the Holy Roman Empire culminated in the Investiture Controversy (over the right to appoint bishops), which led, in 1076, to his excommunication of Emperor Henry IV, who was accused of being behind his brief abduction.

357 Henry IV (r. 1056–1106) had declared Pope Gregory VII deposed at the synod of Worms, held a week before his own excommunication.

358 "Countess Matilda": Matilda of Tuscany (1055–1115), a leading noblewoman and heiress, who supported Pope Gregory VII during the Investiture Controversy.

359 Canossa: Matilda's ancestral castle.

360 Urbanus II (r. 1088–99) in fact succeeded the short-reigning Victor III rather than Gregory VII directly.

361 "the two sons of Henry IV": i.e, Conrad (1074–1101) and his brother Henry (1086–1125), later Emperor Henry V (r. 1106–1125); Conrad joined the papal camp against his father in 1093; Henry was crowned King of Germany by his father to replace Conrad but soon revolted against his father, whom ultimately he deposed.

362 Henry VI (r. 1190–1197) was in fact the son of Emperor Frederick I, while Frederick II was his son.

363 Pope Celestine: i.e, Celestine III (r. 1191–98).

364 Innocent III: reigned 1198–1216.

365 Pope Innocent IV (r. 1243–54) summoned the Thirteenth General Council of the Church at Lyons in 1245 in order to further his attempts to recover from the Holy Roman Empire territories in Italy that Innocent believed belonged by right to the papacy. The Council formally deposed the emperor, although to no practical effect.

366 Frederick II: reigned 1212–1250.

367 Lucius II: during his reign (1144–45), the Senate of Rome established a Commune of Rome that demanded the pope abandon all secular functions; the pope died leading an army against the Commune.

368 "Clement XV": a mistake for "Clement V" (r. ca. 1264–1314).

369 Vienne: on the Rhône in southern France and site of the Council of Vienne, called by Clement V from 1311 to 1312 to address accusations against the Templars, partly in

response to the desire of Philip IV of France, Clement's patron, to confiscate their wealth.

370 "Pope Urban": i.e., Urban VI (r. ca. 1318 to 1389), who in 1384 tortured and put to death certain of his cardinals who wished to declare him incompetent.

371 John XXIII: i.e., the antipope John XXIII (r. 1410–15), whose seat, during the Western Schism, was in Rome.

372 John XXIII was deposed, along with other claimants to the papacy, by the Council of Constance, which was called by Emperor Sigismund; he was accused of heresy, simony, schism, and immorality.

373 Sijjīn: a valley in Hell.

374 "over your eyes there is a covering" (*ʿalā abṣārikum ghishāwah*): cf. Q Baqarah 2:7.

Glossary

Abū Nuwās (al-Ḥasan ibn Hāniʾ al-Ḥakamī) a poet (ca. 140–98/755–813) of the Abbasid period.

Bag-men (khurjiyyūn) the author's term for Protestant missionaries in the Middle East, whether the American Congregationalists of the Board of Commissioners of Foreign Missions, with whom he first came into contact in Beirut, or the British Anglicans of the Church Missionary Society, for whom he worked later in Malta, Egypt, and London. The Congregationalists established their first mission station in Beirut in 1823 (Makdisi, *Artillery*, 81, 83). In December 1823, when their intention to proselytize became clear, Maronite patriarch Yūsuf Ḥubaysh (1787–1845), who had initially received them cordially, ordered his flock to avoid all contact with what he referred to as "the Liberati" or "Biblemen" (Makdisi, *Artillery*, 95–97).

Bilqīs Queen of Sabaʾ (Sheba) in Yemen, the story of whose visit to Sulaymān (Solomon) is told in the Qurʾān (Q Naml 27:22–44).

Druze a monotheistic religious community found primarily in Syria and Lebanon.

emir (amīr) a title (lit., "commander" or "prince") assumed by local leaders in the Arab world; as used in Book One, the term refers most often to the emirs of the Shihābī dynasty of Mount Lebanon.

Fāriyāq (The) the hero of the events described in the book and the author's alter ego, the name itself being a contraction of Fāri(s al-Shid)yāq.

Iblīs the Devil, Satan.

Khawājā a title of reference and address afforded Christians of substance.

kuttāb a one-room school in which children are taught reading, writing, and numeracy.

maqāmah, plural maqāmāt "short independent prose narrations written in ornamented rhymed prose (*sajʿ*) with verse insertions which share a common plot-scheme and two constant protagonists: the narrator and the hero" (Meisami and Starkey, *Encyclopedia,* 2:507). The thirteenth chapter of each book of the present work is described by the author as a *maqāmah*, the plot-scheme in these *maqāmāt* being a debate. See further Zakharia, "Aḥmad Fāris al-Šidyāq."

Market Boss (The) (shaykh al-sūq) the author's term for the Maronite patriarch.

Market-men (sūqiyyūn) the author's term for the Maronite and Roman Catholic clergy, or the Maronite and Roman Catholic churches in general.

market trader (ḍawṭār, plural ḍawāṭirah) the author's term for a member of the Maronite upper clergy.

Maronite of or pertaining to the Maronite Christian community, whose historical roots lie in northern Syria and Lebanon and whose church, while using Syriac as a liturgical language, is in communion with the Roman Catholic church.

Mountain (The) Mount Lebanon, a mountain range in Lebanon extending for 170 kilometers parallel to the Mediterranean coast and the historical homeland of both the Maronite and Druze Lebanese communities.

Qāmūs (al-) *Al-Qāmūs al-muḥīṭ* (*The Encompassing Ocean*), a dictionary compiled by Muḥammad ibn Yaʿqūb al-Fīrūzābādī (d. 817/1415) that became so influential that *qāmūs* ("ocean") eventually came to mean simply "dictionary." The author later published a study of the *Qāmūs* entitled *Al-Jāsūs ʿalā l-Qāmūs* (*The Spy on the Qāmūs*).

Recoiler (The) (al-Khannās) Satan, so called because he recoils at the mention of the name of God.

rhymed prose (sajʿ) "artistic prose, subject to certain constraints of rhyme and rhythm . . . Etymologically, the word referred to the cooing of pigeons" (Meisami and Starkey, *Encyclopedia,* 2:677). First used by pre-Islamic soothsayers, the form developed, often in combination with other types of parallelism, until it became virtually de rigueur by the tenth century AD, and it remained in use into the early twentieth century, "by which time, however, the modern revolt which has now largely swept away this sort of artifice was already growing strong" (idem). The author uses *sajʿ* in the title of the work and most of his chapter titles, in short scattered bursts in the midst of unrhymed prose (especially at moments of drama), and sometimes, as in the four preceding chapters, in sustained blocks. For further discussion of *sajʿ* in this work, see Jubran, "Function."

Sām Seth son of Noah.

Sībawayhi Abū Bishr ʿAmr ibn ʿUthmān ibn Qanbar Sībawayhi (or Sībawayh) (second/eighth century), the creator of systematic Arabic grammar. By the fourth/tenth century, his only work, Kitāb Sībawayhi, was firmly established as the foundation of a grammatical system that has remained essentially unchanged to the present (Meisami and Starkey, *Encyclopedia*, 2:718).

Sulaymān Solomon.

Suyūṭī (al-), Jalāl al-Dīn a prolific polymath (d. 911/1505), much of whose 500-work oeuvre compiles material taken from earlier scholars.

Index

About the NYU Abu Dhabi Institute

NYU
ABU DHABI
INSTITUTE

The Library of Arabic Literature is supported by a grant from The NYU Abu Dhabi Institute, a major hub of intellectual and creative activity and advanced research. The Institute hosts academic conferences, workshops, lectures, film series, performances, and other public programs directed both to audiences within the UAE and to the worldwide academic and research community. It is a center of the scholarly community for Abu Dhabi, bringing together faculty and researchers from institutions of higher learning throughout the region.

NYU Abu Dhabi, through the NYU Abu Dhabi Institute, is a world-class center of cutting-edge research, scholarship, and cultural activity. The Institute creates singular opportunities for leading researchers from across the arts, humanities, social sciences, sciences, engineering, and the professions to carry out creative scholarship and conduct research on issues of major disciplinary, multidisciplinary, and global significance.

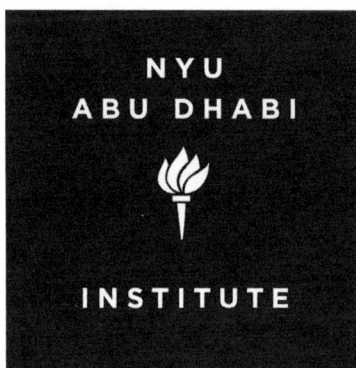

About the Typefaces

The Arabic body text is set in DecoType Naskh, designed by Thomas Milo and Mirjam Somers, based on an analysis of five centuries of Ottoman manuscript practice. The exceptionally legible result is the first and only typeface in a style that fully implements the principles of script grammar (*qawāʿid al-khaṭṭ*).

The Arabic text in the footnotes and margin notes is set in DecoType Emiri, drawn by Mirjam Somers, based on the metal typeface in the naskh style that was cut for the 1924 Cairo edition of the Qur'an.

Both Arabic typefaces in this series are controlled by a dedicated font layout engine. ACE, the Arabic Calligraphic Engine, invented by Peter Somers, Thomas Milo, and Mirjam Somers of DecoType, first operational in 1985, pioneered the principle followed by later smart font layout technologies such as OpenType, which is used for all other typefaces in this series.

The Arabic text was set with WinSoft Tasmeem, a sophisticated user interface for DecoType ACE inside Adobe InDesign. Tasmeem was conceived and created by Thomas Milo (DecoType) and Pascal Rubini (WinSoft) in 2005.

The English text is set in Adobe Text, a new and versatile text typeface family designed by Robert Slimbach for Western (Latin, Greek, Cyrillic) typesetting. Its workhorse qualities make it perfect for a wide variety of applications, especially for longer passages of text where legibility and economy are important. Adobe Text bridges the gap between calligraphic Renaissance types of the 15th and 16th centuries and high-contrast Modern styles of the 18th century, taking many of its design cues from early post-Renaissance Baroque transitional types cut by designers such as Christoffel van Dijck, Nicolaus Kis, and William Caslon. While grounded in classical form, Adobe Text is also a statement of contemporary utilitarian design, well suited to a wide variety of print and on-screen applications.

About the Editor-Translator

Humphrey Davies is an award-winning translator of some twenty works of modern Arabic literature, among them Alaa Al-Aswany's *The Yacoubian Building* and Elias Khoury's *The Gate of the Sun*. He has also made a critical edition, translation, and lexicon of the Ottoman-period *Hazz al-quḥūf bi-sharḥ Abī Shādūf* (*Brains Confounded by the Ode of Abū Shadūf Expounded*) by Yūsuf al-Shirbīnī and compiled with a colleague an anthology entitled *Al-ʿāmmiyyah al-miṣriyyah al-maktūbah: mukhtārāt min 1400 ilā 2009* (*Egyptian Colloquial Writing: selections from 1400 to 2009*). He read Arabic at the University of Cambridge, received his Ph.D. from the University of California at Berkeley, and, previous to undertaking his first translation in 2003, worked for social development and research organizations in Egypt, Tunisia, Palestine, and Sudan. He is affiliated with the American University in Cairo, where he lives.